BRAVE NEW SCHOOLS

BRAVE NEW SCHOOLS

Challenging Cultural Illiteracy through Global Learning Networks

Jim Cummins and Dennis Sayers

St. Martin's Press
New York

ISBN 0-312-12669-7

Library of Congress Cataloging-in-Publication Data

Cummins, Jim, 1949-
    Brave new schools: challenging cultural illiteracy through global
learning networks / Jim Cummins and Dennis Sayers.
        p. cm.
    Includes bibliographical references and index.
    ISBN 0-312-12669-7 (alk. paper)
    1. Educational change—United States. 2. Multicultural education-
-United States. 3. Educational technology—United States.
4. Telecommunications in education—United States. 5. Distance
education—United States. I. Sayers, Dennis. II. Title.
LA217.2.C86 1995
371.3'35—dc20   95-11670
                                                      CIP

Book design by Acme Art, Inc.

10 9 8 7 6 5 4 3

Table of Contents

Acknowledgments

In the pages that follow, we argue that the technological changes that are transforming the realities of virtually everyone in the industrialized countries can either exacerbate the educational disparities between rich and poor or, alternatively, can be harnessed to create communities of inquiry capable of stimulating intellectual, moral, and educational growth among rich and poor alike. Currently, there are more than twice as many children living in poverty in the United States than in any other industrialized country. In arguing for the rights of all children to gain access to the communication tools that are essential for genuine democratic participation and that will define the workplace of tomorrow, we have been inspired by two tireless advocates for children: Alma Flor Ada of the University of San Francisco and Lily Wong Fillmore of the University of California, Berkeley. Both have articulated a vision of society enriched by cultural diversity and have argued passionately for an educational system in which the experience and ideas of *all* students are used as a foundation for learning. We hope that their vision and commitment are reflected, even to some degree, in this book.

Professor Enid Figueroa of the University of Puerto Rico and Dr. Kristin Brown of I*EARN (International Education and Resource Network), cofounders ten years ago, with New York University Professor Dennis Sayers, of the Orillas multilingual learning network, have left their intellectual watermark on every page of this book. We also feel special gratitude for the support and inspiration provided by so many of the veteran teachers of Orillas, chief among them: Arturo Solís of the New Haven Public Schools and Rosita Hernández of the Caguas Public Schools in Puerto Rico; all the teachers of the Orillas Binational Teacher/Researcher Project on Circular Migration (in Puerto Rico, Juan Digna Cuadrado, Lisa Kynoch, Marlyn Peña, Louder Vangas, Ruperta Pizarro, Victor Rodriguez, Teodoro Colón; and in the United States, Miriam Rocca, Ramón Vega, Heather Vega, Nicolé Williams, Nixza Marino, John Marino, William Gerena, Victor Negrón, Pedro Morales, and Paula Murphy); Laura Parks-Sierra and María de Lourdes Bourás of San Diego's Sherman School, pioneers with Rosita Hernández in fostering parental involvement over global learning networks; Dr. Monique Loubert for her assistance in arranging the partnership between Quebec students and their American counterparts in Maine; and Anne-Marie Riveaux of the New York City Public Schools, Tracy Miller of the San Francisco Unified School District (SFUSD), and Juan Carlos Cuellar, staff developer for SFUSD, who provided invaluable help as we researched their efforts to use global learning networks as a tool for reducing interethnic prejudice. Finally, we are grateful to professors Andres Menéndez and Marie Helene Delmestre, among the earliest supporters of Orillas, for their abundant generosity.

Perhaps more than most books, the writing of *Brave New Schools* reflects the subject it treats: intercultural collaborative inquiry through global learning networks. The portraits of these learning networks in action have been sketched, in most cases, by means of the same communications technology that teachers and students used. In some cases, we have worked closely with people we have never met face to face. Narcís Vives, an educator from Barcelona who works with the I*EARN network, provided essential information for the portrait on the children of the Veli Joze refugee camp in Bosnia-Herzegovina. Similarly, Honey Kern of Cold Spring Harbor High School was a most helpful collaborator as we wrote our description of I*EARN's Holocaust/Genocide Project. Dell Salza's readiness to assist on short notice and in the heat of her studies at the Harvard Graduate School of Education made possible the portrait of the Nicaraguan Rope Pump Project. David Eagan, faculty advisor for the Cold Spring Harbor High School's *The Contemporary*, and all the students who edited the Middle East Section of the January and May 1994 issues (especially Kristin Lucas), were the most conscientious of collaborators. Yet none of the fascinating stories these teachers, parents, and students had to offer would have been told without the assistance of Dr. Ed Gragert of I*EARN and Peter Copen of the Copen Family Fund, who so many times pointed us in the right direction as we searched for learning activities that, in their words, "make a difference in the world."

In the academic world, we are beholden to many. University of Arizona Professor Luis Moll's early vision of the potential for intercultural learning of global learning networks, together with his important scholarship on the Soviet psychologist Vygotsky, played a key role in our emerging conception of the power of networking for encouraging educational change. Professor Courtney Cazden of Harvard University's Graduate School of Education was an early advocate (and, equally important, a most cogent critic) of the potential for technology-based "cultural rescue work" with minority students. Professor Sarah Lawrence Light-foot, also of the Graduate School of Education at Harvard, played an influential role in our use of "portraiture" as a compelling approach for presenting the intricacies of social science research to parents, teachers, and concerned citizenry.

Professor William Lee of the University of Southern California introduced the work of Célestin Freinet, the progenitor of today's global learning networks, to the English-speaking world more than a decade ago and we remain indebted to him for his pioneering work. The effort to establish and promote Freinet scholarship in North America has been continued by Professor John Sivell of Brock University in Ontario, Canada, who first translated some of Freinet's work into English, and by Professor David Clandfield, of the University of Toronto, who edited a collection of Freinet's work and is preparing an intellectual biography of Freinet. Discussions with both of these scholars were extremely helpful in preparing the present volume. We are particularly grateful to Professor Clandfield for his detailed and astute comments on an early draft of *Brave New Schools*. We would also like to thank Dr. Anna Uhl Chamot and professors Sonia Nieto and David Bloome of the University of Massachusetts and Professor Nancy Lemberger of Long Island University for helpful comments on the manuscript as well as a number of anonymous reviewers whose suggestions helped shape the book. In addition, a large number of graduate students at both New York University and the Ontario Institute for Studies in Education provided feedback on various aspects of the manuscript and we gratefully acknowledge their input.

Al Rogers, founder of the Global SchoolHouse Foundation, was one of the first to articulate the power of universal access to grass-roots telecomputing, and his vision has inspired us and countless educators around the world for more than a decade. We would also like to thank Sandy McAuley, of the Baffin Divisional Board of Education, whose pioneering work on educational telecommunications in the Canadian Eastern Arctic has demonstrated the tremendous potential of global learning networks for geographically isolated communities.

We are grateful for permission to reprint on page 3 of this volume an excerpt from *Brave New World,* by Aldous Huxley (© 1932, 1960 by Aldous Huxley, originally published by Chatto and Windus of London, reprinted by permission of HarperCollins Publishers Incorporated, Mrs. Laura Huxley, and Random House UK Limited).

Our editors at St. Martin's Press, initially Naomi Silverman and later Michael Flamini, provided encouragement, critical reactions, and clear direction in shaping the book for a broad audience. We very much appreciate their belief in the project and the invaluable support they provided throughout the process.

Finally, to Ioana Cummins and Nathan Hofmann Sayers, who responded, during the many years of our preoccupation with this project, with encouragement, support, humor, and patience, we express our deep-felt gratitude.

—Jim Cummins, Toronto, Ontario
Dennis Sayers, New York, New York
July 1995

I.

Global Networks,
Global Communities

Chapter 1

Introduction

A small boy asleep on his right side, the right arm stuck out, the right hand hanging limp over the edge of the bed. Through a round grating in the side of a box a voice speaks softly. "The Nile is the longest river in Africa and the second in length of all the rivers of the globe. Although falling short of the length of the Mississippi-Missouri, the Nile is at the head of all rivers as regards the length of its basin, which extends through 35 degrees of latitude . . ."

At breakfast the next morning, "Tommy," someone says, "do you know which is the longest river in Africa?" A shaking of the head. "But don't you remember something that begins: The Nile is the . . ."

"The-Nile-is-the-longest-river-in-Africa-and-the-second-in-length-of-all-the-rivers-of-the-globe . . ." The words come rushing out. "Although-falling-short-of . . ."

"Well now, which is the longest river in Africa?"

The eyes are blank. "I don't know."

"But the Nile, Tommy."

"The-Nile-is-the-longest-river-in-Africa-and-second . . ."

"Then which river is the longest, Tommy?"

Tommy bursts into tears. "I don't know," he howls.

—Aldous Huxley, *Brave New World*

For communities nervously about to turn the corner into the twenty-first century, Aldous Huxley's work assumes relevance not only because of his uncannily accurate predictions of technological innovations such as genetic engineering and virtual reality, but because he anticipated and explored the moral dilemmas with which we are confronted as technology progressively unveils its power to us. At a time when the moral certitudes of the past are but distant memories and our gods are elsewhere occupied, we find ourselves increasingly enmeshed by our own creations. The contradictions and tensions that line the pages of *Brave New World* are everywhere laid between the lines of our collective experience as a global community: Individual freedoms ushered in by the new wave of technology are shadowed by the increasing hierarchical control of our lives made possible by the same technology; the images of happiness and fulfillment that beam at us from glossy pages only partially obscure the squalor and hopelessness of our inner cities; the mountains of subsidized beef, butter, and wheat that proudly dot the landscape of wealthy industrialized countries are denied to the children of famine whose blank eyes and skeletal faces silently ask us "Why?" Everywhere we turn we face a choice between the pain of consciousness and the contentment of mental oblivion. The same technology that opens the world to our consciousness frequently closes our consciousness to the world.

The struggle between control and possibility, coercion and collaboration, is nowhere more evident than in our schools. Textbooks and other curriculum materials are designed explicitly to transmit what our society deems important for youth to learn. Teachers are expected to embody and model the values of the wider society. But what are teachers to do when the values of the wider society are violently contested in the streets and in the media; when the moral consensus that gave at least the appearance of coherence to our societies lies fractured all around us? Should teachers continue to transmit officially approved information and skills as if they were neutral reflections of objective reality, or should they help students to analyze issues critically from a variety of perspectives? Will it strengthen or weaken the fabric of nationhood to alert students to perspectives on history and current realities that may be at variance with dominant views? Does the admission of diverse perspectives into the classroom under the guise of "multicultural education" threaten to "disunite America," as suggested by Arthur Schlesinger, Jr., and many other conservative academics?[1]

Teachers in classrooms across the country are making decisions about these issues on a daily basis. Their vision of the society into which they want their students to graduate is sketched in all their interactions with those students. The forms of student participation they encourage in the classroom anticipate the roles they expect their students to play when they graduate into the broader society. The social realities beyond the school-house door have penetrated the classroom cocoon in ways that raise fundamental questions about the functions and directions of the entire educational system.

The escalation of conflict about educational issues is due partly to the fact that previously silenced voices can now be raised and heard as a result of the greater recognition of human rights and freedoms in industrialized societies during the past 30 years. Modern communications technology permits these voices to be amplified, so that they have become harder to ignore. Official versions of history and even the myths that form the foundation of nationhood are being challenged both inside and outside the classroom. To illustrate the point, in the 1990s it is no longer possible to celebrate Columbus's "discovery" of America and to perpetuate the text-book image of Columbus as the pious hero who brought civilization and salvation to the savage inhabitants of this continent without facing an angry rebuttal from the survivors of the genocide that ensued from his arrival. As high school teacher Bill Bigelow notes:

> The Columbus stories [in school textbooks] encourage passive reading, and never pose questions for children to think about. Did Columbus have a right to claim Indian land in the name of the Spanish crown? Were those Indians who resisted violently justified in doing so? Why does the United States commemorate a Columbus Day instead of a Genocide Day?[2]

Not surprisingly, there are risks associated with promoting any form of critical inquiry that has the potential of challenging official versions of events. At the dawn of Western civilization in ancient Greece, Socrates was obliged to drink the cup of hemlock for allegedly corrupting the youth. In the Middle Ages, the guardians of official knowledge instituted the Inqui-sition and piously tortured dissenting voices into silence in the name of God. Today in most industrialized societies, assent to official knowledge is molded in more subtle ways, but educators are still in the front lines of the power struggle between control and resistance. To discuss structures of exploitation and inequality is still to corrupt the youth.

Despite this fact, an increasing number of educators throughout North America and in many other countries are taking this risk. They see it as central to their duty as educators to go beyond the sanitized curriculum they are expected to transmit and to raise with their students fundamental issues about human values and actions. Not content just to reflect their societies and reinforce the existing structure of power, they are actively challenging the ways in which power is negotiated and resources distributed. These teachers, whose pedagogy we will describe in this book, believe passionately in democracy as the cornerstone of Western civilization. They are determined that their students will have the intellectual and cultural tools to participate critically and effectively in the democratic process, whether they are born in migrant camps or in the midst of inner-city urban blight.

Here we aim to analyze this struggle by focusing on three widely debated—though rarely linked—issues: the directions of contemporary educational reform; increasing cultural diversity and immigration; and the global networking possibilities ushered in by the "information superhighway," usually referred to as the "Internet." We analyze the current debates on educational reform in North America and propose alternative directions that promote collaboration between cultures and critical inquiry among students. These alternative directions take advantage of technological advances in telecommunications and microelectronics. However, it is important to state at the outset that we do not *at all* consider this to be a book that centers on educational and communications technology. The kinds of intercultural collaborations we are proposing derive their impact and momentum not from technology but from a vision of how education can enact, in microcosm, a radical restructuring of power relations both in domestic and global arenas.

THE "EDUCATIONAL REFORM" DEBATE

The alarm bells that rang throughout the United States with the publication in 1983 of *A Nation at Risk,* the report of the National Commission on Excellence in Education, gave way almost a decade later to a proclamation of the dawn of a new educational era ushered in by America 2000, the six-point blueprint for educational reform promulgated by former President George Bush. America 2000 reinvented itself as Goals 2000 in the Clinton administration. Goals 2000 added two more points on teacher education and parent involvement, and currently forms the framework for federal educational initiatives in the United States. Signed into law on March 31, 1994, as Goals 2000: Educate America Act, it reads in part:

By the Year 2000—
- All children in America will start school ready to learn.
- The high school graduation rate will increase to at least 90 percent.
- All students will leave grades 4, 8, and 12 having demonstrated competency over challenging subject matter including English, mathematics, science, foreign languages, civics and government, economics, the arts, history, and geography, and every school in America will ensure that all students learn to use their minds well, so they may be prepared for responsible citizenship, further learning, and productive employment in our nation's modern economy.
- United States students will be first in the world in mathematics and science achievement.
- Every adult American will be literate and will possess the knowledge and skills necessary to compete in a global economy and exercise the rights and responsibilities of citizenship.
- Every school in the United States will be free of drugs, violence, and the unauthorized presence of firearms and alcohol and will offer a disciplined environment conducive to learning.
- The nation's teaching force will have access to programs for the continued improvement of their professional skills and the opportunity to acquire the knowledge and skills needed to instruct and prepare all American students for the next century.
- Every school will promote partnerships that will increase parental involvement and participation in promoting the social, emotional, and academic growth of children.

The Educate America Act articulate difficult to contest. Who, for example, would children starting school ready to learn, as go: dramatic improvements in literacy, science, quent goals, are inspiring to contemplate. I among many educators and parents through aspirations, we suggest in this volume that Goals 2000 initiatives, and most of the edu preceding decade, are either naive or cynical: naive to believe that dramatic improvements in educational readiness and achievement will evolve miraculously in the absence of massive investment in the communities that populate the decaying and violent streets of America's inner cities; cynical because proclamations such as Goals 2000 create an illusion of concern and intervention that, in reality, reinforces rather than dismantles the social distribution of power and resources that determines who succeeds and who fails in our schools.

In our view, the recent impetus for educational reform in the United States is likely to have limited, if any, real effect on overall achievement levels. We argue in subsequent chapters that educational reform can be effective only when it actively challenges the real causes of underachievement, which are rooted in the social conditions of schools and communities. For example, goal no. 1 of Goals 2000 rings very hollow in light of the fact that the proportion of U.S. children under age six living in poverty has grown to 26 percent, an increase of about one million children between 1987 and 1992, the year on which these figures are based.[3]

Much of the current discourse on educational reform attempts to orchestrate public consent for reinforcing hierarchical top-down control over what happens in schools. Curriculum and instruction are oriented to produce more efficiently students with adequate functional literacy to meet the needs of industry in an increasingly competitive global economy but insufficient critical literacy to question the structures of power that determine the distribution of status and resources within the society. We argue that the hidden agenda of much of the educational reform movement has been to institute more effective quality control over the products of assembly-line schools while, at the same time, limiting the extent to which, in Brazilian educator Paulo Freire's terms, reading the word might lead students to read the world.[4]

In this sense, the title of our book—*Brave New Schools*—reflects the irony of Huxley's title: The educational reform movement promises to estore the sense of purpose and moral certitude to the educational enterfor the small price of abdication of any pursuit of critical consciousness laborative inquiry, just as in *Brave New World,* happiness was bought ense of freedom. In the chapters that follow, we outline the this Faustian bargain and propose a framework for organizing nstruction that seriously aims to educate *all* children. This alternative framework derives from the groundbreaking efforts of educators in schools that can be described—without a trace of irony—as "brave new schools," where a new pedagogy for intercultural learning is being shaped that is responsive to the economic, scientific, environmental, and cultural realities of today's world.

CULTURAL ILLITERACY: ELITE MONOCULTURAL VS. INTERCULTURAL LITERACY

Just as our title encompasses two senses of "brave new schools," our use of the terms "cultural literacy" and "cultural illiteracy" reflects the sociopolitical dimensions of the struggle over meaning in an increasingly interdependent and culturally diverse world. The term "cultural literacy" attained prominence with the publication of E. D. Hirsch's (1987) book *Cultural Literacy: What Every American Needs to Know.*[5] The book so captured the imagination of policymakers, educators, and the general public that its list of 5,000 items intended to illustrate the common core of knowledge that literate Americans tend to share has formed the basis for textbooks, dictionaries, and even state-mandated curricula (as in Florida). As we argue in chapter 3, Hirsch's specifications for "cultural literacy" are by no means neutral with respect to whose knowledge they represent. They legitimate the economic and political status quo by excluding the knowledge, values, and perspectives that define the identities of the vast range of cultural groups that reside on the margins of the American dream. Hirsch's rallying cry to "circle the wagons" around some supposedly unifying "Canon of Western Culture" reflects the fear that the changing hues of the American cultural landscape will undermine the current economic and political status quo. We argue that the writings of Hirsch and other conservative academics (such as William Bennett, Allan Bloom, Dinesh D'Souza, Diane Ravitch, and Arthur Schlesinger, Jr.) simply intellectualize xenophobia. For these academics, cultural diversity constitutes the enemy within, sowing the seeds of national disintegration more insidiously than any external enemy ever could. From their perspective, it is absurd and tragic that federal and state governments should collude in their own destruction by legitimating diversity through institutional changes such as multicultural education, Afrocentric schools, and bilingual programs. In order to counter the multicultural splintering of the United States and silence discordant voices, it is necessary to infuse the curriculum with officially prescribed cultural literacy. The assumption is that what is taught will define what can be thought.

In our view, this notion of cultural literacy constitutes *cultural illiteracy* in a profound sense. It takes no account of the fact that cross-national and cross-cultural cooperation is crucial for economic, scientific, and environmental progress and for ending ethnically based conflicts around the globe. Cultural literacy in Hirsch's sense is vacuous unless it becomes part of a broader intercultural literacy. This is true as much for white middle-class children as for any other ethnic or racial group.

What Marshall McLuhan termed the "global village" is upon us.[6] We see unprecedented population mobility and intercultural contact resulting from a variety of factors: economic migration, displacement caused by armed conflict and famine, technological advances in transportation and telecommunications, and so on. Intercultural contact within industrialized countries as a result of population mobility is matched by dramatically increased intercultural contact between countries, reflecting increased global economic and political interdependence. Surely this escalation of intercultural contact, both domestically and internationally, cries out for more two-way communication among cultures and the establishment of school programs that promote sensitivity to and understanding of divergent cultural perspectives. Even the narrow discourse of "competitiveness," so prominent in the 1980s' educational reform agenda, would mandate awareness of the cultural perspectives of prospective business clients. Yet cultural literacy curricula orient us inward, averting our eyes from the cultural diversity that characterizes our own countries and our global community. Even more unfortunate, the "facts" of cultural literacy are to be internalized without discussion, exploration, or critical inquiry in much the same way that young Tommy was expected to internalize the cultural literacy of Huxley's *Brave New World.*

We suggest that monocultural curricula in schools and monocultural social policies have reached a point of diminishing returns, even for those "mainstream" groups whose cultures are represented. The transmission of cultural myopia in schools constitutes a recipe for an explosion of inter-group conflict where everyone loses. The Los Angeles uprising of spring 1992 (to protest the acquittal of White police officers who were captured on videotape beating a Black man, Rodney King) illustrates the logical outcome of sustained economic and political discrimination. The fact that the former vice-president of the United States, Dan Quayle, could attribute what was taking place in Los Angeles to the sympathetic depiction of single parenthood on the television program *Murphy Brown* shows just how necessary it is to take seriously the challenge of combatting intercultural illiteracy. In short, Hirsch's monocultural literacy is our "cultural illiteracy." Simply put, schools have a crucial role to play in helping us live and grow together within our global village. For schools to abdicate this responsibility, whether in the name of cultural literacy or educational effectiveness, is to leave students ill-equipped to participate in the democratic process and contribute to their communities in the culturally diverse world of the twenty-first century.

INTERCULTURAL GLOBAL LEARNING NETWORKS

In contrast to monocultural prescriptions for educational reform, we are proposing, as a fundamental catalyst for widespread educational renewal, the adoption on the broadest possible scale of long-distance teaching partnerships across cultures, intercultural networks of partnerships that— to the greatest extent feasible—seek to take advantage of accessible and culturally appropriate educational and communications technology. We argue that such partnerships can promote academic development across a broad spectrum of content and skill areas, including literacy skills development, critical thinking, and creative problem-solving in such vital domains as science and social studies, citizenship and global education, and second-language learning. They also stimulate students' research skills and promote sensitivity to other cultural perspectives.

When we talk of long-distance intercultural teaching partnerships, we are acutely aware that differences in language and cultural experience can themselves create enormous "distances," and not only across continents and oceans or between regions and countries; there are also enormous cultural distances to be bridged within a particular country (and often within a single community) among racial, ethnic, and other immigrant or national minority groups. The diverse cultural enclaves that comprise a single urban center such as Chicago, Los Angeles, Miami, Montreal, New York, or Toronto may live under the same sky but look out on very different horizons. In contrast to those academics and educators who view the increase in cultural diversity as a threat to social cohesion and an occasion for hand-wringing over the alleged demise of the "melting pot," we see diversity as an important resource enabling us to take far greater advantage of technological innovations in promoting educational success for all students.

In the chapters that follow, we present portraits of teachers who are using technological advances to create learning environments that will equip their students with the intellectual and cultural resources crucial for success in the multicultural national and global societies they will help form. They are, indeed, teachers from "brave new schools" who are working collaboratively with colleagues both in their own schools and in distant parts of the globe to establish intercultural learning networks.

At one level, the rationale is very simple: In the world of the twenty-first century, decision making and problem-solving in virtually all spheres—business, science, community development, government, politics—will depend on electronic networks that span diverse national and cultural boundaries. Students whose education has provided them with a broad range of experience in using such networks for intercultural collaboration and critical thinking will be better prepared to thrive in this radically different communications and employment environment than those who have not been provided with access to cross-cultural awareness and problem-solving skills.

At a different level, however, intercultural learning networks provide access to information and possibilities for democratic participation that potentially threaten the top-down control over learning that most societies around the world traditionally have exercised. If textbooks are no longer the only source of information that most students have access to and if students can, in principle, draw from the resources of virtually any library around the world through the Internet, ensuring that students learn only what is considered culturally or politically appropriate may become more difficult. Hence, the initial enthusiasm that greeted the educational potential of the information superhighway has been tempered recently by a certain ambivalence among policymakers because of the reduction of control over learning that it may entail.

We view this potential reduction of top-down control over the learning process as one of the most *positive* aspects of global learning networks. We argue for the importance of withdrawing learning from the prescribed texts controlled by those who exercise power in our societies because educational systems organized according to this model have resulted in staggering failure rates among so-called minority groups. These "minority" groups now represent the majority student population of most large North American cities. The continued failure of our schools to educate these students threatens all sectors of our society. Increasing amounts of gross domestic product will go to fight crime and build prisons to contain those who have been pushed out of schools to the margins of society. Ironically, international economic competitiveness will increasingly depend on even greater numbers of immigrants to supply the intellectual and cultural resources that the schools have squandered.

There are alternatives to this dismal scenario. They require that we reframe education around critical inquiry and the collaborative generation of knowledge in such a way that the experience and cultural contributions of all students are valued. In this scenario, rather than passively internalizing the cultural literacy of socially powerful groups, students actively generate their own intercultural literacy through dialogue and collaborative research with colleagues in their own classroom and in classrooms across the globe.

Teachers and students participating in the learning networks we have observed are clearly not engaged in trivial pen-pal activities; rather, they are conducting significant intercultural learning projects, such as joint surveys on drug abuse, homelessness, and teenage pregnancy in two communities, sharing and analyzing their results, and eventually publishing their findings in their local school or hometown newspapers. By opening their classrooms and their minds to experiences from other cultures, they are not unwittingly turning their backs on their own. In fact, these students have become more aware of their own culture as a result of the contrast they have experienced with another. This is illustrated in a project, described in chapter 2, that involved scores of schools in several countries in which students asked their parents and relatives to help them collect and analyze proverbs and sayings; students then discussed these sayings with many other classes and compiled them in a multilingual publication. In these cases, "high technology" led to intergenerational learning that in turn fostered cross-cultural awareness and, most important, a deeper critical understanding of each student's cultural heritage.

Evidence has shown that this type of long-distance collaboration between teachers and their classes does not require the use of high-cost gadgetry. Yet every one of these team-teaching partnerships does use to some extent "educational technology" and "communications technology"—very broadly defined—ranging from the most rudimentary to much more sophisticated levels. Indeed, in most recent cases we have documented of this type of long-distance teaching partnership, "educational technology" was limited to photographs, audiotapes, and slides, while the "communications technology" utilized was nothing more than the national postal service. This is also the case in the overwhelming majority of instances of intercultural team teaching that have been described by earlier educators over the past several decades, as we discuss in chapter 4.

Recently, computerized electronic mail networks and computer-based conferencing systems have added a far-reaching new dimension to the multimedia mix that can be mobilized in exchanges between schools around the world. Many educators are surprised to learn how little this form of high-tech communication costs. For schools that already have computers and access to a single telephone line, the costs for daily collaboration with a class on the other side of the world can be modest; students in the inner city can be in daily contact with their peers in the global village for as little as a one-time cost of less than $50 for a modem to connect the computer to a phone line. The cost for connection to the Internet, the full-fledged information super-highway, ranges from minimal or none, if routed through universities or other facilitating institutions, to more substantial fees being charged on the open market (amounting to several hundred dollars per year).

But while some form of educational technology and communications technology appears to be necessary and desirable in order to make exchanges between faraway classes more vivid, timely, and engaging, the fact remains that most team-teaching partnerships the world over operate successfully with very low to moderate levels of educational and communications technology—little more than a postage stamp on an envelope with student writings inside. The partnerships are driven principally by the desire of partner teachers to create innovative learning environments that better serve students in today's schools and prepare them for the economic and social challenges that await them when they graduate.

We strongly disagree with the tendency of some educators and policymakers to trivialize (or even to dismiss) the immense potential of intercultural teaching networks as merely another educational technology "fashion." They point to the fate of such previous technological dinosaurs as language laboratories or closed-circuit classroom television, "innovations" that sought to make the curriculum "teacher-proof." Teacher partnership networks, however, depend on teachers' initiative and, if students' motivation is to be sustained, require that joint projects relate directly to issues of relevance to students' lives. Because they are communicating over long distances, teachers willingly adopt educational technology as a kind of cultural amplifier, to "turn up the volume" for their faraway colleagues. However, the technology is but a means to an end, as illustrated by the fact that teacher collaboration over long distances and across cultures flourished long before microcomputers were even dreamed of—indeed, years before television or even radio and films were widely available in the society at large, let alone within classrooms.

CONCLUSION

The chapters that follow tell the stories of educators and students who, throughout most of this century, have engaged in intercultural learning networks. We attempt to highlight the importance of these directions for our collective future as a global community. As our communities and nations emerge into a new millennium, the urgency of intercultural collaboration is painfully obvious.[7] If schools aspire to prepare students for the twenty-first century, their mandate must, by definition, include developing students' capacity and commitment to collaborate across cultural and linguistic boundaries in pursuing joint projects and resolving common problems.

As our examples illustrate, these collaborative projects will require and promote higher-order thinking and literacy skills to a far greater extent than the narrowly focused curriculum envisaged by much of the back-to-basics rhetoric of the educational reform movement. The information superhighway offers unprecedented opportunities for educators to create collaborative learning environments that will stimulate critical thinking skills and academic excellence among *all* students.

Still at issue, however, is the extent to which our societies are truly committed to promoting critical literacy skills among marginalized students and communities. Those who control the distribution of status and re-sources in our societies may not enthusiastically endorse the potential of such an education to enfranchise communities that currently tend not to participate in the democratic process. There are also those who wish to ensure that the information superhighway is harnessed for short-term profit rather than for broader educational and social goals.

In order to argue convincingly for wide-ranging public and educational access to global learning networks and for their specific importance in promoting both equity and excellence in education, it is necessary both to describe how such networks have been used powerfully in the past and to articulate a coherent vision of their potential in the future. The power of global networks derives primarily from their ability to facilitate dramatically learning involving collaborative critical inquiry. Subsequent chapters describe in some detail what collaborative critical inquiry entails, and they attempt to illustrate its central importance in addressing the social and economic challenges we all face as a global community.

Chapter 2

From the Inner City
to the Global Village:
The Emergence of Electronic
Communities of Learning

Global telecommunications is our tool against ignorance in a rapidly
changing world; it empowers people to reach out and make a difference.
—David Barzilai, Student,
Lexington Public High School,
Lexington, Massachusetts,
at the First Global Classroom Youth Congress

In this chapter, we present case studies—portraits, if you will—of "brave
new schools" that have established long-distance teaching partnerships
relying on modern computer networking. Some would ask: Why speak of
technology, let alone computer technology, when textbooks—even pencils
and paper for that matter—are in such short supply, and when school
buildings remain dilapidated after decades of neglect? Moreover, there are
glaring inequities of access to technology and networking resources for
teachers and students, both within industrialized countries and in schools
around the world. Indeed, a teacher in New York City may face similar
difficulties in getting connected to a computer network as an educator in
China. Yet a teacher five miles away in Westchester County, New York,
has immediate access to sophisticated technology that permits her students
to interact with peers around the globe.

Inequity of access to technology resources, including computer networks, simply mirrors the unequal distribution of every other human and material resource in public education, especially in countries like the United States, where educational funding is inextricably tied to local property taxes.[1] There are also obvious inequities of access to all forms of technology between industrialized and Third World countries.

While access to sophisticated technology is not essential for engaging in intercultural learning networks, as illustrated by the extensive networks established by Célestin Freinet in France earlier this century (see chapter 4), equity of access *is* a central issue for any serious attempt at educational reform in today's schools. It is important to recognize that modern computer-based telecommunications networks—frequently referred to as the information superhighway or the Internet—do indeed open up entirely new possibilities for collaboration that Célestin Freinet and many other pioneers of global learning networks could never have imagined in the 1920s.

What is the Internet? The best way to conceive of the Internet is as a "network of networks," specifically, a worldwide computer meganetwork comprised of hundreds of local computer networks. The Internet represents a radical change from stand-alone computers that can run only single computer programs, such as word processors, spreadsheets, or databases. While all these programs make your personal computer a powerful tool, networking takes these tools and magnifies their power immensely.

A single microcomputer on a desk—or an even more powerful minicomputer or computer workstation located in the corner of a room—may be an invaluable resource for the handful of people who use it; yet it remains a tool with all the obvious limitations imposed by the local and specialized interests of the few people who utilize that particular computer as a stand-alone resource. However, personal computers can be wired together into a local area network (LAN), creating a community of users—for example, all the computers at a single university, or every desktop in a private corporation, or each user within a nonprofit organization—all of whom share wider, mutual interests. Indeed, every time the circle of common interests is widened across computing networks, more and more people can take advantage of locally based yet mutually shared resources.

The Internet extends this logic one decisive step further—in fact, to its ultimate and logical conclusion. By linking any and every network that chooses to become part of the Internet into a network of networks, the Internet provides the possibility of communicating and of sharing locally developed information resources instantaneously between continents. Equally as significant, the network of networks over which information resources are shared also can carry electronic messages (called e-mail for short) between distant correspondents, delivered nearly instantaneously.

As each day passes, it becomes ever more crucial for parents and educators to confront this momentous transformation of networking technologies and to examine critically its potential impact on the schooling of all our children. We must also understand why it is so important to ensure equitable and universal access for educators and students. In this chapter, we focus on two global learning networks in particular precisely because they illustrate in a dramatic way the barriers that have been overcome by public school educators in securing access to computer networking resources when funds are short as well as the promise that can be realized when full networking access is brought within the reach of every teacher and student.

Universities have subsidized the participation of academics and researchers on the Internet so steadily over the last decade that many workers in higher education have come to take for granted their access to its resources. Not so with educators at the elementary and secondary levels. Indeed, the key issue that overrides all others in the kindergarten through grade 12 (K-12) networking arena is the very access of public school teachers to the Internet itself. Unlike academics, researchers, commercial enterprises, and even nonprofit organizations, classroom teachers confront a formidable and often daunting task in their attempts to link students to the Internet. At the heart of this challenge is the decaying infrastructure of the schools: It is hard enough to get a classroom painted, let alone have a phone line installed in a classroom or even get access to a line somewhere in the school. And full connectivity costs dearly considering the limited funding available for education. The kind of Internet connectivity that academics have come to take for granted is sold on the open market for anywhere from $200 to $400 a year.

Despite many impressive proposals, including Vice President Al Gore's much-touted National Research and Education Network (NREN), which seeks to connect every elementary and secondary classroom in the United States to the Internet, for huge numbers of classroom practitioners in the United States and elsewhere access to networking is severely limited.

Direct Internet access is limited to the relative handful of educators who secure accounts through their personal connections among professors in schools of teacher education at nearby universities.

Teachers now resort to one of three options if they wish to engage in global networking activities:

1. Free or nearly free electronic bulletin board systems (BBSs), which act as "gateways" to the Internet but which restrict connectivity to the exchange of electronic mail between distant colleagues;

2. Prepaid subscriptions for full access to Internet-based services through not-for-profit organizations such as the Association for Progressive Computing, a confederation of Internet computer networks devoted to peace, environmental, and other issues focusing on social responsibility, costing around $200 a year per teacher account; or

3. High-cost educational networks targeted at teachers and promoted by profit-taking commercial concerns such as Microsoft and giant telecommunications industry companies, costing anywhere from $300 to $1000 per class each year.

In her review of research on computer equity issues, researcher Delia Neuman discusses not only computers but also "teleconferencing, interactive television, electronic mail, and expanded telecommunications networks." She warns that

despite the promise of emerging technology, it is important to remember that technology and equity are not inevitable partners. . . . The literature on computer equity reveals that many students—not only minority, disadvantaged, and inner-city but also female, handicapped, and rural— have been hampered by inequitable access to computers and by widespread patterns of inequitable distribution and use of computers within and across schools.[2]

What is the potential of global learning networks and why is equitable and universal access so crucial for the society that our students will form in the next millennium? The eight portraits to be sketched in this chapter illustrate how educators and students are jointly creating forms of teaching and learning that use the new communications technology in unique ways to amplify literacy and intellectual skills collaboratively with peers in culturally and geographically distant settings.

The portraits in this chapter focus on the nature and status of computer networking at the end of the twentieth century. Our aim is to understand the expanded potential of networked computing resources for enabling teachers and students to engage in the *collaborative critical inquiry* that, we argue, is crucial for preparing students for full democratic participation in their society. These eight global learning projects confront a variety of issues that all sectors of society face on a daily basis, including the need to reduce racial prejudice and ethnic strife in order to cooperate productively to achieve mutually beneficial goals; the kind of intergenerational learning between young people and their elders, extended family, and community that promotes successful learning of basic literacy skills; and the importance of promoting awareness and solidarity between students and their peers in war-ravaged countries and areas of the world disrupted by natural disasters.

The portraits are drawn from two computer-based global learning networks—I*EARN (the International Education and Resource Network), and Orillas (short for the Spanish phrase *De Orilla a Orilla* [From shore to shore])—two networks that have attempted to explore the potential of computer networking for developing among students a capacity to analyze social issues more deeply and to collaborate with peers in exploring resolutions to these issues. I*EARN learning projects have taken advantage of full Internet access and offer a fascinating view of the educational potential that can be realized through geographically distant communities of learning. Orillas has concentrated on multilingual global learning while working to keep the costs of telecomputing as low as possible in order to increase the numbers of students who can participate from poorer school districts in North America as well as from industrializing countries.

I*EARN is one of the largest groups of educators using the Association for Progressive Computing (APC) confederation of networks, which is concerned with peace, environmental, conflict resolution, health, and public interest issues. It is composed of the subnetworks Alternex in Brazil, Chasque in Uruguay, ComLink in Germany, Ecuanex in Ecuador, GlasNet in Russia, GreenNet based in London, IGC (itself comprised of PeaceNet, EcoNet,

ConflictNet, and LaborNet) in San Francisco, Nicarao in Nicaragua, Pegasus in Australia, NordNet in Sweden, and The Web in Ontario, Canada.

I*EARN's purpose is to facilitate educational projects designed to empower young people from kindergarten to twelfth grade to work collaboratively in different parts of the world through global telecommunications networks. According to Peter Copen, its founder, "The most fundamental purpose of I*EARN is to have the students learn that they *can* make a difference in the world."[3] I*EARN now includes hundreds of schools in over 20 countries, including Argentina, Australia, Brazil, Britain, Canada, China, Costa Rica, Finland, Hungary, Indonesia, Israel, Japan, Jordan, Kenya, Korea, Mexico, Netherlands, New Zealand, Spain, the United States, and the newly independent states of the former Soviet Union and the former Yugoslavia. Like Orillas, I*EARN attempts to maintain a balance of schools inside and outside North America in order to insure intercultural diversity.

De Orilla a Orilla is an international teacher-researcher project that has focused on documenting—through serious research involving teachers—promising practices for intercultural learning over global learning networks. Since 1985, Orillas has been an international clearinghouse for establishing long-distance team-teaching partnerships between pairs or groups of teachers separated by distance, forming "sister" or "partner" classes. Orillas team-teaching partnerships are multilingual (in English, French, Haitian, Japanese, Portuguese, and Spanish) and multinational (with schools in Puerto Rico, Quebec, and the United States, but also in English-speaking Canada, Costa Rica, France, Japan, and Mexico).

The collaborating teachers make use of electronic mail and computer-based conferencing to plan and implement comparative learning projects between their distant partner classes. Such parallel projects include dual community surveys, joint math and science investigations, twinned geography projects, and comparative oral history and folklore studies.[4] Often teachers in Orillas electronically publish their students' collaborative work over the Internet.

Research on Orillas has focused on those networking activities which effect social change, validating community traditions (such as oral history and folklore) in the schools, antiracist education, and linguistic human rights, while allowing teachers to explore the classroom practicalities of teaching based on collaborative critical inquiry. Robert DeVillar and Chris Faltis in *Computers and Cultural Diversity* judged Orillas "certainly one of the more, if not the most, innovative and pedagogically complete computer-supported writing projects involving students across distances."[5] In our view, Orillas remains—after more than a decade—the leading global learning network project working to explore and expand the theoretical and practical boundaries of multilingual, intercultural learning.

Both Orillas and I*EARN concentrate on intercultural learning. Perhaps the most important factor in the success of the communities of learning created by these two networks is their insistence on a process of democratic and decentralized decision making in both day-to-day work and long-term planning. Both networks recognize that far too often in the past educational technology has been dominated by some North Americans' patronizing we-know-best attitude when working with educators from other nations. The three cofounders of Orillas, Enid Figueroa of the University of Puerto Rico, Kristin Brown of the University of San Francisco, and Dennis Sayers of New York University, have worked together for over a decade to assure that every country and culture participating in this multilingual network has a voice in shaping its direction.[6]

Similarly, I*EARN is governed by the I*EARN Assembly, composed of one representative from each of its centers around the world, which in turn elects a five-person executive committee that serves as I*EARN's board of directors. Each member of the executive committee is from a different country, thus assuring that one cultural perspective never dominates decision making. Both I*EARN and Orillas take advantage of computer networking to spread day-to-day decision-making responsibilities far and wide around the world. Yet both networks recognize the value of face-to-face contacts in solidifying their communities of learning. I*EARN's Assembly and executive committee meet annually in a different country, and Orillas has organized numerous two-week summer institutes where teachers are invited to Puerto Rico to work with colleagues in designing and testing collaborative networking projects.

TWO WAYS TO CREATE
GLOBAL COMMUNITIES OF LEARNING

First, we contrast two radically different approaches to exploring the educational potential of the Internet. Teachers and students can participate in activities that involve dozens of schools and thousands of students, as in the first portrait, which focuses on a huge global learning activity that centered on bringing relief assistance—and ultimately the release of laughter—to children in the refugee camps of war-torn Yugoslavia. Yet productive learning partnerships also can occur between as few as two teachers who can fine-tune their collaboration to suit the special learning needs of their students, as we witness in the exchange between a class in Quebec City in the French-speaking Canadian province of Quebec and another class in northern Maine on the United States–Canadian border.

Portrait 1:
THE VELI JOZE REFUGEE
CAMP IN SAVUDRIJA, CROATIA[7]

In January of 1993, a group of volunteer relief workers from Catalunya in Spain belonging to a pacifist organization called MOC (Moviment d'Objectors de Consciencia [Conscientious Objectors' Movement]) were set to travel to Veli Joze, a refugee camp located in Savudrija, Croatia, that had been set up by the Croatian military to house Bosnian refugees. Before they left, Narcis Vives, an educator from Barcelona, heard of their trip and contacted Miquel Colomer of the MOC. Vives asked if the Catalan volunteers would be interested in taking a donated computer and a modem to Croatia to install in one of the makeshift "schools" the Croats permitted to operate, with little material or human support, for the 500 children living inside Veli Joze. Colomer agreed and set up a computer station in the refugee camp. There, a boy named Sanel Cekik wrote a message about the impact of the war on himself and on his family, and sent it out over the modem to schools around the world.

Sanel Cekik's electronic mail message was to unleash a chain reaction of social action around the world. But first it had to be translated from Sanel's mother tongue, Bosanki, a dialect of Serbo-Croatian, to a language more familiar to others. The educators in Barcelona quickly resolved the problem posed by this language barrier. They conjectured that by sending out a call for a translator of Bosanki over a number of international networks, some bilingual student would respond who came from a family where this dialect was still spoken at home.

They had guessed correctly. Tanya Lehmann, a student from Cold Spring Harbor High School in Long Island, New York, was taking part in several projects through the I*EARN global learning network, and she and her family understood Bosanki. She wrote back to the educators in Barcelona on February 22, 1993:

> I was involved in translating Sanel's letter because I am working on a project dealing with the abuses of human rights occurring around the world. . . . We are very interested in the events taking place in the former Yugoslavia, we are very excited that we were of some help to you.
>
> I will be very happy to translate your letter to Sanel. I will send a copy of the translation to you and Narcis.

Here is the translation of Sanel Cekik's letter that Tanya to Narcis Vives in Barcelona.

> The war slowly but surely came to our city. After some time, it happened; the Serbs took over the city and as everywhere they started with their terrible torture. My incident is next. One night in my apartment where unfortunately was my father, came four Serb soldiers. First they beat him. (My father is 60 yrs old). Then they made horrible wounds on his back, on his forehead, his hands with razor blades. The next day when I came and saw him in this condition, I was very shaken. This picture is going to forever stay in my mind as the pictures of many other people and children who were killed by the Serbs. A message to the whole world from me and all the children, my friends, and from all other refugees. Thank you for all the help. Stop this damned war!!

The English translation of Sanel's letter reached hundreds of schools around the world because Vives posted it on a variety of global computer learning networks, including the APC networks, Free Educational Mail (FrEdMail), and the European Schools Project (ESP), where it was translated into many other languages besides English. The reaction was overwhelming. Students everywhere began sending electronic mail messages to the refugee camp. Here are some of their reactions.

Dear Sanel,

I come from Australia. Our class read your letter and I felt upset on how the Serbian soldiers could do something so horrible. Our class is writing to the Australian Government to try to end the war. My dad was in the Vietnam war and he got wounded and my dad doesn't talk about it much but you were there when the Serbian soldiers attacked your dad so you're in a different situation but it's still disgraceful what happens in the world.

Dear Sanel,

I am 13 years old. I live in Duluth, Minnesota. . . . I am really sorry that this war is going on and I hope it gets over soon. I am not just writing this because my teacher told me to, I am writing because I want to. Some people say that this war is just going to go away, but I don't think that it is going to. In my thoughts I think that this war is wrong. People who want to fight don't need guns or knives, what they need to learn is how to fight with words. I just want you to know that I feel really bad for all of you and I hope this war gets over soon.

Dear Sanel,

I am an Australian girl, shocked and repulsed by the present state you and your family have been put in. The brutality and lack of mercy shown by the Serbian soldiers has sickened and disturbed us. Most people my age know little of the tragedies you face but we would like to broaden the international knowledge of the war. Personally I don't know the whole story behind the war and I can't honestly say I can relate to what's happening but I do sympathize and would like to do all in my power to help. I think the world should be more aware of the atrocities others face. As an Australian I can write to the government to increase public awareness, and perhaps the United Nations. We (our class) just want to tell you that people do know what's happening, you are not alone. . . .

With the flood of international concern pouring into his camp, the Croatian Army director decided to pull the plug on the computer the refugee children had been using to communicate with youth around the world. But the Catalan teachers and volunteers knew that the awareness Sanel's letter had evoked could not be allowed to vanish. They tried to come up with creative ways to perpetuate the interest and commitment that had been mobilized in classrooms in so many countries. Narcís Vives posted this electronic message to students and teachers:

> Now the camp's director doesn't allow telecommunications being used there because he loses control of the information leaving the camp. Anyway, we will try to use other ways. Every twenty days some volunteers leave Barcelona, Catalunya, Spain to Veli Joze, Croatia with a lot of messages and drawings. The Bosnian children also send us hand-written messages and drawings which we will share with you if you are interested.[8]

Though electronic mail was no longer possible, Vives was offering to serve as a conduit for the concern that Sanel's message had awakened in classrooms around the world. Mail—electronic and otherwise—began pouring in to Barcelona, including drawings, photographs, videotapes, class projects, and school materials.

Then the whole team of Catalan volunteers and teachers organized yet another way to harness technology to amplify the interest that Sanel's letter had generated. They called for an International Day of Solidarity with Veli Joze on February 26, 1994, the highlight of which would be a simultaneous videophone conference call (sponsored by I*EARN and the Copen Family Fund) between children at Veli Joze and students from two cities in New York and eight schools in Barcelona. Preparations for the Day of Solidarity were complex. In order to expand the number of schools around the world that could participate, Vives sent out a request for drawings and messages of solidarity—written in any language—to be faxed to Barcelona no later than February 24. In the hectic days preceding the activities, Vives wrote:

> I have received messages and drawings related to Veli Joze from Australia, Israel, Chile, Russia, Denmark, Germany, Holland, Croatia and different states in the United States: New York, Georgia, Massachusetts, Texas, Minnesota, Washington, Florida, Ohio.[9]

Early in the morning of February 24, two Catalan teachers and a professional clown left Barcelona with a videophone, all the drawings and messages of solidarity that had arrived from around the world, and another computer and modem. Their destination was the Veli Joze Refugee Camp in Savudrija, Croatia. There they would set up an art exhibit and prepare the necessary equipment for the videophone conference call and the computer teleconference that would take place on February 26, the Day of Solidarity.

That day was filled with activities, many of which were technology-mediated, but with a decidedly human touch. In Veli Joze, the teachers plugged in their videophone—a slow-scan video camera embedded in a standard telephone receiver designed to project photos of speakers and simple texts during phone conversations—and teachers and students in New York and Barcelona saw and spoke with Sanel Cekik himself for the first time. Teachers and other children at Veli Joze answered questions from their international interlocutors and supporters. After the conference call, the Catalan teachers plugged in their computer and modem and conducted a live computer teleconference in which the Veli Joze students could communicate simultaneously with students in six different schools by typing messages that would be read in Catalunya.

But activities of solidarity were not limited to technology-mediated communication. Vives writes:

> [In Catalunya, students] could see some slides from Veli Joze and together in the playground of the school we sang Bob Dylan's song "Blowing in the Wind" with more than 40 guitars and flutes being played by children from different schools.
>
>   In Veli Joze at this same time a Catalan clown called Tortell Poltrona was acting for the children. Later, they could also see an exhibition of drawings and writings. . . .
>
>   Now the solidarity day has gone, but not our solidarity. We will look for the best ways to help. They certainly need money, food . . . but in my opinion what they need the most is love, a lot of people sending them messages, drawings, asking them to do things, motivating them. We still don't know if we will have telecommunication facilities (the Catalan teachers are negotiating with the camp authorities this fact). Anyway, every 20 days a group of Catalan volunteers go to and come from Veli Joze. They can [still] send and bring messages.[10]

Vives was correct; the Day of Solidarity would continue to reverberate in the refugee camp. The Catalan Tortell Poltrona, one of the clowns who was there that day, wrote—in Catalan—of his experience at Veli Joze and its aftermath. There was so much interest in his remarks that they were later translated into several languages by his colleagues in Catalunya. Here is the English translation:

With my performance watched by over 700 people, most of them children, I could determine the value of a clown in such a situation where humour is the medicine and laughter the cure.

In the camps, most of the inhabitants are children, and most of them are orphans. A high rate of psychological and physical tension exists among the people, but the need to laugh never dies, and so, by creating smiles instead of tears, even for only a short period, we can raise the life standard in these depressing camps.

This was not so easy for me, as performer, since the audience was racked with bitter and tragic memories, but once I had one smile, the laughter followed quickly, as though the sun had broken through the storm.

Today, medicine and science recognizes more and more the therapeutic importance of laughter. If laughter is so vital for society under normal conditions, its necessity in conflict situations is obvious.

After this experience we arrived in Barcelona with the decision to organize expeditions of artists to such under-privileged children, not only in war-torn Yugoslavia, but in all situations where children have lost their rights to be children.[11]

Poltrona's performance before hundreds of young interned refugee children was captured on videotape, eventually to appear in a widely circulated video production available from the Southwest Educational Development Laboratory, a regional educational research organization under contract with the U.S. Department of Education.

Poltrona went on to organize Clowns without Borders, a nonprofit organization of artists and performing artists and clowns designed to raise money for refugee camps in war-torn Bosnia-Herzegovina and to visit the camps regularly. To date, different performers have made 23 trips to dozens of camps; moreover, contingents have been sent to Pakistan, Chiapas in Mexico, Brazil, and several countries in North Africa. The performing arts and technology-mediated communication have joined in the effort to respond to the misery engendered by ethnic strife. Narcís Vives summed up their impact:

> The group of teachers that give support to Clowns without Borders and another NGO [Non-Governmental Organization] called Musicians for Peace who have recently joined the project want to continue giving support to the clowns' and musicians' trips, and would like to try once again sending computers and modems to the refugee camps. In fact, we have identified 32 Bosnian refugee camps in Croatia. Three of them would welcome telecommunication facilities to all the world. We are now trying to raise the money to get these computers and modems.[12]

The fleeting glimpse of an end to repression and global strife that seemed at hand at the end of the 1980s has been eclipsed by eruptions of brutal conflicts around the world. For the students and teachers, themselves from many different cultural and linguistic backgrounds, who communicated with their peers in Bosnian refugee camps, "ethnic cleansing" is no longer an abstract concept; it has a human face that brings home to them the personal and collective costs of intolerance and racism. This communication, while uncomfortable, has generated a resolve among many students to understand the roots of discrimination and to confront its manifestations in their own societies.

Portrait 2:
A PARTNERSHIP BETWEEN
CLASSES IN MAINE AND QUEBEC CITY

In the 1992-93 school year, two classrooms (one in northern Maine, close to the border between the United States and Canada, and the other in Quebec City, the capital of the province of Quebec in Canada) were among more than 100 classes that participated in partner-class projects through their involvement with the Orillas multilingual computer network. Their partnership offers special lessons to all parents and educators who are concerned that so few students graduate from high school truly fluent in a foreign language—a skill that could make or break the future career opportunities for many students who will confront a global economy upon graduation.

Both classes were composed of upper elementary grade school children, and neither group had used computer learning networks previously. Here the similarities between the classes ended. The class in northern Maine was composed of students from a francophone background bordering the French-speaking province of Quebec. Their teacher was interested in her pupils recovering the cultural and linguistic heritage of their parents and grandparents through contact with French speakers in Quebec. The students in Maine saw their partnership with the Quebec class as an opportunity to practice their written French, but also as a way to learn more from their parents and elders who still spoke French at home. The teacher of the class in Quebec City, on the other hand, was pleased at the opportunity to sharpen her students' English skills by working on projects with native speakers in the United States.

With these language learning goals in mind, the two teachers proposed a bilingual "language policy" to guide their interschool exchanges: The Maine class would attempt to use French whenever possible, but could always resort to English to express complex ideas, while the Quebecois would employ French for most of their written exchanges, practicing their English whenever they felt comfortable. With this language policy in place, the classes began their work on parallel learning projects in a way that encouraged the acquisition of a new language in both settings.

For their first joint activity, neither group of students knew the exact identities of their counterparts; the classes exchanged "mystery cultural packages" containing soil samples, photos, and examples of local flora and fauna, individual and class photographs without identifying information, and other clues by means of which the partner class might deduce the location of their faraway colleagues. This informal ice-breaking activity was followed by a more formal joint student journalism project that resulted in a student magazine at year's end that both classes had worked hard to make fully bilingual—writing, critiquing, revising and translating—in French and English for each and every student author.

Unlike many classes in the Orillas global learning network, these classes had the advantage of being located relatively close to each other—a mere three-hour school bus ride apart, in an area of the world where such distances seem trivial. Thus, at the end of the school year, the teachers made the arrangements for the Maine class to visit Quebec City. Imagine the feelings of the American students as they met their partner class for the first time face to face. They experienced firsthand that the distant class-mates with whom they had collaborated in French and in English for nearly a year, and upon whom they looked as competent and highly proficient models for learning French as a second language, were deaf. Indeed, their first language was LSQ ("Langue de Signe Quebecois," or French Cana-dian Sign Language) and their second language—a language these pro-foundly deaf students had never heard—was French.

The partnership between the classes in Maine and Quebec City highlights in a dramatic fashion several important elements of binary collaborations (where just two teachers collaborate) and their considerable potential for promoting second-language acquisition and foreign language learning. In class-to-class partnerships teachers have more chances to shape their exchange in ways that suit the particular learning needs of their students. Successful class-to-class partnerships seek to take full advantage of two key elements of networked collaborations that at first would seem antithetical to foreign language acquisition: distance and asynchronous communication.

Distance, in the context of class-to-class exchanges, creates the possi-bility of collaboration with an unknown but knowable audience, principally through written communication. The inevitable cultural differences that exist between distant groups require clarity of written communication in disclosing local realities. Distance also provides multiple occasions for receiving questions from distant colleagues concerning these written com-munications as well as for querying their culturally bound, "home-grown" versions of reality. In the Maine/Quebec City partnership, geographic and cultural distances stimulated a vigorous year-long communication that focused on diverse local realities. Even though students shared a franco-phone heritage, for one group that heritage was a living reality while for the other it was a cultural and linguistic tradition in danger of fading into another kind of distance, the distance of memory. In a sense, communica-tion over geographic and cultural distance had created a context for cultural rescue work.[13]

Although an electronic message may arrive on the other side of the globe seconds after it is sent, e-mail is asynchronous. Asynchronicity—that is, communication that does *not* occur in "real time"—offers the advantage of permitting language learners to reflect on their responses, something that is rarely possible in face-to-face communication. They can take advantage of the calm of off-line composition to refine their electronic mail responses. Since partner classes are working on parallel learning projects, both familiar words and the language structures in which vocabulary items appear are being recycled constantly. Most applied linguists view communicative interaction as perhaps the most important ingredient in second-language acquisition.[14] The communicative interaction we have observed in sister-class partnerships is no less intense than in face-to-face contact. However, it has the additional advantage of encouraging learners to pay attention to language structures and to generate precise vocabulary in ways that usually are not possible in the immediacy of face-to-face communication.

In short, asynchronicity allows second-language learners the extra time they need to elaborate and polish written texts based on "models" of native speakers of the target language, while seeking and relying heavily upon assistance from their local language and cultural resources in the form of teachers, peers, and community members. In the Maine/Quebec City exchange, the deaf students took perhaps the fullest imaginable advantage of the extra time provided by asynchronicity to compose and refine their written communications to their U.S. counterparts with extensive assistance from their local language and cultural "experts," that is, their hearing teachers, parents, and the community in which they lived. Indeed, they— as language learners—in turn became the models for "native-speaker" input for their distant classmates in Maine.

The deaf students, themselves learners of French as a second language, could assume the "expert" role of high-quality "native-language" informants for the students in Maine owing to the asynchronicity of telecomputing and the greater time available for reflection, revision, and capitalizing on assistance from local French speakers. We as parents and teachers need to rethink our assumptions concerning language learning in the context of global learning networks. In the world of the future, there will be little economic opportunity for anyone who cannot speak more than one language. Yet our schools currently do a very poor job in preparing any students to speak additional languages. Ironically, global learning networks hold tremendous potential for breaking this cycle of failed language teaching by helping us benefit from the genuine language learning resources we have close to home.

FAMILIES AND COMMUNITIES LEARNING TOGETHER: BECOMING LITERATE, CONFRONTING PREJUDICE

Many people are surprised to learn that one of the most common forms of collaborative learning taking place over computer-based global networks centers on activities that draw children and their families into learning partnerships across generations. The three portraits that comprise this section are drawn from ten years of experience of the Orillas network and are based upon the writings and research of its codirectors, Enid Figueroa, Kristin Brown, and Dennis Sayers.[15]

These portraits focus on intergenerational learning in two or more languages. We believe they illustrate how high technology can be enlisted not only to promote students' awareness of their families' and culture's oral traditions, but also to confront deep-seated prejudices. Global learning networks can foster the kind of robust communication between youth and their elders that breathes new life into classroom learning, building bridges not only between generations but between the community and school.

Portrait 3:
CONFRONTING INTERETHNIC PREJUDICE IN NEW YORK AND SAN FRANCISCO SCHOOLS[16]

Andrew Hacker's book *Two Nations: Black and White, Separate, Hostile, Unequal* (1995) forcefully documents that much remains unchanged more than 40 years after the landmark *Brown v. Board of Education* decision by the U.S. Supreme Court in which "separate but equal" schools for African American children were declared unconstitutional. In many urban centers, few white families are left in inner cities, and conflict has increased among minority groups who see themselves competing for increasingly scarce resources.

In this portrait, we examine the way in which teachers in inner-city schools have used global learning networks to bridge cultural distances and reduce interethnic prejudice. In doing so they revisited the Contact Theory advanced by social psychologist Gordon Allport in 1954, which argued that prejudice could be reduced through cooperative learning in which students of different racial backgrounds worked together interdependently to achieve common academic goals.[17]

Sheridan Elementary is a recently integrated school located in a predominantly African American neighborhood in San Francisco. In response to a court-mandated desegregation order, immigrant students from the primarily Latino Mission District have been bused to Sheridan in recent years. As in many other inner-city schools, teachers face the challenge of educating an increasingly diverse student population while at the same time counteracting the negative effects of prejudice between the different ethnic groups at their school.

Relations are most strained between the two largest groups at the school, the African Americans and the immigrant Latinos. At Sheridan, as at other newly desegregated schools in the San Francisco Unified School District, the Latinos usually are placed in bilingual education classes while the African Americans are placed either in "regular" classes or in "English Language Development" classes along with other linguistic minorities (Asians, Filipinos, Russians, and other students of European backgrounds).

The social distance between the African American and Latino students is exacerbated at Sheridan Elementary because the school is under construction, with portable classrooms nearly filling the playground. Students have little chance to meet even during recess. The Latino students are not only isolated but fearful, conscious of the resentment their presence causes in the community and in the schools. Juan Carlos Cuellar, a bilingual resource specialist for the school district, points out that strained relations in the desegregated schools reflect tensions in the broader society: "U.S.-born minority students such as African Americans, Chicanos, Asian Americans and Native Americans have been hardened by their own difficult experiences in the dominant U.S. culture. They see themselves as pitted against the new arrivals, and are not very welcoming of the new immigrants."[18] Ms. Tracy Miller, a teacher at Sheridan Elementary, reports overhearing on the playground such negative comments from African American children as "You can't sit here because you're Latina," and Latinos reacting with "You can't play because the black might rub off on me." Ms. Miller feels these prejudices stem from attitudes learned at home and are worsened through nonproductive interactions during school hours.[19]

In the fall of 1993, Cuellar and Dr. Kristin Brown, Orillas codirector and a telecomputing consultant for California school districts, met to explore the role that telecommunications might play in addressing the academic and social problems faced by students in San Francisco's newly desegregated schools. Previous research conducted in Orillas classrooms had shown that carefully planned projects conducted over global learning networks could lead to the reduction of negative attitudes toward recently arrived Puerto Rican students among U.S.-born Latinos.[20]

In creating partnerships for the San Francisco teachers, Brown and Cuellar would carefully select distant bilingual classes that included Latino students from the Caribbean who are themselves of African descent. As they recall their first conversation:

> Since the partner classes in New York or Puerto Rico would include Spanish-speaking Latino students of African descent, we would be linking San Francisco's Latino students with faraway colleagues who in many ways were like them—students who spoke the same mother tongue and shared the experience of learning English as a second language—but whose physical attributes and pride in their African heritage more closely resembled their African American schoolmates. In this way we hoped to provide a bridge between the African Americans and the Latinos who saw one another everyday at school but whose interactions were distorted by fears and deep-seated prejudice.[21]

As a result of this initial strategy session, Cuellar and Brown set to work recruiting teachers who would be interested in participating in year-long Orillas team-teaching exchanges designed to confront prejudice between groups in their schools.

At Sheridan Elementary, Tracy Miller's third/fourth-grade bilingual class was paired with Anne-Marie Riveaux's third-grade bilingual class at P.S. 19 in Brooklyn, New York. The teachers would stay in touch using a variety of technologies including computers and electronic mail, fax, telephone, videotapes, audiotapes, and photos. Ms. Miller's class was composed entirely of Latino students. As the students explained to the partner class in an introductory note,

Nosotros somos de varios paises de América Latina, México, Nicaragua, El Salvador y Guatemala. Todos nosotros somos bilingues. Hablamos inglés y español.

[We're from various countries in Latin America. . . . All of us are bilingual. We speak English and Spanish.]

Ms. Riveaux's class in New York, composed predominantly of African Caribbean students, replied that (like the students in San Francisco) they also spoke Spanish and some English but that "most of our students are from the Dominican Republic, with Puerto Rico, Colombia, Ecuador, and Venezuela represented in the class as well." Ms. Riveaux described her own Caribbean roots, explaining that although she grew up in New York, her mother is from Puerto Rico and her father came from Trinidad. Both classes were eager to get to know better the students in the other class. Their teachers hoped that by getting to know their distant counterparts, students in both classes would get to know themselves and their classmates better.

Both teachers felt that a video exchange could accomplish several goals. Videos would allow students to introduce themselves while providing an informal setting within which students could begin drawing comparisons between Latin American and Caribbean cultural traditions. The two teachers came to an agreement. In Ms. Miller's class, students would create a video about indigenous celebrations of El Dia de Los Muertos (the Day of the Dead); in Ms. Riveaux's class, students would produce a video about traditional games passed down through oral traditions within their families and communities.

It was at the end of October in 1993 when Tracy Miller's class began planning the video they would send to Ms. Riveaux's class. On everyone's mind were the upcoming cultural activities they had planned for the Day of the Dead on November 2. Not surprisingly, then, they selected this topic as the theme of their video. Because the Latino students in Ms. Miller's class realized that the students in Ms. Riveaux's class might not know about the Day of the Dead, they composed an explanation to read at the beginning of their video:

En California las comunidades latino-americanos celebran el Dia de los Muertos haciendo altares en las galerías de los centros culturales. Además se organiza una procesión dentro de la comunidad en la noche.

Para los altares los niños cortan papel picado y hacen figuras de papel picado. También hacen máscaras de "papier-mâché". En los altares ponen comida y lo que le gusta al muerto en el altar. Se hace una variedad de artes dramáticas y visuales para festejar esta celebración.

[In California the Latin American communities celebrate the Day of the Dead by making altars in the galleries of cultural centers. In addition, processions are organized through the community at night. For the altars, children make designs and figures out of cut tissue paper. We also make masks of "papier-mâché." Food and whatever the dead would like is placed on the altar. The festivities include a variety of dramatic and visual art for this celebration.][22]

In the class students began discussing what else they might show their new friends in New York. As Ms. Miller recalls, their ideas poured forth: "We could teach them the 'Naranja Dulce' [sweet orange] song, we'll show them the masks we're going to make, we can tell them about the field trip we have planned to visit the Mission Cultural Center, we'll tell them about the altar we're making in our class and the people in our families who we are remembering."

Activities in the classroom took on a new level of excitement as the students planned how they would sequence the video for their partner class. They would begin it with a dance behind masks and then later reveal who they were. This way the other class also would have a chance to learn about Mexican masks. As they would later explain in their video:

We make masks by cutting strips of plaster material that people use to make casts for broken bones. We put Vaseline all over the face so it doesn't stick to the skin. Then we wet the material and put it on the face and leave the strips on about ten minutes. It feels cold and scary. Later we paint the masks.

Next the students created a brightly colored altar in the corner of their classroom, covering cardboard boxes with fuchsia and blue fadeless paper and cut tissue-paper designs and then balancing skeleton puppets on top made from cut paper and brads. On the front of the altar they prominently displayed one of the well-known Day of the Dead prints by Guadalupe Posada, a Mexican artist from the early twentieth century. The print the students chose to display was La Catrina, the prototype of an aristocrat—a fancy lady with feathers and flowers in her hat—"a fancy *dead* lady" the students liked to point out, adding "because everybody dies."

This flurry of activity and excitement caught the attention of other teachers and students at Sheridan, who asked if they could stop by the room to see the altar (which was becoming more elaborately decorated each day as students brought in artifacts, photos, and other items by which to remember the dead in their families). In the teachers' lounge, Ms. Miller discussed the video exchange with Ms. Hornsby, an African American teacher of a second-grade class composed predominantly of African American students with a few Chinese and Filipino students and one Native American child. These teachers were good friends and were both interested in improving race relations at the school. Both saw an opportunity for bringing their classes together and expanding the original scope of the project in order to get the African American students into direct, productive contact with the Latino students. They saw the power of global learning networks to act as a catalyst for change at the local level.

And so Ms. Miller's class (Room 17) formally invited the students from Ms. Hornsby's second grade class (Room 7) to see their altar. They also invited Ms. Hornsby's class on the day they had set aside to film the video for the partner class in New York. While Mr. Cuellar set up the video camera, the students of Room 17 proudly taught the students from Room 7 the song "Naranja Dulce, Limón Silvestre," a traditional Day of the Dead song. They wrote the words on the board, so the two classes could sing it together on the video. All the students wanted the video to come out well and so were constantly whispering instructions to Mr. Cuellar about how to arrange the room to get the best takes.

As Mr. Cuellar started taping, Tracy Miller began by explaining the altar to their distant audience in New York City, providing her introduction in English so Ms. Hornsby's class would understand but also taking advantage of the "teachable moment" to have all the students pronounce key words in Spanish, such as *ofrenda* and *pan de muerto* (meaning offering, and bread of the dead).

Ms. Miller: Greetings to our friends at P.S. 19 in New York. We are very excited. We are here today with Ms. Hornsby's class to talk to you about our altar.

A lot of people call this *ofrenda*. In many countries in Latin America and in Mexico this is a national holiday, and people don't have to go to school or work because on this day they visit the cemeteries and they decorate the graves with skeletons and candles and bread of the dead, or *pan de muerto*, which is supposed to look like a mummy. The reason they put food on the altar is because people in the land of the dead are going to come back and visit us and so we need to have some food for them to eat because they are going to be very hungry and very thirsty. We have on our altar also a glass of water. My students have brought things to the altar remembering the people they knew who have died.

At this point Ms. Miller picked up one of the items on the altar and signaled to a young girl from Mexico sitting in front of her. Coralia jumped up. Ms. Miller continued, "For example, Coralia has brought a little house she made of cardboard and a little figure of a chicken. Coralia will tell you about it."

Coralia (in Spanish): *Porque a mi abuelo le gustaba pintar houses y a mi abuela le gustaba dar de comer a las gallinas.*

And Ms. Miller motions to Mario, a bilingual student in the class who translates: "Her grandfather liked to paint houses and her grandmother liked to feed chickens."

Ms. Miller continues, "Lydia will tell you why she brought a cup," and motions to Lydia, who explains, *"Yo traje esta taza porque a mi tia le gustaba tomar mucho café y por eso le traje la taza para que la recuerde."* Mario translates: "Her aunt really loved to drink coffee and so to remember her aunt she put a coffee cup on the altar."

"Now Jesse will explain what he brought," Ms. Miller says as the tape continues.

Jesse: I brought this because I have a photo of my grandfather that died. Here is his picture. That's him. He died because he had a heart attack. Tomorrow I'm going to bring a little plastic horse for the altar because he liked to ride a horse.

Ms. Miller: José will go next.

José: El nombre de mi tío es Juanito. Mi tío murió cuando yo tenía dos años y el vivía solo en una casa de piedra y mi abuelita le llevaba de comer a la casa de tío Juanito.

Mario: The name of my uncle is Juanito. My uncle died when I was two years old and he lived alone in a stone house and my grandmother brought food to the house of my uncle Juanito.

Ms. Miller: Jessica will tell how they celebrate in Guatemala.

Jessica: In Guatemala they celebrate the Day of the Dead with food, water and flowers and they go to Chichicastenango where the Indians are. They go to church with their friends and relatives, and they go to the cemetery where the old people died, and after that they go to the church and put food and water.

Everyone notices that this time it is not one of Ms. Miller's students who has her hand raised to speak but a student from Ms. Hornsby's class. Ms. Miller calls on Winnie. Winnie begins shyly, "We have the same thing but it's not the same." Ms. Miller realizes that she hasn't introduced Winnie as she had each of the others who have spoken in front of the video camera. So she says, "Winnie Young will tell us how they remember the dead in her homeland, China."

Winnie: We got two ways in our family. One is to go to the cemetery to put some food and flowers. Another way we celebrate is in the house. At home the people who died, we put their picture on the top of the wall and we put the food and flowers and something else by this. The other day when we celebrate we put some paper things in the fire so that they burn.

After Winnie breaks the ice, an African American boy from Room 7 raises his hand. Ms. Miller calls on him and he says his uncle has died. After Ms. Miller introduces him, Renell continues:

Renell: What we do is call all our family up and send them invitations to come over to the city of San Francisco. They come on Friday and first when they come we do fun things together but on Saturday morning about

11 we go to the graveyard and give my uncle flowers and after that we stare at the grave and then we just leave and go have a barbecue and we usually just get together, like eat and other good things. I like remembering my uncle and another thing . . . some people don't like to remember in my family because they think it's tragic but it's a good thing to remember your family because they'll always be dead. Except for the spirit, he'll always be dead. It's a good thing to remember your family.

Everyone in the classes at Sheridan was eager to know if Ms. Riveaux's class in New York would like their video. Soon a package arrived in the mail from New York. Inside they found a note in which the partner class said they were excited to receive the video. It had inspired Anne-Marie Riveaux's third graders to create a class altar also and discuss the universal theme of life and death. Tracy Miller's class was excited to learn that the package also included a video. The students in Ms. Riveaux's class had taped students playing the games they had learned from their families and parents. Ms. Miller's students watched animatedly and eagerly, making comments about each game as they took delight in seeing games that they were familiar with, games like the ones that they had played in Mexico before they arrived in the United States.

The partner teachers (now expanded to include Ms. Riveaux in New York and Ms. Miller and Ms. Hornsby in San Francisco) decided that their next joint project would be to make a book of games collected from the families in all three classes. Ms. Riveaux wrote:

When I first introduced the idea to my students they were so excited at the thought we were going to be playing games. Little did they know that by playing games we were going to be learning so much. When I mentioned it to the parents on open school night, they showed much enthusiasm also. The children went home and worked with parents on writing up their reports. When they brought them in, the children came in front of the classroom and told us about their game: how to play it, their experience working with a relative on the project, and memories of when they played the game in their homeland.[23]

Ms. Riveaux faced a difficult situation at the beginning of the year: Students were being moved in and out of her class so frequently that they felt rejected and had lost any sense of community. She shared with the other teachers the value of the games project, describing it as "great community-building activity with my class."

For the teachers at Sheridan, the most attractive aspect of the games project was the opportunity it provided for drawing parents' traditional knowledge into their curriculum. Ms. Hornsby was already doing a thematic unit on families and ancestors; what better way to complement her unit than to ask children, equipped with tape recorders, to interview their parents about the games they had played as children, folk games passed down through countless generations? And since folk games were universal while remaining culture-specific, what more powerful way to help their students discover a common humanity across cultural differences?

The hardest part at both schools was finding a place to teach one another the folk games they were collecting. New York City public schools often lack even asphalt playgrounds, and Ms. Riveaux's was no exception. Sheridan Elementary was "under construction" that year. As it turned out, the common area at both schools turned out to be the cafeteria before or after lunch. The teachers at Sheridan rearranged their schedules so that both their recreation periods fell in the morning when the cafeteria was free. They were careful to assign their students to small groups, consisting of some African American and some Latino students. In these small groups, the students would teach each other folk games, with the "expert" bilingual students doing the translating—causing their status to soar among their peers.

Ms. Hornsby's class began by showing Ms. Miller's students how to play Mancala, a game from Africa. Then Ms. Miller's class showed Ms. Hornsby's students how to play *Haciendo Cuadritos,* a pencil-and-paper strategy game. Day after day, the students moved from cross-cultural marbles, to jacks, tops, and hopscotch, all simple, enjoyable, pleasurable games. Here is what the students wrote about what it meant to them to share them:

> Nos gusta aprender las costumbres de otros estudiantes. Por eso, la unidad Juegos Tradicionales es perfecta para nuestra clase. Compartimos juegos de Nicaragua, El Salvador, y Guatemala con el salón 7 mientras que ellos nos enseñan juegos originando de África.

> [We like to learn the customs of other students. For this reason, the unit on "folk games" is perfect for our class. We share games

from Nicaragua, El Salvador, and Guatemala with Room 7 while they teach us games originating in Africa.] [24]

Reflecting the bilingual character of their learning context, one student wrote in *both* languages:

Hemos aprendido que muchos de los juegos tienen algo en com n. De hecho, todos nosotros tenemos algo en com n y todos nosotros podemos ser amigos. Después de participar en este programa, Mario Riva expresó lo que aprendió así: "In this world there is a friend for everyone!"

[We have learned that many of the games have something in common. In fact, we all have something in common and we all can be friends. After participating in this project, Mario Riva expressed what he had learned in this way: "In this world there is a friend for everyone!"] [25]

And the African American students in Room 7 also knew they were doing something important while enjoying the pleasure of sharing folk games. They wrote:

We began our games unit to help us with social studies, multiculturalism, and conflict resolution. By sharing games with one another, we have learned that we all have something in common—we like to have fun together! We have all made new friends through sharing the games our parents played as children. This is a project we'd like to continue. [26]

But their teachers knew the real question was: Would their newfound friendships, based on short-term intercultural sharing, actually *last* longer than the school year? There were some signs they did. A year later, Ms. Hornsby and Ms. Miller continue to collaborate. Ms. Miller now has two African American girls in her bilingual class (former pupils of Ms. Hornsby) since their parents *demanded* that their children be given the opportunity to learn Spanish by studying with Spanish-speaking students. Last reports were that the two girls were learning Spanish as a second language, and according to Ms. Miller, "They love it and think it's great." And for the first time ever at Sheridan Elementary, Latina girls have joined the Girl Scout troop, originally organized by African American and European American mothers. Who are the new recruits? *Every single girl* in Ms. Miller's bilingual class this year. Perhaps Tracy Miller deserves the last word on the potential of global learning networks for reducing prejudice:

> We still need to do so much more, to integrate the classes themselves, to have after-school programs where all students play and work together. It's a very slow process, but there was real understanding, and one thing leads to another. Some schools don't do anything. But this was a good starting point.[27]

Portrait 4:
THE SHERMAN SCHOOL AFTER-SCHOOL COMPUTER COURSE FOR PARENTS AND THEIR CHILDREN

This portrait illustrates a team-teaching partnership with just three schools. It is particularly interesting because of the wide range of ages, languages, and literacy skills of the participants. While most Orillas partnerships take place between school-age children, this example describes the experiences of a group that included both parents and children.

Sherman Elementary is located in Barrio Sherman in San Diego, California, in a neighborhood principally composed of Latino, African American, Cambodian, and European American communities. During the 1989-90 school year, ethnic and linguistic minority parents and their children from this school participated in an Orillas telecommunications exchange with other groups of parents and children from Denver, Colorado, and from Caguas, Puerto Rico. At the start of the school year, Sherman School planned an after-school computer course for both parents and their children. All parents, regardless of their linguistic or academic backgrounds, would be welcome; indeed both the teacher of this literacy class, Lourdes Bourás, and the school contact person, Laura Parks-Sierra, had worked extensively with students in the Orillas Project in previous years and had discovered the effectiveness both of using computers for a variety of communication activities and of having students work in teams.

The design of the parent-child literacy course would be similar to the approach already used in the Orillas network: Local partners would work on the computer, learning to use it both as a writing tool (word processing) and as a communication tool (telecommunications). Next, the many local partners who made up the Sherman School literacy course would form another kind of partnership with distant partner classes, using electronic mail. Finally, what they wrote eventually would be published locally in a newsletter distributed in the community. The only difference between previous Orillas projects and this literacy course would be that this time the local partnerships would be made of a parent or caretaker and his or her own child.

The "computer" course was announced at school to all second-through sixth-grade students. On the first night of the class, dozens of parents appeared. Several confided that they were tired after long days at work and of caring for their families. They might not have left the house, they admitted, except for the insistence of their children for whom computer time is a favorite activity. However, by the end of the evening many commented that they were intrigued with the prospect of learning how to use a computer with their children, and particularly the idea of communicating with other parents and children in far-off places.

At the outset, there were some difficulties just in learning to use word processing and other software programs. Explanations to the group seemed labored: The teacher was fluent in Spanish and in English, but English speakers initially expressed some impatience at having to wait for the lessons to continue during what seemed like lengthy translations; they complained of time "wasted" or "taken" from more important, computer-related tasks. Moreover, Ms. Bourás reported her sense that, during initial computer projects, whoever was at the keyboard assumed control, creating barriers for others to join in as full participants.

Yet once communications from the distant parent groups began to arrive, some interesting changes seemed to take place in parents' and students' attitudes, both toward engaging in computer-based collaborations and toward language use. The group, faced with the task of representing and describing San Diego in response to the initial questions from the distant groups, became more cohesive.

To help introduce themselves to their partner groups in Colorado and Puerto Rico, the Sherman School parents and children decided to make and send a "culture package" that featured a book to which everyone could contribute, regardless of their level of literacy in their mother tongue or in English. For example, the Cambodian family in which parents could not speak, read, or write English brought in the most pictures, hand-drawn sketches, and magazine articles. Together, parents and children elaborated a clear picture of the book they wanted to send; the parents and children worked in teams to create the different sections and then shared their writing and the pictures they had gathered with the rest of the group. As the parents learned to help one another, they could draw on the model of how their children had helped them all along, especially in terms of computer skills and English literacy. All the text had been typed in and printed out using computers. The parent/child-authored book had become a "seamless" group product where the individuality usually expressed in the concept of "sole authorship" had become unimportant.

Moreover, the Spanish speakers' status changed when most of the messages began arriving over the computer in Spanish. As the group logged on to the electronic mail system to read messages from Colorado and Puerto Rico, parents and children pulled their chairs as close as possible to the computer to read the text. Suddenly, proficiency in Spanish became highly prized as messages that everyone was so interested in reading scrolled by in Spanish. English speakers now saw the importance of devoting time to translation, even insisting that translation be done carefully to ensure that everyone understood the incoming messages. English-speaking parents who previously had worked on their own sought seats next to Spanish speakers, and were active in assuring that the teacher had translated every detail (at times, double-checking with their local bilingual/bicultural "expert"). In Ms. Parks-Sierra's words, "These discussions really seemed to bring the group together."

Thus the concept of teamwork was expanding. To be sure, all teams did not function identically. Some parents and their children "shared" equally all stages of writing (prewriting, drafting, and revising and editing) and translating (from their home language to English and back). Other teams divided the writing task in a variety of effective ways, with some parents playing the key role of topic "definers" in the home language while their children, who sat at the keyboard, acted as English language interpreters and "refiners." One child described this relationship to his intergenerational co-authors:

Dear parents and children,
Our names are Keovong, Maria and Eam. I am Keovong the one that is

typing because I am good at typing. I was born in Philippines and
my parents are from Cambodia. My mom come to computer class. My mom
is writing in Cambodian and someone will translate it in English or
Spanish. My dad used to come with me to the computer. Many of my
people had died in Cambodia. My land has been taken by the bad people.
But now I am far away from my home land and I am safe in San Diego.
Your new friend,
Keovong Sar[28]

This was just the first stage in what might be termed a "nested sequence
of intergenerational collaborations," where children and parents interacted
and later communicated their new understandings to other parents and
children. Next, there would be closer collaboration between different
linguistic groups, as parents and children translated for one another and
began to share their differing cultural and linguistic skills.

Unlike previous courses for parents sponsored by the Sherman School,
the high attendance in the Parent-Child Computer Course justified continuing it for the entire academic year. Parents and children attributed this,
in large part, to the communications with the faraway parent groups and
the parents' continuing interest in what the distant partner classes would
write. By the end of the year, the Sherman School parents and children had
created numerous collaborative publications. Here we list those publications, along with key excerpts:

- A bilingual booklet of parent-teacher conference guidelines distributed to all of Sherman School's parents and teachers.

  Tu participación es importante: ¿Qué es una conferencia familiar?
  Una conferencia familiar es cuando nos reunimos con los maestros
  de nuestros hijos para hablar sobre su aprovechamiento escolar y su
  comportamiento en la escuela. Es el momento de aprender más
  acerca de nuestros hijos y sus maestros.

  [Let's Lead the Way: What is a Family Conference?
  A family conference is an update on your child's progress and to
  discuss their future goals. It is a network between teacher, student
  and parents."][29]

- An international collection of articles on self-esteem and technology, for which the Sherman School Computer Class worked with university professors, psychologists, teachers, and other parents and children from North and South America.

> I think that a computer is good for children as well as adults because it let you put down your thoughts and feelings and express your opinions. . . . I think it's great that the children are learning about computers and how they work and how to use them and write their own stories and to read what they have written. I think it gives them a good feeling inside to know that they did it and that they are as important as we are.
>
> —Christyl McCorley [African American mother with two children in the computer class]

> In response to the question, on learning by technology, it is my personal belief that it is a good way to prepare our children and ourselves to meet the future for it is changing daily. It is nothing to be afraid of, it is like turning on your television or dialing your phone. The difference is that here you are upon something new, and if you do not have familiarity with the equipment, it's natural to feel unease about technology.
> . . . In the case of computers, at first you may feel not capable to be able to manipulate its system. As you start playing the keyboard, you begin to get a much better feeling about what you are doing. It then becomes a challenge between you and the system, until you are able to master it.
>
> —Hector Reynoso [Mexican American parent]

- A community newspaper—the product of collaboration with teachers and administrators and children at Sherman School. (Original spelling and punctuation is retained in the following anonymous article written by other mothers in the class.)

> An Exemplary Mother
> Eam is originally from Cambodia, she is medium high has a beautiful black hair and is always smiling. She started coming to the computer

class almost from the beginning. She never missed a class and she always had a positive attitude toward everybody. Eam looks so young that you will never believe she is thirty six years old. She was a mother of nine children, but three of them died in the war in Batanbag, in Cambodia.

Eam was 15 when she got married, even though this sounds too young, this is normal for Cambodians. . . . Eam didn't want to have children right away but contraceptive methods were not very advanced in Cambodia so she got pregnant right away. Her new family grew fast and she had to work harder and harder, since in Cambodia your children depend very much from the mother's care. It was fascinating talking with Eam and getting to know such a different culture, but what makes this story more fascinating is the fact that no matter where in the world we are or where do we come from the importance of being a caring and loving parent is always the key for our future generations. And Eam is one of these great mothers that has helped six children grow up with an incredible future in front of them.

As parents recognized the many resources and talents of their local and distant colleagues, they realized how much they could accomplish if they pooled their efforts in new ways. They gained greater confidence in their ability to publish newspapers and write books. They came to see that other parents would be interested in what they had to say and that together they had the potential to effect change in their local community through the sharing of their distant voices. And bilingual literacy skills emerged without having been explicitly "taught" in these intergenerational long-distance partnerships.

Portrait 5:
LA ESCUELA ABELARDO DIAZ MORALES AND THE "ORILLAS INTERNATIONAL PROVERBS PROJECT": USING TELECOMMUNICATIONS TO CONDUCT FOLKLORE INVESTIGATIONS

Teachers in Orillas can participate by engaging in at least one of three very different types of activities: (1) the exchange of cultural packages through the postal service to help the participating classes get to know one another; (2) partner-class projects involving joint investigations resulting in a single product based on contributions by both classes; or (3) group projects involving many teachers and their classes, which usually result in an Orillas-wide publication.

The following portrait describes a group project in which many Orillas teachers participated. Group projects are designed to take advantage of the rich possibilities for intercultural learning provided by an international network. Over this network, a community is created of teachers interested in a single theme dealing with an issue of global interest, such as the environment, human rights, or the loss of oral traditions. Group projects are particularly suited for themes that benefit from multiple perspectives on a single issue or in which collective effort can create impressive bodies of information that students can analyze later or patterns and regional differences.

In 1989, Orillas announced a group project whose goal was to collect and analyze proverbs. It is important to note that the categories proposed were simply suggestions, based on the previous experiences of successful team-teaching partnerships. In all Orillas projects, teachers are invited to design and shape the activities according to their local needs. Here we provide a close-up of one particular class in Puerto Rico and then describe different ways in which other teachers have adapted the project to their own curriculum.

La Escuela Abelardo Diaz Morales, named after a distinguished Puerto Rican educator, is an elementary school in Caguas, Puerto Rico. Its students are proud of their computer lab, the walls of which never fail to catch the eye of the visitor. On these bulletin board walls are photographs of students and their teachers, flags of Mexico and California, illustrated maps, richly colored student artwork, a collection of Yaqui legends from the Southwest, and several issues of the student-produced newspaper, *Cemí.* The bulletin boards trace the history of this school's participation in Project Orillas.

Each year since 1986, the computer writing teacher, Rosa Hernández, has engaged in a long-distance team-teaching exchange with a teacher in another part of the world, using a classroom computer, a modem, and a computer network. Networking also has made it possible for Ms. Hernández and her students to stay in touch with the wider group of Orillas teachers and to participate in a variety of Orillas group projects, including a survey of endangered species, an international human rights project, and several intergenerational folklore investigations, such as the Proverbs Project, originally presented to Orillas teachers in the following project announcement.

ANNOUNCING: INTERNATIONAL PROVERBS PROJECT
from Kristin Brown, Dennis Sayers, and
Enid Figueroa Orillas Co-Directors

Orillas is sponsoring a multilingual proverbs contest. We invite your students to participate in one or more of the following categories:

- BEST DRAWING illustrating one of the following proverbs: "Those who live in glass houses should not throw stones" or "It takes all kinds to make the world go around".
- BEST ORIGINAL FABLE Students pick a proverb, write an original story illustrating that proverb, then give the proverb at the end of the story as the "punchline."
- GREATEST NUMBER OF "ANIMAL" PROVERBS SUBMITTED BY A SINGLE CLASS Example, "A barking dog never bites." Helpful hint: Ask the parents and relatives of your students to help out!
- GREATEST NUMBER OF CONTRADICTORY PROVERBS SUBMITTED BY A SINGLE CLASS Example, "There's no place like home" contradicts "The grass is greener on the other side of the fence."
- BEST ORIGINAL ESSAY ON "WHAT'S WRONG WITH THIS PROVERB" Pick a proverb you don't agree with and write an essay explaining what is wrong with the views it projects. Not all proverbs are wise; some of them say terrible things about others. For example, the sexist proverb "A woman's place is in the home" suggests that women should only do housework. Other proverbs are racist, ageist, or ridicule people with handicaps.

The contest is open to students of all grades and speakers of all languages. By identifying proverbs whose social, moral or political views are obsolete, by searching for modern examples to illustrate noble or wise proverbs, and by exploring under what circumstances seemingly contradictory proverbs are true, we can all help define the "collective wisdom" of the 20th century, and beyond.

At the end of the semester each participating class will receive a booklet containing selected student essays, photocopies of the drawings, and a list of all the proverbs collected.[30]

Over the next few weeks, Ms. Hernández's class, like many others throughout the Orillas network, gathered proverbs, focusing especially on ones containing animals. The list grew as students collected proverbs from parents, older brothers and sisters, grandparents living at home, neighbors, and other nearby relatives. During the school's spring break, the week of Semana Santa (the Holy Week preceding Easter), when families travel to other parts of the island to visit friends and relatives, the list grew most dramatically. Just before the vacation, Ms. Hernández printed out for each student a copy of the animal proverbs collected up to that point. When the students returned to school the following week, their lists were well worn and much longer. "Nearly a hundred animal proverbs!" they exclaimed when they had finished adding the new proverbs to the old.

The class discovered that the task of categorizing the proverbs they gathered by theme was not as easy as it first appeared. The students debated the meanings of the proverbs and eliminated duplicates while making note of the frequency of use of each proverb. They identified different versions and regional variations, and compared notes with their classmates about the contexts in which their parents and grandparents actually used the proverbs. As they continued to gather and analyze proverbs, they stayed in touch with other classes on the network.

In other classes, teachers and students had integrated the project into their own curriculum in a variety of ways. In Watsonville, California, for example, the proverbs project was used to build parent involvement in the school's bilingual program. A migrant farmer parent at Watsonville and his kindergarten child wrote the following critique of a proverb:

Vale más un pájaro en mano que ver cien volando
    No estamos de acuerdo con este refrán porque las personas no
    nos debemos conformar con lo que tenemos sino luchar y
    esforzarnos para vivir mejor cada dia.
                    —Por los padres de Angélica Pérez García,
                            Kinder, Watsonville, California

[A bird in the hand is worth two in the bush
    We don't agree with this proverb because people shouldn't be
    satisfied with what we have but instead should struggle and
    make an effort to make each day better.]

—by the parents of Angélica Pérez García,
Kindergarten, Watsonville, California]

In a bilingual fifth/sixth-grade class in Connecticut, students worked on a unit on fables, first reading fables in Spanish and English written by Samaniego, Aesop, and La Fontaine, then writing their own fables that illustrated some proverbs the class in Puerto Rico had collected. In this class, students chose proverbs that reflected their own experiences. Here is one story/fable they wrote illustrating a proverb and tying it to academic learning.

El mismo perro pero con diferente collar
    Había una vez una maestra llamada Ms. Caraballo. Le estaba
    enseñando a sus estudiantes de tercer grado como multiplicar.
    Ella les enseñaba todo lo necesario a sus alumnos.
        "Bueno estudiantes," dijo la Sra. Caraballo. "¿Cuánto
    es 2 X 3?" Solo una estudiante levantó su mano y dijo, "Seis."
    Todos los estudiantes entendieron eso, menos Pedro.
        "Maestra," dijo Pedro, "Yo no sé como hacer eso."
        "Bueno Pedro," dijo Ms. Caraballo amablemente. "Esto
    es como si tu dijeras 3 + 3, pero en otra forma. Como si
    dijera 3 + 3 + 3 que es lo mismo que 3 X 3, que es igual que
    9, pero en otra forma."
        "Ahora ya entiendo," dijo Pedro. "Es como mi abuelo me
    dijo del refrán—'el mismo perro pero con diferente collar.'"

[The Same Dog but with a Different Collar
    Once there was a teacher named Ms. Caraballo. She was teaching
    her third-grade students to multiply. She taught her students
    everything they needed to know.
        "Okay, students," said Ms. Caraballo. "How much is 2 X
    3?" Only one student raised her hand and said "six." All the
    students understood this, except Pedro.

"Teacher," said Pedro. "I don't know how to do that."

"Well, Pedro," said Ms. Caraballo in a friendly way, "it is like saying 3 + 3 but in a different form. Just as 3 + 3 + 3, 3 X 3, and 9 are all different ways of saying the same thing."

"Now I understand," said Pedro, "it's just like the proverb my grandfather taught me—'The same dog but with a different collar.'"]

At another school, a sixth-grade class asked students at other grade levels to illustrate familiar proverbs. They then classified the drawings in terms of whether each illustration was based on a literal or figurative interpretation of the proverb. The teacher was excited to note that for the first time in all her years of trying to get her upper-elementary level students to understand the textbook terms "literal and figurative speech," her students had announced in class, "Now we understand, Sra. Druet, it's like the way you can be talking about the horse's mouth and really it has nothing to do with a horse."

In other classes, this folklore project evolved into a lesson on sophisticated editorial writing. Proverbs are controversial by nature. They cannot be separated from the inequities of power relationships within the social fabric from which they have developed and in which they inextricably exist. In several classes, students wrote about proverbs they could not agree with. In the following examples, students from New York draw on their own experiences as they critique proverbs that they feel are unfair. The least favorite proverb among students in the United States was "A woman's place is in the home." A New York student explains:

El lugar de la mujer es en el hogar

Yo, Martha Prudente, no estoy de acuerdo en que la mujer esté en el hogar. Eso era el pensamiento de los tiempos antiguos. Así era como mis padres pensaban pero yo no, porque soy rebelde. Sí yo voy a tener un hogar pero sí quiero trabajar, voy a trabajar. Y pienso ser enfermera antes de casarme y después yo sigo trabajando en mi carrera.

[A woman's place is in the home.

I, Martha Prudente, do not agree that a woman's place is in the home. This kind of thinking is old-fashioned. This is

```
how my parents thought, but not me because I am a rebel. Yes,
I will have a home, but if I want to work I will work. I hope
to be a nurse before I get married and afterwards continue
working in my career.]
```

Cervantes once referred to proverbs as "short sentences drawn from long experience." The International Orillas Proverbs Project just described stems from a long-standing and continuing interest on the part of Orillas teachers in exploring folklore in networked classrooms. The teachers involved in the project concluded that proverbs provide an excellent vehicle for students to share cultural and linguistic knowledge for the following reasons:

- Proverbs are universal.
- The families of students are involved, encouraging oral histories.
- Children from families who have immigrated to North America and elsewhere can build links to their (in some cases, disappearing) culture, and learn to take pride in their rich proverbial heritage.
- Analyzing proverbs encourages discussion, critical thinking, and a deromanticized appreciation of culture.
- Students studying Spanish as a foreign language gain from the cultural knowledge embodied in proverbs.
- Young students can participate as the amount of text to be shared is small and easily entered in the computer.
- Proverbs can encourage much longer writings, such as opinion statements or modern fables.
- A database can be used to categorize proverbs by themes in order to facilitate cross-cultural comparisons.
- Collecting proverbs is a provocative yet discrete task resulting in a rich, concrete product.

In this project, telecommunications made it possible for bilingual students from diverse regions to collaborate rapidly in a wide-ranging investigation of proverbs. Moreover, the students created materials that classroom teachers everywhere were able to use to stimulate reading and writing skills, often across two languages. Folklore collections of all kinds can be instrumental in building bridges between schools and families and within the wider community of speakers of a particular language—both among the diaspora of local immigrant communities, and their cultures of origin around the world. Yet they also can bring cross-cultural awareness and language skills to students who otherwise would never have access to people from distant lands and other worldviews. Once again, students from every background stand to benefit from participation in global learning networks.

INTERCULTURAL CONNECTIONS IN THE BORDERLANDS OF TIME AND SPACE

Global learning networks also afford students and teachers unprecedented opportunities for confronting the living reality of injustice in distant lands or the not-so-distant past, all the while drawing connections between the social inequities they discover elsewhere and those within their own communities. Both Orillas and the I*EARN global learning network offer many examples of this type of critical learning. We have chosen three for this final section of portraits.

First, we examine the I*EARN's international Holocaust/Genocide Project as a multifaceted activity that took full advantage of the global reach of telecommunications to bring home to students the history of the Holocaust and to provide concrete lessons on how we all bear a responsibility, in one student's words, to assure that "the suffering which occurred in the Holocaust serves as a shield for future victims" of prejudice and intolerance.

Second, we trace the development of the Nicaragua Rope Pump Project in which students around the world joined together to raise funds for digging sanitary wells refitted with simple but effective water-drawing technology. In the process, they learned important lessons about underdevelopment and the painful legacies of neo-colonial domination as played out in the personal lives of their "distant classmates" in Nicaragua.

In the final portrait, we consider the intense controversy surrounding *The Contemporary,* a student publication that dared to print a frank exchange of views between an American teacher working in a Palestinian school and teachers and students in Israeli and Palestinian schools, based on electronic mail exchanges. In all three portraits, we provide extensive examples of students' writings over electronic networks in an effort to trace how their awareness of distant social issues evolved to the stage at which they could see the relevance of these issues for their daily lives.

Portrait 6:
THE HOLOCAUST/GENOCIDE PROJECT

The Holocaust/Genocide Project (HGP) is one of many I*EARN initiatives that focus on using telecommunications for raising and confronting issues of prejudice and intolerance in schools around the world. Since January 1992, under the mentorship of Gideon Goldstein representing I*EARN in Israel, it has involved schools in Argentina, Australia, the newly independent republics of the former Soviet Union, Israel, Poland, and in the United States, California, New Mexico, New York, Washington State, and Wisconsin. As one of its student coordinators describes the project in its annual publication, *An End to Intolerance:*

> The HGP enables students to use telecommunications to share information on an international level about history, literature and art, as well as emotional responses concerning genocide. Students have the opportunity to discuss the Holocaust of WWII and learn about the murder of eleven million people. Surprisingly, many people do not know about the Holocaust according to a recent Associated Press article, and that is one thing that we want to change.[31]

The youth who participated in the Holocaust/Genocide Project have exploited networking possibilities more than students in any of the other projects discussed in this chapter. Full-service Internet access for teachers and students essentially offers two broad areas of networking capability: on-line access to information in the form of databases and documents stored in computer archives around the world, and the means for communicating and collaborating with people who share common concerns and interests.

The Holocaust/Genocide Project is a textbook example of how—without using textbooks—these two kinds of connectivity can be woven together to create contexts for critical thinking and empowerment that help students confront such deep-seated social problems as racism and intolerance.

The pages of *An End to Intolerance* are replete with evidence of students' growing ease and expertise at utilizing the Internet to advance their project's goals. In order to conduct the basic research for the detailed articles they wished to publish on the Holocaust and to identify the resources and materials that would be annotated and reviewed, students used the network to locate and consult numerous databases. One database consulted was the Holocaust and Fascism Archives located in Victoria, Canada, where 2,500 Holocaust-related documents are stored. Using the Internet, students were able to connect via Canada to Jerusalem, where a descriptive menu of the holdings there allowed them to examine each document and decide which ones they wanted delivered by electronic mail back to their schools in seconds.

Another database accessed was the Holocaust and Genocide Bibliographic Database, available from the Institute on The Holocaust and Genocide in Jerusalem, with 9,000 citations principally from 1980 onward, when the field began to emerge.

In addition, the computer catalog of the library and archive collections of the Leo Baeck Institute (LBI), located in Leipzig in the Deutsche Buecherei in Leipzig, the German equivalent of the U.S. Library of Congress, was consulted. The LBI holdings include volumes rescued from Jewish libraries. The LBI archives materials ranging from poetry and fiction authored by German Jews, Jewish community histories, and more than 750 periodicals published by Jews from the eighteenth to the twentieth centuries that document the cultural heritage of the German Jewish community before its decimation by Hitler's "final solution."

The students not only made connections to key historic documents; they also connected with people who shared their belief in the importance of Holocaust studies in education. They signed up for the Holocaust LISTSERV, a discussion group that broadcasts electronic messages written by any member to all others in the group, thus creating an on-line forum. Here students could observe and join in on the discussion taking place among both experts and newcomers like themselves to Holocaust studies, and they discovered that the "veterans" were more than glad to give advice and answer questions about the research the students were conducting. Thus the Internet not only provided students with access to information but also served as an entree into a community of learners where apprenticeships between experts and novices are created constantly.

Computer networking led to productive collaborations with faraway colleagues, albeit through the reading of words framed in the cold medium of a computer screen. But face-to-face contact with other learners also grew out of the networking activities of the Holocaust/Genocide Project. Certainly, the Poland/Israel Study Mission could never have been coordinated so quickly without networked communication. This mission included an Australian teacher, a teacher from California, a student from Seattle, together with 5 students and a teacher from Cold Spring Harbor in New York, and a contingent of 35 Israeli students. Once in Poland, they visited Holocaust memorials in the Warsaw Ghetto as well as in the Majdanek, Auschwitz, Birkenau, and Treblinka death camps. They then journeyed to Israel with their new friends. The American and Australian students stayed with host families in the evenings after visiting Israel's memorial sites for Holocaust victims and centers of Holocaust documentation during the day.

These students and teachers traveled across the world in an encounter provoked by a global networking project, one that linked schools determined to bring Holocaust studies alive in the classroom. Closer to home for the Americans, students in the Holocaust/Genocide Project received information about the recently opened Holocaust Museum in Washington, D.C., and arranged to travel there. Nor was human contact limited to group travel to faraway places. Student authors learned through the Internet of survivors closer to home whom they subsequently met and whose testimony heightened the personal meaning of the essential facts and statistics they were gathering. They learned about professional authors who had published fiction and nonfiction and arranged to interview them. For example, interviews were published in *An End to Intolerance* with Ruth Minsky Sender, whose works include *The Cage, To Live,* and *The Holocaust Lady,* as well as with Inge Auerbacher, author of *I Am a Star,* who provided a firsthand account of Kristallnacht drawn from her childhood memories. In other words, students were not just consuming information, they were generating new knowledge and understanding through collaboration and critical inquiry.

Teachers and students who have participated in the Holocaust/Genocide Project have produced a great deal of written material; thus, antiracist education has been linked to literacy development throughout. *An End to Intolerance* has included student-authored articles on the history of the Holocaust, interviews with Holocaust survivors, book reviews, reviews of hate music in the United States and Germany, editorials on the Holocaust denial movement, and poetry and fiction inspired by students' Holocaust studies. But aside from their annual publication, other writing collaborations also have developed between teachers and students. Using research conducted by students over the Internet, students and teachers have jointly authored numerous lessons plans that have been grouped into Holocaust teaching units. These interdisciplinary lesson plans, involving language arts, social studies, math and science, and the arts, have focused on understanding the history both of the Holocaust and of contemporary genocidal threats around the world. The students and teachers distribute their units—again using the Internet—to classrooms around the world, as a way of giving back what they have learned to the growing movement of Holocaust studies in schools.

"Through computer conferencing and e-mail," writes Honey Kern, a teacher coordinator of the project, "the HGP has enabled my students to have global, ongoing discussions about the sensitive topic of Holocaust/Genocide and to relate these discussions to the way we treat each other as human beings."[32] Kern asserts firmly that networking has served as a catalyst for a new kind of antiracist learning in her classroom. She insists that the magic is not in the computers, but in the encounters they provoke with living history and between reflective people. But the last word should go to the students of the Holocaust/Genocide Project:

> . . . both students and teachers on the HGP are dedicated to making
> a difference and proving to the world that racism and prejudice
> no longer have a place in our world.
>
> —Joey Bergida, grade 10

> While working on this telecom project, I have learned many things
> . . . children who are educated to respect other cultures, races
> and religions generally grow into tolerant adults who raise tolerant
> children.
>
> —Reema Sanghvi, grade 11

> I have been working on the Holocaust/Genocide Project for over
> two years. In that time, I have learned how many people are unaware
> of what happened 50 years ago, and do not know what is still
> happening today. My main reason for working on the Holocaust/Geno-
> cide Project is to educate people about these events and at the
> same time, help to solve what seem to be unsolvable problems of
> ignorance and prejudice.

The project has opened my eyes to the misconceptions that people
have about other cultures. However, at the same time, it makes me
feel better to know that there are other people willing to work
hard to try to bring an end to ignorance.

—Jen Harris, grade 12[33]

Portrait 7:
THE NICARAGUA ROPE PUMP PROJECT (I*EARN)

Dell Salza is an educator who coordinates the I*EARN project in the Boston
area, "a collaborative project of 12 public school systems in the greater
Boston area working to make social responsibility a core element of the
K-12 school program."[34] She journeyed to Nicaragua in the summer of
1991, as part of a group sponsored by Habitat for Humanity, an international organization concerned with meeting the needs for decent housing
in the United States and Third World countries. Another important reason
for her trip was to visit the grave of her cousin, Benjamin Linder, an engineer
who had been building small hydroelectric power plants in northern
Nicaragua when he was killed by the Contra rebels in 1987.

Salza also visited villages away from the capital of Managua to
experience community life in the countryside. One central fact of life
was common for *campesinos* (peasants) in villages even as close as 30 miles
from Managua: Community life revolved around the daily struggle to
get water from wells. Many families send one or more members, often
youngsters, to walk up to several miles in order to haul home the day's
water supply.

Having to work hard to take care of daily necessities is common in
countries like Nicaragua, ravaged by years of war as well as economic
blockades and pressures from the U. S. government after the Sandinistas
overthrew the Somoza dictatorship. Citizens there also face the difficulties
of surviving in an underdeveloped economy, owing to decades of single-
crop monoagricultural dependence in volatile world markets.

But the problems of water distribution involve more than the miles
that people—mostly women and children—walk to supply their families
with water. Many of the wells in Nicaragua are open and unsanitary: Dirty
buckets and contamination by leaves, soil, insects, and other airborne agents

are commonplace, as are the diseases they cause. Salza learned that the incidence of cholera, which had already reached plague proportions in Peru and other parts of Latin America, was on the rise in Nicaragua due in part to the widespread problem of contaminated water. Highly contagious, cholera creates severe and often fatal dehydration as its victims experience diarrhea and vomiting simultaneously. Rehydration is an emergency medical procedure requiring access to health care services that are virtually nonexistent in most Nicaraguan villages.

Salza spoke with friends and colleagues in Nicaragua who worked for a nonprofit development organization in Nicaragua called El Porvenir (The Future), affiliated with Habitat for Humanity. She discovered that wells could be "renovated" with easily available technology, using concrete, wood, a single wheel, and a length of rope with little metal cups knotted into the rope at regular intervals. With donated community labor, a sanitary well could be built for $100 to $250. Returning to Boston, Salza set about using telecommunications to generate widespread interest in improving the quality of life of communities in Nicaragua. Two schools in Massachusets were the first to raise enough money to build the first two wells, but as a result of Internet communications, interest spread rapidly in schools throughout the United States and as far away as China and Spain. Here is an electronic mail note from across the continent in Oregon that chronicled one school's participation in the words of a fifth-grade student.

ROPE PUMP PROJECT

This whole project started with a slide show presentation given to us by Dell Salza. She visited our school and told us about her trip with her family to Nicaragua. She explained to us how desperately rural Nicaraguan villages need a bike rope pump. The pumps are going to provide families with clean water, instead of dirty, infected water.

When Dell was explaining this, I became very interested. I thought about what might happen if these families didn't get the clean water that their families so badly needed to live. Her slide show was very interesting, and very inspiring.

Kids from one of our fifth grade leadership groups organized brief presentations for all the classes about the jog-a-thon that our whole school was going to do. They also told us information about conditions in Nicaragua and the great need for these pumps. We got pledge sheets and began signing up people to pay us money for jogging for rope pumps.

Everywhere we went in the school, we saw pictures and posters on the walls. Then I knew that this was truly a school-wide, team effort. The pumps cost $100.00 each, and I wished we could earn a lot, because I felt really badly for the people in Nicaragua and I wanted to help.

The jog-a-thon was a big success, with each grade jogging for an hour around the school. Throughout the day during the jog-a-thon, we had a water shuttle where kids had to carry buckets of water 50 meters. Every student, from Kindergarten to fifth grade, carried water at least once for 50 meters. Every 40th trip of 50 meters, down and back, we rang a bell to announce we had reached four kilometers. That's the distance that one girl from Nicaragua had to walk to get water every morning. When the bike rope pump was installed in her village, she wrote a thank you letter saying that since the pump had been installed, she didn't have to walk four kilometers every morning and could now go to school.

Our teacher, Mr. Snook, collected all the money for a week or so, then sent a big check to El Porvenir in care of Dell Salza. The Jog-a-thon raised $2,143.00 . . . that's 21 pumps! I was so excited! I couldn't believe that our school had bought 21 pumps!

This is the best thing that our school has ever done! I hope other schools will do this, too.

Thank you Dell Salza for presenting this to us!

Sincerely,
Kristi Kraus, Fifth Grade, Sunset School,
West Linn, OR [35]

Here is the letter from Nicaragua that Kristi Kraus was referring to:

Dearest Friends,
We hope to find you well enjoying good health. We, here in this region of Tierra Colorada, find ourselves very happy because we have a well

with a rope pump. And now, thank God, we do not have to walk 4 kilometers every day to be able to have water now that you have helped us with this project. We thank you for now we do have a well and we ask that you continue to back us with the projects of the region.

I am a thirteen year old girl who was to go for water, but now, thanks to you, I do not have to think of going so far. I am in the third grade.

I say goodbye lovingly,

—Leyla del Carmen Campos Luna

In the first year of what became known as The Pump Project, schools from the I*EARN Network raised more than $2,500 in Massachusetts alone for villages in Nicaragua. In its second year, the Pump Project was offered as part of The PLANET Network, a consortium of six educational telecommunications networks committed to humanitarian projects. In that year, over $4,000 was raised from six I*EARN schools and three schools in TENET (Texas Educational Network). To date $10,000 have been raised to build wells throughout Nicaragua.

Electronic letters detailing the building of the wells and the workings of the Water Committees, the village cooperatives that organized the construction, were exchanged between Nicaraguan students and their counterparts in North America and other countries. These letters were sometimes handwritten, and then keyed in after being carried to the closest computer with networking access. One girl from Nicaragua wrote:

Tierra Colorada

Dear Friends of North America,

We hope you are all enjoying good health. We here in the area of Tierra Colorada are very happy that we now have a well with a rope pump. Thank God we have water and are able to bathe ourselves, do washing, etc.

We are very happy that our brothers and sisters from North America helped us with the construction of the well that we now have and of course with the help of all the community, the enjoyment, the happiness of having a well in our community makes us feel happy, but very happy as when we perform a piece of work or assignment in our small school which we visit every day even though it is far away in another community.

I say goodbye with much happiness. This is the first letter I have written. I am a girl of ten years of age.

—Ivania Vancza Campos

But it is important to underscore that the Pump Project was concerned with much more than teaching philanthropy to North American students. Salza asserts that the Pump Project "has tremendous possibilities for interdisciplinary and intercultural lessons."

We hope the cultural benefits will come from the way that teachers are able to integrate learning about Nicaragua into their curriculum as they work with students on this project. We think there are great possibilities for learning depending on what teachers and students decide to do with it. They will also have letters and possibly photos from the people in the cooperatives building the pumps and telling about the difference it has made in their lives. The work that you are doing in writing about this project will educate everyone who reads what you have written about the culture of Nicaragua.[36]

Schools participating in the project received instruction manuals in Spanish that described how the rope pumps are constructed. In some cases, students followed illustrations and instructions written in Spanish by relying on their local Spanish-speaking classmates to help with the translation, reversing negative attitudes toward speakers of Spanish that exist in so many North American schools.

Based on projects like this, controversial issues such as comparing the disparity of access to health services in industrialized and developed countries and the benefits of culturally appropriate technology became commonplace in social studies and science classes. Dr. Ed Gragert, executive director of I*EARN, spoke of the impact of this project:

The important aspect of this story is that the U.S. and Nicaraguan children learned that they could make a meaningful difference in the world. They also learned about another culture as well as many other academic skills such as geography, social studies, writing, and technology. The Nicaraguan child learned that she is part of a global village—she is not alone. She also became a teacher to the North American students, demonstrating the democratic potential of global telecommunications between children in countries of the North and South.[37]

Students everywhere who were touched by this project learned that international solidarity, combined with local community-based organization and appropriate technology, could generate both health and knowledge.

Portrait 8:
THE CONTEMPORARY

The Contemporary is a unique student-edited magazine that has been an integral part of the I*EARN computer-based global learning network for about five years. Based at the Cold Spring Harbor High School on Long Island in New York, it was originally a newsletter but is now printed in a magazine format. This new format has been made possible by donations from patrons and sponsors, which have permitted the purchase of desktop publishing software and a laser printer. What is immediately impressive about *The Contemporary* is that its articles are drawn not only from students at Cold Spring Harbor High but from young people from a wide international spectrum. As its editors write:

> *The Contemporary (TC)* is a student news magazine, international in scope, that aims to provide teenagers with a way to learn about issues of national and global importance as the first step toward understanding how youth can have an impact on the direction taken by our world. Of special concern to *TC* is the publication of articles that focus on telecommunications projects that allow students to play an active role in addressing some of the problems that our world faces.[38]

Yet even these intriguing characteristics do not arrive at the heart of what makes *TC* such a unique student publication. What is most remarkable about *The Contemporary*, in our view, is its unflinching willingness to explore the potential of computer networking for raising and discussing difficult issues from a variety of perspectives. Even though at times these issues of national and global importance were controversial in nature, student editors continued to write about them. However, they were soon to find out that encouraging debate around a hotly contested topic in another part of the world would lead to volatile confrontations about their self-expression closer to home.

The January and May 1994 issues of *The Contemporary* featured Middle East Sections that included writings of Palestinian and Israeli teachers and students. As Kristin Lucas, the eleventh-grade editor of these special sections, recounts:

> At the start of my project, my goal was to inform students around the world about recent developments in the long-lived Middle Eastern crisis. Our global news magazine, The Contemporary, was used as a vehicle for the promotion of this goal. I set out with the belief that students from Israel and the Occupied Palestinian Territories needed to realize the similarities in their hopes and fears in order to pave the way for a more peaceful future. Because of communication and time barriers, and the sensitivities involved, I was unable to set up a true dialogue between Israeli and Palestinian students, which had originally been the plan. However, I feel that the work done in this direction along with the articles published in the January issue of TC are important steps in this direction. Trying to get two groups who are deeply opposed to each other to communicate was certainly a challenging task.[39]

Through computer networking, students had established contacts with the Ramallah Friends School located in Occupied Palestinian Territories (OPTs). As described by Rory Phimister, an American teacher there, the Ramallah Friends School was atypical in many respects:

> Although bound by the Israeli enforced curriculum which censors teachers and bans books, patronage by the international Quaker movement has afforded the school a degree of autonomy not enjoyed by other Palestinian institutions. . . . [Yet] in this situation of military occupation where human rights violations are a feature

of daily life and where the young people know only the experience of confrontation and resistance, the application of the Quaker principles [of nonviolence] is a central challenge for teachers at the Ramallah Friends School.[40]

Phimister attempted to express his colleagues' efforts toward resolving this contradiction between the principles of nonviolence and the day-to-day realities of living and learning in a politically polarized and brutally violent social context.

Respect for the individual begins with respect for the self. In an environment of humiliation and fear, an acknowledgment of pain is required, both in the self and in others, if the concepts of respect for the individual and the equality of all persons are to be achieved. Thus the encouragement of self-expression and the development of communication skills, without the denial of pain, is considered of particular importance within the Ramallah Friends School curriculum.[41]

Here are two examples of what students at Ramallah sent to the student editors of *The Contemporary* as they sought to communicate their daily reality while acknowledging the pain of life in the Occupied Palestinian Territories. Often they spoke of the pain associated with Israeli-enforced curfews and of being denied access to education for long periods of time.

We must change the world, because we know we can't survive in it the way it is. Let's rip out the weeds of pain and hate and plant the sprouts of love and hope. This planet has seen enough wars, enough dying and enough suffering.

—Ashraf Hussein (18 years old)

As Palestinians, we have not had the freedom of education or even of movement. At the beginning of the intifada, our schools were closed for almost two years. The Israelis thought they could stop us from learning, but we continued to study at home and in people's houses where we made classrooms. Still, many children suffered

from this. The Israelis also put us under curfew a lot. Curfew is
when you cannot leave your house or you will be arrested or even
shot. Curfews can last from three days to six weeks. During curfew,
you cannot go to school, you cannot buy food or go to the hospital,
and you cannot go to work to make money.

—Ammar Jadallah (14 years old)[42]

These and many other testimonies from teenagers of the harsh realities
of life in the Occupied Territories were sent to the student editors of *The
Contemporary* at Cold Spring Harbor High in preparation for the January
1994 issue. As editor of the Middle East Section, Kristin Lucas recalls the
hard work that followed:

My next step was to get Israeli students to respond to the
Palestinians' writings. This required an inordinate amount of letter
writing to contacts which sometimes did not even respond. Eventually
though, with the help of I*EARN staff members, I did receive some
great responses from Israeli students.[43]

Raphi Amram, executive director of the Israel Arts and Science Academy, reacted to the Palestinian teacher and the Ramallah students' writings
soberly:

Nobody said it was going to be easy. The road to peace is as stony
as the hills surrounding Jerusalem, and undoing what has been done
until now is proving difficult and bloody. There is good reason
for it to be called a "process," arriving at "peace" is never easy
for anyone. The murders—the chain of killings—are causing more
than just sorrow and loss; people from all political persuasions
have their many reasons to protest each and every step of the
way.[44]

Israeli students' responses to the Palestinian writings spanned the
spectrum, from those who saw no alternative to Israeli control of the
Occupied Palestinian Territories to others who found Israel intransigent
and obdurate in the struggle for peace in the Middle East. Among them:

The occupied lands are not being held because of our greed, they are being held for our safety. We have never started a war, and always were on the defensive side. We are peaceful people, and we wish there were no wars and no need for people to suffer. If we could assure our safety without holding those lands, only then could we consider seriously the future of these areas.

—Alon Yacobi (11b)

—Itay Erez (11b)

For thousands of years the Jewish people, as an "occupied" nation, fought for independence and a state of their own. They helped the British to take over the land of Israel from the Ottoman Empire, and then fought against the British in any way they could to win a homeland. They even used terrorism and violence in their efforts to get the land that they counted as their own.

Once Israel was created, wars with Arab states followed, and as a result many territories were occupied by the Israeli army. And, for over 25 years now, we have assumed the role of occupiers.

Israelis as former subjects of foreign governments . . . have not shown understanding in this regard. We personally believe that the Palestinians need to get their own independent state in order to build a proper life.

—Yeal Rav-Hon

—Hila Levy[45]

With these responses—delivered over electronic mail—in hand, Kristin Lucas thought the Middle East Section January issue was nearly ready for publishing. But she was to learn that by opening a dialogue around such a controversial issue, her work had only begun. She writes:

I then edited this material and proceeded with the layout portion of my project. After I had finished the layout of my section, Rory [Phimister of Ramallah Friends School] sent a message threatening to withdraw the Palestinian articles!! He was upset with the Israeli section being paired with the Palestinian one and was offended by some of the details in articles written by myself and a classmate. I spent seven periods (out of nine) that day trying

```
to keep my project together. The finished project in TC consisted
of two separate sections of articles: one Palestinian and one
Israeli.⁴⁶
```

Though Kristin had the satisfaction that her hard work had resulted in a provocative and controversial counterpoint of opinions, she and her student editor colleagues remained frustrated that a more extensive dialogue had not taken place.

The staff of *The Contemporary* wanted a more in-depth give-and-take between students and educators, one that went far beyond a single response to a teacher and his students from Ramallah Friends School. They decided to exploit telecommunications more fully as a means to foster a more probing, lasting exchange of views. Therefore, along with the Middle East Section, they published this notice:

> Beginning with the Spring issue of 1994, *TC* will also post within its teleconference a series of controversial topics and invite students to submit their views concerning these issues. *TC* intends to use the dialogues that develop among the students interested in the subjects posted as the foundation for a series of articles in its next issue.⁴⁷

That is, Kristin and her colleagues decided to exploit the technology to an even greater extent. Instead of relying on letters and articles sent through electronic mail, they opened a computer conference area on the network called "iearn.tc," hoping this time for a more extensive and true back-and-forth dialogue. At the time they had no idea how the pressure of world events would soon raise the political tension in the Middle East to unprecedented levels, which in turn would provoke a flurry of responses in the "controversial issues dialogue" teleconference they were planning to set up.

On February 23, 1994, Baruch Goldstein murdered 50 Arabs and wounded many others with automatic weapon fire as they prayed in the Al Ibrahimya Mosque in Hebron. Turmoil ensued in Israel and the Occupied Palestinian Territories. The massacre derailed the nascent peace process. Demonstrations by Palestinians led to beatings and killings by occupying forces; Israeli authorities invoked extensive curfews in the Occupied Territories; and members of extremist groups from both sides carried out reprisal murders. Kristin Lucas wrote: "Immediately after the massacre, a pair of discussion topics were posted . . . to give students in I*EARN a chance to talk about this horrible incident and the effects it has had."[48] She continued:

> The Palestinian and Israeli students and teachers who have expressed their views in the iearn.tc teleconference about the Hebron massacre deserve much credit for doing so during what is a sensitive and critically important time for all of them. While the contributors clearly disagree on many of the points they commonly discussed, their open sharing of their feelings about the recent violence at least represents a step towards understanding. The maintenance of lines of communication is necessary if peace is ever to be reached between Palestinians and Israelis.[49]

Western media coverage of the events provoked a heated and extensive debate between Palestinian and Israeli students. Raanan Keren, an Israeli high school student from Maalot, wrote:

> The Western media is always at the scene when both Israelis and Arabs are killed and the coverage is much more in favor of the Palestinian side in the opinion of Israelis. My opinion, in general is that the Palestinians deserve a country, and I support the Labor Party and Prime Minister Rabin, but I don't like the way the Palestinian students put things as if they are poor and all the world is against them.[50]

A Palestinian student from Ramallah Friends school disagreed:

> Dear Raanan Keren,
> I believe the Western media is not always on the scene when both Arabs and Jews are killed and the coverage is in favor of the Israelis. The few times that the coverage is in the Palestinians' favor, it is because a Palestinian is the one who reported the incident. . . . When an Israeli is killed, the Western media is always there because it is rare that an Israeli is killed, while Palestinians are shot and killed everyday. . . . It is not important that the media covers this or that. What is important is that the killings stop. I respect your opinion that the Palestinians deserve a state.
>
> —Ali Hussein [51]

Two Israeli students, Ran Feldman and Eran Pax, were not in agreement that the killings of Palestinians received little media coverage. "A recent example," they wrote, "is the Israeli TV coverage of the massacre on the day of the massacre, all day long, and for days after, it was covered by TV, radio and newspapers." Their comment provoked a response from a Palestinian student:

> I'm responding to Ran Feldman and Eran Paz on the issue of media coverage. . . .
>
> The question is not whether it is covered, but how it's covered. What I mean by this is that when Palestinian youth (freedom fighters) are murdered by Israeli soldiers the message sent out to the world is, "The solder killed the terrorist in self-defense." But is that really a logical description? How can you compare a stone to a gun? Who is the terrorist in this situation?
>
> —Maha Jabar, Ramallah Friends School[52]

All the debate surrounding media coverage provoked one Israeli student—who wished to remain anonymous, likely because his or her opinions would have sparked resentment and debate among Israeli classmates—to dispute the frequent press descriptions of Baruch Goldstein as an insane assassin who acted alone.

> I believe that the massacre was not the action of a lone lunatic but one taken by a gunman acting under the influence of a radical minority group. This group deserves to be condemned and outlawed, but the entire Israeli population should not be blamed for this act of violence because it did not reflect the sentiments of many of the people who are hoping for peace. Similarly, the extremists among the Palestinians should be condemned for their violence, not all the Palestinian people.
>
> —Anonymous[53]

The Contemporary published these and numerous other electronic mail messages in its May 1994 issue, all drawn from the teleconference dialogue between Israeli and Palestinian students, and included many reactions from students in Australia and New York as well. The extended dialogue between students was followed by several pages drawn from the diary of Rory Phimister offering a firsthand account of the harshness of life during the Israeli-imposed curfews and the many disruptions in his students' education caused by repeated interruptions in their studies.

That issue of *The Contemporary* also published letters from students in other countries sharing their opinions, drawing lessons from what they were reading to realities in their own countries. Phoebe McDonagh, a student from Australia, wrote:

> In my country we have many people from different backgrounds and have grown to communicate and accept everyone. This all sounds like Australia is a loving and understanding country but the sad truth is that our native Australians, the Aboriginals, are the last ones to become accepted and treated equally. It has taken 200 years for this, and we still have a long way to go.[54]

In a similar vein, Kristin Lucas compared the crisis with the history of the United States.

> Over . . . several hundred years, the Native Americans were persecuted, and the settlers overtook their sacred land. The government has tried to compensate the Native Americans for their losses to a degree, but much damage has been done to these people, and the scars are many. Looking back on my forefathers, it is difficult to decide if they were villains or saints. From one aspect, they were land-hungry conquerors who drove away the helpless natives; yet the other side tells me to appreciate their courage and spirit in establishing the country where I reside.[55]

Thus, the heated dialogue that *The Contemporary* had begun with a focus on political turmoil over land disputes in the Middle East led students in faraway countries to extrapolate lessons about their own countries' expansionist origins.

With this, the last issue of the school year, student editors of *The Contemporary* felt they had achieved their goal of using telecommunications for opening and sustaining an extensive dialogue between antagonists in the decades-old conflict in the Middle East during a period of intense political crisis. As Kristin Lucas wrote:

I have had the opportunity to accomplish what many other students may never have a chance to attempt. Even though I do not have the influence to reverse the sometimes harsh sentiments of the people, I would like to come away thinking that at least I did something to try to help the peace process along. . . . Many people do not have the opportunity to tap directly the minds and hearts of their peers who live thousands of miles away in troubled lands. I am very thankful to have had this opportunity and to have worked on a project that has strengthened my communication skills and provided me with some of the most valuable lessons one can learn in life.[56]

With the publication of the January 1994 issue, the student editors of *The Contemporary* had no idea of how world events would make their efforts to provoke discussion on controversial issues remarkably timely. Similarly, as they published their May 1994 issue at the close of the academic year, they had no inkling of the controversy their efforts would continue to provoke—and this time closer to home—nor of the lessons they would continue to learn from defending their attempt to open dialogue on sensitive issues.

Peter Copen is head of the Copen Family Fund, which has supported the I*EARN Network since its inception in 1989. His vision was to explore the potential of telecommunications to give youth a voice in shaping and improving the world. To this end, he established I*EARN and provided funding from the Copen Family Fund to underwrite some of the network's activities during its formative years, until I*EARN had established a clear identity and could become self-sufficient. This support took many forms, including contributing seed monies for special projects.

While *The Contemporary,* in its five years as a publication, had made great progress toward becoming self-sufficient through its own efforts and by seeking patrons and supporters, the Copen Family Fund also had provided generous financial support from the outset. Though edited and published by students at Cold Spring Harbor High, over the years *The Contemporary* had become much more than a simple high school magazine or the mere product of an after-school journalism club. Indeed, through its steady reliance on contributions from young writers around the world gathered via telecommunications, *The Contemporary* had grown to be a highly visible presence within the entire I*EARN network.

In recognition of this achievement, the I*EARN Network's board of directors, composed of Peter Copen and representatives from all participating countries, had designated *The Contemporary* as an Annual I*EARN Project "so as to provide schools within our network with convenient access to an on-going telecommunications project with an established record of success in working toward I*EARN's goal of improving the welfare of the planet." [57]

The problem was that the Middle East Section in the January and May 1994 issues had provoked controversy not only between Israelis and Palestinians. Peter Copen met in person with the faculty advisor and editorial staff at Cold Spring Harbor High to voice concerns and a personal point of view concerning their coverage in the Middle East Sections. The meeting took place in June 1994. It must be stressed that Peter Copen was not in any way discussing "pulling the plug" (as the Croatian refugee camp director had done in Portrait 1); rather, he spoke to the students as a respected mentor who had genuine personal concerns about how best to handle controversial issues in the fledgling network he had founded.

Some were procedural: He felt the *TC* editors had short-circuited open discussion by not the posting to the "iearn.tc" computer conference the long diary written by the American Rory Phimister about his emotional reactions to the disruption of his Palestinian students' education during the curfews in Ramallah. Open debate in the computer conference might have shown that what the *TC* editors viewed as a moving account others could view as "inflammatory." In some cases, he felt, authorship of articles was not clear, creating confusion as to whether the American teacher or his Palestinian students was doing the writing; nor were Phimister's views balanced by those of Israeli teachers.

But other concerns were more substantive. In Copen's view, the editors of *The Contemporary* had departed from their original mission, which he viewed as one of serving as an outlet solely for the self-expression of young people. Finally, he expressed his opinion that the controversial nature of the topics covered by *The Contemporary* might generate disagreements within I*EARN and jeopardize the willingness of some schools to continue participating in the network, a natural concern for a growing community of learners.

After the meeting, the staff of *The Contemporary* met and drafted the following response to Copen's concerns. It provides rich insights into the kind of critical thinking that students can achieve within the context of global learning networks using telecommunications.

> We have devoted a great deal of time to discussing and thinking about Mr. Copen's criticisms. Our thinking at the time we put this section together was as follows:
>
> . . . Regarding the point that I*EARN seeks to provide a space where youths can be empowered to work toward the resolution of global problems, feel safe in so doing, and be encouraged to "hear" each other, we thought that the core of the MES [Middle East Section] (the five-page dialogue between Palestinian, Israeli, American and Australian students) served that purpose as well as could be expected given the explosive nature of the issues being discussed. We sought to give all interested parties a chance to state their views and respond to each other. Did the contributors "hear" each other? Well, most seemed to listen but few seemed to hear very well. Did we try to make the MES a safe place to conduct such a discussion? Yes, but we realized that when feelings run as hot as they do in the Middle East, there may be no such thing as a safe place to discuss the subject. Does that mean we did not make a contribution to the resolution of the problems discussed? No. We feel progress in this instance ought to be measured simply by the fact that the contending parties at least talked to each other and read what each other was feeling and thinking. Dialogue (no matter how contentious it may seem) is the first step toward resolving any problem. . . .
>
> Does the fact there were adult contributors in the MES run contrary to I*EARN's goal to empower youth or diminish/overshadow the contributions made by students? We don't think so. TC has always had some adult contributors in each issue of the magazine. Why is this the case? TC's goal is to educate students, and whenever possible to have students take the lead in working towards this goal, but we do not feel that this goal in any way precludes the use of adult writings to stimulate student thinking or focus attention on a particular point of view.[58]

Thus, the debate provoked by The Contemporary through its use of telecommunications to open dialogue on controversies in a distant land was brought home to Cold Spring Harbor High, and provoked further learning into the qualities of courage required to persevere in the struggle to confront complex issues with a history of hatred, prejudice, and intolerance between peoples. Even more important, by squarely confronting these issues not only in distant lands but close to home, both the students and the I*EARN Network matured as a result. As Peter Copen wrote:

> Although some of the students may have, and indeed did, interpret our meeting as a desire to edit them, that was never my intention. It precipitated a very important outcome, though, which was the agreement by everyone involved that it made sense to have TC (as well as I*EARN) issue disclaimers about student publications. The disclaimers would create more clear and open space for expression as well as comments and criticism.[59]

As a student on the Editorial Board, Celeste Perri should have the last word. She expressed her heightened appreciation of the power of open and free discussion as she and fellow students prepared to shape the world of the future:

> I think I approach and view the world a lot differently now. I think free and open communication among the youth of our world is a wonderful thing; perhaps with this experience some students will prize dialogue more dearly in the future when our generation is the generation that is making the world's decisions. Hopefully, if we try to understand each other more, we might be more willing to talk things out instead of going to war over them. Wars are stupid, they are pointless. In the end, it is not who is wrong or right that counts, it's who's left. There are no winners.[60]

CONCLUSION

It is clear from the eight portraits we have presented that computer-based networks have the potential to greatly magnify the reach and impact of intercultural learning across both cultural and geographic distances. These portraits are not isolated instances of educators using global learning networks to forge a new approach to teaching and learning that is responsive to the challenges we and future generations face. Many other such portraits could have been adduced from hundreds of documented cases, whether drawn from modern global learning networks or from decades of examples that have preceded the advent of computers and networking. Yet—as with any innovation in education—without an overarching conception of how to shape learning in the direction of the sort of critical inquiry that prepares our youth for the future, global learning networks will merely lead to trivializing, superficial classroom practices that do little to reverse patterns of student, teacher, and community disempowerment.

From a series of different perspectives, each of the following chapters attempts to outline a framework for conceptualizing global learning networks as contexts for student, teacher, and community empowerment. Chapter 3 considers the implications of the alleged "literacy crisis" and the narrowly conceived drive for educational reform of the past decade. In chapter 4, we examine the origins and development of global learning networks in the pioneering work of European educators Célestin Freinet and Mario Lodi.

Chapter 5 makes explicit the conception of learning and teaching that we have termed "collaborative critical inquiry." We argue that the teaching of literacy must place issues of cultural and linguistic diversity at the core rather than on the periphery of its concerns. Our times demand a rigorous approach to the teaching of reading and writing, but at the same time one that embraces rather than ignores issues of cultural identity.

Finally, chapter 6 returns to the issue of where we are headed on the information superhighway. Technology advocates from the business community view educational consumers who can be reached electronically as enormous untapped markets. On the other hand, many exponents of a more critical and progressive perspective on curriculum and pedagogy have rejected the information superhighway as merely another corporate plot to maximize profits at the expense of the public good. While sharing many of the concerns of these critics, we contend that global learning networks have the potential for creating, nourishing, and sustaining the genuine learning communities so desperately needed if we are to confront the social, cultural, economic, and ecological challenges of the coming years.

Chapter 3

Beyond Functional Literacy:
The Dilemmas
of Educational Reform

This is a world that is losing its faith in the one true mission of progress and development, or at best is sheepishly defensive about it. It is a world where the West and its cultural canon is well on the way to losing its messianic race pretensions even though they still harbour an anachronistic sense of their own self-importance. It is a world of fragmentation, of cultural diversity, of multiple gender identities, of half a dozen different types of families, no one of which commands a majority adherence, of subcultures and styles and fads. It is a world where there are thousands upon thousands of specialist magazines speaking in specialist tongues and where there are some cities that have sixty television channels for aficionados of all sorts of peculiar discourses from pentecostalism to pornography. It is a world where a dozen or more languages might be spoken on one city block, where the television brings live coverage to that same block of what is happening at the ends of the earth.

—Mary Kalantzis and Bill Cope,
The Powers of Literacy: A Genre Approach to Teaching Writing

Confronted by the bewildering diversity and moral complexity just sketched by Australian scholars Mary Kalantzis and Bill Cope, educators throughout the industrialized world are attempting to redefine their roles and priorities. A cacophony of discordant voices clamors for ascendancy outside the schoolhouse door. The terms "reform" and "restructuring" are on everyone's lips, but few can agree on the nature of the required reforms or the image of the student who will emerge after more than a decade of compulsory education. What should this student know? What values should she or he espouse? What job-related skills should be developed at school in order to maintain a nation's competitive edge in the global economy? How should the ability to think critically about social issues be fostered? Or should it be fostered at all? How should schools respond to the often conflicting demands of diverse cultural, linguistic, religious, and sexual orientation groups that their particular perspectives be incorporated into the curriculum? The differences that have always characterized our societies are suddenly out in the open and can no longer be denied.

Public schools serve the societies that fund them, and they aim to graduate students with the skills, knowledge, and values necessary to contribute to their societies. In other words, an image of the future society that students will help form is implicit in all the interactions between students and educators in school. The dilemma for educators at the turn of the millennium is that no consensus exists in the broader community about the nature of the society schools should be attempting to promote. We are in the midst of cultural, economic, and existential changes that cloud our collective future as a human race. Small wonder then that schools should have become the battleground for competing visions of that collective future.

The cultural changes have confronted schools with the dilemma of whose history should be taught and legitimated in the curriculum. In universities and schools across the Western world, the descendants of the colonized, the vanquished, and the enslaved are attempting to reclaim their histories and identities, previously consigned to footnotes on the pages of dominant group history. These insurgent voices demanding multicultural education, Afrocentric schools, and bilingual education are repudiated vehemently by policymakers and media commentators who interpret them as a serious threat to social cohesion and national unity.

The economic restructuring of Western societies associated with the advances in microelectronics and telecommunications that have ushered in the "Information Age" has similarly occasioned vigorous debates during the past decade about the purposes and methods of education. Schools have been castigated for their presumed failure to develop the literacy and numeracy skills required in the workplace of the future. The major impetus for most of the business elite who plunged into school reform efforts in the 1980s in many Western countries was the conviction that economic prosperity and even national security were being jeopardized by the absence of quality control over the products of schooling.

With respect to existential realities, the fleeting celebration of the "new world order" proclaimed by former President George Bush subsequent to the collapse of Eastern Bloc communism and the restoration of the friendly dictatorship in Kuwait after the Gulf War has proven illusory. The "new world order" was intended to signal the dawn of an era of peaceful global relations enforced, where necessary, by the United States in its newfound role as the sole superpower. However, a few years later, the new world order lies in tatters. Incomprehension at the horrors abroad and fear of violence at home grip the United States. The technological wizardry that allowed us to experience the "virtual reality" of being in "the eye of the bomb" screaming toward Iraqi targets is impotent to terminate the savagery erupting around the globe or to alleviate the starvation that continues to afflict the populations of many developing countries. Persistent economic malaise, unemployment, and inner-city misery in Western industrialized countries similarly mock the declaration of a new world order.[1]

As parents contemplate these daunting realities and wonder what the future holds for their children, education assumes a new urgency. While education by no means guarantees economic security, the prospects of a decent job and good wages without high levels of education are remote. High school graduation is no longer sufficient to ascend the ladder of social mobility; university degrees and other forms of advanced qualifications are increasingly being demanded by employers eager to maximize their "human resources" in an age of unprecedented technological change. Hence the concern and anger of many parents when they are bombarded by media reports of an education system in decline characterized by ineffective instruction, falling academic standards, and rampant school violence. At a time when rigorous instruction is most needed, educators are presented as fickle and subject to every passing pedagogical whim.

Not surprisingly, educators tend to see the issues differently. They point to the fact that schools are increasingly expected to solve the social problems of a society in disarray: More than a quarter of American children entering school are living in poverty; the 350,000 children annually born to mothers addicted to cocaine during pregnancy enter school with major behavioral and academic difficulties; classrooms are increasingly populated with abused and/or neglected children, reports of which tripled between 1976 and 1987 to 2.2 million.[2] Literacy and numeracy are not the only topics crucial to students' future; more immediately relevant for many students may be finding out how to protect themselves from the specter of AIDS. In addition to these challenges, educators are expected to mold a common allegiance and sense of national identity out of the diversity of cultures, languages, religions, and sexual orientations represented in their classrooms.

As they contemplate the sobering and conflictual reality of both their classrooms and the world outside, educators are faced with the necessity of defining more precisely their roles as shapers of the next generation. How can they establish forms of interaction with their students so that both students and educators can better understand their personal histories and explore more fully options for shaping a sane collective future? How can this focus on understanding and social action be reconciled with the need to develop the literacy and numeracy skills students need to compete in an increasingly competitive job market?

This tension between the purpose of education in drawing out the intellectual and personal potential of children and its role in preparing a workforce for the industrial needs of society has characterized debates on schooling since the beginnings of mass formal education. In general, it is fair to say that the goal of personal and intellectual enrichment has not been problematic for children of elite groups in society while, for the general population, public education has been oriented primarily to economic and, in some contexts, religious goals. Schools were instituted to produce workers with the skills required by industry, and literacy also was promoted by many organized religions in order to facilitate access to the truths of holy books, such as the Bible or Koran, considered essential for salvation.

In this chapter, we try to chart the general directions our schools should be pursuing if they are to respond to the realities of the twenty-first century. Our central point is straightforward: We currently have a window of opportunity to expand and radically transform the educational possibilities available to *all* students in our schools. We described in chapter 2 the types of high-level critical inquiry that students are capable of undertaking when they collaboratively investigate issues of real significance for their lives with peers in geographically distant settings. The electronic networks not only provide unprecedented access to informational resources, they also, and more significantly, encourage the formation of communities of learning that transcend previous limitations of time and space. As we illustrated, participation in these learning communities can be intensely motivating for students to read more, write more, and ultimately think more.

As the infrastructure of the information superhighway is being erected, we have the opportunity to ensure that all North American students have freedom of access and freedom of movement to explore forms of learning and thinking that have the potential to transform their lives. We are not suggesting that access to the Internet by itself is sufficient to increase students' learning opportunities. However, we believe that when access to communities of learning is combined with forms of teacher-student interaction that are very different from those that exist in most schools today, there are immense possibilities for expanding students' intellectual, cultural, and political horizons.

If the cost of linking schools to the Internet is built in to the overall process of establishing the information superhighway, it will be absorbed with minimal financial pain or even awareness. Under these conditions, ensuring relatively equal access between rich and poor schools will not be problematic. However, if the information superhighway is privatized indiscriminately to the highest bidders, whose interests lie in short-term profit, the tax burden of providing free access to all schools will be prohibitive. Rich schools will have the funds to pay for access, poor inner-city and rural schools will not.[3]

The window of opportunity to provide all schools across the country, whether wealthy or impoverished, free access to the Internet will close probably before the turn of the century. Thus, understanding why the provision of such access is crucial for the long-term development of our societies and articulating the forms of instruction that will help translate students' access into intellectual and academic growth is urgent. We believe we are at a crossroads: We can continue to travel the path of perpetuating historical patterns of exclusion, whereby increasing numbers of students are consigned permanently to the margins where they are likely to drain the economic and cultural potential of the society (through welfare, crime, and incarceration); alternatively, we can recognize that the best interests of all members of society lie in having a highly educated population that is capable of participating in the economic and democratic development of the nation.

Although the choice between these alternative scenarios may appear obvious, the United States historically has opted for the former, with dropouts from urban school systems reaching as high as 70 percent in New York City.[4] To choose the latter option would entail a radical rethinking of the social priorities of the 1980s. As documented by journalists Donald Barlett and James Steele, economically elite groups (the top 2 percent in income levels) have benefitted enormously from these priorities, while many middle-class families have been pushed into the expanding ranks of the poor.[5] The enormous social and economic costs of these trends for the next generation have been largely ignored by politicians and media alike.

The power relations that determine the distribution of status and resources in society have strongly influenced the ongoing debates on educational reform that have raged in the United States and Canada for more than a decade. Implicit in these debates are opposing conceptions of the kind of society we envision and the kind of literacy we expect our students to develop in the course of their schooling. Specifically, the capacity for collaborative critical inquiry that we wish to encourage through participation in computer-mediated communities of learning is anathema to many of those who have been most vocal about the need for educational reform. Their conception of literacy is restricted to what is frequently termed "functional literacy"—the forms of literacy required to function effectively as a worker and consumer. The impetus for educational reform during the Reagan/Bush years was fueled by the perception that there was a decline in functional literacy among the youth and that this constituted a "literacy crisis" for the society.

In this chapter, we highlight two major aspects of the educational reform debates that have been founded on the presumption of a literacy crisis. First, we examine the credibility of the "competitiveness" argument linking the nation's economic health to the allegedly inferior products of schooling. Although this claim has had a powerful impact on school reform efforts, its credibility is increasingly suspect in view of emerging data that challenge virtually all its premises; for example, there is no evidence that educational standards have dropped over the past three decades; there is no evidence that North American workers are "uncompetitive" in comparison to their European or Asian counterparts; there is no evidence of a shortage of workers with the high levels of literacy and numeracy allegedly required by the workplace of the future. University graduates are still driving taxis across North American cities. These credibility gaps suggest that there is a more covert agenda at work than the simple desire to improve the nation's educational system.

The second dimension of the reform debates that we discuss is the ambivalence toward issues of diversity within the reform movement. Policymakers have been unwilling to accept the logical implications of the fact that educational underachievement and consequent low literacy levels are phenomena that predominantly affect marginalized and excluded communities in our society. In other words, the "literacy crisis" is a direct consequence of a power structure that has systematically denied educational or social advancement to marginalized groups. This is clearly not a recent development, and it assumes the proportions of a "crisis" only because at this historical juncture, advantaged groups perceive their vested interests threatened by the "fact" that the literacy levels of workers, an increasing proportion of whom are of minority background, are inadequate to cope with the expanding literacy demands of the workplace. As noted, the credibility of this rationale for school reform has become increasingly suspect; however, there is little doubt that it has been internalized as "fact" by the general public and many policymakers and businesspeople.

The proposed solutions are contradictory because, in order to reverse patterns of minority underachievement, a realignment of the current paradigms of power in our society is required. While these modifications to the power structure may be in the best interests of socially advantaged groups in the long term, in the short term they require some degree of equalization of power relations that, not surprisingly, is resisted by the currently advantaged sectors of the society. Hence, there arises the contradiction whereby issues of diversity frequently are viewed as marginal to educational reform efforts whereas the logical premises of the entire impetus for reform would suggest that they should be central.

What kinds of instruction will reverse the underachievement of minority students? While instruction alone is unlikely to reverse the legacy of economic and social discrimination in our inner cities and migrant camps, certain kinds of instruction can contribute significantly to this process. Specifically, strong academic growth can result from instruction that encourages students to use language powerfully to analyze social issues that affect their lives. This orientation to language is usually termed "critical literacy," and we examine its relevance in the next section.

FUNCTIONAL, CULTURAL
AND CRITICAL LITERACIES

While different theorists have distinguished a variety of forms of literacy, for present purposes it is sufficient to distinguish *functional, cultural,* and *critical* literacies.[6] The term "functional literacy" has entered the lexicon of business and educational policymakers concerned about the gap between the "products" of educational systems and the needs of business. Functional literacy implies a level of reading and writing that enables people to function adequately in social and employment situations typical of late twentieth century industrialized countries. As such, it is defined relative to changing social demands. For example, the level of literacy required to be a car mechanic 30 years ago was minimal compared to what is required today. As the technology changes ever more rapidly, mechanics require a high level of literacy skills to read the complex technical manuals that guide the automotive repair process.

The term "cultural literacy" usually is associated with the work of E. D. Hirsch. His book *Cultural Literacy: What Every American Needs to Know* became a best-seller and spawned the *Cultural Literacy Dictionary* and a series of curriculum materials for grades 1 through 6 outlining the essential knowledge that students at each grade need to know in order to be "culturally literate."[7] Cultural literacy emphasizes the need for shared experiences, knowledge, and expectations in order to comprehend adequately texts, media, or patterns of social interaction within particular communities. In contrast to functional literacy, where the emphasis is on *skills,* cultural literacy focuses on the particular content or knowledge that is required to understand texts or social situations. For example, many recent immigrants may lack the cultural literacy to fully interpret typical situation-comedy programs on American television, just as many middle-class European Americans may lack the cultural literacy to interpret rap music.

Not surprisingly, the process of defining what constitutes cultural literacy is not politically neutral any more than the content of IQ tests or curricula in general can be considered politically neutral. Cultural literacy prescriptions almost inevitably legitimate the knowledge and values of those social groups that do the prescribing and delegitimate the knowledge and values of marginalized groups. As expressed by researcher Michael Apple:

... it is naive to think of the school curriculum as neutral knowledge. Rather, what counts as legitimate knowledge is the result of complex power relations and struggles among identifiable class, race, gender, and religious groups. Thus, education and power are terms of an indissoluble couplet. It is at times of social upheaval that this relationship between education and power becomes most visible. Such a relationship was and continues to be made manifest in the struggles by women, people of color, and others to have their history and knowledge included in the curriculum.[8]

Apple's point is illustrated in a statistical analysis conducted by elementary school teacher Bob Peterson of Hirsch's curriculum series *What Your First (through Sixth) Grader Needs to Know.* This analysis "shows that 82% of the pages devoted to literature and poetry have Euro-American selections. Of those that deal with non-European cultures 37% have animals as main characters, compared to 11% of the Euro-American selections. The not-so-subtle message is that stories about non-European cultures are not as serious."[9]

While notions of functional literacy and cultural literacy typically have been presented as politically neutral and divorced from issues of power and resource distribution in the society, critical literacy is explicitly focused on issues of power. As expounded originally in the work of Brazilian educator Paulo Freire, critical literacy highlights the potential of written language as a tool that encourages people to analyze the division of power and resources in their society and work to transform discriminatory structures. Freire's organization of literacy classes for Brazilian peasants was so threatening to the military junta that seized power in Brazil in 1964 that he was imprisoned and eventually exiled. The power of literacy to promote reflection and social action also was recognized in the early years of the United States, when it was illegal to teach slaves to read.

Critical literacy is defined by researcher Ira Shor as follows:

Habits of thought, reading, writing, and speaking which go beneath surface meaning, first impressions, dominant myths, official pronouncements, traditional cliches, received wisdom, and mere opinions, to understand the deep meaning, root causes, social context, ideology, and personal consequences of any action, event, object, process, organization, experience, text, subject matter, policy, mass media, or discourse.[10]

In short, critical literacy reflects the analytic abilities involved in cutting through the surface veneer of persuasive arguments to the realities underneath and analyzing the methods and purposes of particular forms of persuasion. Clearly, the ability to think critically in these ways is crucial for meaningful participation in a democratic society. If consent can be manufactured effortlessly through media persuasion, then democracy merges into totalitarianism. By the same token, it is hardly surprising that those who have the power and resources to influence the media are, at best, ambivalent toward critical literacy. To put it crudely, the less critically literate a population is, the easier it is to manufacture consent for policies and programs that are in the interests of the rich and powerful; policies and programs, for example, that have increased the gap between rich and poor in the United States such that the top 20 percent of households earn 48.2 percent of the nation's income while the bottom 20 percent earn only 3.6 percent.[11]

As middle-class families also have been big losers in the redistribution of wealth that took place in the United States during the 1980s, critical literacy skills should be of particular importance to middle-class students. Barlett and Steele report that the middle class (defined as families in the $20,000 to $50,000 income group) shrank from 39 percent in 1980 to 35 percent in 1989. Those who earned less than $50,000 a year (85 percent of all Americans) averaged yearly increases of 2 percent during this period; those earning $1 million or more pocketed yearly increases of 243 percent.[12]

It seems clear that the vast majority of the population has a strong vested interest in becoming critically literate themselves and in ensuring that their children have the opportunity to become sufficiently literate to minimize the potential for exploitation. Critical literacy enables individuals to challenge disinformation and become more socially involved in the democratic process. It also encourages marginalized communities to become more aware of the value of their own cultural heritage. This fact is illustrated in the comments of one Latino parent who participated in a Spanish-language family literacy project organized by Alma Flor Ada together with the Pajaro Valley School District in Watsonville, California:

> One of the fathers said: "I have discovered that my children can write.
> And I bring another story [written by his child]. But also, I have

discovered something personal. I have discovered that by reading books one can find out many things. Since my children want me to read them the stories over and over again, I took them to the public library to look for more books. There I discovered books about our own culture. I borrowed them and I am reading, and now I am finding out things I never knew about our roots and about what has happened to them and I have discovered that I can read in Spanish about the history of this country and of other countries."[13]

Many theorists have emphasized the close relationship between literacy and cultural identity.[14] Specifically, particular literacy behaviors that affirm the individual's sense of cultural identity will be acquired more easily and with more personal involvement than those that serve to deny or devalue cultural identity. This relationship is illustrated in Signithia Fordham's study that reported that academically successful Black students felt obliged to adopt "racelessness" or "acting White" as a strategy for academic achievement:

> . . . within the school structure, Black adolescents consciously and uncon-
> sciously sense that they have to give up aspects of their identities and of their
> indigenous cultural system in order to achieve success as defined in domi-
> nant-group terms; their resulting social selves are embodied in the notion of
> racelessness. Hence, for many of them the cost of school success is too high;
> it implies that cultural integrity must be sacrificed in order to "make it." For
> many Black adolescents, that option is unacceptable. For the high achievers
> identified in this paper, achieving school success is not marked only by conflict
> and ambivalence . . . but with the need to camouflage efforts directed at
> behaviors that the group identifies as "acting White."[15]

A focus on critical literacy is essential for students, such as those described by Fordham, who opt out of the pursuit of academic success because they see conformity to the expectations of educators as undermining their sense of self. They resist this devaluation of identity. However, students have no need to resist literacy instruction that is affirming of identity and encourages them to discover how their individual and collective identities have developed and been shaped over many generations. This pursuit of one's own personal and collective history inevitably entails becoming aware of how power and resources have been distributed in society and how schools and other societal institutions historically have reflected the values of the wider society. For example, racial segregation in schools was not just an educational policy; it reflected patterns of power relations in the wider society and the value assigned to different cultural and racial groups. Students from marginalized groups are likely to engage in academic efforts only when they are convinced that educators are committed to helping them reverse historical patterns of social and educational inequality. Otherwise, if the odds remain stacked against them, why should they bother to play the game?[16]

In short, instruction that ignores or denies students' cultural identity is unlikely to be successful in improving academic achievement. Unfortunately, most reform efforts have paid only lip service to issues of diversity and cultural identity.[17] The emphasis on functional and cultural literacies, to the exclusion of critical literacy, has perpetuated the sanitized curriculum that will continue to be resisted by those groups whose identities it distorts. Our analysis suggests that functional and cultural literacy among marginalized groups will be promoted effectively only through a focus on critical literacy. The dilemma for many of those who are attempting to orchestrate educational reform is that for more socially powerful groups, critical literacy among workers or students is no more welcome today than it was in the era of slavery.

This dilemma can help us understand some of the contradictions in the rhetoric of educational reform that we address in the next section.

THE COMPETING DISCOURSES
OF EDUCATIONAL REFORM

The debates on educational reform can be viewed in terms of competing discourses that are aimed at mobilizing public opinion to support particular policies and programs. We are using the term "discourse" to refer to the ways in which language is used to create what is generally accepted as "common sense," thereby orchestrating consent for initiatives that are in the interests of particular groups. Thus, discourses are intimately linked to patterns of power relations in a society. In fact, they constitute the predominant means of both establishing and resisting power and status relations among social groups. Internalized discourses can be viewed as computer programs in our heads that allow for certain propositions to be processed in highly automatized ways and accepted as valid while propositions that are inconsistent with the internalized discourse are rejected automatically. They constitute what can be thought and what counts as truth or knowledge. A major focus of schooling in virtually all societies is the transmission of internalized discourses that are consistent with, and reinforcing of, national, cultural, or religious identities.

The relationship between discourse and power can be illustrated with countless examples from the world of politics. For example, the discourse of anticommunism was so firmly entrenched in the American psyche from the McCarthy era in the early 1950s to the fall of communism in the late 1980s that it was almost impossible to comprehend the notion of a democratically elected Marxist government, such as that of Salvador Allende in Chile in the early 1970s. Marxism had been established in people's minds as synonymous with evil and totalitarianism and in absolute opposition to democracy. The internalized anti-Communist discourse was effective in legitimating and minimizing public dissent to the CIA-inspired overthrow of Allende's government in 1973. No evidence was required to establish the "truth" that if the government was Marxist, it was of necessity totalitarian and oppressive and therefore should be overthrown in the name of freedom. In Chile (as well as many other countries around the globe), the tragic irony was that the excesses of the military dictatorship of General Pinochet, which replaced the Allende government, matched the worst of Stalinism.[18]

Current educational discourses are more subtle in their effects than those that have legitimated military adventures abroad; they nevertheless exert a huge impact on the lives of communities who live in poverty and who are ill-served by the educational opportunities available to them. We argue in the following sections that educational discourses that attempt to legitimate the continued exclusion of marginalized groups from the mainstream of American life have reached a point of diminishing returns even for the socially powerful groups whose interests they are intended to serve. Middle-class communities have a particular stake in critically analyzing these discourses because it is they who will bear the brunt of the social and economic costs generated by the creation of an ever-increasing underclass.

Three major interrelated discourses on literacy have emerged during the recent debates on educational reform in North America. These concern worker literacy and business competitiveness, literacy instruction in schools, and literacy achievement of marginalized groups.

WORKER LITERACY AND BUSINESS COMPETITIVENESS

Many of the educational reform reports of the 1980s in the United States explicitly related the difficulties of American industry in competing against Asian countries to the inadequacies of the human resources that American industry had to draw on, specifically the low levels of worker "functional literacy." The low literacy of workers was, in turn, attributed to the failures of American schools to transmit basic literacy and numeracy skills in an organized and sequential way. In fact, the imperative for reform was sparked by the widespread perception that educational standards in the United States were in decline for a number of years and, as a result, American business interests were placed in jeopardy in an increasingly competitive world economy. As expressed in *A Nation at Risk:* "Our once unchallenged preeminence in commerce, industry, science and technological innovations is being overtaken by competitors throughout the world."[19]

The recommendations of *A Nation at Risk* and most subsequent reports have focused primarily on raising standards and graduation requirements, eliminating the "curriculum smorgasbord" of "soft" subjects in favor of a common core curriculum for all students, and increasing the amount of time that students are expected to spend learning the "basics." The thrust has been toward "getting tough" with students and teachers in order to increase the rigor in curriculum materials and instruction.[20]

More than a decade after *A Nation at Risk* was published, it is clear that this ongoing discourse of "competitiveness" and "functional illiteracy" constitutes what researcher Larry Cuban has called "the Great School Scam."[21] Workers and educators became scapegoats for the economic difficulties of North American industry in the 1980s and the prodigious waste of human and economic resources by government and business during that period. Two obvious examples are the savings and loan scandal and escalating military expenditures during the Reagan/Bush administrations. As a number of commentators have noted, the discourse of educational reform, and particularly the myth that "bad schools cause a bad economy," diverts attention from the failure of government to allocate resources to the social infrastructure essential for healthy human development.[22] The cyclical economic woes of the United States and Canada have complex causes, most of which are unrelated to the quality of schools. In Cuban's terms:

Better to tell the truth: schools are important but not critical to economic competitiveness in a global economy. Better to say clearly that public education is the only social institution in a democracy that has as its central purpose the production of thoughtful citizens who have a sense of their individual rights and of their community responsibilities. . . . Finally, it is better to point out now that the myth of a corporate formula to save schools, which currently dominates public policy, will do precious little for big-city schools that continue to hemorrhage one-third to one-half of their students to the streets.[23]

Cuban also has pointed out that if schools were to blame for the faltering economy of the late 1980s and early 1990s, then logically they should get the credit for the thriving economy of the mid-1990s. He poses the rhetorical question: "Now that America outstrips Japan and Germany in labor productivity, economic growth, and share of world merchandizing exports, why haven't public schools received the educational equivalent of the Oscars?"[24]

Several investigators also have cast doubt on the claim that North American industry is facing an impending skills shortage. Iris Rotberg of the National Science Foundation in Washington, D.C., points out that there is little evidence of any shortage in the supply of scientists and engineers.[25] Brian O'Reilly, writing in *Fortune,* talks about a "worldwide glut of skilled workers" and discusses the fact that companies are seeking to tap this "vast new supply of skilled labor around the world."[26] Jonathan Weisman's analysis of a variety of economic data similarly refutes the corporate premise of a crisis in the supply of skilled labor. He concludes that

. . . studies of the most sophisticated corporations in the U.S. have consistently failed to find a skills shortage. Instead, what is emerging is a picture of corporate America hiding decades of mismanagement behind the presumed faults of the education system. The education reform movement has largely accepted this rhetoric about an inadequate work force and has argued for educational improvement on economic grounds. In so doing, however, . . . [t]hey have been trying to overhaul the entire education system for business' sake, rather than focusing their attention on the truly disadvantaged, whose abysmal education really does hinder productivity.[27]

The rush to blame the schools for the nation's allegedly low levels of literacy ignores the fact that literacy levels in most Western countries have been rising rather than falling. In Canada, for example, national statistical data suggest that "Canadians are better educated than ever before. Steady improvements in levels of educational attainment occurred over the past few decades. More younger Canadians today have university degrees and fewer have less than a Grade 9 education than did earlier cohorts."[28]

Lawrence Stedman and Carl Kaestle similarly point out that the apparent test-score decline in the 1970s that so concerned U.S. educational reformers was due to a variety of factors other than educational quality (including the fact that more minority students were staying in school rather than dropping out) and by the late 1970s the decline in standardized test scores had ended, well before "the reformers issued their reports, and before the legislatures passed their post-1980 reform bills."[29] Thus, they argue that the alleged decline in educational standards that precipitated the reform movement was actually a fabricated crisis.

The same conclusion emerges from a comprehensive study of U.S. education conducted by scientists at the Sandia National Laboratories.[30] Sandia, one of the largest scientific and engineering laboratories in the United States, has no particular hidden agenda in the educational arena. The findings of their report (publication of which was delayed for three years by government agencies) refuted almost all the premises underlying the 1980s educational reform movement.

Consistent with Stedman and Kaestle's conclusion, the Sandia report found that the apparent decline in Scholastic Achievement Test (SAT) scores arises from the fact that more low-achieving students are taking the test. Every ethnic group taking the test is performing as well or better than it did 15 years ago. In fact, if SAT scores are controlled for gender and students' ranking in class so that the test population is equivalent to those who took the test in 1975, the results show a 30 point improvement in scores. Similarly, National Assessment of Educational Progress (NAEP) scores show no evidence of decline over time.

With respect to other indicators, the United States fares well in comparison to other countries. For example, when reentry to high school is included in calculation of high school completion rates, the United States shows a high school completion rate of 85 percent, which, according to the authors, is among the best in the world. Only Belgium and Finland exceed the United States in percentage of 17-year-olds enrolled in school. In addition, the United States continues to lead the world in the percentage of young people obtaining bachelor's degrees. Fifty-seven percent of U.S. youths attempt postsecondary studies, which is about double the Japanese rate and equivalent to the high school graduation rate in the United States in the early 1950s. The authors discredit international comparisons of educational achievement on the grounds that differences in educational goals, philosophy, and culture make meaningful comparison very difficult; in particular, many other countries "weed out" low achievers prior to the upper levels of secondary school.[31]

The Sandia report warns against complacency, despite the surprisingly positive "report card." Among the major challenges facing education are the difficulty of finding national consensus about educational directions, improving the performance of minority and urban students, and adjusting to demographic changes and immigration.

In short, there is an enormous credibility gap in the discourse linking schools and the economy. It is clear that this discourse has been mobilized primarily for political purposes that have little to do with actually improving education. Cuban suggests that for business leaders and national public officials, the major function of this "educational swindle" was to avoid "harsher public judgements about inept governmental and corporate policies and helplessness in the face of intransigent economic cycles."[32] In the Canadian context, William Hynes has similarly attributed the corporate agenda in education to the effort to displace blame for economic problems and divert attention from the real shortcomings of schools, namely "the fact that its benefits and pains are shared very unequally, and that this inequality is based on class, race, locality and sex."[33]

In both the U.S. and Canadian contexts, the issue of social control also is implicated. Improving the "output" of public schools will result in an even greater skills surplus than exists at present, resulting in a buyer's market whereby highly skilled people can be hired cheaply and controlled more effectively.[34] In addition, discrediting the public schools likely will increase support for privatized schooling with its double attraction for business of profit possibilities and reductions in tax burden.[35] Finally, a back-to-basics orientation in the classroom will minimize the possibility of critical literacy skills being developed, particularly among marginalized communities. This, in turn, will facilitate a smoother "democratic" process, better business climate, and greater national unity. In spite of rhetoric about the need for higher-order thinking skills, business elites have minimal interest in fostering critical thinking and articulate communication among marginalized communities.

In view of this reality, it is hardly surprising that the competitiveness discourse is closely associated with vehement attacks on the process of literacy instruction in schools, a topic to which we now turn.

LITERACY INSTRUCTION IN SCHOOLS

Several interrelated issues related to the teaching of reading and writing have emerged in the educational reform debates. First, it is assumed that educational standards and test scores have declined during the past 30 years. For neo-conservative commentators, a major culprit to emerge in this perceived decline of student literacy and numeracy is the proliferation of "progressive" "child-centered" teaching methods and the alleged unwillingness of educators to teach "basic skills" and content in a direct, no-nonsense fashion.[36] When applied to reading instruction, this issue manifests itself in the perception that schools have virtually abandoned systematic instruction in phonics in favor of "whole-language" methods that eschew direct instruction in the subskills of reading; since students are denied access to the building blocks of reading, it is hardly surprising (according to this view) that they don't learn to read very well. A parallel argument is beginning to be heard against "process" approaches to writing instruction; since process writing instruction has abandoned direct systematic instruction of vocabulary, spelling, and grammar in favor of allowing students to "discover" these aspects of literacy in the process of writing, it appears hardly surprising to critics of this approach that students have meager vocabularies and that their grammar and spelling are substandard.

Finally, with respect to content instruction, there is a common perception (and some evidence) that American students are profoundly ignorant of their own culture and history (as well as anybody else's culture and history).[37] This usually is attributed to the failure of American educators to transmit to students the essential shared knowledge base necessary to participate effectively in American society (Hirsch's "cultural literacy").

The inference drawn by both academic and media commentators is that educators should desist from their permissive and "progressive" ways and start to *teach*.

Clearly, issues related to the content of instruction, general orientations to pedagogy, phonics versus whole-language reading instruction, and traditional versus process approaches to writing are complex from both educational and sociopolitical perspectives. These issues are by no means new; the pendulum of educational discourse has swung frequently between the extremes of traditional versus progressive pedagogy.[38]

The premise of the neo-conservative attack on literacy instruction in schools is that literacy levels have been declining. As is clear from the data reviewed earlier, however, this premise is totally inaccurate. Unfortunately, accuracy is minimally important to the construction of mythologies, and the mythology of declining literacy standards and ineffective literacy instruction usually has been reinforced by attributing the "literacy crisis" to the child-centered permissiveness and social unrest of the late 1960s. However, as Stedman and Kaestle point out, the greatest student protest took place between 1968 and 1971, whereas the greatest decline in standardized test scores occurred between 1971 and 1978:

> Blaming the decline on the effects of social unrest in the schools may be fashionable, but the middle to late 1970s were years of educational retrenchment, characterized by a renewed emphasis on the basics, the spread of statewide competency testing and moves to end social promotion. We can hardly blame the test declines of the 1970s directly on activist educators who, frustrated by their inability to change schools, had effectively abandoned their efforts by the mid-1970s.[39]

A further point is that virtually all the empirical data show that instruction in schools has changed very little over the course of this century.[40] According to John Goodlad's analysis of more than 1,000 elementary and secondary classrooms, the typical American classroom configuration involves:

> the teacher explaining or lecturing to the total class or a single student, occasionally asking questions requiring factual answers; the teacher, when not lecturing, observing or monitoring students working individually at

their desks; students listening or appearing to listen to the teacher and occasionally responding to the teacher's questions; students working individually at their desks on reading or writing assignments; and all with little emotion, from interpersonal warmth to expressions of hostility.[41]

Sirotnik has similarly commented that the teaching and learning process "appears to be one of the most consistent and persistent phenomena known in the social and behavioral sciences . . . the 'modus operandi' of the typical classroom is still didactics, practice, and little else."[42] He notes that teacher lecturing or total class work on written assignments continue to emerge as the primary instructional patterns and suggests that "navigating back to the basics should be easy. We never left."[43]

In other words, while arguments for child-centered or experience-based pedagogy have been prominent in the academic literature for a considerable period of time, in fact long before the term "whole-language" was coined, actual practice in U.S. schools has remained relatively unaffected by such arguments. However, despite their relatively minimal impact, child-centered instruction frequently has been made a scapegoat for the perceived failings of American education.[44] In the present context, they provide a convenient scapegoat for the neo-conservative attempt to reassert control over the curricular "input" and human "output" of education. The need to reassert control has been precipitated by the increasingly determined efforts of marginalized groups to inject their experiences and perspectives into the school curriculum through bilingual programs and multicultural education.

LITERACY ACHIEVEMENT OF MARGINALIZED GROUPS

The relationship between equity issues and literacy has been prominent in U.S. educational debates since the 1960s. In recent years, there has been grudging acknowledgment that minority group educational underachievement is related to the "literacy crisis" because it is difficult to avoid the fact that minority groups are massively overrepresented in the "functionally illiterate" category. For example, a survey by the National Assessment of Educational Progress (NAEP) in the United States reported that at each of the three literacy levels (basic—score of 200, intermediate—score of 275, and advanced—score of 350), European Americans performed better than Latinos who in turn performed better than African Americans.[45] Newman and Beverstock suggest that "this division implies an alarming trend, considering the fact that minorities who have been economically and educationally disadvantaged comprise an increasingly large percentage of the population." They also note that literate skills involving thinking and problem-solving at the 275 level and above on the NAEP scale will be increasingly required in the workplace of the twenty-first century: "the scales of difficulty also demonstrated that complex and demanding tasks—those that are expected to characterize work in coming years—may be beyond the current skills of many young adults. For example, workers often will be expected to use information on computer screens, make calculations, consult documentation, and then type new instructions."[46] These activities reflect skills at or above the 275 level on the NAEP scale, a level that only 78 percent of European Americans, 57 percent of Latinos, and 39 percent of African Americans attained.

A more recent NAEP study reported that Black, Hispanic and American Indian students in grades 4, 8, and 12 performed considerably worse than White or Asian/Pacific Islander students on measures of reading proficiency.[47] The scores for these groups were (not surprisingly) in the same range as for "disadvantaged urban" students. The differences in reading proficiency between "disadvantaged urban" and "advantaged urban" students were immense; for example, at the fourth-grade level, the former group obtained a score of 188 on the reading measures compared to a score of 240 for the latter.

The shift in rhetoric during the 1980s from an emphasis on equity to a focus on "excellence" signaled a shift in the way minority underachievement data was interpreted by conservative academics, policymakers, and media commentators. The public discourse shifted to absolve schools and society from responsibility for minority group underachievement and once again to attribute school failure to minority students' own deficiencies, deficiencies of their families, or to cynical manipulation by minority group politicians. Thus, while schools are castigated for their failure to promote adequate literacy and academic excellence and for their cavalier attitude to accountability, it is minority students and their communities that are largely blamed for their poor school performance. Conservative groups believe that if broader societal institutions are at all responsible for minority group underachievement, it is only to the extent that politicians and educators have caved in to "ethnic demands."[48]

Thus, within the mainstream educational reform effort, there has been minimal analysis of the causes of academic failure among marginalized groups. Most media commentators do not move much beyond an analysis that blames the victim and exhorts teachers to be more effective. In fact, under the guise of promoting "excellence," the neo-conservative educational agenda during the 1980s abdicated even any pretense of promoting equity in educational opportunity, let alone in educational outcomes. Simply put, in the short term, it is cheaper to import the human resources needed by industry than to make the enormous investment to rebuild the social and educational infrastructure devastated by more than a decade of policies that have transferred wealth from the poor and middle class to the rich, as documented conclusively by Barlett and Steele.[49]

Diversity has remained an uncomfortable issue even for many schools that are attempting to engage in a participatory and democratic restructuring process rather than a "top-down" process. This is illustrated by the findings of a major research project conducted by the advocacy group California Tomorrow involving 73 Californian schools that were in the process of restructuring. The sample included a variety of restructuring models based on the work of James Comer, Henry Levin, and Theodore Sizer, as well as other initiatives funded through California's 1991 school restructuring legislation (SB 1274).[50] The study revealed a lack of discussion about issues of culture and identity and "heavy barriers to bringing diversity and equity issues into the school's plans to better serve their students."[51] In spite of genuine commitment, the agenda for the reform process was largely determined by the concerns of educators from the dominant group; the voices of marginalized groups were rarely heard. In many schools, parents and instructional aides who were capable of adding to the knowledge base about issues of language, culture, and race in the lives of the students were excluded from significant participation in the restructuring process. The report suggests some of the reasons why dialogue about diversity and equity was missing:

> Four-fifths of California's teachers are white. Most do not come to work with firsthand knowledge of the communities and cultures of their students. Most

speak only English. . . . Teacher education programs are far behind the times in providing teachers with the knowledge about second language acquisition, about the impact of racism in students' lives, and about the diverse cultural backgrounds of the students in the public schools. We found more direct, lively dialogue and consideration of issues of race, culture and language in schools where prior to restructuring, there had been a tradition of strong bilingual programs or multicultural education and community embeddedness. . . . Generally, however, it appeared to us that in many schools, people were unaware that there is a perspective, a knowledge base that is missing around their table. They do not know that they do not know.[52]

We believe that an analysis of the causes of minority group underachievement is central to any genuine effort to restructure education for the twenty-first century. In this regard, an obvious contributor to the pattern of underachievement is poverty, a phenomenon that has increased dramatically during the past decade in both the United States and Canada.[53] However, in addition to factors associated with poverty and economic discrimination, the systematic undermining of students' cultural identity within schools plays a significant role. As a result of this persistent devaluation of identity, marginalized communities frequently have internalized a sense of ambivalence in regard to the value of their culture and a sense of futility with respect to the possibility of improving their lives through democratic participation.[54] As Andrew Hacker concludes in his book *Two Nations: Black and White, Separate, Hostile, Unequal,* "legal slavery may be in the past, but segregation and subordination have been allowed to persist."[55]

The treatment of marginalized groups as "internal colonies" is exemplified by the fact that the three groups in the U.S. context that experience the most pronounced educational difficulty (African American, Latino, and Native American students) each have been subordinated for centuries by the dominant group.[56] In the Canadian context, the academic difficulties of First Nations (Native) students and minority francophone students outside of Quebec illustrate a similar pattern. In Scandinavia, the underachievement of Finnish minority students in Sweden is similarly linked to the fact that Finland was colonized by Sweden for several hundred years.[57] As in most colonial situations, upward mobility for marginalized communities has entailed a process of denial of identity, exemplified by the students in Fordham's study who identified academic achievement with "acting White."

The devaluation of identity in the broader society has been reflected in the interactions between educators and students in school. A variety of structural and attitudinal factors operating in schools have contributed to students' difficulties and resistance. Among them are:

- Segregation and tracking practices that provide students with "a watered-down curriculum due to low expectations, along with the least experienced teachers . . . [in] schools that are most often overcrowded, underfinanced and ill-equipped."[58]
- Exclusion of all aspects of students' culture and language from the school together with discouragement of parental participation.
- Curriculum that fails to reflect the experience and realities of culturally diverse students, together with instruction that actively discourages any critical refection on the content to be internalized.

The clear implication of these patterns is that educational reform efforts that pay only lipservice to causes of underachievement among marginalized groups are unlikely to be successful. A focus only on technical skills of reading and writing fails to address the continuing legacy of a coercive power structure. In short, for marginalized communities, functional literacy can be attained only through critical literacy.

THE PARADOX OF EDUCATIONAL REFORM

At this point, the paradox of educational reform and the dilemma for socially powerful groups can be discerned. Raising the overall literacy levels of the population, and by implication within the neo-conservative discourse the competitiveness of American industry, necessitates reversing the pattern of school failure among minority students—particularly because the overall proportion of these students in the population is rising dramatically. Reversing school failure, however, is unlikely to come cheaply; it will entail not just educational expenditures but also massive investment in a social infrastructure in inner cities and poor rural areas that has been decaying for the past 25 years. In other words, the long-term goal of making American industry competitive through upgrading educational achievement would require that there be some reversal of the income distribution pattern of the past 15 years where funds have been transferred from poor to rich. In a similar vein, historian Paul Kennedy has pointed out that "any attempt to alleviate homelessness and poverty in the inner cities—and the rural South—might cost a great deal of money, and a transfer of resources from the better off (who vote) to the poor (who don't)."[59]

Not surprisingly economically advantaged groups resist this scenario. Yet it is increasingly clear that their agenda of preserving a power structure that disadvantages the majority of Americans is self-defeating and is rapidly reaching a point of diminishing returns. The costs of maintaining the status quo (e.g., the need to incarcerate more and more people) have outstripped the costs of shifting to a more collaborative sharing of power through more equitable investment in education and social programs. Educator Harold Hodgkinson points out that more than 80 percent of prisoners in the United States are high school dropouts, and each prisoner costs taxpayers a minimum of $20,000 a year. A decent education would have given people a stake in preserving the social system rather than dismantling it and would require only a fraction of the escalating costs of incarceration.[60]

The fiscal absurdity (not to mention the human injustice) of pushing minority students out of school can be seen in some of the data marshaled by Gary Natriello, Edward L. McDill, and Aaron M. Pallas in their aptly titled book *Schooling Disadvantaged Children: Racing Against Catastrophe.* In a conservative calculation of the cost to the nation of high school dropouts, they conclude: "Each year, then, the estimated cost to the nation of the dropout problem is approximately $50 billion in foregone lifetime earnings alone. Also associated with this cost are foregone government tax revenues, greater welfare expenditures, poorer physical and mental health of our nation's citizens, and greater costs of crime, as well as a variety of social costs to which it is difficult to attach dollar figures."[61] They also note that "each dollar invested in early prenatal care can reduce the cost of infant care by more than three dollars."[62] Estimates of the financial returns on Head Start programs also suggest that every dollar spent on a Head Start child will result in savings of $7 through reduced need for special education, welfare, incarceration, and so on.[63]

The short-term thinking that characterizes social policy in the United States is evidenced by the fact that there is little reluctance to spend public funds on prisons, even though the country incarcerates its population at a rate six times greater than that of Australia and ten times greater than that of the Netherlands.[64] Similarly, the costs of more adequate social and economic programs designed to combat poverty and educational failure usually are viewed as prohibitive by the same politicians who, with minimal dissent or even debate, committed $157 billion of taxpayers' money (for starters) to "resolve" the savings and loan scandal and whose trillions of dollars of wasted military expenditures never required justification.[65] These policy decisions served the interests of the rich and powerful at the expense of the vast majority of American citizens.

The effort to preserve what is essentially a coercive power structure has given rise to patterns of discourse whose logical contradictions are immediately apparent. As one example, consider the orientation of neo-conservative groups (such as the cultural literacy movement or organizations such as U.S. English) to the development of bilingual and multilingual abilities among students. Within the discourse of competitiveness, there have been many calls to improve foreign language instruction. Since global economic, scientific, and environmental interdependence is clearly a reality, many business and educational leaders view cross-cultural sensitivity and the ability to communicate in international languages as an essential component of the human resources that business requires to thrive (and survive) in the global marketplace. These abilities could be viewed as dimensions of a "global cultural literacy," the lack of which is seriously hampering North American competitiveness in a shrinking global economy. However, there is vehement rejection of any suggestion to expand and reorient bilingual education programs to promote bilingual students' literacy skills in their primary language. Rather than developing the "home-grown" linguistic and cultural resources of the nation, groups such as U.S. English insist on using foreign-language instructional methods that, for generations, have proven ineffective for the vast majority of students. The financial investment required to make bilingual education available on a wider scale to both majority and minority students would be minimal compared to the investment required to train monolingual and monocultural adults to operate effectively in cross-cultural business, diplomacy, or security-related endeavors.[66]

A reasonable hypothesis is that this apparent absence of good business sense is due to the majority group's reluctance to reinforce bilingual students' cultural identity. To acknowledge that their bilingualism is a valuable cultural and economic asset would effectively reverse the historical pattern of devaluation of identity. An expansion of bilingual education would transfer status and power (as well as jobs) to minority groups that have the linguistic and cultural abilities to work in such programs. There is also a fear that if the economic advantages of bilingualism are acknowledged, monolingual children will be disadvantaged in the future job market in comparison to the bilingual children of minority groups. Hence the contradictory call for more effective foreign-language teaching while simultaneously insisting that schools eradicate all "un-American" languages that students may happen to speak fluently on entry to school.[67]

Similar contradictions are evident in other aspects of the rhetoric of educational reform:

- The call for better development of problem-solving and critical thinking abilities contradicts the simultaneous insistence that teachers get back to basics and transmit information in a didactic way that allows for minimal student language use, let alone critical thinking.
- The call for better reading and writing skills development contradicts the reduction in amount of classroom time that students can spend reading literature or amplifying their experience through writing (as advocated, for example, by many whole-language approaches to literacy).[68]
- The insistence that education is fundamental to business competitiveness contradicts the simultaneous reduction in government funding and corporate contributions for public education.[69]

As a result of these contradictions, much of the educational reform discourse obscures rather than clarifies the directions required to reorient our schools for the challenges of the twenty-first century. The sociopolitical agenda underlying this discourse is designed to preserve the societal power structure while accommodating minimally to the perceived need to upgrade national literacy levels. More specifically, the unstated goals are to (a) promote sufficient functional literacy to meet the needs of industry in an increasingly technological work environment; (b) promote cultural literacy and cultural identities that are in harmony with the societal power structure so that what is in the best interests of elite groups is accepted as also being in the best interests of marginalized groups; and (c) limit the development of critical literacy so that students do not develop the ability to analyze disinformation and challenge structures of control and social injustice.

Clearly, a fundamental change in social mindset and orientation to educational reform is required if our society is to address the changing cultural, economic, and existential realities that are fast approaching.

RESTRUCTURING FOR WHAT?
THE RAPIDLY CHANGING CONTEXT OF EDUCATION

Cultural Realities

The dramatic increase in cultural diversity in Western industrialized countries shows no signs of abating as refugees from political conflicts and devastated economies continue to seek asylum. In addition, falling birth rates in most Western countries have resulted in greater immigration to maintain population levels and stimulate economic growth. For example, Canada increased its annual immigration from 84,302 in 1985 to 250,000 annually (about 1 percent of the population) in the early 1990s. As a consequence, students from linguistically and culturally diverse backgrounds now constitute about half the school population in cities such as Toronto and Vancouver.

In the United States, immigrants' share of total population growth represented 39 percent between 1980 and 1990, compared to 33 percent in the previous decade and just 11 percent between 1960 and 1970.[70] These trends are expected to continue. For example, the Asian American population is expected to increase dramatically, from 8 million in 1992 to 16 million by 2009, 24 million by 2024, and 32 million by 2038. Latinos will account for more than 40 percent of population growth over the next 60 years and become the nation's largest minority in the year 2013. African Americans are expected to double in number by the year 2050.[71]

Consistent with these projected growth trends, the proportion of culturally diverse students is rapidly increasing in U.S. urban centers. To illustrate, the National Coalition of Advocates for Students estimated that by the year 2001, minority enrollment levels will range from 70 to 96 percent in the nation's 15 largest school systems.[72] In California, so-called minority groups (e.g. Latinos, African Americans, Asian Americans) already represent a greater proportion of the school population than students from the so-called majority group. By the year 2030, half of all the children in the state are projected to be of Latino background while European Americans will compose 60 percent of the elderly population, a reality that Paul Kennedy terms "a troublesome mismatch" that raises the prospect of "a massive contest over welfare and entitlement priorities between predominantly Caucasian retirees and predominantly nonwhite children, mothers, and unemployed, each with its vocal advocacy organizations."[73]

These changing cultural realities have immense relevance to educational restructuring in Western countries. In the first place, increased diversity at home and globalization internationally highlight the importance of promoting additional language competence in schools. Bilingual and multilingual individuals are likely to be more attractive to employers faced with providing service to a linguistically diverse clientele in societal institutions (hospitals, seniors' homes, airports, schools, etc.) as well as to those engaged in international trade. While English is spreading rapidly as a second language throughout the world, Senator Paul Simon's dictum "You can buy in any language, but you can't sell in any language" still holds. The internal logic of the "international competitiveness" discourse might suggest that in an increasingly interdependent world, it is the monolingual/monocultural individual who is "culturally illiterate" and ill-equipped to prosper in the global economy.

Second, increased diversity has highlighted the need to develop more effective ways of promoting intercultural cooperation and understanding in our education systems. Educators concerned with preparing students for life in the twenty-first century must educate them for "global citizenship." The potential to achieve this goal is obviously greater in a classroom context where cultural diversity thrives than in a classroom context where cultural diversity is either ignored or suppressed.

Third, as we argued already, educational success for culturally diverse students will occur only in school systems that promote pride in students' cultural identities and respect for other cultural realities. This is illustrated in Lawrence Stedman's reanalysis of the "Effective Schools" research literature. Stedman analyzed case studies of schools that achieved grade-level success with low-income students and maintained this success over several years. A major characteristic of these schools was their focus on cultural pluralism. Effective schools acknowledged and reinforced the racial and ethnic identity of their students and provided opportunities for culturally diverse parents to become involved in their children's learning and participate in school governance.[74]

In summary, there are compelling reasons why schools should abandon their long-term orientation to diversity as a problem to be overcome in favor of a focus on diversity as a societal resource to be nurtured.[75] Communication across cultural and linguistic boundaries is essential not only for economic development in the twenty-first century but also to resolve potential intergroup conflicts in both the domestic and international arenas. Even minimal investment in bilingual programs for both majority and minority students and a focus on infusing multicultural awareness across the curriculum can contribute significantly both to the nation's economic competitiveness and to its ability to collaborate internationally in resolving global problems.

Economic and Scientific Realities

Although there is little credibility in the neo-conservative "literacy crisis" rhetoric, it is true that the major economic and scientific changes that our global society is undergoing entail significant implications for our educational systems. The nature of our society, and particularly the nature of the workplace, has changed dramatically in recent decades. Just as, over the long term, the Industrial Revolution in the 1800s created the need for a much broader range of literacy and numeracy skills than had hitherto been the case, the technological changes associated with the current Information Age require that many workers employ literacy skills that are far beyond those their parents needed.

Even in jobs where high levels of literacy are not required for adequate job performance, employers have raised educational standards for applicants. For example, many employers now require higher levels of education for low-level and low-paid jobs in the service sector, which represented the fastest growing segment of the job market in Western industrialized countries during the 1980s. This trend appears to be related to the perception that the "trainability" of workers is essential for businesses to adapt in a flexible manner to a rapidly changing economic environment.[76]

In a similar vein, economist Robert Reich has highlighted the importance of *symbolic analysis* skills in an economy that is shifting from high-volume to high-value production.[77] These skills are:

- Abstraction—the capacity to order and make meaning of the massive flow of information, to shape raw data into workable patterns.
- System thinking—the capacity to see the parts in relation to the whole, to see why problems arise.
- Experimental inquiry—the capacity to set up procedures to test and evaluate alternative ideas.
- Collaboration—the capacity to engage in active communication and dialogue to get a variety of perspectives and to create consensus when that is necessary.

Canadian social commentators Maud Barlow and Heather-Jane Robertson provide a more skeptical perspective on the workplace of the future. They point to the worldwide glut of skilled labor and the dim prospects for any significant immediate increase in North American jobs that would require "symbolic analysis." Recent job creation has involved primarily service sector jobs, often part time and for minimum wage. They point out that business has a short-term vested interest in keeping levels of unemployment high:

> The reality is that high unemployment keeps up competition for jobs, thus keeping wage demands and inflation down, which is good for business. . . . It is against this backdrop that business demands for structural change in how and what we teach young people must be considered. Simply put, if we knowingly train young workers for jobs that don't exist, i.e. if we train a glut of young people for the jobs available, knowing that the resulting competition will drive down wages and create conditions that may be good for business, but not for anyone else, we are sowing the seeds of great social unrest.[78]

Barlow and Robertson suggest that the long-term interests of business and of the entire society are better served by promoting full employment and decent living standards so that the bulk of the population will have money to pump back into the economy. This scenario would promote long-term economic stability (which is good for business) and social cohesion rather than the "spiritual and cultural impoverishment" and social upheaval that is the inevitable outcome of current economic trends.

Educator Arthur Wirth also highlights the inevitability of social unrest if present trends in business and education continue. Industry and schools face clear choices as we approach the twenty-first century. He points out that during the 1980s leaders in industry and labor

> began to see the long-standing tradition of top-down, expert-controlled, scientific management as the source of problems, rather than as the solution to problems. They were probing various forms of workplace democracy . . . as alternatives. At the same time, policy makers in American education, under the leadership of Secretary of Education William Bennett, were rushing in the opposite direction. The linchpin of educational reform, Bennett argued, was measurable accountability—expert-designed, centrally monitored instruction and testing.[79]

Wirth suggests that this model of top-down control (which he terms "automating") is counterproductive for both business and schools in the postindustrial economy. Competitiveness can be ensured only by bringing workers into active participation and by shifting "considerable learning and power to people at work." This second option, which would require workers with skills of symbolic analysis, he terms "informating."

Wirth argues that the real literacy crisis resides in the fact that an increasing proportion of American children (largely from low-income minority communities) are denied access to schooling that will promote skills of symbolic analysis. The growing polarization between wealthy and impoverished confronts U.S. society with a choice of alternative futures:

> The first, our present path, is to maintain a society wounded by class divisions and unequal access to learning. For the near future this approach might be made to work. The upper echelons may see the society handicapped by an impoverished non-white sector that is largely "out of it" and by many workers with only mediocre education and training. But for the moment they can keep America in the competitive race by choosing the high-tech, centrally administered "automating" option. . . . This option is based on the bet that the middle and lower-middle classes can be kept in line by the diversions of consumption and by playing on racial fears.

But social divisiveness could become increasingly troublesome. By the year 2020, the top fifth may well earn more than 60% of American income, while the bottom fifth may drop to 2%. Well-educated elites will withdraw further into their secure enclaves, living a life with excellent health care, challenging work, effective schools, global travel, and electronic linkages. The urban and rural poor will live largely out of sight in their decaying communities. The despair and hopelessness of their children will be facts of life—as will be the human waste of warehousing thousands of youths of color in prisons. A stepped-up security apparatus may be required to contain them.[80]

These trends are already well under way, as evidenced, for example, by the dramatic increase in security-related employment during the 1980s (workplace supervisors, police, judicial and corrections employees, private security personnel, the armed forces, and producers of military and domestic security equipment).[81]

According to Wirth, there is an alternative to this nightmarish scenario; specifically, "the best bet for American social well-being is a population equipped with symbolic analysis skills, tempered by ecological awareness and a deep appreciation for the values and traditions of democracy." Creation of the world-class schools necessary to provide the population with access to symbolic analysis skills "would require an investment in education comparable to what has been spent on building a high-tech military machine."[82]

In short, genuine educational reform that responds to the economic and scientific realities of the twenty-first century would require the reversal of two fundamental ways in which the educational system has served the societal power structure. First, it would require significant long-term investment in the education of marginalized communities; a major step in this direction would be to equalize the amount of per-pupil expenditure between school districts within states; many states have almost a three to one ratio between high-expenditure and low-expenditure districts.[83] The long-term economics of this investment are attractive when compared to the economics of escalating crime and incarceration. However, in the short term they are unpalatable to elite groups that benefit from the transfer of resources from poor and middle class to rich.

Second, the effort to maintain control of the "products" of schooling by controlling what can be taught would have to give way to models of schooling based on collaboration and critical thinking. Passive internalization of inert content—which, as noted earlier, research suggests is the predominant mode of learning in U.S. classrooms—does not promote the kind of active intelligence that is required to create high skill jobs in the changing economy.[84] By contrast, active intelligence is central to the kinds of projects that we described in chapter 2, in which students worked together to define an issue, carried out research, critically interpreted the resulting data, and then collaborated in searching for solutions to the problems identified. These students are developing the skills of symbolic analysis that will help secure them decent jobs and promote job creation through the economic expansion made possible by a highly skilled workforce.

In summary, the neo-conservative educational reform movement, with its emphasis on testing, accountability, and back to basics, has oriented many schools away from the learning realities of the twenty-first century. This apparent paradox derives from the accurate assessment by the neo-conservative establishment that individuals who have developed critical literacy skills are less subject to manipulation and control. Their dilemma is where to draw the line between indoctrination that stultifies and the (at least partial) intellectual emancipation of students implied by some versions of the twenty-first-century workplace. Promotion of critical literacy and economic participation for all students might, in fact, result in dramatically increased democratic participation, a prospect far from congenial to those who currently control the resources and power within the society, particularly in view of the growing demographic strength of marginalized communities.

Existential Realities

By "existential realities," we are referring to the increasing sense of fragility that characterizes our relationship to both our physical and social environment. For example, a perusal of virtually any newspaper anywhere in the world will quickly show the extent of environmental deterioration and the enormity of the global ecological problems that our generation has created for our children's generation to resolve. Similarly, the "new world order" of peaceful coexistence that seemed at hand with the end of the Cold War has been overtaken by eruptions of brutal conflicts around the world. The summer 1992 riots directed against refugees in Germany or the Los Angeles uprising a few months earlier protesting racism in the United States are manifestations of the enormous pressures that lie just beneath the surface of the social fabric of Western industrialized countries.

Despite these changed existential realities, many schools appear dedicated to insulating students from awareness of global issues rather than communicating a sense of urgency in regard to understanding and acting on them. In most schools across the continent, the curriculum has been sanitized such that students rarely have the opportunity to discuss critically, write about, or act upon issues that directly affect the society they will form. Issues such as racism, environmental pollution, genetic engineering, and the causes of poverty are regarded as too sensitive for fragile and impressionable young minds. Still less do students have the opportunity to cooperate with others from different cultural and/or linguistic groups in exploring resolutions to these issues.

A major reason why schools try to maintain a facade of innocence in relation to social and environmental issues is that such issues invariably implicate power relations in the domestic and international arenas. Promoting a critical awareness of how power is wielded at home and abroad is not a task that society expects educators to undertake. In fact, as we have argued, renewed demands for a core curriculum and for imposition of "cultural literacy" can be interpreted as a way of controlling the information that students can access so as to minimize the possibility of deviant thoughts. In the shadows of the list of facts that every American should know is the list of facts that every American must be *discouraged* from knowing. Prominent among these is the history of imperialism and colonialism of Western powers from 1492 to the present. Also, students receive little incentive or encouragement to explore cultural and artistic work that focuses on social issues in ways that might challenge mainstream perceptions or sensibilities.

In this regard, Christian fundamentalist alliances have exerted a major influence in exorcising what they view as Satanic influences from the curriculum. Despite the fact that the Christian Right represents a numerically marginal group, few school districts are eager to be targeted for what frequently ends up being an expensive and divisive battle. While members of the business elite have promoted sanitization of the curriculum to remove "frills" (such as the arts) that they view as detracting from the learning of "basic skills," the religious Right has promoted supersanitization, campaigning to remove not just obvious targets such as sex education, the teaching of evolution, and multiculturalism but also whole-language approaches to literacy, creative writing, cooperative learning, and any form of instruction that might reduce the effectiveness of indoctrination.[85]

Clearly, these perspectives are at the opposite end of the spectrum from what we are advocating. The extremes to which cultural chauvinism can be taken are illustrated in the case of the fundamentalist school board of Lake County, Florida, which decreed that teachers can discuss other countries only if they make clear that America is the "best of the best"; the rationale there was that if students felt that the United States was inferior or equal to other countries then they would have no motive to go to war to defend it.[86] Needless to say, this is hardly a good starting point for developing intercultural literacy. While this example is extreme, it illustrates the pressures that educators are facing in their efforts to develop critically literate citizens who can cooperate across cultural, linguistic, and racial boundaries in the workplace, the broader society, and in the international arena.

In summary, we have argued that students must be encouraged to focus their developing literacy skills on the analysis and resolution of both local and global problems. Such a focus is not in any sense in opposition to the acquisition of more basic literacy and numeracy skills. In fact, for many students, promotion of critical literacy may be a necessary condition for development of functional literacy. Students will be more motivated to learn when they can appreciate the relevance of the content to their own lives.

Our analysis also suggests that issues related to the organization of society, specifically the division of resources and power, be taken off the taboo list of what is appropriate to explore in school. Students whose communities have been marginalized will increasingly perceive the omission of these fundamental issues as dishonest and hypocritical, and this will reinforce their resistance to achievement under the current rules of the game. By contrast, a focus on critical inquiry, in a collaborative and supportive context, will encourage students to engage in learning in ways that will promote future productive engagement in their societies. The research, critical thinking, and creative problem-solving skills that this form of education entails will position students well for full participation in the economic and social realities of their global community. Excluding students from the learning process at school is pushing us toward a society where everyone loses because every dropout carries an expensive price tag for the entire society.

In the next chapter, we explore the history of intercultural learning networks that have promoted skills of collaborative critical inquiry among their students. These projects, carried out in many countries for most of this century, illustrate the feasibility and the potential of the alternative directions that we believe educational reform should pursue.

Chapter 4

Blueprints from the Past: The Intercultural Learning Networks of Célestin Freinet and Mario Lodi

When we live very close to our surroundings and to people, we eventually come not to see them. . . . But thanks to the questions sent from our distant colleagues, our eyes are opened. We question, we investigate, we explore more deeply in order to respond with precise verifications to the inexhaustible curiosity of our distant collaborators, based on a natural motivation. This gradually leads to an awareness of our entire geographic, historic, and human environment.

—D. Gervilliers, C. Berteloot, and J. Lèmery, *Las correspondencias escolares*

When Michelle Gonsalves in San Diego and Arturo Solís in New Haven first joined their classrooms by e-mail in September 1986, neither realized that their first small step toward sister-class exchanges was following a well-trodden path blazed decades earlier by the pioneers of intercultural networking, European educators Célestin Freinet and Mario Lodi. We have much to learn today from these early pioneers. Although terms such as "e-mail" and "computer" had not entered the lexicon of any language, the intercultural learning that took place in their classrooms was as profound as that arising from the computer-mediated exchanges that we described in chapter 2.

Too often in North American classrooms today, increasingly sophisticated technological machinery is used for trivial purposes for want of a coherent instructional and social vision to drive it. We believe the kernel of that vision is to be found in the practice and writings of Freinet and Lodi.[1] In this chapter we explore the lessons of the past.

We begin with three short vignettes that sketch networking experiences spanning more than half a century. First we revisit Michelle Gonsalves and Arturo Solís as they discover the myriad instructional and learning possibilities opened up by sister-class exchanges. Then we travel 30 years back in time to the plains and valleys of northern Italy, where Mario Lodi was similarly discovering how minds can meet over geographic and cultural distances. Finally, 40 years earlier, we visit a tiny village in the French Alps and Célestin Freinet, whose vision transformed the educational experiences of students and teachers in the 10,000 schools in 33 countries that participated in the learning network of the Mouvement de l'École Moderne (Modern School Movement).

Vignette 1:
NEW HAVEN, CONNECTICUT
AND SAN DIEGO, CALIFORNIA, 1986

Arturo Solís of Truman School in New Haven, Connecticut, and Michelle Gonsalves of Valley Center School in San Diego, California, were bilingual teachers working with Spanish-speaking students; Mr. Solís's students were of Puerto Rican descent, while Ms. Gonsalves's were of Mexican heritage. Together, their fourth-grade students formed a long-distance partnership, using their classroom computers to send electronic mail. But they did much more than exchange letters. These students wrote and published newspapers together over the course of a school year, using all of the latest classroom technologies related to print and publishing. Besides sending e-mail, the students also used the national postal service, since they regularly exchanged "cultural packages" filled with snapshots, maps, postcards, drawings and mementos. These cultural packages often were accompanied by a student-produced videotape focusing on a key aspect of school or community life. The students named the tapes "video letters."

As the Spanish-speaking students in the bilingual classes watched the videos they had exchanged, they were quick to note differences between

Puerto Rican and Mexican dialects of Spanish. They followed up this insight with an investigation of proverbs common to each country. By asking their parents and grandparents about the proverbs they heard repeated every day in their homes and communities, the children discovered they had much in common with their distant correspondents. The parents of children from different nations, separated by thousands of miles, had passed along the collective wisdom of countless generations using the same folk sayings; where there were differences, these served to highlight intriguing contrasts between Mexican and Puerto Rican cultures. Both groups discovered that proverbs are one important way that immigrants maintain their cultural identity in their adopted country.

Vignette 2:
VHO, ITALY, AND CERTALDO, ITALY, 1960

Mario Lodi taught in the plains village of Vho and Bruno Ciardi taught in mountainous Certaldo. Although separated by hundreds of miles, their elementary school students collaborated closely in a variety of student journalism projects culminating in the publishing of newsletters. Both Lodi and Ciardi felt strongly that student journalism, shared between two classes, could serve as a catalyst for their students' emerging literacy skills, in effect transforming their classrooms into literacy learning laboratories.

They took this general principle to its logical conclusion. Proceeding from the principle that "adult" technologies, especially those associated with communication and the printed word, belonged in the classroom and, what is more, under children's control, Lodi and Ciardi actually taught their students how to operate state-of-the-art printing machinery. But the students took charge of much more than machines; they became responsible for putting their world into words and then putting these words before the world. *Il Mondo* (The world) and *Insieme* (Together), their student-written and edited newspapers, were published nearly everyday for a readership of fellow students, parents, and even subscribers in ten countries, week after week, for years.[2]

Letters were one important way the young reporters stayed in touch. But to say that the students had pen pals would be to trivialize their relationship. A Vho student, when writing to a friend in Certaldo, in a very real sense *became* that friend for her classmates. She was responsible for letting everyone in her class know how her friend was doing, for keeping them posted. These running updates about distant friends were like portrait studies, periodically undraped for classmates and carefully pondered for emerging features of character rendered by the young artist's caring hand.

The partner classes also exchanged audiotapes and added a slightly different twist to this technology: The students dubbed them "spoken letters." The transcripts of these group discussions around a single microphone reveal a fascinating blend of rehearsal and improvisation. One tape began with a song by the students from Vho. Each student in turn asked after his or her friend in Certaldo. The tape continued as Carolina, for example, reassured her faraway friend Claudio that her father, hospitalized after being gored by a bull, was improving. Finally, the Vho students left the tape recorder running while they viewed numbered slides that had been taken in Certaldo and that had been included in the last cultural package the Certaldo students had sent to them. The Vho students reacted freely, telling about the striking differences between the mountain village's pastoral economy and their own familiar farms. Earlier that school year, the Vho students also had sent slides of their village, with a taped running commentary. Thus in spoken letters, students revealed their worlds to distant friends and to themselves.

Many fascinating collaborative projects developed serendipitously. Like the students in New Haven and San Diego, it was through recordings that students first noticed the marked differences in dialect between the two villages, leading both partner classes to launch a sophisticated linguistic investigation into Italian dialects. They jointly developed a common system for writing their dialects and then tested their new scheme by investigating, recording, and transcribing lullabies from each village's communal traditions. Thus, both partner classes served as catalysts in the creation of new knowledge with their distant correspondents.[3]

Vignette 3:
LE BAR-SUR-LOUP, FRENCH MARITIME ALPS, AND TRÉGUNC, FINISTÈRE, FRANCE, 1924

Célestin Freinet taught in a public school in the southern French village of Le Bar-sur-Loup. His students had regular contact with a partner class taught by René Daniel in the Breton village of Trégunc. Like the Italian classes, the French students had learned how to print up their writings, and each class mailed their neatly printed news articles every other day to their distant colleagues. And every week, the two classes exchanged "cultural packages." The ones that arrived for Freinet's class in Le Bar-sur-Loup, for example, brought flowers, fruits, perfumes, seashells, fossils, photographs, local toys, figurines, ribbons and lace, and costumes from a coastal village to his students' tiny town in the Alps. Célestin Freinet wrote a single entry in his diary on the day the first cultural package arrived: *"Maintenant, nous ne sommes plus seuls"* (Now we are no longer alone).[4] Dated October 28, 1924, this diary entry marks the beginning of the history of global learning networks.

STARTLING DIFFERENCES AND A PROFOUND SIMILARITY

These three vignettes have taken us on a journey backward through time, from the end of this century back to its beginning and the birth of global learning networks. Viewed chronologically:

1. Célestin Freinet and René Daniel taught in the 1920s, and their classes used printing presses to produce enough copies of student writings to share with a partner class and eventually with the thousands of schools that participated in the Mouvement de l'École Moderne (Modern School Movement).

2. Mario Lodi and Bruno Ciardi, teaching in the 1950s and 1960s, employed typewriters and mimeograph machines in their class-rooms. Il Movimento di Cooperazione Educativa (the Cooperative Education Movement) was founded in 1951 by a group of teachers to promote widespread interest in Freinet's approaches within Italian public schools. Their goal was to adapt Freinet's pedagogy to the realities of Italian schools and to use the most current educational technologies relevant to writing and communication.[5] Later we describe the Italian Cooperative Education Movement as one of many examples of how Freinet's pedagogy of intercultural learning partnerships was adapted in other European countries, as well as in Africa, Asia, and Latin America.

3. Finally, while these French and Italian innovators networked via their national postal services, in 1986 Arturo Solis and Michelle Gonsalves made use of computers, first to compose and publish, and then to exchange student writings over the Orillas network. (See chapter 2.)

In spite of these differences, all three projects are linked fundamentally by the six teachers' common vision: to create a fertile ground for their own and their students' learning by sharing curricular activities with a distant partner class, activities that nevertheless remained firmly rooted in community-based learning.

In the next section, we examine the groundbreaking work of Célestin Freinet who, though he remained a rural elementary school teacher all his life, nevertheless founded what remains the largest long-distance global learning network in history. Freinet, together with thousands of collaborators in the Modern School Movement, developed an approach to teaching that continues to shape the practice of educators throughout Europe and Latin America and in many African and Asian nations as well.[6]

CÉLESTIN FREINET'S MODERN SCHOOL MOVEMENT: THE ORIGINS OF GLOBAL LEARNING NETWORKS

As chronicled in the documentary writings of Célestin Freinet's lifelong teaching companion and wife, Élise Freinet, the beginnings of global learning networks could hardly have been more humble or inauspicious. In 1920, Célestin Freinet began his 46-year-long career as an elementary school teacher in a one-room rural schoolhouse located in the French Maritime Alps. Six years later, Freinet established the Modern School Movement, which, by the time of his death in 1966, involved 10,000 schools in 33 nations.

It was within the context of this network of schools that Freinet was to refine an evolutionary approach linking day-to-day classroom practice with an ongoing discussion of reflective teaching among thousands of educators, an approach that has influenced generations of teachers and countless thousands of students and parents on every continent.[7] Yet although both Célestin and Élise Freinet's many writings have been translated into 17 languages, their thought remains largely unknown in the English-speaking world. Until 1990, none of their writings had been published in English.[8]

Beginnings of Freinet's Pedagogy

Célestin Freinet developed three complementary teaching techniques, each of which encouraged students to engage with their classmates, their families, and community members. The first technique was the "learning walk." Weather permitting, students would join Freinet in exploratory walks throughout the town and its environs. During these walks, they would gather information and impressions about community life that formed the basis for subsequent classroom activities in reading and writing, science and math, and social studies. As a regular follow-up activity to these walks, the students authored, as a group, what Freinet called "free texts." These writings turned into "pretexts" for taking action within their local community to improve living conditions. The students designed a new village fountain and built a modest hydroelectric dam in a local stream, both in response to needs they had come to see in their learning walks.[9]

At first, all their group writings were merely collected in a folder. But soon after, Célestin Freinet introduced his second technique, classroom printing, which helped the students place even more value on their writing. His elementary students became expert at producing hundreds of typeset copies of their writings for their families and friends.

But the birth of long-distance teaching partnerships and of the Modern School Movement itself can be precisely dated with the introduction of the third of Freinet's techniques: interschool networks. Célestin Freinet met René Daniel, a colleague from a neighboring province who became interested in Freinet's techniques, and they agreed to exchange "culture packages" as well as writings their students had authored and printed. This interschool exchange in October 1924 marks the beginning of the uninterrupted history of intercultural teaching partnerships, extending far beyond Freinet's lifetime.[10]

The Structure of "Interschool Networking" in the Modern School Movement

The actual arrangements that evolved within the Modern School Movement for exchanging student work are especially interesting in light of the fact that present-day educational networking projects such as Orillas and I*EARN have come to structure their electronic message exchanges in a remarkably similar fashion, although employing sophisticated computer conferencing technology unimaginable in the 1920s.

In Freinet's teaching network, two teachers in distant schools were matched to form a "twinned" or "sister-class" partnership according to their own common teaching interests and the grade levels of their students. Then several of these partnerships were joined to form a "cluster," with an effort toward representing as many national regions and countries as possible. Partner classes engage in two kinds of exchanges: monthly culture packages of maps, photos, tapes, schoolwork, and local memorabilia; and joint projects, which may best be described as identical long-distance team-teaching units. Partner-class teachers and their students plan and jointly execute these curricular projects *at both sites,* sharing such activities as international student journalism, joint science projects, dual community surveys, contrastive geography investigations, and comparative oral histories.

Thus, each class in a cluster enjoyed a special relationship with its partner class, characterized by frequent exchanges. However, every class in the cluster also maintained a less extensive but regular exchange with hundreds of other students by sending monthly samples of exemplary work to all cluster classes. In this way, all students were assured of a wide audience for their writings among colleagues in numerous regional and international schools. Thus, using a "network" no more sophisticated than various national postal services to exchange curricular projects, Freinet established team-teaching partnerships and clusters among 10,000 schools around the world. In fact, so many teachers in Freinet's network organized to demand government support for their interschool networks that to this day French teachers pay *nothing* to use the national postal service for educational projects. The same basic approach of creating clusters out of dyads has continued to the present day, although electronic mail and faxes have replaced the printing press and national postal service in many Freinet classes.[11]

Toward reflective teaching

A frequent theme in both Célestin and Élise Freinet's writings about teaching and teachers concerns the distinction they drew between *methods,* on the one hand, and *techniques,* on the other. Freinet's critique of *methods* was a response to two "top-down" forces that he felt placed unrealistic demands upon teachers: first, the extremely powerful French educational bureaucracy with its centralized, lockstep curriculum; and second, the highly structured methodologies of many curricular reformers, which to Freinet's thinking had ceased being innovations by becoming codified, packaged fads.

In the place of fixed methodologies, Freinet espoused what he termed "techniques." In Freinet's conception, techniques serve to establish a new kind of relationship between students and teachers. This interactive relationship is one that provides teachers with the kind of invaluable, continuous feedback so essential if they are to reflect upon and improve their practice. These techniques included classroom printing, community photography, use of slide/tape shows, and the like. "Methods," on the other hand, work to impede the general improvement of teaching by encouraging uncritical imitation of preestablished curricula.

Central to Freinet's goal of promoting massive educational change was an ongoing, evolving effort *by teachers and parents themselves*—not the central educational authorities or traveling consultants and experts. Genuine educational reform requires the development of techniques and instruments capable of reaching the majority of classroom practitioners while offering a realistic prospect for the long-term professional development of all teachers, from novice to veteran educators, in collaboration with parents. As Célestin Freinet wrote: "Our techniques, as their principal goal, must respond to the necessities of our public schools. Far from descending either from imaginary projects or from pedagogical theories, they must ascend exclusively from the base, from our own work, and from the life of the children in our transformed classes."[12]

Among dozens of techniques, Freinet accorded central importance to the special brand of collaborative teaching that develops in the context of what he termed "interschool networks." As Élise Freinet noted: "The introduction of new techniques in the public schools and their optimum performance will be greatly facilitated by the human network that links each school with many others: *interschool networks*. It would be impossible to overemphasize the central importance of this pedagogical technique."[13]

Interschool networking was seen as especially important for two reasons. First, networking was the central technique through which all other techniques were first developed, then tested, and finally disseminated.

Second, like all the techniques developed by Freinet and his colleagues, collaborative teaching via networking enabled educators to provide feedback to each other, the type of feedback that encouraged them to reflect upon the way they conducted teaching in their classrooms. It also encouraged teachers to reflect on how their teaching could contribute to beneficial social change in their communities and societies.

Freinet described the rich context for reflective teaching that is provided by interschool networks as that of a scientific laboratory where teachers could discard the rigidities both of fixed curricula and of the latest teaching method in fashion. Instead, interschool networks would allow teachers to collaborate in the development of new techniques with their colleagues and thus remain vital as learners of teaching:

> Contrary to what usually occurs with methods which are patented internationally, we do not present an immutable framework, nor a ceremony from which a teacher may not deviate for any reason on earth upon pain of undermining and betraying the spirit in whose name this rigidity was imposed.
>
> Instead we offer: techniques which we have fully tested, which teachers have created in large part, perfecting and adapting them to their needs; . . . [and] the principles for organizing the classroom life and work of the students, comprising both the permanent collaboration of teachers and the generalized practice of interschool networks.[14]

Freinet and his colleagues in the Modern School Movement were the first to conceptualize the enormous potential inherent in global learning networks for building coherent educational theory from their reflective classroom practice. By rejecting fixed methodologies and by focusing attention on techniques and technologies that shape new social contexts for learning, their goal was nothing less than the creation of a popular pedagogy to promote educational reform. And this, on a massive scale.

The Acquisition of Literacy through Interschool Networking

In chapter 3, we were concerned with various conceptions of literacy and their implications in today's world. Let us examine more closely how Freinet and his colleagues in the Modern School Movement viewed the acquisition of literacy. The challenge, as Freinet saw it, lies in making the goals of writing less abstract and more social.

> If drawing, like all artistic expressions . . . is sufficient unto itself because it produces beauty and inspires emotion, writing does not have the same engaging quality. The child doesn't seek it out or use it unless it is used for an evident goal, unless it is motivated by an organic necessity; otherwise, it becomes like an exercise bicycle, mounted on a stand, with its wheels turning in a vacuum, never achieving the movement which would be the normal consequence of pedaling.[15]

Freinet's solution to the problem of how to embed writing within a meaningful, goal-directed activity involved the use of a classroom technology—the printing press (for producing multiple copies of student writings)—together with the creation of a distant audience for young writers through interschool exchanges of printed texts, letters, and packages containing tapes, photographs, maps, and items of local interest. "Having something to say, writing to be read, to be discussed, to be responded to critically—this is the grand motivation we should be seeking, and which is realized through classroom printing and interschool networks."[16]

> Writing makes no sense unless one is obliged to resort to it in order to communicate beyond the reach of our voice, outside of the limits of school. We have incorporated, in a practical way, this motivation through the sequence of our techniques: free [oral] expression; classroom printing of texts; illustration; production of student newspapers sent to parents and interchanged with other schools; and a far-reaching exchange of free texts between schools with an unimaginable educational impact.

Thus literacy learning, in Freinet's conception, requires a carefully defined and wide-ranging social context. In Freinet's schools, this highly structured context—the combination of locally rooted learning shared with an unknown but knowable faraway audience through the use of classroom technologies—served to foster the discipline and commitment students needed to master the difficult reading and writing skills required to "take charge of this instrument [of written language] in order to adapt it to their own uses."[18]

In many of his writings, Freinet stressed that his goal was not to avoid direct instruction in the technicalities of language mechanics such as spelling, grammar, and punctuation. Rather, he sought to create a context whereby the teacher's intervention answered a *felt learning need* of the students. In this regard, interschool networks played a central role: "Wherever this powerful teaching technique of interschool networking is introduced, it becomes immediately evident to what extent this natural technique is superior to the artificial contrivances which are arrayed in order to provoke in students the interest and discipline necessary to assure the acquisition of the essential academic skills."[19]

The learning of literacy skills in Freinet's approach grows out of the complex interplay between students' greater familiarity with highly *contextualized,* locally produced writings of their classmates, in the first instance, together with their desire to understand the more *decontextualized* texts that they receive from distant partner classes.

> If, on the one hand, the child . . . creates new texts to satisfy her need for self-expression, utilizing words and expressions without worrying herself about the technicalities of syllables and letters, then on the other hand the practice of interschool networking places reading in an entirely different context. Now that the task is to decipher a written page, there is a totally different motivation, but equally personalized. . . .
>
> This is the moment in which the child really moves into decoding and becomes aware of it as a process. Familiar words are immediately discovered and ones that have never been seen are carefully analyzed. . . . Students want our intervention, even an exercise sheet, as an aid in easily decoding those words that might clarify for them what they want to know. The teacher's observations and help with syllabification are not an imposed system, but rather a necessity integrated with something lived, and therefore received with the same enthusiasm for everything that extends the child's life.[20]

In Freinet's approach to the teaching of literacy, the exchange of texts between faraway classes was an integral, complementary component of a two-part process of literacy development. First, students wrote spontaneously about familiar realities; later, as they shared writings with their distant colleagues, a felt need was created that powerfully motivated further learning about language mechanics. Thus the introduction of *distance* into the literacy equation allowed Freinet to create a unique approach to teaching reading and writing. The desire to communicate with a distant audience generated a motivation powerful enough to sustain the effort of mastering the difficult mechanics of reading and writing; this motivation was reinforced by the powerful printing technology to which students had access.[21]

In the next section, we examine how Freinet's pedagogy was taken up and adapted by Mario Lodi and his colleagues in Italy.

THE WORK OF MARIO LODI AND THE ITALIAN COOPERATIVE EDUCATION MOVEMENT

The Cooperative Education Movement was founded in 1951 by a small group of teachers to promote interest in Freinet's approaches within Italian public schools, while adapting these approaches to the latest available technologies relevant to writing and communication.[22] During the next 20 years, the Cooperative Education Movement attempted to discover and promote what they termed "an Italian way"; that is, while affirming the basic tenets associated with Freinet's approaches, they sought to adapt the French pedagogue's techniques to the realities of Italian schools, avoiding slavish imitation of the original French models and the (by then) outmoded technologies. Here we describe the Italian Cooperative Education Movement as one of many examples of how Freinet's approach to global learning networks was adapted in other European countries, as well as in Africa, Asia and Latin America.

Mario Lodi was to become the Cooperative Education Movement's most visible advocate with the publication of his *Il Paese Sbagliato* (1977) (The mistaken country). This book was widely read in Italy and later would be translated into Spanish, French, and German, establishing Lodi as one of the most influential European educational reformers of recent times, following and yet transforming the tradition of Freinet and the Modern School network. Incredibly, the writings of both Freinet and Lodi remain largely unknown in the English-speaking world. Lodi's is an unusual educational manifesto, elegant in its simplicity. It is written in a reflective style displaying immense respect for the intricacies of children's learning.

Il Paese Sbagliato is a country school teacher's diary, spiced with liberal samples from students' dialogues, writings, and group projects over the course of five years at an elementary school in the village of Vho.

Lodi placed special emphasis on two of Freinet's classic techniques: student journalism and interschool networks. Students themselves, with the teacher as facilitator, would elaborate their own alternative to the regimentation of the state-mandated, required textbook. Through the rich and varied social process of producing a student newspaper, Lodi helped students develop their own "free text" in collaboration with distant colleagues, by tapping into the funds of knowledge that students and their communities already possessed, thereby generating new syntheses and understandings. In Lodi's classroom, typewriters and mimeograph machines replaced Freinet's movable-type printing press. The newer, cheaper technologies gave students more direct control over every aspect of the publishing process, while allowing for even more frequent publication.

Another new technology, audiotape recording, played a large role in adapting Freinet's approaches to the multilingual realities of Italian schooling. Like many European countries, Italy is a patchwork quilt of often mutually incomprehensible regional dialects, while the language of the larger society and of schooling remains standard Italian. The exchange of audiotaped recordings between Italian classes encouraged students to compare dialects. "The tape recorder records our ideas in familiar language. In this way the colloquial language, that for centuries has been dominated and subjugated by written language, takes precedence over the written language whose rules have been imposed upon us by the dominant class."[23]

Later, the students would use tape recorders to conduct local oral history projects in collaboration with their distant correspondents. In this way, the two classes developed a greater appreciation of the rich linguistic heritage of their respective dialects, dialects that schools typically have suppressed in favor of standard Italian. Lodi, in fact, vehemently disagreed with the traditional educational policy in Italy forbidding the use of regional dialects in schooling:

> To start out where the children are simply means to accept them with everything they bring with them from their homes, but also to value what they bring and to help them understand that what they possess is impor-

tant, and that while they are in school we will be working with and building upon what they bring.

Our school will not destroy so as to construct afterwards, but rather we will cause their heritage to grow. The difference is substantial. In the first case, a basis is created for a lack of confidence, both in oneself and in one's previous experiences away from school, while in the second the basis is created for self-confidence that serves as the foundation for all knowledge that will come later.[24]

For Lodi, these were not empty words. While the students in his Cooperative Education Movement spoke a multitude of regional Italian dialects, they communicated with other students in the learning network by sharing audiotapes in standard Italian. These students engaged in countless projects in which examples of proverbs, folklore, and traditional games in their native dialects were contrasted between partner classes. Thus, although the students used standard Italian to communicate with sister classes, they did not have to reject their mother tongues which were dialects; on the contrary, the focus was on developing a deep awareness of how language works, with the contrast between dialect and standard forms *enriching* students' overall linguistic abilities. This recognition that students' native dialects and languages can and should provide a platform for constructing fluency in the language of the wider society was a key aspect of Lodi's approach to interschool networking, and has important implications in today's schools, as we shall show in the next chapter.

The sharing of audiotapes also was viewed as an especially effective way of lowering the threshold for young authors to enter the world of writing. Composing a group audiotape required a considerable amount of planning, so as not to leave out important details or to include unnecessary repetitions. Lodi felt that the exchange of tape recordings, while squarely based on existing oral language skills, placed demands on students that were similar to those of written compositions:

a) to communicate with someone who isn't present, to whom it is necessary to be explicit and explain everything;

b) to plan the speech, anticipating its parts and assigning them to different speakers;

c) the impossibility of using gestures, facial expressions, and other indicative movements that simplify the understanding of oral language so much; and

d) not receiving an immediate reply and having to wait for one.[25]

Thus, composed by groups of students for a distant audience, the audiotapes served as a bridge between oral language skills and formal writing.

This sort of "bridge building" between the types of knowledge acquired at home (here, facility with spoken language) and the kinds of learning associated with schooling (in this case, writing) is a hallmark of both Freinet's and Lodi's approaches to education. Interschool networks, collectively organized, form a crucible within which young writers can fuse elements from personal, family, and community life. The children can bring the printed text (whether typeset or mimeographed) back into the home to share with their parents. The literacy process comes full circle, since children share *between generations* the very reading skills that they have learned in their schools but that are rooted in the oral language they have learned at home. In this fashion, even illiterate parents can be involved in powerful ways in the development of their children's literacy.

Similarly, audiotapes composed by groups of students build upon oral language skills to span the artificial distance between knowledge developed at home and "school learning." Lodi took care to keep the language of the home vital within a school setting, both out of an appreciation for its intrinsic value and as a powerful tool with immense potential for promoting academic learning. Of equal importance, in Lodi's view, this respect for the home language served to encourage the kind of personal communication between generations about sensitive issues that becomes of critical importance as children approach adolescence.

Thus, Mario Lodi, just like Célestin Freinet, brought the technologies associated with writing and the spoken and printed word into public schools. First they established a social context to motivate writing about topics around genuine personal and community interest, and later they widened the audience available to young authors far beyond the classroom and town to a vast intercultural and global learning network.

In the next section we examine how Freinet's legacy has continued into present-day France.

FREINET SCHOOLS IN CONTEMPORARY FRANCE

William B. Lee, an American teacher educator at the University of Los Angeles, provides us with an especially rich insider's view of today's Freinet classrooms. Lee has closely observed Freinet classrooms over the course of the last two decades and was the first educator to publish an assessment of Freinet's pedagogy in English.[26] While he conducted research in France during the 1980s, Lee's sons attended a Freinet school for two and a half years. In the 1990s, he returned to investigate Freinet's pedagogy through extensive classroom observations. Thus Lee's later account offers a unique perspective on Freinet pedagogy and the atmosphere in the classrooms of teachers who adopt this approach to teaching. Lee speaks with a special authority—from the point of view both of a parent and of an educational researcher. He writes:

> The walls display the life of the class. The children's work overflows from the bulletin board and adorns almost every available space. Artistic endeavours abound: drawings, paintings, and collages, as well as creative written work, both prose and poetry—often products of the class printing press and usually handsomely decorated. While faxes and electronic mail now supplement the printing press, the more routine and "low-tech" aspects of life in a Freinet school are in evidence also. The carefully completed and neatly written homework (in ink of course) serving as an example of how all assignments should look.

Nor is direct instruction in language mechanics ignored.

> Seemingly out of place amidst these creative efforts are large posters illustrating formal lessons of grammar: conjugation of regular and irregular verbs, agreement of subject and verb, and sentences dividing words into groups resembling the little practiced and often discredited American practice of diagramming sentences. Almost all of these words and phrases are taken from the children's work and are reminders to them that effective communication and creative expression must conform to rules of correct usage.[27]

We can see clear continuity with the approaches developed in the early years of the Modern School Movement. As we have seen, in Freinet's literacy pedagogy there are moments when free expression is encouraged, as for example during and after the "learning walks" when students create the "free texts" centering on community issues. But there are also times when the issue of language mechanics comes to the forefront of concerns, as when free texts are printed and distributed in the community and sent off to a distant class; or when students demand lessons on grammar as they attempt to decipher the writings of their distant partner class.

But Lee stresses that what makes Freinet pedagogy unique is not the simple admixture of creative expression with a healthy dose of structured grammar instruction. Rather it is the way in which this approach to teaching engages and confronts the daily realities of the lives of the children and their community.

> Also exhibited on the classroom wall are individual or committee reports accompanied by postcards, photos, drawings, clippings from newspapers and other forms of documentation. The common denominator of the topics is that they are of interest to the children and often have an impact on their lives and the lives of their families.[28]

In one classroom, the students' interest in local issues led them to keep close track of the workings of the city council.

> One teacher reported that when the children took notes the council members became nervous. Also dealt with are current social and economic issues such as unemployment (Christopher's father is out of work. Why?), inadequacy of local parks and playgrounds, pollution, nuclear power, children living in poverty and famine in Africa.[29]

Far from avoiding complex social issues, Freinet's approach to critical literacy brings these realities into sharper focus and encourages students to exercise the powerful tools of literacy in direct social action on issues that have an impact on themselves, their families, and their communities.

WHAT CAN WE LEARN FROM
THE WORK OF FREINET AND LODI?

The modern reader, upon first confronting the separate elements of Freinet's pedagogy, is repeatedly struck by their contemporary quality. For example, his focus on cooperative learning and small-group work foreshadows the research interests of many contemporary scholars, both in regular education programs and in technology-mediated learning.[30] Freinet's concern with student- and group-authored writing prefigures much of the work by recent researchers into the "writing process" in school settings.[31] Similarly, educators will recognize that Freinet anticipated the current "teacher-as-researcher" movement by his insistence that teachers should experiment, modify, and validate new teaching approaches through careful observation in their own classrooms and in cooperation with colleagues.[32]

However, focusing on these multiple parallelisms actually can obscure the true achievement of the Modern School Movement network. What is unique about Freinet's pedagogy is not merely that its constituent elements, considered separately, presaged many of our contemporary preoccupations, but rather that Freinet synthesized such a range of educational practices into a fully articulated approach to teaching, a symbiosis that is very much more than the sum of its parts, and one that addresses in new ways concerns that remain vital today.

Of central importance is the complementary emphasis on "distancing" and social action in Freinet's pedagogy. Distancing refers to the increased awareness of the social, cultural, historical, geographic, and linguistic realities of one's own community as a result of the need to describe these realities in response to questions from distant peers. In the words of Gervilliers and his coauthors:

> The student, because she needs to describe them, develops an awareness of the conditions of her life, of the life of her town or her neighborhood, even of her province. . . . She had been living too close to these conditions and through interschool exchanges she has distanced herself from them in order to better comprehend the conditions of her life.[33]

Yet "distancing" is not the only outcome. Students also discover multiple opportunities for purposeful engagement with their day-to-day reality. According to Freinet, reflective distancing leads to social action: "interschool networks . . . are conducive to a true cultural development, offering to all individuals several possibilities of action over their surroundings, and causing a profound engagement with human beings and with things past, present and future."[34]

For Freinet, school-to-school exchanges were not an end in themselves. Rather, partnerships between faraway classes served as the indispensable precursor to a more profound and active engagement with social realities much closer to home. In other words, students in the educational communities inspired by Freinet and Lodi and their colleagues were developing not just literacy in a generic sense but rather a *critical literacy* that was being stimulated constantly by the collaborative inquiry undertaken by students in distant classes.

We view this collaborative critical inquiry as the intellectual fuel that drives any serious intercultural networking project. Freinet's pedagogy provides a model that current computer-mediated networking endeavors would do well to heed if their intercultural exchanges are not to degenerate into ultimately meaningless pen-pal correspondence or formulaic interactions.[35]

CONCLUSION

Educators since the time of Plato have recognized the power of literacy to expand human consciousness. But they also have recognized that access to literacy involves access to power. Plato wrote of what was in his day the "newfangled" technology of writing, "Those who acquire it will cease to exercise their memory and become forgetful; they will rely on [it] to bring things to their remembrance by external signs, instead of on their own internal resources."[36] He went on to roundly criticize the invention of writing because it was designed to replace a human response with a manufactured artifact. Even worse, this technical innovation threatened to cheapen all learning by further democratizing access to knowledge.[37]

Plato clearly saw that literacy was a tool for critical thinking that posed dangers to the established social order if placed in the wrong hands, or in the hands of too many. In large part, the teaching of literacy has unfolded according to Plato's scenario. Throughout the centuries during which the technologies associated with reading, writing, and communication have evolved continuously, access to the power of literacy has been regulated by a series of ever-present gatekeepers. The gatekeepers have ranged from scribes under the strict control of religious and political leaders to the enforcers of the pre–Civil War laws in the United States that in many states made teaching a slave to read and write a crime punishable by imprisonment or death.[38]

It is useful to be reminded of how access to literacy has intersected with power relations in the society. A particularly vivid example is cited by John Willinsky in discussing the volatile debates that took place in England during the early part of the nineteenth century about extending schooling and literacy to the working class.[39] As expressed by a Conservative member of Parliament:

> However specious in theory the project might be of giving education to the laboring classes of the poor, it would in effect, be found to be prejudicial to their morals and happiness . . . instead of teaching them subordination, it would render them factious and refractory . . . it would enable them to read seditious pamphlets, vicious books, and publications against Christianity; it would render them insolent to their superiors; and in a few years, the result would be that the legislature would find it necessary to direct the strong arm of power towards them.[40]

Freinet's pedagogy directly challenged the ambivalence about extending literacy to all sectors of the society. Not only was literacy instruction rooted in students' authentic experience and stimulated by their desire to communicate with real audiences of peers, it also was powered by the most advanced communications and literacy technology available in the wider society. Nearly five centuries after the introduction of the printing press in Europe, Freinet bought one for his rural classroom. Then he found one other teacher who shared his vision, and together they created the first long-distance learning partnership so that students in both classes could exercise fully their critical literacy skills by comparing worlds and realities.

From this modest beginning, and despite ever more sophisticated technological innovation throughout this century, Freinet's Modern School Movement remains the largest technology-based community of learning in history. It achieved and maintained this status only as a result of its integration of technology with a pedagogy of collaborative critical inquiry.

Today, we have much more sophisticated communications technologies than were available in Freinet's time. However, we are still plagued by the same ambivalence about extending critical literacy to all sectors of the society. As Freinet's Modern School Movement demonstrates, combining access to advanced communications technology with a pedagogy of collaborative critical inquiry can nurture the development of intellectually powerful and socially committed individuals.

We turn in the next chapter to exploring in more depth what collaborative critical inquiry entails.

Chapter 5

Instructional Landscapes: Putting Collaborative Critical Inquiry on the Map

The will to learn is an intrinsic motive, one that finds both its source and reward in its own exercise. The will to learn becomes a "problem" only under specialized circumstances like those of a school, where a curriculum is set, students confined, and a path fixed. The problem exists not so much in learning itself, but in the fact that what the school imposes often fails to enlist the natural energies that sustain spontaneous learning—curiosity, a desire for competence, aspiration to emulate a model, and a deep-sensed commitment to the web of social reciprocity.

—Jerome S. Bruner,
Toward a Theory of Instruction

To the many parents who have watched their children's enthusiasm for school dwindle as they progress through the grades, these words, written by the most eminent cognitive psychologist of his generation, ring as true today as when they were penned 30 years ago. The endless litany of the ways in which schools are failing, recited dutifully by countless school reformers, fail to grasp this one essential truth: If instruction does not mobilize students' intrinsic will to learn, very little will be learned. The turgid prescriptions of most of the 1980s' school reform reports focused only on extrinsic motivation—the rewards and punishments used to control students' and teachers' behavior. As any parent can testify, children are capable of prodigious feats of creativity and learning outside of school—

whether it is the internalization of every baseball statistic since the beginning of time, mastery of computer programming and "hacking" techniques, or the ability to compose poetry or songs (e.g., rap) that address immediate aspects of children's lives. Yet, in school, students are as often penalized as rewarded for these talents because they do not mesh with the prescribed curriculum. Shakespeare's characterization of schooling from *As You Like It* is still apt:

> At first the infant
> Mewling and puking in the nurse's arms,
> And then the whining school-boy, with his satchel
> And shining morning face, creeping like snail
> Unwillingly to school.

What has gone wrong? Why is it more the exception than the rule that schools succeed in activating students' intrinsic will to learn? Why do suburban affluent schools succeed better in this regard than schools that serve the poor? Clearly, the huge gap in funding between rich and poor schools is part of the answer. Access to more resources in the form of children's literature, computers, and field trips facilitates making school an exciting place to be. Similarly, the insecurity and violence that characterize inner cities make schools marginal in many students' lives.

However, there are other reasons why school has become irrelevant to many students, particularly in poor areas. Primary among these is the monocultural transmission-oriented instruction that continues to dominate American classrooms.[1] Paulo Freire has termed this approach a "banking" education because the teacher's role is to deposit information and skills in students' memory banks.[2] This form of instruction has been especially pervasive in remedial programs for so-called disadvantaged students. In most compensatory programs, minimal attempts are made to relate curriculum content to students' experience, students are expected to internalize what to them is frequently irrelevant content through drill and practice activities, and there is usually little encouragement for students to pursue guided inquiry on issues that are of importance to them.

Our goal in this chapter is to argue that the educational potential of computer-mediated learning networks can be realized only within a context of collaborative critical inquiry. A community of learning must be created in the classroom where students and teachers jointly investigate issues that are of relevance to them in their lives and of broader social significance. By contrast, if students' voices are silenced in the classroom, they also will be muted in electronic communication. If no knowledge is generated in the classroom, little can be communicated to distant peers. If students are being trained to become consumers, technology will merely increase the effectiveness of that training.

In other words, if global learning networks are to contribute significantly to children's education, we must have a clear vision of what role they will play in fostering both the immediate instructional and the broader social objectives of schooling. How will they contribute to literacy development and to civic involvement? We suggest that their impact will range from minimal in certain kinds of traditional schooling environments to highly significant in contexts that aim explicitly to transform students' possibilities for personal and social development through the use of collaborative critical inquiry.

Collaborative critical inquiry was illustrated in practice in the interactions described in chapter 2. It is important to state at the outset that this is not the "soft" child-centered pedagogy caricatured by many back-to-basics advocates. Rather what we are advocating for all grade levels is nothing less than the rigorous pursuit of knowledge that is typically required among university graduate students. We believe that students at all grade levels, whether in wealthy suburban or low-income schools, "gifted" or "remedial" tracks, are capable of collaborative critical inquiry and will benefit academically from it. In the absence of collaborative critical inquiry, global learning networks will soon lose their appeal for both teachers and students. Students' enthusiasm will peter out if there is no intellectual challenge, and, under these conditions, computer networking will have minimal impact on their academic achievement. The corollary is that global learning networks can act as a catalyst for collaborative critical inquiry in the classroom.

Although labels inevitably oversimplify and obscure the gray edges of any category, for the sake of convenience we will contrast three orientations to pedagogy—traditional, progressive, and transformative—in order to locate collaborative critical inquiry within the shifting sands of pedagogical fashion. Traditional and progressive orientations have vied for ascendancy at regular intervals throughout this century, while the focus on the transformative potential of education is a more recent phenomenon and strongly influenced by Paulo Freire's work.

Each of the three orientations incorporates a set of instructional and social assumptions. Instructional assumptions are concerned with the conceptions of language, knowledge, and learning that underlie various forms of teaching; social assumptions focus on the ways in which the curriculum addresses relations of culture and power.

Most proponents of traditional and progressive pedagogies tend to focus more on instructional than on social dimensions. They see their instructional recommendations as socially neutral and nonideological. By contrast, advocates of transformative pedagogy argue that all forms of instruction entail social assumptions, whether acknowledged explicitly or not. The forms of thinking and literacy that are encouraged in school anticipate the forms of civic participation that students are being prepared to undertake upon graduation. Transformative pedagogy explicitly aims to prepare students to participate fully in the democratic process and to uphold the principles of human rights and social justice that are enshrined in the constitutions of most Western industrialized countries.

TRADITIONAL PEDAGOGY

Instructional Assumptions: Just the Facts

As discussed in chapter 3, much of the current impetus for educational reform derives from the conviction that "child-centered" (or progressive) instruction has resulted in a lowering of academic standards. These claims lack credibility both because there is little evidence of falling academic standards and because child-centered instruction penetrated only a small minority of U.S. classrooms, albeit substantially more in Canada and other English-speaking countries (Australia, Britain, and New Zealand). Despite the lack of evidence for its claims regarding child-centered approaches, traditional "back-to-basics" instruction is appealing to many parents who find security in getting straight answers about what their children will be taught and what standards they are expected to attain at different stages of their education.

With respect to assumptions about language and literacy, traditional approaches reduce language to its component parts and argue that the components of language should be taught individually, starting with simple elements and progressing to more complex forms. Thus, explicit phonics instruction is a prerequisite for reading development; grammar, vocabulary, and spelling must be taught before students can start writing; and curriculum content should be transmitted clearly and sequentially for students to internalize.

These traditional assumptions about learning and teaching have dominated the education of "disadvantaged" students during the past 30 years. We would argue that this approach has contributed significantly to the mixed results obtained in many compensatory programs. Initially these programs were founded on the assumption that inner-city children were "culturally deprived" or suffered from verbal deficits insofar as they spoke either limited English or a nonstandard variety of English (e.g., "Black English"). Thus, many educators aimed to eradicate children's deficient prior learning and transmit more appropriate language and cognitive skills in its place. Children's prior experience or cultural knowledge was seldom used as a foundation for learning since the goal was to "fix" those who were assumed to have been damaged by their prior experience.

Parents also were viewed as a source of their children's problem. Thus many programs made only minimal efforts to involve parents as equal partners in their children's education. Finally, because poor inner-city children were considered incapable of conceptually challenging learning, many compensatory programs were based on drilling children in low-level literacy and numeracy skills. Researchers Jere Brophy and Thomas Good, for example, articulated the underlying assumptions of many remedial programs in asserting that underachieving low-income students need more control and structure from teachers, increased review, drill and practice, and lower-level questions than their higher-achieving middle-class peers.[3] These assumptions have also been built into computer-based programs for low-income students.[4]

Although few cognitive psychologists currently endorse these instructional assumptions, they have been revived through E. D. Hirsch's Cultural Literacy curriculum. Hirsch is unapologetic about endorsing a transmission approach to instruction: "Young children enjoy absorbing formulaic knowledge. Even if they did not, our society would still find it essential to teach them all sorts of traditions and facts. Critical thinking and basic skills, two areas of current focus in education, do not enable children to create out of their own imaginations the essential names and concepts that have arisen by historical accident."[5]

Despite the persistence of transmission approaches in classrooms, research has increasingly pointed to its limitations as an instructional philosophy. The change of emphasis is clear in the contrast between the just-cited views expressed by Brophy and Good in 1986 and Brophy's (1992) current perspective. He points out that much of the earlier "effective schools" research was limited as a result of its reliance "on standardized tests as the outcome measure, which meant that it focused on mastery of relatively isolated knowledge items and skill components without assessing the degree to which students had developed understanding of networks of subject-matter content or the ability to use this information in authentic application situations." More recent research suggests that "students develop new knowledge through a process of *active construction*" where thoughtful discussion, and not just teacher lecturing or student recitation, is crucial for understanding. He also emphasizes the importance of "authentic tasks that call for problem solving or critical thinking, not just memory or reproduction" and instruction that enables students to relate what they are learning to their lives outside of school. Finally, Brophy suggests that in effective schools "the teacher creates a social environment in the classroom that could be described as a learning community where dialogue promotes understanding."[6]

Other researchers also have emphasized the creation of classroom and schoolwide learning communities. Richard Prawat, for example, suggests that the criteria for judging teacher effectiveness have shifted from delivering good lessons to being able to build or create a classroom learning community in which students and teachers engage in animated conversations about important intellectual issues.[7]

Unfortunately, typical U.S. classrooms still appear to be intellectual light-years away from "animated conversations," if the results of large-scale research conducted in the 1980s are to be believed.[8] Kenneth Sirotnik, for example, argues that the predominant instructional pattern comprising a lot of teacher talk and a lot of student listening in a "virtually affectless environment" suggests that "we are implicitly teaching dependence upon authority, linear thinking, social apathy, passive involvement, and hands-off learning."[9]

In short, while transmission of information and skills is one legitimate aspect of schooling, it is wholly inadequate as the predominant instructional approach. It reduces students to passive consumers of information and rarely, if ever, invokes what Jerome Bruner called children's intrinsic will to learn. This is particularly the case for low-income students whose culture usually is absent from what is being transmitted.[10]

Social Assumptions: Intellectualizing Xenophobia

Traditional approaches to curriculum and instruction aim, to a greater or lesser extent, at controlling the knowledge and skills transmitted to the next generation. While skills transmission is motivated primarily by the needs of the economy, culture transmission is a means of maintaining identity across generations—ensuring that the next generation thinks like ours. Although this is most evident in the attempts of the religious Right to censor curriculum materials that they deem objectionable, it also is manifest in Hirsch's curriculum and to a large extent in all curricula that aim primarily to transmit specific values and factual content. Whereas the religious Right has focused on eradicating certain facts and ideas from various curricula, other curricula (such as Hirsch's) simply omit facts and ideas that don't conform to the developers' preferred view of the world. No construction of history or selection of literature can claim to be "objective," but developers seldom admit this openly.[11]

James Moffett has written insightfully about the effort to control processes of cultural transmission based on his experience as one of the authors of an English textbook series entitled *Interaction* that, in 1974, was the object of a tumultuous confrontation between Christian fundamentalists and the school board in the district of Kanawha County, West Virginia. The school district included the city of Charleston together with highly conservative fundamentalist Christian rural areas in the Appalachian Mountains. Moffett analyzes the roots of xenophobia as follows:

> In plain human terms the protestors feared losing their children. Books bypass the oral culture—hearth and ethos—and thus may weaken local authority and control. Perhaps all parents fear having their children mentally kidnapped by voices from other milieus and ideologies. The rich range of ideas and viewpoints, the multicultural smorgasbord, of the books adopted in Kanawha County were exactly what fundamentalists don't want. They believe that most of the topics English teachers think make good discussion are about matters they consider already settled.

The invitation to reopen them through pluralistic readings, role-playing, values clarification, personal writing, and open-ended discussion can only be taken as an effort to indoctrinate their children in the atheistic free-thinking of the Eastern seaboard liberal establishment . . . the real enemy is simply the outsider, the Other.[12]

Moffett highlights the limitations of viewing education as cultural transmission since, whether the curriculum is Eurocentric, Afrocentric, or designed to transmit any other cultural tradition, "transmitting any heritage entails selecting some ideas, frameworks, and values and excluding others. Exclusion is built into the very idea of education as cultural transmission." Exclusion, furthermore, "practically defines ethnocentricity—the failure to identify outside a certain reference group," and this almost inevitably results in bigotry and intolerance.[13]

Moffett argues that schools should promote students' capacity to transcend the blinders of a single cultural perspective. Instruction should focus not so much on transmitting culture as on challenging the exclusivity of cultures:

Not only does the whole society transmit the culture anyway, not only does schooling debase it in trying to synopsize and select for it in its overcontrolled way, but this very effort militates against another educational goal—open inquiry, learning to think for oneself—that, ironically, we attribute to our Western heritage. . . . Transmit the culture, OK, but subordinate that to transcending the culture. . . . The world is warring right and left because the various cultures strive so intently to perpetuate themselves that they end by imposing themselves on each other. . . . The secret of war is that nations *need* enemies to maintain definition, because differences define.[14]

As a means of transcending rigid cultural boundaries and expanding identity, Moffett advocates the widest possible range of reading for students rather than just one preselected reading program: "Great books, yes, but youngsters need to experience *all* kinds of discourse and all kinds of voices and viewpoints and styles—hear out the world. Our heritage, OK, but we need to encompass *all* heritages, cross cultures, raise consciousness enough to peer over the social perimeters that act as parameters of knowledge."[15]

Contrast this perspective, which is fundamental to the present volume, with the cultural chauvinism evident in Arthur Schlesinger, Jr.'s, insistence on the superiority of European heritage:

> Whatever the particular crimes of Europe, that continent is also the source—the *unique* source—of those liberating ideas of individual liberty, political democracy, the rule of law, human rights, and cultural freedom that constitute our most precious legacy and to which most of the world today aspires. These are *European* ideas, not Asian, nor African, nor Middle Eastern ideas, except by adoption.[16]

We believe the issue is not which group has the right to claim certain ideas and ideals as its own—largely a misguided and futile exercise—so much as the rigor and consistency with which particular societies practice these ideas and ideals. Few groups or regions of the world either now or in the past look particularly impressive by this criterion (as evidenced by reading any Amnesty International report). If appreciation of the European tradition of respect for human rights, cultural freedom, and individual liberties is to become anything more than the pious mantra recited by Schlesinger, Diane Ravitch, and others, an agenda of human rights, cultural freedom, and individual liberties must be pursued actively within the schools as the birthright of every citizen. Future citizens should be taught how to become vigilant in protecting this legacy and identifying abuses of power both in our own societies and in others. In other words, a central goal of schooling that aims to honor the European democratic tradition should be to promote critical literacy in the pursuit of social justice.

Why is it that we can search in vain through the pages of William Bennett, Allan Bloom, Arthur Schlesinger, Jr., and the others who trumpet the superiority of European traditions and find no mention, let alone endorsement, of critical literacy? Why is any significant treatment of human rights, supposedly intrinsic to the European tradition, in the school curriculum anathema to these same patriotically correct commentators (to borrow Robert Hughes' apt phrase)? Why is the most prolific and ardent North American proponent of human rights, linguist Noam Chomsky, despised as a virtual dissident by the conservative establishment if he is simply attempting to realize this long-standing European commitment to human rights?

In summary, traditional pedagogy aims to indoctrinate, both in its instructional and social goals. Facts are to be memorized, religious or cultural truths internalized, inquiry circumscribed, and contradictions obscured. The goal may appear laudable—to build a strong culture—but a culture whose identity is based on ignorance of all around it is living in a fool's paradise.

PROGRESSIVE PEDAGOGY

Instructional Assumptions: The Search for Meaning

Within the scope of progressive pedagogy, we are including the major instructional approaches that derive their inspiration from John Dewey's thought, identified today in North America primarily as whole language and process writing. Also within the scope of progressive pedagogy are approaches deriving from the work of cognitive psychologists who emphasize active student inquiry as central to academic and cognitve growth. All of these approaches share Dewey's emphasis on the importance of student experience; for learning to occur, students must integrate new information with their prior experience. Only in this way can new information become meaningful.

Whereas traditional approaches decomposed language—broke it up into its component parts for easier transmission—progressive approaches insist that language can be learned only when it is kept "whole" and used for meaningful communication in either oral or written modes. Within the traditional curriculum, knowledge is viewed as fixed and inert; in progressive pedagogy, it is seen as catalytic in the sense that new information acts to stimulate further inquiry. Learning in traditional pedagogy is largely memorization; learning in progressive pedagogy is constructed collaboratively through interaction with peers and teachers.[17]

Whole-language approaches emphasize extensive reading of authentic literature as fundamental to literacy development. In this they are supported by an extensive body of research showing that the amount of reading that students do inside and outside school is strongly related to their academic progress.[18] This is hardly surprising, since only in books do we find the less-frequent vocabulary that is required for academic achievement in higher grade levels. It is no coincidence that this is also the kind of vocabulary that appears in standardized tests of reading and verbal IQ.[19]

Progressive pedagogy also is closely allied with small-group cooperative learning. This instructional strategy involves small groups of students from a range of cultural backgrounds and with a diversity of educational talents and attainments working together to attain a common learning objective through activities based on interdependent cooperation. Extensive research suggests that cooperative learning enhances academic development and social relationships in the classroom.[20]

A variety of "inquiry" or "constructivist" approaches to learning that draw their inspiration from the social learning theory of Soviet psychologist Lev Vygotsky (who died in 1936) also share many of the principles of progressive pedagogy.[21] What Denis Newman and his colleagues call "the construction zone" (or in Vygotskian terms, "the zone of proximal development") is the interpersonal space where minds meet and new understandings are constructed, thereby enabling the child to advance cognitively. It is easy to see how this emphasis on the importance of social interaction and collaborative inquiry fits with the notion of the classroom as a community of learning.

The importance of creating classroom and schoolwide communities of learning that focus on acceleration of student progress rather than remediation is reinforced by the success of the Accelerated Schools Project, initiated by Stanford University professor Henry Levin.[22] This project, currently implemented in more than 300 schools across North America, rejects remediation for low-income students and instead argues that what works for so-called gifted and talented students will work for all students. Curriculum and instruction build on students' experiences, interests, motivations, culture, and observed abilities. Language use is emphasized across the curriculum, and the development of higher-order literacy skills is fostered from an early age. A focus on experiential learning (learning by doing rather than learning by listening), problem-solving, peer tutoring, and cooperative learning are also central to instruction in accelerated schools. There is also a strong focus on parents as partners in a shared educational enterprise, with parents expected to contribute significantly to their children's engagement in learning.

Accelerated schools (at both elementary and middle-school level) have shown substantial increases in student achievement in places as diverse as San Francisco, Los Angeles, Seattle, New Orleans, Missouri, and Illinois.

Levin cautions, however, that usually about six years is required for a school to make the full transformation from a conventional to an accelerated school because major changes in school organization are required. Central among these changes is a shift from "top-down" to "bottom-up" decision making with teachers taking collective responsibility for decisions they will implement and evaluate.

We are in general agreement with the pedagogical principles underlying a whole-language, inquiry-based progressivist pedagogy; at this point, they are in the mainstream of educational research and theory in North America (although not by any means in the mainstream of classroom practice). However, we also concur with critics of whole language when they suggest that some children require more explicit forms of instruction and corrective feedback than that frequently envisaged in whole-language approaches. Specifically, children also need explicit instruction in how to use language powerfully to achieve social goals.[23] This would entail developing competence in the conventions of different genres (report writing, formal letters, etc.) and an awareness of how language is used in a wide variety of social contexts. In African American educator Lisa Delpit's words, teachers must learn not only how to "help students to establish their own voices, but to coach those voices to produce notes that will be heard clearly in the larger society."[24]

We see the provision of explicit instruction to develop students' awareness of language as complementary to whole-language instruction rather than in opposition to it. In the same way, we agree with Australian educators Mary Kalantzis and Bill Cope that there is a legitimate role in the classroom for encouragement of both deductive and inductive reasoning and the explicit exposition of content and ideas despite the fact that whole-language theorists seldom emphasize deductive reasoning and teacher exposition.[25] We believe it is not difficult to avoid the excesses occasionally identified in the implementation of whole-language and process writing approaches by insisting on the importance of explicit instruction to guide students' critical inquiry and their use of both written and oral language.

Social Assumptions: Implicit Acceptance of the Status Quo

Progressive pedagogies, by and large, do not have much to say about larger social realities.[26] Their focus is on the child, either as an individual or within the classroom learning community. However, as educator Maria de la Luz

Reyes points out, the failure of some whole-language educators to focus on these larger social realities often carries considerable costs for culturally and linguistically diverse students.[27] Students' culture and language become invisible and inaudible to the teacher, resulting in programs that fail to take their background experience into account. This one-size-fits-all assumption clearly contradicts a basic principle of whole-language philosophy, namely, that instruction should mesh with students' experience and, in fact, validate and extend that experience. Thus, this is a problem of implementation rather than basic philosophy.[28] However, without explicit attention to issues of diversity, it is likely that many whole-language classrooms will be just as monocultural and blind to students' realities as are most traditional classrooms. In both cases, the cultural and linguistic resources that culturally diverse students bring to school are squandered and lost to the society as a whole.

Where progressivist instruction is allied with multicultural education, the multicultural focus frequently is limited to "celebrating diversity"— promoting tolerance and acceptance that is aimed at increasing students' self-esteem but that does little to challenge inequities of power and status distribution in the society.

In short, progressivist pedagogy usually focuses narrowly on the teaching-learning relationship and fails to articulate a coherent vision of the broader social implications of instruction. Tolerance and acceptance of cultural difference often are implied, but critical reflection on students' own experience and critique of social realities are not.

TRANSFORMATIVE PEDAGOGY

Transformative pedagogy uses collaborative critical inquiry to relate curriculum content to students' individual and collective experience and to analyze broader social issues relevant to their lives. It also encourages students to discuss ways in which social realities might be transformed through various forms of democratic participation and social action.

We see the principles of transformative pedagogy as central to realizing the potential of global learning networks. The intercultural interactions portrayed in chapter 2, which were fueled by critical inquiry into social issues, illustrate transformative pedagogy at work.

In this type of pedagogy, the instructional goal of promoting critical literacy is tied closely to the major social goal of encouraging democratic participation. Thus, we will analyze its instructional and social assumptions together. In illustrating the practice of transformative pedagogy, we draw primarily on the publication *Rethinking Our Classrooms: Teaching for Equity and Justice,* a special issue of the periodical *Rethinking Schools.*[29]

Instruction for Critical Literacy and Social Participation

One of the editors of *Rethinking Our Classrooms,* fifth grade teacher Bob Peterson, illustrates the difference between traditional, progressive, and transformative (critical) pedagogy by contrasting the likely response of a teacher from each of these orientations to a student who brings in a flyer about a canned food drive that is being organized during the December holiday season.

> The traditional teacher affirms the student's interest—"That's nice and I'm glad you care about other people"—but doesn't view the food drive as a potential classroom activity.
>
> The progressive teacher sees the food drive as an opportunity to build on students' seemingly innate sympathy for the down-trodden, and after a class discussion, has children bring in cans of food. They count them, categorize them and write about how they feel.
>
> The critical teacher does the same as the progressive teacher—but more. The teacher also uses the food drive as the basis for a discussion about poverty and hunger. How much poverty and hunger is there in our neighborhood? Our country? Our world? Why is there poverty and hunger? What is the role of the government in making sure people have enough to eat? Why isn't it doing more? What can we do in addition to giving some food?[30]

In other words, transformative pedagogy shares a common instructional orientation with progressivist pedagogy (with some qualifications) but incorporates an explicit focus on social realities that relate to students' experience. It also is informed by a coherent vision of the kind of society it hopes students will promote—one founded on principles of democracy and social justice—and classroom instruction is oriented to building students' awareness of democratic ideals and giving them the academic and critical literacy tools they will need for full participation.

The editors of *Rethinking Our Classrooms* articulate eight interlocking components that are reflected in curriculum and classrooms oriented toward collaborative critical inquiry.[31] We paraphrase from their description of these components.

- Grounded in the lives of our students. All good teaching begins with a respect for children, their innate curiosity, and their capacity to learn. Regardless of what subject is being taught, ultimately the class has to be about students' lives as well as about a particular subject. Students should probe the ways their lives connect to the broader society and are often limited by that society.

- Critical. Students must learn to pose essential critical questions: Who makes decisions and who is left out? Who benefits and who suffers? Why is a given practice fair or unfair? What are its origins? What alternatives can we imagine? What is required to create change? Through this type of inquiry, students learn to think about advertising, cartoons, literature, legislative decisions, military interventions, job structures, newspapers, movies, agricultural practices, or school life.

- Multicultural, antiracist, pro-justice. A social justice curriculum must strive to include the lives of all those in our society, especially those who have been marginalized or excluded historically. A rigorous multiculturalism should engage students in a critical analysis of the roots of inequality in curriculum materials, school structure, and the larger society.

- Participatory, experiential. Whether through projects, role-playing, simulations, mock trials, or experiments, students need to be mentally and physically active. Students also must be stimulated to develop their capacity for democratic participation through questioning, challenging, decision making, and collaborative problem-solving.

- Hopeful, joyful, kind, visionary. The ways we organize classroom life should seek to make children feel significant and cared about— by the teacher and by each other. Unless students feel emotionally and physically safe, they won't share real thoughts and feelings.

- Activist. A critical curriculum should reflect the diversity of people from all cultures who acted to make a difference, many of whom did so at great sacrifice. We want students to come to see themselves as truth-tellers and change-makers, capable of acting in pursuit of social justice.
- Academically rigorous. Far from devaluing the vital academic skills young people need, a critical and activist curriculum speaks directly to the deeply rooted alienation that currently discourages millions of students from acquiring those skills. Critical teaching aims to inspire levels of academic performance far greater than those motivated or measured by grades or test scores. When children write for real audiences, read books and articles about issues that really matter, and discuss big ideas with compassion and intensity, "academics" starts to breathe.
- Culturally sensitive. These days, the demographic reality of schooling makes it likely that white teachers will enter classrooms filled with children of color. Teachers must be prepared to learn from their students and to call on parents, culturally diverse colleagues, and community resources for insights into the students and communities they seek to serve.

Consistent with a collaborative critical inquiry orientation, a major component of Peterson's practice (and that of other critical educators) derives from Paulo Freire's problem-posing approach. Students and teachers jointly pose substantive, challenging questions for the class to try to answer. Many of these questions are written down in a spiral notebook and, when feasible, discussed by the entire class. To illustrate:

> In a reading group discussion, for example, the question arose of how it must have felt for fugitive slaves and free African Americans to fear walking down the street in the North during the time of slavery. One student said, "I sort of know how they must have felt." Others immediately doubted her statement, but then she explained.
>
> "The slaves, especially fugitive slaves, weren't free because they couldn't walk the streets without fear of the slave masters, but today are we free?" she asked. "Because we can't walk the streets without fear of gangs, violence, crazy people, drunks, and drive-bys."[32]

Peterson also notes how critical thinking can be integrated with diverse subject matter. Math can be integrated with social studies, for example, by having students

> tally numbers of instances certain people, viewpoints, or groups are presented in a text or in mass media. One year my students compared the times famous women and famous men were mentioned in the fifth grade history text. One reaction by a number of boys was that men were mentioned far more frequently because women must not have done much throughout history. To help facilitate the discussion, I provided background resources for the students, including biographies of famous women. This not only helped students better understand the nature of "omission," but also generated interest in reading biographies of women.
>
> In another activity I had students tally the number of men and women by occupation as depicted in magazine and/or TV advertisements. By comparing their findings to the population as a whole, various forms of bias were uncovered. . . .[33]

These examples illustrate the potentially unlimited scope of collaborative critical inquiry and how it can be integrated with basic numeracy and literacy skills. The different cultural perspectives represented in the classroom become important resources for insight into the social issues that surround the classroom.

In summary, classrooms oriented to collaborative critical inquiry draw on the extensive instructional research showing that cooperative learning and active student inquiry are highly effective in promoting higher-order cognitive and academic skills. However, unlike many progressivist approaches that share these instructional orientations, transformative approaches also incorporate an explicit vision of the social goals toward which instruction is directed. This societal image takes seriously the ideals of documents that define the moral nature of different societies (such as the U.S. Constitution or the Canadian Charter of Rights and Freedoms) by emphasizing the central role of education in preparing students for democratic participation and the pursuit of social justice.

A focus on social justice requires that students become aware of how relations of culture and power play themselves out in our societies. We turn now to a more detailed examination of intercultural learning and the implications of crossing (and failing to cross) cultural boundaries.

CROSSING CULTURAL BOUNDARIES:
INTERCULTURAL LEARNING AS CORE CURRICULUM

Let us first look at the picture of schooling in the United States that emerges from one of the most in-depth examinations of schooling ever carried out in North America. Entitled *Voices from the Inside,* this investigation of four schools concluded that "a pervading sense of despair" characterized the experiences of students, teachers, and other school staff. Two central themes emerged from the investigation and ran through all the other problems identified: first, the nature of relationships formed between educators and students, and second, issues of race, culture, and class. The authors, Mary Poplin and Joseph Weeres, report that:

> Participants feel the crisis inside schools is directly linked to human relationships. Most often mentioned were relationships between teachers and students. Where positive things about the schools are noted, they usually involve reports of individuals who care, listen, understand, respect others and are honest, open and sensitive. Teachers report their best experiences in school are those where they connect with students and are able to help them in some way . . . Students of color, especially older students often report that their teachers, school staff and other students neither like nor understand them. Many teachers also report they do not always understand students ethnically different from themselves.[34]

With respect to issues of race, culture, and class, the authors note that many students perceive schools to be racist and prejudiced, from the staff to the curriculum; teachers are divided on this issue, some agreeing that students are right about racism, others disagreeing. The report goes on to note: "In our schools, as in the nation's schools, most students are increasingly bicultural and sometimes bilingual. Yet most who teach are monocultural and monolingual. Students have an intense interest in knowing about one another's culture but receive very little of that knowledge from home or school."[35]

The authors also emphasize the need for a radical rethinking of teaching and learning. Students (particularly those past fifth grade) report that they are bored in school and feel that what is taught has little relevance to their lives and their futures. Teachers feel pressure to teach the mandated curriculum, and they themselves often are bored by it. Students have clear views about the kinds of instruction that would motivate them to learn: "Students from all groups, remedial and advanced, high school to elementary, desire both rigor and fun in their schoolwork. They express enthusiasm about learning experiences that are complex but understandable, full of rich meanings and discussions of values, require their own action, and those about which they feel they have some choice."[36]

Student descriptions of the most boring and least relevant schoolwork focused on activities that stick closely to standardized materials and traditional transmission teaching methods. In addition, students of color seldom see the knowledge that they bring from their communities represented in the curriculum, which results in alienation and reduced involvement in learning.

The study's findings suggest that the cultural membranes that weave themselves in every direction throughout our schools are frequently made rigid and calcified into cultural barriers as a result of instruction that marginalizes issues of diversity to the periphery of the curriculum. This process is not by any means inevitable. Alternatives to monocultural curricula enable these cultural membranes to remain permeable—capable of two-way communication with the outside—and to be nurtured and evolved as a result of this exchange.

In other words, this study strongly suggests that if schools are to fulfill their goals of developing literacy skills among all students and preparing them to participate effectively in their societies, then they must focus on stimulating intercultural learning. Intercultural learning must start with teachers themselves. By encouraging students to talk and write about their experiences, teachers will begin to appreciate the cultural knowledge their students bring to school. Incorporation of this knowledge into the curriculum will provide students with opportunities to learn from each other and to develop a critical appreciation of their own culture and that of their peers. Lisa Delpit has expressed the fundamental importance of a multicultural orientation in addressing issues of underachievement:

> If we plan to survive as a species on this planet we must certainly create multicultural curricula that educate our children to the differing perspectives of our diverse population. In part, the problems we see exhibited in

school by African American children and children of other oppressed minorities can be traced to this lack of a curriculum in which they can find represented the intellectual achievements of people who look like themselves. Were that not the case, these children would not talk about doing well in school as "acting White." Our children of color need to see the brilliance of their legacy, too. [37]

We are not talking here about the "feel-good curriculum" focused only on self-esteem that has been so (justifiably) maligned by many parents and educators. Rather, we are proposing that our schools, from grades K through 12, adopt the rigorous pursuit of knowledge and insight into social and cultural issues that is aspired to in university liberal arts graduate schools where students are expected to read widely and analyze and synthesize issues in critical and informed ways. We have observed students doing precisely this in the context of global learning networks where the opportunities for research and intercultural interaction are maximized.

Faced with the overwhelming urgency of moving our schools in this direction, we must ask why our societies are so obsessed with controlling rather than unleashing our students' will to learn. We believe that, once again, James Moffett has put his finger on at least part of the answer:

Literacy is dangerous and has always been so regarded. It naturally breaks down barriers of time, space, and culture. It threatens one's original identity by broadening it through vicarious experiencing and the incorporation of somebody *else's* hearth and ethos. So we feel profoundly ambiguous about literacy. Looking at it as a means of transmitting our culture to our children, we give it priority in education, but recognizing the threat of its backfiring we make it so tiresome and personally unrewarding that youngsters won't want to do it on their own, which is of course when it becomes dangerous. . . . The net effect of this ambivalence is to give literacy with one hand and take it back with the other, in keeping with our contradictory wish for youngsters to learn to think but only about what we already have in mind for them.[38]

The fear of multicultural education has the same roots. The crossing of cultural boundaries knows no bounds. It potentially allows the Other to infiltrate and therefore must be controlled. The dilemma, of course, for those who fear these border crossings (to use Henry Giroux's term) is that our economic and social survival as a nation is increasingly dependent on crossing these cultural borders. Unless our students cross the cultural boundaries both within and beyond our national borders and, by so doing, develop a broader sense of identity, they will be ill-prepared to address the myriad social and ecological problems their generation will face.

Giroux has articulated what he terms "border pedagogy" to highlight the central role this process of crossing borders should play in any discussion of educational reform. He suggests that schools need to "create pedagogical conditions in which students become border crossers in order to understand otherness in its own terms." Crossing these ideological, political, and cultural borders allows new identities to be fashioned in the borderlands that result. In Giroux's terms, not only "are borders being challenged, crossed, refigured, but borderlands are being created in which the very production and acquisition of knowledge is being used by students to rewrite their own histories, identities, and learning possibilities." This form of intercultural learning requires a psychologically safe and socially nurturing environment that recognizes "how fragile identity is as it moves into borderlands crisscrossed within a variety of languages, experiences and voices." [39]

The failure of schools to navigate these borderlands, let alone teach their students how to do so, is poignantly expressed by a high school student in Poplin and Weeres's study: "This place hurts my spirit!" As Poplin and Weeres forcefully argue, both our education and social systems will remain in crisis until we honestly face up to these issues. [40] In other words, issues of cultural diversity must be at the core rather than the periphery of our educational endeavors.

A first step in this direction is to expose the conservative paranoia about multicultural education as fundamentally misguided and distorted. The most vehement arguments against multicultural education almost always identify it with extreme views that attempt to replace Eurocentric curricula with equally chauvinistic and ethnocentric glorifications of alternative cultural traditions. Some extreme versions of Afrocentric curricula have received the bulk of criticism in this regard, but these same critics could equally identify the curricula in some private religiously oriented schools (Catholic, Christian fundamentalist, Islamic, Jewish, etc.) as falling within this category. What the critics of multicultural education fear is intercultural exploration and critical literacy. If any critical literacy is permitted, it can only be directed outward, toward the Other, never inward.

Contrary to the distorted accusations of its critics, multicultural education is a strong force against this form of cultural separatism. Art critic and historian Robert Hughes lucidly expresses its significance in helping students see through and reach across borders:

> Multiculturalism asserts that people with different roots can co-exist, that they can learn to read the image-banks of others, that they can and should look across the frontiers of race, language, gender and age without prejudice or illusion, and learn to think against the background of a hybridized society. It proposes—modestly enough—that some of the most interesting things in history and culture happen at the interface between cultures. It wants to study border situations, not only because they are fascinating in themselves, but because understanding them may bring with it a little hope for the world. . . . To learn other languages, to deal with other customs and creeds from direct experience of them and with a degree of humility: these are self-evidently good, as cultural provincialism is not.

Hughes goes on to say that in a globalized economy, the future lies with "people who can think and act with informed grace across ethnic, cultural, linguistic lines." [41] The students we have observed participating in intercultural global learning networks are receiving such an apprenticeship.

CONCLUSION

The instructional landscape of North American education is littered with the intellectual debris of battles long ago lost and won; dead issues, false dichotomies, divine revelation, Communist plots, paranoid delusions masquerading as fact—all have had their day in the revolving rhetoric that has attempted to shape the form of American and Canadian schooling. We can continue to recycle this tired rhetoric and watch our schools decompose further. Or we can recognize that our best interest—perhaps even our future—lies in burying the cadavers of the past and embarking on a very different journey, a journey that will take us collectively across cultural, linguistic, and racial frontiers that at one time loomed in the distance like the edge of the world. If we do not summon up the confidence in our own cultures to explore these distant cultural regions, our own cultural borders will surely implode, as they did in Los Angeles in the spring of 1992.

Although we cannot pinpoint what our ultimate destination will be, we have at least a precise map and some promising directions to explore. Neither intercultural learning nor collaborative critical inquiry are new. From the pioneering work of Freinet and Lodi in Europe and the many educators and students in North America who are currently pursuing critical inquiry in the borderlands of our collective cultures, narratives have emerged to guide us. A technology also has emerged to, literally, speed us on our way.

Thus, we have practical examples and the outlines of a transformative pedagogy of collaborative critical inquiry that can realize the potential power of intercultural learning. Our society will reap enormous advantages by including all social groups in this process of cultural exchange and ensuring equality of access to these forms of learning. However, in opposition to this, some powerful groups fear genuine literacy, are paranoid about cultural infiltration, and evince a myopic drive to maximize their personal resources at the expense of the common good.

In chapter 6, we focus directly on the new technology and chart alternative directions that we believe will open up very different social and instructional landscapes beyond our current horizons.

Chapter 6

Superhighway to Where?

> In the world that is coming, if you can't navigate
> difference, you've had it.
> —Robert Hughes, *Culture of Complaint*

Open a newspaper any day of the week and it's likely that at least half of the news content will fall into one of three categories:

- Issues related to the way we negotiate difference; in other words, contacts and controversies related to cultural, ethnic linguistic, racial, religious, age, gender, and sexual orientation differences that form the fabric of our domestic and global communities. Some of these stories may be hopeful and inspirational—of individuals and communities coming together across the boundaries of difference; more frequently, they document the brutal consequences of our failure to navigate difference in regions as unfamiliar to most Europeans and North Americans as Rwanda and Chechnya and as familiar as New York, Los Angeles, Toronto, Berlin, and Belfast.
- Issues related to youth and the efforts that adults make to socialize youth through education. Educational reform has assumed urgency in many Western countries as a result of dramatic changes in the global economy and the fact that technological changes have increased the literacy demands of many occupations while deskilling others. Rhetorical wars have raged over whether we are suffering from a skills shortage or a skills surplus; the only thing that most people agree on is that as a society we are suffering and that schools

    should help alleviate that suffering by educating youth for jobs (that may or may not be there).

- Technology: The word conjures up both promise and threat. Several times a day we experience new conveniences brought about by technology—for example, when we go the supermarket or the bank machine or contact our colleagues by fax or through the Internet. Yet while we enjoy the convenience, the critiques of authors such as Neil Postman ring true that technology is not only facilitating our lives and culture but also shaping them in ways that may limit our perspectives and vision.[1]

    In this volume we have tried to establish links between these three phenomena that so preoccupy our collective attention as we approach a new millennium. We believe that we have reached a crossroads in each of these three areas and that the choices we will make in the next few years carry enormous implications for our societies. In the next sections, we briefly recapitulate the arguments that we have made to this point and outline the educational options we face as humanity enters an era of unprecedented cross-cultural contact and technological revolution.

NAVIGATING DIFFERENCE

We believe that public policy must acknowledge that the tribal instincts that contributed to our survival in previous evolutionary eras are now one of the greatest threats to our collective survival. Differences of all kinds that previously were suppressed are now out in the open, and so is the fear of difference. As a result of technological changes and dramatically increased international mobility, contacts across difference (cultural, racial, linguistic, religious) are virtually impossible to avoid. Faced with the reality of diversity at home and abroad, we can choose to turn inward, adopt a chauvinistic provincialism under the guise of "cultural literacy," and erect barriers that insulate us from the voices and perspectives of the Other. The consequences will be an escalation of intolerance and strife.

    Alternatively, we can recognize that new evolutionary imperatives are at work. "Survival of the fittest" has shifted from the biological to the social sphere. The groups that will survive and thrive in the new millennium are those that have learned how to work together across difference, who can use the strengths of each social group to achieve new collective insights, and who devote their energies to generating power through collaboration rather than depleting it through coercion.

This distinction between coercive and collaborative relations of power is central to any attempt to shift into a new paradigm for navigating difference. Coercive relations of power assume that power is a fixed quantity and that if one person, group or country gets more, then less is left for others; in other words, power relations are subtractive in nature, and there is a constant struggle for advantage in asserting and imposing one's power. The 697 percent increase in income that those earning between $200,000 and $1 million arranged for themselves during the 1980s in the United States at the expense of the middle-class and poor illustrates the subtractive nature of coercive relations of power.[2]

By contrast, collaborative relations of power recognize that power does not have to be viewed as a fixed quantity, that it can be reciprocal and additive rather than subtractive. As parents of young children, close friends, and lovers well know, power can be generated in interactions between people or groups such that participants are affirmed in their identities and develop a greater sense of efficacy to effect change in their lives or social situations. In this sense, we can define "empowerment" as the collaborative creation of power.

Perhaps the major challenge for us as individuals and as a global society is learning how to work together across cultural and linguistic differences in ways that generate empowerment for all participants. To shift to this new paradigm entails a challenge to the ways in which coercive relations of power have operated in our society. We believe that it is crucial to move public policy in this direction because the consequences of continued coercive relations of power are all too evident. As we suggested, this paradigm of power relations is rapidly approaching a point of diminishing returns, even for those groups that are currently in an economically advantageous situation. Even the most ardent social Darwinist can compute the economic consequences (not to mention the human costs) of continuing the current level of policing and incarceration of those who have been excluded from meaningful social participation.

We have illustrated in chapters 2 and 4 the empowerment and intellectual enhancement that can be generated among students when interactions are structured appropriately across cultural, linguistic, national, and religious boundaries. These interactions can contribute to mutual understanding, respect, and tolerance but, even more important, they can bring into focus for participants new dimensions of their own histories and identities. As Célestin Freinet so frequently stressed, contact and collaboration with distant peers enables students to view their own culture at a distance and so achieve greater appreciation of its strengths and possible limitations. We believe that this strengthening of one's own identity through cultural exploration offers far greater prospects for individual and collective human development than the alternative attempt to protect one's identity through isolation and chauvinism.

Today we have the opportunity to make cultural exploration a vital part of every child's educational experience through ensuring that all schools have access to the Internet. Appropriately structured, this cultural exploration will provide not only an apprenticeship in navigating difference but also stimulate the academic skills and critical literacy required for employment and effective democratic participation.

EDUCATIONAL FUTURES

We have analyzed the contradictions in the discourse of the neo-conservative education reform movement in order to identify the real agenda behind the rhetoric. Virtually all of the rationales advanced for reforming public education in the service of greater economic competitiveness lack credibility. In the first place, as the Sandia report demonstrates, there is little evidence that academic standards have dropped during the past 30 years; nor is there evidence of any skills shortage in the labor market; if anything, there is a glut of skills in the global economy and too few high-skilled jobs to go around.[3] The call for a renewed back-to-basics instructional approach ignores the fact that traditional transmission models of instruction continue to dominate classrooms across the United States.

The instructional agenda of these back-to-basics reformers is oriented to narrowing the curriculum to impart only the very basic functional literacy required by industry (despite their rhetoric of the need for higher-order thinking and critical literacy skills) and to ensure that only official versions of history and current events get transmitted. Within this sanitized curriculum, there is no room for either critical inquiry or any serious form of multicultural education. In other words, the goal is to produce compliant consumers for capitalism. These students will lack both the critical literacy and the inclination to use the democratic process to challenge the distribution of power and resources in their societies. It has become just as important to narrow the curricular options for the middle class as for the poor because currently many in the middle class are being squeezed into the ranks of the poor, as Donald Barlett and James Steele so clearly demonstrate.[4]

An additional goal behind much of the "competitiveness" rhetoric appears to be to discredit public schooling and thereby advance the cause of privatized education. An expanded private school system has the double attraction for business of reduced taxes (since fewer tax dollars will be required to support a shrunken public education system) and significant profit possibilities in managing and supplying technology to the private system.

Advocates of these directions are minimally concerned that their vision of short-term profit will likely entail long-term social and economic costs to contain and/or incarcerate the alienated dropouts of an even more impoverished public school system. Once again the blinders of social Darwinism obscure the impending catastrophe of entrenching a two-tier society in which the bottom tier, the permanent underclass, has no stake in preserving a society that has essentially excluded it.

While we reject the false premises and contradictory solutions of the neo-conservative educational reform effort, we are nevertheless adamant about the urgency to restructure schools to respond to the challenges of the next century. We believe that any genuine effort at educational reform must focus primarily on increasing the achievement levels of students from marginalized communities, since these are the students who currently are not being served adequately by our educational system. Clearly, increasing the equity of financial allocation between schools in impoverished and wealthy areas is an important step in this process. However, transforming the entire mission and ethos of the schools—so that diversity is seen as a resource and education becomes a process of cultural exploration and intellectual inquiry rooted in respect for the experiences that students and communities bring to school—is probably even more important. As several research studies have shown, even schools committed to genuine reform have some way to go in recognizing the need to affirm diverse cultures and languages and tap into the funds of knowledge that are abundantly present in students' communities.[5] If this diversity is not affirmed, relationships across the boundaries of race and class will continue to be strained. Cultural boundaries become barriers, and self-protective hostility replaces collaborative action.

A pedagogy of collaborative critical inquiry is a prerequisite for making schooling relevant to marginalized students' lives and engaging them in academic effort. The forms of participation that are encouraged in the classroom reflect educators' vision of the contributions they are preparing students to make in the wider society. Fostering students' ability to think critically about complex social issues and take collective action to shape their societies is an explicit goal of collaborative critical inquiry.

This does not imply any neglect of "core" academic content such as science, math, or English. On the contrary, students' intrinsic will to learn about these content areas is enhanced by seeing their relevance to their own lives and to the social issues confronting their communities and societies. Thus, our proposal is for the rigorous intellectual inquiry more often associated with the curriculum of universities than with that of grade schools.

Clearly, collaborative critical inquiry is not dependent on any form of sophisticated technology. However, as our examples illustrate, the potential of collaborative critical inquiry to transform students' learning and amplify their cultural awareness is enhanced when it operates within the context of global learning networks.

In short, our vision of educational reform is hopeful and positive. We believe that the academic involvement of currently underachieving students can be enhanced dramatically by using tools such as the Internet in the service of collaborative critical inquiry. We are also sufficiently realistic, however, to recognize why curricula remain sanitized and why collaborative critical inquiry is still uncommon as an instructional strategy, especially for marginalized students. Ruling classes always have viewed the democratization of literacy with suspicion, and as James Moffett and others have pointed out, little has changed today.[6]

Thus, educational reformers face a dilemma: If we invest in the diverse cultural, linguistic, and intellectual capital that *all* students bring to school, we can create a highly skilled workforce amply endowed with the capacities for symbolic analysis. This workforce will have far greater ability to create wealth through innovation and manipulation of information than is now the case. As a consequence, it will have greater financial assets, which will spur consumption and further production. Far less expenditure will be required on welfare, police surveillance, and incarceration, saving our societies billions of dollars annually.

Why have we as a society consistently resisted pursuing this path? We believe the answer lies in our refusal to abandon coercive relations of power that have historically kept marginalized communities "in their place." The educational scenario we have sketched requires the active pursuit not just of functional literacy but of critical literacy. It also requires that educators foster confidence among *all* students in their own intellectual abilities and in their cultural knowledge, thereby reversing the message of intellectual and cultural inferiority that many marginalized groups have received both in school and in the broader society.

In addition, our emphasis on *collaborative* critical inquiry requires that the educational process encourage students to reach across boundaries of difference and extend their own identities by establishing contact and solidarity with others. Such an educational system that encourages solidarity and the collaborative creation of power in the borderlands between different marginalized communities is likely to be viewed with alarm by those who traditionally have used a strategy of "divide and conquer" to maintain their powerful status.

Finally, there is the threat of democratic participation. The pedagogy we have outlined has as an explicit goal the promotion of students' ability and willingness to contribute to their societies through civic participation. We take seriously the democratic legacy of Western civilization and its concern with human rights and social justice. However, unlike many commentators such as Arthur Schlesinger, Jr., who fear the impending disintegration of America as a consequence of the infiltration of the Other in the guise of cultural diversity, we recognize that throughout the history of Western civilization, concern with human rights and social justice has been honored more often in the breach than in the observance. We believe that education has a crucial role to play in reversing this gap between the ideal and the real; through dialogue, research, and critical inquiry, students can come to a greater understanding of why the noble ideals of Western civilization (and other civilizations) have been so difficult to realize in practice.

In this regard, the pedagogy we propose is explicit about the contributions that students will be capable of making to their communities and societies. Unlike the purveyors of (mono)cultural literacy and other forms of "banking" education, we believe that education should enable *all* students to collaborate in pursuit of the "common good," human rights, social justice, and democratic participation. If our schools abdicate the cultivation of critical literacy, the next generation will be even more subject than ours to manipulation by those who control the media (and many other resources in our society). The more consent can be manufactured through media persuasion and omission of divergent perspectives, the more democracy merges into totalitarianism.

In short, computer-mediated learning networks can act as a catalyst for collaborative critical inquiry that is fundamental in preparing students to participate actively in a democratic society. Hence, we are adamant about the importance of ensuring that all schools have access to this technology and to the instructional strategies required to use it fruitfully. Universal access, when combined with a transformative pedagogy, represents a small but significant step toward promoting collaborative relations of power in the educational system.

TECHNOLOGY

Clearly we believe that certain forms of technology can be powerful tools to facilitate intercultural learning and collaborative inquiry. We have described how intercultural inquiry through the Internet can serve as a means of challenging traditional forms of indoctrination and disempowerment of marginalized students and communities. In endorsing computer-mediated learning networks, we may appear to have chosen some strange bedfellows. Many of the most ardent advocates of technological expansion in education, such as Chris Whittle, former chairperson of Whittle Communications of Channel One fame and John Golle, chief executive officer of Educational Alternatives, Inc., are enthusiastic precisely because they see technology as a more efficient "delivery system" than teachers in producing a reliable supply of "adaptable, flexible, loyal, mindful, expendable, 'trainable' workers for the 21st century."[7] In other words, their educational vision seldom extends beyond transmission of facts and skills and inculcation of a value system that will enable students to know their place within their society. Their understanding of the learning process is about as sophisticated as the technological wizards in Huxley's *Brave New World* who attempted to program the essential facts about the River Nile into Tommy's resistant brain.[8]

Essentially, these myopic visionaries are unconcerned about student learning. Corporate promoters of technology see it as an unalloyed good that will simultaneously rescue education from the imprecision of human delivery systems and garner significant profits for private investors. Technologically based instructional delivery will require fewer expensive humans, thereby realizing profits based on the same per-pupil expenditure as conventional schooling. In Douglas Noble's words: "Corporate leaders view schools as the last major labor-intensive industry ripe for colonization and modernization. Public schools, finally, represent for them an expensive public monopoly overcome by bureaucratic inefficiency and abysmal productivity."[9]

While we may agree about the bureaucratic inefficiency of much public education, technology delivery systems are far from our vision of an education system that responds to the challenges of the twenty-first century. We share the concerns of many critics of the regime of technology.[10] Maud Barlow and Heather-Jane Robertson, for example, in discussing what they term the "disinformation highway," express their concerns as follows:

> To reach young people, as consumers, as future workers, as the social architects of tomorrow, business is looking to the powerful medium-of-choice for kids, high technology. Information is increasingly delivered not by books and teacher lectures but by computers and telecommunications (which are less easily regulated to reflect the consensus standards set by boards, parents, and governments). Technology is becoming the way to bypass the system and go directly to students with a message. While this is as true for environmentalists, labor groups, and others trying to persuade young people to their view, no other sector will have as much financial access as corporations to ride the highway into the schools.[11]

While not disputing the essentials of their analysis, we feel that Barlow and Robertson and others who view encroaching technological invasion as yet another corporate plot to subvert democracy underestimate the potential of relatively low-tech access to the Internet as a forum for resistance to coercive relations of power. We view the opportunities that technology offers to bypass "the system" as positive, since any system, whether controlled by governments, unions, or corporations, is intended to limit access to information and alternative perspectives. Our concern as educators is not to persuade students to our point of view but to allow them access to alternative perspectives so that they can arrive at their own informed judgments. Learning how to control, rather than being controlled by the technology, is essential to education in the twenty-first century.

As Michael Apple points out, even Channel One offers teachers and students opportunities to promote a critical orientation to media and societal power relations:

> Channel One offers critically oriented teachers an opportunity to do some very interesting educational work with students in middle schools and high schools. It provides the context for a serious deconstruction—*with students*—of its content and form, of its ethics of selling students as audiences, and of its interests. It does offer technology that students themselves can "play" with, using the VCR and the monitors to broadcast their own productions and meanings, and to make parodies of and reconstruct "the news."[12]

The dismissal of the information superhighway by critics of the left ignores the fact that it is here to stay and will play a determining role in the life of every student who graduates in the next millennium. Rather than abandoning the field to narrow corporate interests, it seems imperative to us to articulate how powerful a teaching and learning medium it can be when aligned with a pedagogy of collaborative critical inquiry. Furthermore, it is crucial to insist that we emulate the vision of schools in France throughout much of this century, where collaborative critical inquiry has been facilitated by free access to the national postal service. If we believe that education has a role to play in shaping the future of our societies, then our national interest with respect to both economic and democratic participation is clearly served by ensuring that all schools have basic access to the Internet for purposes of intercultural learning.

Building this right of access into the national infrastructure is well within the power of governments. In fact, such access was a key element of the proposal for a National Information Infrastructure advanced by the Clinton administration. This proposal would have established a National Research and Education Network (NREN) that would have provided every elementary and secondary public school in the nation access to the Internet. Stephen Hodas has described the importance of this initiative in these terms:

> The proposed deployment of the K-12 NREN offers us as citizens, technologists, and educators an unprecedented opportunity to assist in shaping a new expression of civic and pedagogical culture. More than this, the decisions that are made or not made over access, equity, rights, and responsibilities will fully define the social, cultural, and economic opportunities of several generations of students. The K-12 NREN, as a policy design and a policy settlement, will have concrete, sententious consequences for our children. It can be a progressive force for change, equity, and restructuring or a regressive distribution of resources and influence to those already most in possession of them. These alternatives will depend on how it is construed and financed, how conceived and implemented, but in any case its impact on pedagogy will be profound.[13]

Yet when the measure came to a vote in the Democratic-controlled Congress, the administration bowed to the threat of a Republican filibuster and to pressure from the former Bell Telephone companies and other telecommunications conglomerates that are fighting to charge for Internet access while permitting no subsidies for education or any other purposes.[14]

Thus, the debate about the ultimate destination of the information superhighway continues. The issues are clearly drawn: restrict access to those individuals and schools that can afford to pay for it (at an estimated cost, according to some analysts, of about $120 per month);[15] or provide low-cost access to schools and individuals as a means of ensuring that it becomes as universal a means of communication as the telephone and can be used to promote the intercultural learning and intellectual development that our society so desperately needs to preserve its democratic foundations.[16]

The final words on the potential and pitfalls of the Internet for our social and educational systems belong to Ralph Nader, who has long championed the rights of North American consumers:

When the new computer information technologies were first developed, there was great concern that these systems would be used to enhance the power of the state and large corporations to place citizens under surveillance, invading personal privacy and, through various methods of manipulation, reducing our personal power and sovereignty as consumers, workers, and citizens. While these concerns remain, there is good reason for a more optimistic view of the new technologies. In recent years a number of citizen groups have experimented with the use of computer networks as a tool for monitoring government agencies and organizing citizens. Today, using the Internet, it is possible to obtain information on a wide range of important topics and share it among literally millions of persons at a very low cost. The communications are often interactive, allowing citizens to talk to each other, exchange feedback, offer pointers, and debate facts, strategies, and values.[17]

Clearly, issues of culture, education, and technology merge at the crossroads of the twenty-first century. Do we plan for the common good by enabling *all* students to navigate difference, develop intellectually and academically, and gain expertise in employing technology for enhancing democratic participation, or do we curtail the development of these social, intellectual, and technological skills in order to restrict potential challenges to the current distribution of power and resources in our society?

II.

A Guide to the Internet for Parents and Teachers

Internet Basics

Access to the Internet: Getting Connected

For parents, teachers, or students new to the Internet, the key element in successfully making your first connection to this "network of networks" is to find someone locally to help you. Luckily for those interested in educational networking, most school districts have computer coordinators who would be glad to lend a hand as you learn how to set up your computer for connecting to the Internet. Here we attempt to avoid technical jargon in order to provide an extremely basic "primer" for educational networking, offering advice that your local computer expert can help you interpret.[1] Once connected, you will quickly forget all the intricate settings and incomprehensible manuals it took to dial into a computer network for the first time. But until you are beyond the threshold of that first connection, be sure to line up a local expert.

A second order of business is purchasing any one of the several excellent handbooks now available on the Internet, a selection of which are provided in the list of references at the end of this guide. These handbooks provide detailed instructions for each of the Internet communication tools. Here we discuss some of the major Internet communication tools, leaving aside for your own exploration other communication tools which have more intricate commands and are best learned from detailed handbooks (such as USENET, "FTP" and "Archie"). Our goal in this guide is to provide an overview of the kinds of resources available over the Internet and a sampling of the communication tools you can use to find those resources.

Any personal computer, no matter what brand, and from whatever country, can connect to the Internet. Beyond having a computer, there are five requirements that you will need to address. Your local school district's computer coordinator or an educational software specialist at your local computer store can provide invaluable advice and specific suggestions about how to meet each requirement. You will need:

1. A word processor
2. A modem and cable that connects your computer to a phone line. Modems come in various speeds. While 28,800 bits (letters) per second (bps) now is considered the standard by some, many use 14,400 or 9400 bps. Slower 2400 bps modems often can be bought at a discount price, far under $100.
3. A telecommunications software program to run your modem and dial the phone. Many of these computer software programs are available as either "shareware" (low-cost programs that you can use for free until you decide they are good enough to support with your check) or commercial programs (usually costing under $100). In either case, paying the low shareware registration fee or buying your own registered copy of a commercial program is the best idea, since a manual and on-line support is often available. Your local computer expert can help you set up this software program to match the requirements of your modem and those of the Internet service provider you have chosen.
4. A telephone line. Any regular phone line will do, such as are found in most homes. Yet schools often are wired differently and pose special problems for telecommunications. In older buildings, often the only regular phone connection is in the principal's office; and in newer buildings, switchboards and push-button dialing phones block direct access to the dial tone you will need. These are questions to work out, either by making connections from your own home or by finding work-arounds thanks to the ingenuity of your local educational computer experts.

    The ideal access method is to have a direct phone line installed in a teacher's room or the school's computer lab. Aside from installation cost, the only other fee is the monthly service charge for the phone line. Local calls to your Internet service provider are all that will be made on the line. Barring this, some teachers take disks to the principal's office and send off their students' writings once a week, but this can be awkward. Often parents and teachers prefer to connect from home, since time is hard to find during the normal working or teaching day.

5. Access to an Internet service provider. This is dealt with in the next section of this guide.

While it is possible to use any personal computer, no matter how humbly equipped, to connect to the Internet, the possibilities that open up for global learning networks are broader with a setup that includes a high-capacity hard disk, as much random access memory (RAM) as possible, a high-speed modem, and a color monitor with speakers. A parent, teacher, or student with such a computer setup would be in an ideal position to take advantage of the new multimedia programs, such as Netscape or Mosaic, for exploring the Internet. Nevertheless, even the most rudimentary computer equipment can make possible the kind of collaborative critical inquiry we have discussed; each of the portraits in chapter 2 used only the most basic computing resources.

Choosing a Local Telecommunications Service Provider: Three Levels of Connectivity

There are three levels of connectivity to the Internet. While this sounds simple at first—merely choosing between three increasingly costly alternatives—a parent or educator needs more information to make an informed choice. An informed consumer needs to take into account the two types of resources available over the Internet and the various tools for accessing these resources, and their costs.

First, it is important to realize that the Internet provides access both to *human* resources and to *information* resources; in other words, the Internet can connect you with people you can come to know, or it can help you locate information that you need to have. In either case, this access takes place through the use of several Internet communication tools. While these human and information resources often are interrelated (the people you meet help you find information resources you had no idea about, and often information you discover will point you to other people who share your interests), it helps to keep in mind the basic division between making human connections and making information connections as you decide on a local Internet service provider.

Second, we need to survey briefly the range of communication tools available for global learning networks in order to understand their pros and cons for accessing either human or information resources. Under the huge umbrella of the Internet, most communication that takes place between computer networks falls into two basic categories: electronic mail (e-mail), which is passed, stored, and sorted from one computer to another until reaching its final destination; and remote access, where long lines of communication are opened directly between a "user" on one network and a database or program that runs on a different network, a line of communication which, in fact, passes through countless other computer networks.

E-mail is by far the most common type of communication over the Internet. It is relatively cheap since it merely requires the rapid opening and closing of connections between networks lasting only microseconds. Packets of mail are shunted from place to place around the world, finally to be stored within the addressee's "electronic mailbox" on a local (for them, but distant for you) computer network until he or she has the time to "log in" and read the waiting message.

Remote access, on the other hand, takes place in what is called "real time." Remote access means that an open connection is established and maintained between one local computer network and another faraway computer network through dozens of other networks. This open connection lasts for as long as a local user wishes to interact with the particular faraway computer system. It is therefore comparatively more costly than e-mail.

In both cases, the Internet works for two basic reasons. First, international standards have been set where each participating computer network agrees to use similar systems of "addressing" (the technical term is "communication protocols") for the exchange of information. Second, "connect costs" are distributed across *all* participating computer networks. Each network can achieve global connectivity individually simply by agreeing to pay the connect costs between itself and its closest neighboring networks. In effect, each computer network agrees that if it passes anyone else's e-mail along to its destination, then everyone else will help it distribute its e-mail. And if it allows an open line of communication through its network to anyone who wants to use remote access tools to interact with a computer system somewhere else on the planet, then other systems will return the favor.

In the case of e-mail, a special type of addressing called TCP/IP (Transport Control Protocol/Internet Protocol) has become the de facto standard. All computers on the Internet can interpret an e-mail message with an address such as

SAYERS@acfcluster.nyu.edu

or

JCUMMINS@oise.on.ca

as saying something like "Please place this message in the mailbox of the person named SAYERS who gets messages over the ACF computer network that is running at New York University, an educational institution," or "Do me the favor of putting this note in the mailbox of JCUMMINS who picks up messages at the network run by the Ontario Institute for Studies in Education, an institution in Ontario, Canada."

Similarly, remote access is made possible only because every network participating in the Internet agrees to run similar computer programs at each site (programs with exotic names ranging from Gopher and Veronica, FTP and Archie, Telnet, WAIS, the World Wide Web, etc.). With all these standards for e-mail and remote access in place, the Internet—as a network of networks—offers a staggeringly broad range of telecomputing possibilities far beyond the reach of any of its single component networks.

What does all this mean when it comes time to choose your local Internet service provider?

Some service providers offer Level 1 connectivity to the Internet, or access through "gateways." To connect with these service providers, you use your modem to dial them up. These service providers are not really part of the Internet itself, but are free-standing computer systems that hand your electronic mail over to the Internet through a gateway where it is then routed from one network to another until reaching its final destination; when a correspondent sends you e-mail, it is picked up off the Internet by your service provider at its gateway and delivered into your personal electronic mailbox. Some of these service providers are commercial (e.g., America Online, Prodigy, CompuServe) and some are free. (Your local public school district may run a service called a computer bulletin board system that may be able to pass e-mail to and from the Internet through a gateway.)

Level 1 connectivity means that you are limited to the services that your service provider allows. The basic service is e-mail, and since this is where much of the "action" takes place over the Internet, it is certainly a good place to start. But you are likely to want access to more sophisticated Internet communication tools before long. Some level 1 service providers may offer these Internet communication tools but charge an extra premium for using them; other service providers concentrate strictly on no-frills e-mail.

Level 2 connectivity means that when you dial up your service provider, you are connecting to a host computer that is part of the Internet itself. This host computer provides you an electronic mailbox for your e-mail, just as the level 1 service providers do, but it typically also offers

Telnet, Gopher, World Wide Web, and other remote access services. This more complete array of services commands a higher price. Some teachers buy one account and share it among themselves in an effort to economize; for example, Cold Spring Harbor High School, featured in several of the portraits in chapter 2, has engaged in sophisticated networking projects for years by using a single Internet account for the entire school.

With level 3 connectivity, your computer itself—or more likely, your school district's computer—is actually part of the Internet and has a coded address that any Internet computer can directly reach. It becomes possible to participate in the highest-tech projects on the Internet, such as the Global Schoolhouse or CoVis (described in Internet Resources for K-12 Education). While most parents, teachers, and students will be connecting to the Internet through level 1 or level 2 service providers, it is important to advocate within your school district and board of education for level 3 connectivity in each school building. In every case, your local school's computer coordinator will be able to tell you where to begin looking for Internet service providers in your area.

Internet Communication Tools and Learning How to Use Them

We will distinguish between two types of Internet communication tools: those that connect people and those that help gather information resources.

THE "PEOPLE CONNECTION" TOOLS

These tools include electronic mail (or e-mail) and LISTSERVs. Over 90 percent of all activity over the Internet takes place through e-mail. Sending e-mail requires having the Internet address of a correspondent (or a group of correspondents; see LISTSERVs, below). Preparing e-mail is a bit different from getting a letter ready for the postal service. First, you address your "electronic envelope" with the Internet address of your correspondent and then you write a message (or insert a previously written message in the "envelope"). Your message is sent by passing mail packets from computer network to computer network, opening and closing circuits all along the way. Because each transaction takes only nanoseconds to complete, e-mail is the fastest and cheapest way to communicate over the Internet. It is even possible (though somewhat tedious) to use e-mail to access other more sophisticated Internet communication tools, as we describe later.

LISTSERVs use e-mail to create discussion groups of people with common interests. The guiding principle of LISTSERVs is simple but powerful. A host computer somewhere on the Internet runs the LISTSERV program that is devoted to a particular special interest topic, say, for example "deaf education." Without charge or fee, you can subscribe to the LISTSERV by sending a short message to the *subscription address* for that discussion group. From that moment on, you will be placed on the subscribers' list for that LISTSERV and will receive every message that anyone sends to the LISTSERV. Moreover, any message you send to the *participation address* of that LISTSERV will be placed in the electronic mailbox of every other subscriber to that LISTSERV. As a result, a discussion group is created between a broad range of people often with a wide variety of experiences yet interested in the same topic, ranging from students, parents, and teachers to internationally recognized experts in a particular field.

THE "INFORMATION CONNECTION" TOOLS

While electronic mail works by quickly moving packets of information through switches between computer networks, remote access tools require an open line of communication between one computer network and another—in the process often tying up numerous computer networks in between. These communication tools therefore cost more money to operate. We consider two basic classes of remote access tools, Telnet and information displayers such as Gophers and World Wide Web browsers. More difficult-to-use tools (such as the File Transfer Protocol, or FTP) should be explored with the help of any of the books listed in the references section.

Telnet: This is the most basic of the remote access Internet communications tools, since it performs its own special function while also permitting you access to other Internet communications tools, such as Gopher (discussed next). Telnet allows you to connect from your own service provider to another remote computer and, once there, actually to run another computer program as if you were right in that computer network yourself, miles away. These computer programs range from specialized programs that can search databases (see ERIC discussion, below) to microworlds where students can explore alternative realities based on specific subject areas, such as mathematics and science.

Information Displayers: The Internet is replete with hundreds of thousands of fascinating documents. How to access them? Several remote access tools allow a parent or teacher to find a wealth of information that can transform the educational experience of students in schools. Two of the most important of these information displayers are Gophers and World Wide Web information browsers.

Gopher: This is one of the most common of the information displayers. The name stands for an Internet communications utility that "goes for" documents located within its own menus or any other Gopher around the world. There are Gopher sites on hundreds of networks, many devoted to K-12 educational issues. Each Gopher lists its information offerings in the form of menus for you to select from. Once you find some information you want, you can have it mailed back to you electronically instantly.

The World Wide Web (WWW or "The Web"): This information displayer is based on the concept of "hypertext." Instead of the menus that Gopher provides, the Web uses "browsers" which highlight key words in its "homepages." By clicking on these key words, a parent or educator can be linked to another computer resource anywhere in the world. While Gophers handle mostly "text documents" composed of nothing but letters, numbers, and punctuation, the Web also allows the well-equipped user to see graphic displays, even video clips, and hear sound that is linked to a text—the Internet version of a "slide/tape show."[2]

ERIC: A Case Study on Exploring with Internet Tools

To explain more about how Internet tools work, we narrate the fictitious story of a parent and teacher, whom we will name Olga Reyes, as she explores the Internet making connections with both people and information. This is a composite scenario, drawn from typical examples of educational computer networking activities.

In particular, we will observe Ms. Reyes as she uses two of the major Internet communications tools for exploring perhaps the richest source of educational information in the world—the Educational Resources Information Center (ERIC) system. But before meeting Olga Reyes and discovering what she, as a parent and teacher, is interested in finding over the Internet, let's first become acquainted with ERIC.

ERIC is the largest and most frequently searched education database anywhere, with more than 800,000 records and 30,000 new accessions each year. Sponsored by the U.S. Department of Education's Office of Educational Research and Improvement, ERIC is comprised of 16 subject-area clearinghouses located at host universities:

- Adult, Career, and Vocational Education, Ohio State University, Columbus, with its adjunct Clearinghouse on Consumer Education
- Assessment and Evaluation, Catholic University, Washington, D.C.
- Community Colleges, University of California at Los Angeles
- Counseling and Student Services, University of North Carolina, Greensboro
- Disabilities and Gifted Children, Council for Exceptional Children, Reston, Virginia
- Educational Management, University of Oregon, Eugene Elementary and Early Childhood Education, University of Illinois, Urbana
- Higher Education, George Washington University, Washington, D.C.
- Information and Technology, Syracuse University, Syracuse, New York

- Languages and Linguistics, Center for Applied Linguistics, Washington, D.C., with its adjunct Clearinghouse for ESL Literacy Education
- Reading and Communication Skills, Indiana University, Bloomington, Indiana
- Rural Education and Small Schools, Appalachia Educational Laboratory, Charleston, West Virginia
- Science, Mathematics, and Environmental Education, Ohio State University, Columbus, Ohio
- Social Studies/Social Science Education, Indiana University, Bloomington, with its adjunct Clearinghouses on Art Education and U.S.-Japan Studies, Bloomington, Indiana
- Teaching and Teacher Education, American Association of Colleges for Teacher Education, Washington, D.C.
- Urban Education, Teachers College, Columbia University, New York, New York, with its adjunct Clearinghouse on Title 1

Information specialists employed by the 16 subject-specialty clearinghouses help keep the ERIC database vital and current for each particular area of interest by acquiring and reviewing key educational literature. The 800,000 items in the database fall into two major categories: 350,000 abstracts of educational journal articles (documents beginning with EJ numbers), and 450,000 abstracts of nonjournal education documents (those with ED numbers).

For the first category, articles in more than 800 educational journals are reviewed and abstracted by educational resource specialists each year, saving educators everywhere valuable time and effort in the unceasing struggle to stay current in their rapidly changing fields. The second category includes an enormous variety of educational documents: research reports, conference papers, educational program descriptions, opinion papers, teaching guides, evaluation studies, tests and questionnaires, instructional materials, and bibliographies. Particularly useful are the "ERIC Digests," specially commissioned state-of-the-art summaries, usually no more than two pages in length, concerning current theories and practice on important educational topics. More than 1,200 other ERIC Digests are available, and new titles are produced each year. Digests are often in question-and-answer format and include a list of additional resources for more information.

In the past five years, ERIC has attempted to make as many of its information resources as possible available over the Internet. The ERIC Clearinghouse on Information and Technology, located at Syracuse University in New York, has played a leading role in this effort. We will watch as Olga Reyes explores these ERIC resources located on the computer network at Syracuse University, using two of the most common Internet communication tools, e-mail and Gopher.

EXPLORATIONS: AN "INTERNET SCENARIO" FROM K–12 EDUCATION

Our composite teacher is Ms. Olga Reyes, a fifth-grade classroom teacher in a suburban school district bordering a large metropolitan area. Besides being an involved parent in her son's education at the local high school, Ms. Reyes is constantly looking for new strategies to encourage more parent involvement in the education of the students enrolled in her own class. Her students come from a variety of backgrounds, mostly African American and European American, but every year she has a number of students from Spanish-speaking families and a few students whose families have arrived from other countries in the last several years. Hence, Ms. Reyes is always interested in finding new ways to include multicultural approaches in her teaching.

In her state, there has been a recent push toward "inclusion"—that is, toward mainstreaming into regular classroom settings students with special learning needs who formerly were assigned to separate special education classes. Ms. Reyes therefore is intensely interested in learning about these children's special learning needs. Lately, she has started using cooperative learning activities (creating small groups of students from different cultural backgrounds and varying levels of academic ability) to foster both achievement and intercultural learning. Also, in another effort to reach *all* the students in her class, Ms. Reyes has been experimenting recently with "thematic units" that organize all content-area instruction (language arts, math and science, social studies, and creative arts) around a single unifying concept. Since she will herself be exploring the Internet in the coming months, Ms. Reyes has decided that her next thematic unit will be focused on the unifying concept of "explorations."

Now she is hoping to use the Internet to find information resources that will help her as a teacher and a parent and to make connections with parents and educators with similar interests. She has contacted her district's computer coordinator, who gave her some tips about how to buy and set up a modem, cable, and software to use with her home computer, since the only phone line in her school is in the principal's office, and she prefers to connect from home, away from the inevitable interruptions if she were to connect from the school office. The coordinator recommended a good basic handbook on the Internet and gave Ms. Reyes the phone numbers of local Internet service providers. Ms. Reyes called up and got a full-service account on a host network called "INTERCOM" (a fictitious name) for $15 to $20 per month. A few days later, she received her "Username" and secret "Password" in the mail along with a manual explaining the commands she would use once connected to the Internet service provider. The computer coordinator had mentioned to Ms. Reyes that the nearby university's School of Education might provide free Internet connections for local K-12 teachers starting the following school year; however, Ms. Reyes wanted to get started right away and chose to subscribe to her own Internet account.

Ms. Reyes turns on her computer and modem and starts her telecommunications software program. She follows the menu of that program to enter the local telephone number for INTERCOM, her Internet service provider, into a dialing log so that she can dial automatically in the future. She presses the Enter/Return key, and immediately from her modem she hears a dial tone and then the musical tones of a telephone number being dialed, followed by a few rings, a two-pitched beep, and miscellaneous noises. Finally, the word "CONNECT" appears on her screen. A welcoming message scrolls by and then pauses as the host network of her Internet service provider waits for her to type in her Username and Password.

Striking Out: The First Connection to the ERIC Gopher

Ms. Reyes is ready to begin exploring the Internet. Her first task is to get an overview of the educational resources available to her. The computer coordinator had mentioned the ERIC Internet site located at Syracuse University and suggested using the "Gopher" Internet tool to visit there and to browse through its resources. Because she has purchased a full-service Internet account through her local Internet service provider and since it had installed its own Gopher program locally, she can go directly to the Syracuse University Gopher. She types

```
gopher ericir.syr.edu
```

and immediately the host network makes connections, from her town and through numerous other networks on the Internet, until she is connected to Syracuse University directly. (By the way, she is *not* paying for a long-distance call to make this connection, only the local call to her INTERCOM host computer.)

The following Gopher menu appears on her screen:

```
Internet Gopher Information Client v2.0.14


      AskERIC - (Educational Resources Information Center)

--> 1. News and Information about ERIC and AskERIC/
    2. Map of the Library/
    3. Search AskERIC Menu Items <?>
    4. AskERIC Toolbox (under construction)/
    5. Frequently Asked Questions (FAQ's)/
    6. AskERIC InfoGuides/
    7. Lesson Plans/
    8. Education Listservs Archives/
    9. ERIC Clearinghouses/Components/
   10. ERIC Digests File/
   11. ERIC Bibliographic Database (RIE and CIJE)/
   12. Bibliographies/
   13. News & Announcements of Interest to Educators/
   14. Other Education Resources/
   15. Education Conferences (Calendars and Announcements)/
   16. Electronic Journals, Books, and Reference Tools/
   17. Internet Guides and Directories/
   18. Gophers and Library Catalogs/


 Press ? for Help, q to Quit, u to go up a menu     Page: 1/1
```

Ms. Reyes surveys the menu and sees a list of "directories" to further menus, each directory signaled by the "/" at the end of the menu item.[3] At the bottom is a short "Help" message, and on the right she sees that this is a simple one-page menu.

First, Ms. Reyes presses the "?" key and reads the instructions for moving around Gopher menus. It's easy enough; she just uses arrow keys to move to the directory and presses Enter/Return, and a new menu of options appears. When she finishes reading the Help screen, she presses "u" to go "up" to the original Main Menu. She uses her arrow keys to move to the directory labeled "Map of the Library." She presses Enter/Return until the map is on her screen. The map is a large document, and she decides (rather than reading it all on-line) to get a copy through e-mail and read it when she has more time off-line. To do this, she presses the "m" key. This is what she sees on her screen.

```
  Map of the AskERIC Virtual Library   (updated 1/16/95)      (81k)1%

+--------------------------------------------------------------------+
                          Map of the Library
                          Updated: 1/16/95
1. News and Information about ERIC and AskERIC/
              1. The AskERIC Service for Educators.
+ --------Map of the AskERIC Virtual Library (updated 1/16/95)-------- +
|                                                                    |
| Mail current document to:                                          |
|                                                                    |
|---------------------------------------                             |
| [Help: ^-][Cancel: ^G]                                             |
|                                                                    |
+ ------------------------------------------------------------------ +

              2. Map of the AskERIC Virtual Library (updated 9/16/95).
              3. Search AskERIC Menu Items <?>
4. AskERIC Toolbox (under construction)/
+ ------------------------------------------------------------------- +

        [Help: ?]    [Exit: u]    [PageDown: Space]
```

Ms. Reyes types her full Internet address, <Reyes@intercom.com>, and presses Enter/Return, and in less than one second the 31-page "Map of the AskERIC Virtual Library" is mailed to her electronic mailbox located on her local INTERCOM host network!

Now it's time to quit her first five-minute Gopher session, go get the map in her electronic mailbox, and read it more carefully. She quits the Gopher program by pressing "q," then types "Mail" and pulls the map into her home computer from the host network of INTERCOM through a process called "downloading." (We discuss downloading and uploading in a later section of this guide, "Saving Precious Time on the Internet.") After she disconnects from INTERCOM's host computer, she opens the map document with her word processor and prints it out. Once off-line, Ms. Reyes pages through the map and surveys all the ERIC resources that she can obtain instantly through e-mail.

ERIC's array of information resources is truly amazing. Paging through the ERIC map, Ms. Reyes finds seven different types of resources: ERIC Infoguides, curriculum units and lesson plans, ERIC Digests, the AskERIC Service, parent involvement resources, professional discussion groups, and class-to-class partnering resources.

"ERIC Infoguides" are compiled by specialists at the 16 ERIC clearinghouses. These guides cover a huge range of topics from cooperative learning, multicultural education, and all the subject areas Ms. Reyes teaches her students, including a particular interest of hers, parent involvement. Most important, the ERIC InfoGuides give an overview of the Internet resources available on a particular topic, with contact information for the particular clearinghouse that specializes in that issue, including their free "800" phone number and the contact address (both regular mail and e-mail). Each InfoGuide concludes with an annotated listing of ERIC documents (many of them free or low cost) that can be obtained directly from that clearinghouse.

Another resource is a listing of more than 1,000 teacher-tested curriculum units and lesson plans. Gopher will search through them according to keywords Ms. Reyes supplies and then gather the ones that fit her criteria into a customized menu so she can review them for adaptation to the realities of her own classroom. The more than 1,200 ERIC Digests are still another resource. The digests are two- to four-page state-of-the-art summaries for classroom practitioners of the latest educational research, written by world authorities who have been commissioned by ERIC. These too can be searched through by keywords. (Ms. Reyes's computer coordinator refreshed her memory on how to use Boolean logical expressions such as AND and OR to refine her searches.) Gopher gathers the appropriate digests into a single menu so each one can be examined for its usefulness.

The AskERIC Service is like an electronic reference librarian for K-12 teachers. AskERIC is an Internet-based question-answering service for teachers, library media specialists, and administrators. Anyone involved with K-12 education can send an e-mail message to AskERIC at `askeric@ericir.syr.edu`. Drawing on the extensive resources of the ERIC system, AskERIC staff will respond with an answer within 48 working hours. Educators may have questions about primary and secondary education, learning, teaching, information technology, or educational administration.

Numerous menu items hold a wealth of material on the vital topic of parent involvement, especially the directory for the National Parent Information Network. Along with a weekly bulletin on parental involvement, this directory provides information on "PARENTS AskERIC," a new ERIC service for parents looking for information to facilitate their children's developmental and educational experiences.

Professional discussion groups are listed. One directory, "Education LISTSERVs Archives," itemized a number of LISTSERVs devoted to discussion between education professionals on a variety of topics. By subscribing to these LISTSERVs, a teacher can enter into dialogue with like-minded educators focused on a single topic.

As Ms. Reyes explored the discussion among educators that had been stored in the archives for INCLASS, a forum for teachers using the Internet in their classrooms, she learned of another LISTSERV that seemed particularly exciting. IECC, for "Intercultural Email Classroom Connections," is devoted to making team-teaching partnerships based on shared curricular projects between distant educators at the same grade level and with common interests.

With so many resources to explore, Ms. Reyes decides to plan her next Gopher sessions; after all, the faster she can get on-line, collect material from the Internet, and then get off-line, the more likely her Internet connect costs will be minimal. She decides to explore the ERIC Gopher as outlined. In other words, she will start by exploring the first three options, which have to do with collecting information resources, and then she will investigate the "people connections" by using e-mail both to subscribe to LISTSERVs and to take advantage of AskERIC and PARENTS AskERIC.

Exploring the "Information Connection"

Ms. Reyes logs on to the INTERCOM host computer and types `gopher ericir.syr.edu` and immediately is transferred to the computer at Syracuse University that runs the ERIC Gopher. She selects the directory for "AskERIC InfoGuides," presses Enter/Return, and a new menu appears on her screen.

```
                       AskERIC InfoGuides

  —> 1. New - Fall 1994 AskERIC Infoguides/
      2. AskERIC InfoGuides on Library Technology (12/2/94)/
      3. Search AskERIC InfoGuides <?>
      4. AIDS Education
      5. African History - 1
      6. African History - 2
      7. American History
      8. Anthropology
      9. Arts Therapy
     10. Astronomy
     11. Authentic Assessment
     12. Business Information
     13. Business and Economics
     14. Central and South American Indians
     15. Chemistry
     16. Chemistry for Kids
     17. Child Abuse
     18. Children's Literature


   Press ? for Help, q to Quit, u to go up a menu    Page: 1/4
```

Ms. Reyes examines each InfoGuide, as she did in her first Gopher session, by using the arrow keys to move to interesting titles and pressing

Enter/Return; for each of the InfoGuides that seems relevant to her interests, she presses the "m" key (for "mail") and electronically sends it from Syracuse University back to her mailbox on the INTERCOM host computer. In this fashion, she gathers InfoGuides on parent involvement; on all the subject areas she teaches her fifth graders, including mathematics and science, language arts, social studies and the creative arts; on approaches to teaching, such as multicultural education and cooperative learning; and on how to better serve students with special needs in her classroom.

Next, Ms. Reyes uses the "u" key to move back "up" to the Main Menu of the ERIC Gopher, and selects the directory called Lesson Plans. She is presented a new menu of 16 directories, but she remembers from studying the ERIC Map earlier that under these 16 directories there are more than 1,000 teacher-tested curriculum units and lesson plans. These are far too many resources to explore individually, so she selects the first option, Search AskERIC Lesson Plans <?>, and is presented with this screen.

```
                        Lesson Plans

   —> 1.  Search AskERIC Lesson Plans ?
       2.  Astronomy: Curriculum Unit for Intermediate Elem. Students/
       3.  CNN Newsroom Daily Lesson Plans/
       4.  The Discovery Networks' Educator Guide/

+ ———————————— Search AskERIC Lesson Plans——————————+
|                                                        |
| Words to search for                                    |
|                                                        |
|————————————————————————————                           |
|                                                        |
| [Help: ^-][Cancel: ^G]                                 |
+————————————————————————————————————————————+

       13. Social Studies/
       14. Units from the Minn. Valley National Wildlife Reserve/
       15. Misc. Lesson Plans & Curriculum Units (from StemNet)/
       16. Television and Violence (from SchoolNet)/
```

Since Ms. Reyes is planning a curriculum unit on the theme of exploration, she types in this word for Gopher to "go for" any of the 1,000 lesson plans and units that mention that word. In seconds, Gopher presents her with a customized menu listing all these lesson plans and units. Here is the first of six screens filled with potentially useful teaching ideas.

```
            Search AskERIC Lesson Plans: exploration

  —>1.  Mod5cont.txt
     2.  Art History and creating masks (K-8)
     3.  I'm "Inclined" to See Exploration", studying sphere motion
         (9-12)
     4.  Stress Effect of Feelings (3)
     5.  Introduction
     6.  Exploring seeds in fruit (1-3)
     7.  1/24/95+ Exploring Space
     8.  "Potential & Kinetic Energy"
     9.  Contents.txt
    10.  CD Rom
    11.  Studying "Newton's Laws", Exploration & Application (9-12)
    12.  Math - Index
    13.  Mod5secB.txt
    14.  Learning about "Probes", Exploration & Application (8-12)
    15.  mini-lesson on family ties with history (7-12)
    16.  Geography, Your state and climate (6-12)
    17.  Cultural Awareness Activity (4-9)
    18.  "Mirror Image Exploration", study of reflected light (9-12)


     Press ? for Help, q to Quit, u to go up a menu    Page: 1/6
```

Ms. Reyes browses through these lesson plans, looking for ones that are appropriate for her thematic unit. She finds dozens of teaching ideas for every subject area (language arts, math and science, social studies, and creative arts) each of which centers on some aspect of her unifying concept of "exploration." Once again, she electronically mails her selections back to her mailbox by pressing "m".

Using the "u" key to move back "up" to the Main Menu, Ms. Reyes next explores the directory called "ERIC Digests," where she does a search for "multicultural education" and "cooperative learning." Gopher searches through the more than 1,200 invaluable two-page state-of-the-art summaries for the ones that deal with these topics and presents her with another customized menu. She mails several digests back to her mailbox at INTERCOM where she will collect them later.

Moving back up to the Main Menu, Ms. Reyes now selects the directory for "Education Listservs Archives." She reads on her screen:

```
                  Education Listservs Archives

      —> 1.  BigSix/
          2.  ECENET-L/
          3.  EDNET-List/
          4.  EDPOLYAN-List/
          5.  EDTECH/
          6.  Education Policy Analysis Archives/
          7.  HS-COMPUTING/
          8.  Higher Education Processes Conferences Archive/
          9.  INCLASS/
         10.  ISED-L/
         11.  ISLMA-List/
         12.  K12ADMIN-List/
         13.  K12Pals/
         14.  KIDSPHERE-List/
         15.  LM_NET/
         16.  MIDDLE-L/
         17.  REGGIO-L/
         18.  SAC-List/


      Press ? for Help, q to Quit, u to go up a menu    Page: 1/1
```

The school district's computer coordinator had told Ms. Reyes that LISTSERVs can be forums where she can share ideas and resources with other teachers from around the world. Also, they serve as "partner teacher clearinghouses" that help match up teachers to work on common class-to-class projects over the Internet. But she is not certain which ones she should join to begin with. In this menu of directories, she can browse through recent exchanges on each LISTSERV *before* subscribing. She decides that the EDNET discussion group talks about many of the issues she is interested in herself, and she makes a note of the *subscription address* and the *participation address* for this LISTSERV. As for a "partner teacher clearinghouse" LISTSERV, she makes note of both the subscription and participation addresses for the K12PALS LISTSERV as well.

Finally, she explores the Gopher menu that is devoted to parent involvement issues. First, she returns to the Main Menu and selects "Other Education Resources." There she is given another menu, where she selects "National Parent Information Network." Here is the menu she then sees.

```
       National Parent Information Network

  --> 1. NPIN Now Available on WWW
      2. Welcome to the NATIONAL PARENT INFORMATION NETWORK
      3. Parent News (updated weekly)/
      4. Short Items Especially for Parents/
      5. PARENTS AskERIC/
      6. Ideas for Community Programs and Activities/
      7. The Market Place/
      8. Resources for Parent Educators/
      9. ERIC Digests/
     10. ERIC Bibliographies/
     11. About NPIN and ERIC/


   Press ? for Help, q to Quit, u to go up a menu    Page: 1/1
```

While Ms. Reyes finds many resources helpful as she explores this directory, she is especially intrigued by the information she finds under "PARENTS AskERIC" and "Parent News (updated weekly)." PARENTS AskERIC is a question-answering service sponsored by ERIC on topics especially pertinent to child development, child care, parenting, and child rearing. Any parent who sends an e-mail question to the Internet address

askeric@ericir.syr.edu

will receive an answer from an ERIC specialist within 48 hours. The AskERIC Service, Ms. Reyes learns, has been available since 1992 and handles 350 queries a day, mostly from teachers with questions about primary and secondary education, learning, teaching, information technology, or educational administration. In the last year, the AskERIC service has expanded to include specialists who work exclusively with parents who are looking for information to facilitate their children's developmental and educational experiences.

The *Parent News* directory contains both the latest issue and all the back issues of a weekly newsletter with information pertinent to parental concerns. Ms. Reyes knows that she will want to return to the Gopher of the National Parent Information Network often, but she will want to read *Parent News* every week. Because she doesn't want to have to page through so many levels of menus every time she logs on, she moves to the *Parent News* directory and, following the suggestion of her local computer coordinator, presses the capital letter "A" (for "Add a bookmark for this entire Menu"), followed by Enter/Return. Next, she presses the lowercase letter "a" (for "add a bookmark for this particular menu item"). Finally, she presses the letter "v" (for "view your bookmarks"), and she sees her first customized menu of bookmarks.

```
                            Bookmarks

 —> 1.  National Parent Information Network
    2.  Parent News (updated weekly)/


      Press ? for Help, q to Quit, u to go up a menu Page: 1/1
```

In the coming weeks, she will add many more of her favorite directories to this "bookmark" menu, which is stored on her host computer at INTERCOM. Anytime she wants to skip to one of these favorite items, she will simply press "v" to View the bookmarks instantly.

Ms. Reyes is now ready to quit the ERIC Gopher at Syracuse University, and presses "q" for "quit." She quickly gathers all the e-mail that was waiting for her back at her INTERCOM mailbox, pulls it into her home computer (see the section "Downloading and Uploading," below), and then logs off. As she will discover later after printing them out off-line and reading them, in 30 minutes she has collected many important resources.

Exploring the "People Connection"

In the next days, Ms. Reyes will learn just how powerful a tool the Internet can be for making *personal* connections with other parents and teachers, aside from its clear value as an *information*-gathering resource. In her role as a teacher, she took advantage of AskERIC's question-answering service by sending a query to `askeric@ericir.syr.edu`. She wrote an e-mail message asking about cooperative learning techniques and how they can be used to reduce prejudice in classrooms, and received an answer when she checked her e-mail the next day. In her capacity as a parent, she wrote another e-mail query about how parents of secondary school students can confront the specter of drug abuse: she quickly received a list of useful resources from an ERIC specialist on parent issues, well before the promised 48-hour deadline.

Ms. Reyes also joined two LISTSERVs, ECENET-L (a forum for educators and parents concerned with early childhood and elementary education) and IECC (the "partnering" service for teachers and students). Every LISTSERV has two addresses: a subscription address and a participation address. The subscription address for ECENET-L is

`LISTSERV@vmd.cso.uiuc.edu`

and the participation address is

`ECENET-L@vmd.cso.uiuc.edu`

To subscribe, Ms. Reyes sent a single message to the subscription address that contained only the words "subscribe ECENET-L Olga Reyes." Similarly, the subscription address for IECC is

`IECC-REQUEST@stolaf.edu`

and the participation address is

`IECC@stolaf.edu`

To subscribe to IECC, she sent a message to the subscription address that said only "subscribe IECC Olga Reyes."

Once she subscribed, Ms. Reyes began to receive e-mail from each LISTSERV. She could see immediately that each provided a very different kind of forum. On ECENET-L, she heard from elementary school educators from around the world on a variety of topics relating to the theory and the practicalities of teaching, including one of her most central concerns, parent involvement. Elementary-level teachers, parents, and university professors all discussed issues of common interest on an equal footing. Her e-mail reactions to the discussion topics were encouraged with spirited replies.

When she read IECC, she sensed immediately that here the ground rules were completely different. The entire purpose of IECC is to make class-to-class collaborations. Therefore, in IECC, Ms. Reyes read announcements from teachers about projects they were inviting another teacher to join. Subscribers to IECC were expected to contact anyone they were interested in working with *directly* at their personal e-mail address, so as not to clutter the LISTSERV with extraneous e-mail messages "closing a deal" between partner teachers.

Ms. Reyes sent a short message describing the explorations theme unit that she was planning, inviting another teacher to join her. She received an answer from a teacher in another country, and they began corresponding regularly as they coordinated activities between their classes around that theme. Eventually both classes compared the early colonial history of both countries, with a special focus on the impact of the arrival of European settlers on indigenous peoples and the social costs of economic expansion. By the end of the marking period, their classes were drawing connections between their joint study of earlier explorations and complex contemporary issues, such as the social implications of diverting economic resources toward space exploration.

Saving Precious Time on the Internet

All teachers know that the one of their most precious resources is time, something that no parent has enough of. In the first blush of excitement over exploring networked resources, it is important to remember that a major goal should be to spend *as little time as possible* connected to the Internet. One clear reason is to keep costs down; Internet service providers bill for a flat monthly rate with an additional "connect time" charge. (Another reason is that the Internet is fascinating terrain that can lure new users away from other important responsibilities!) Here we provide some tips on how to get the most out of each hour you spend on the Internet.

DOWNLOADING AND UPLOADING: PLANNING SEQUENCED INTERNET SESSIONS

Using your "connect-time" efficiently means planning and sequencing your Internet sessions to take advantage of off-line time for reading over information you have gathered earlier and for preparing e-mail responses. Downloading and uploading are two of your most important vehicles for accomplishing this goal.

As you explore the Internet, you will find information of many types, and you will mail these documents back to your personal mailbox on your local service provider.[4] But that information is still not "yours," since it remains on the host computer, not in your personal computer. Downloading is the process of moving the document from your mailbox on a local host computer to your own personal computer at work or at home. The term originated in the idea of "pulling down" information from a larger computer to a smaller computer. Downloading is a way for you to transfer a document into your own computer at a rate of at least 72,000 to 1,728,000 letters per *minute*, faster than most people can read, so that then you can examine the document at your leisure without running up a bill. It is not at all difficult, and you can learn the specifics of downloading by following along in the manual that came with your telecommunications software program.

One of the most common ways of downloading is "capturing."[5] While connected to your Internet service provider, you follow the host computer's commands for reading your mail. You notice a document you want to capture. If the document is long and you decide to read it while connected to your host computer, you are running up costly connect-time charges. A better idea is to quickly download the document to your own computer, disconnect from the host computer, and read it on your own time.

At this point, while reading your mail, you need to prepare your home computer to receive that document. You use the menu of your telecommunications software program to find the command for "capturing," "receiving text," or "opening a buffer"—the exact words will vary for each program. When you select the "capture" command, the program will ask you to give a name to the file you are about to create on your hard disk or floppy disk. Choose a name that describes the document you are about to capture. Once this "capture" file is opened, *everything that moves across your screen will be saved there.* Now you can page through the document in your mailbox, knowing that it is being collected on your own computer as you do so. When you are finished, you use a command from your telecommunications software program to close the "capture" file. At this point, you can disconnect from the host computer and exit your telecommunications software program. To read the document you have just captured (or even print it out), start your word processor and simply open the "capture file" that you created minutes before.

We have discussed how to get e-mail efficiently; what about sending e-mail? Again, it is extremely inefficient and costly to type your e-mail messages while on-line, even for a good typist. Like a typewriter, on-line typing usually allows you to correct mistakes only by backspacing, which means that typing while on-line is good only for short responses to messages you find in your mailbox. A better idea is to prepare e-mail messages on your personal computer with a word processor *before* you log on to your host computer and then send the polished message when you make your next on-line connection. In a way, uploading provides you with a way to "type" on-line automatically at a speed of at least 72,000 to 1,728,000 letters per minute, without a single mistake.

Uploading is a similar process to downloading, but in reverse. The term comes from the idea of transferring a document "up" to a larger computer from a personal computer. The first step in uploading is to write your message with your word processor. Then you must save it in a special way. Find the menu item for "saving" in your word processor and look for a command that says "save as ASCII," "save as a text file," or, with WordPerfect for MS-DOS computers, use the "DOS In/Out" command, Control-F5. Give the message a special "filename" you won't forget. Then exit your word processor, start up your telecommunications software program, and dial the number of your Internet service provider's host computer.

Once you log on, go to the mail section of your host computer and prepare the "electronic envelope" of your e-mail message just as you normally do—that is, with the correct Internet address of your correspondent. You are preparing the host computer to receive the message you wrote a few moments earlier. Once the "envelope" is ready, use the menu of your telecommunications software program to find the command for "transferring a file" or "sending a file." Your program will ask you for the name of the file that you want to transfer or send; type in the exact name of the message you prepared. Once you have done this, you will see your message *automatically* "typed" into the e-mail envelope, like a player piano moving the keys to make a melody. When you message finishes scrolling by on the screen, you can send the message as you normally would if you had typed it yourself on-line.

Thus, learning to use networking efficiently means thinking of *pairs* of Internet sessions; simply put, two sessions are better than one. In the first of your sessions, gather resources using Gopher, World Wide Web, or another Internet information displayer, then download them from the host computer to your personal computer, along with any other e-mail correspondence and LISTSERV messages you want to respond to. Disconnect and read them *off-line,* and then write e-mail responses at your leisure. Finally, in the second of your sessions, log on, upload the e-mail messages you have just written, and disconnect. The next time you log on, you are likely to have answers to your e-mail message. You then can repeat the cycle of downloading information and e-mail messages, responding off-line, and uploading your replies.

E-MAIL AND LISTSERV MANAGEMENT TECHNIQUES

You probably will use e-mail more than any other communication tool. There is a saying "Write a letter, get a letter" which certainly holds true for e-mail, as well; but if you subscribe to a LISTSERV, the adage should be changed to "Write a letter, get plenty of letters." Your first rule of thumb should be never to use your electronic mailbox as a place to store e-mail. Download every e-mail that you want to keep and then delete it. This also makes good economic sense because most Internet service providers will charge you extra when you exceed your personal storage limit.

While LISTSERVs may be a wonderful resource for meeting and dialoguing with parents, educators, and students who share common interests, an active LISTSERV will clutter up your electronic mailbox quickly. This is because even after you disconnect from your host computer, other members of the LISTSERV are constantly sending messages that arrive in your mailbox at any hour of the day or night. Once they arrive, the messages are stored in your mailbox by chronological order; even if you subscribe to just a few LISTSERVs, reading through your e-mail can become like trying to play poker with several different decks of cards all shuffled together.

There are ways to avoid this frustrating aspect of LISTSERVs. One absolutely essential step is to *keep* the first welcoming message that comes to your mailbox when you initially subscribe to a particular LISTSERV. This message contains such vital information as how to:

- "Unsubscribe." (Nothing is more maddening than to be unable to quit a LISTSERV, and to have to keep deleting messages you no longer want.)
- "Stop delivery" if you go away on vacation or will be unable to log on to your host computer for any length of time.
- Arrange to have a "Digest" of all the messages for that particular LISTSERV delivered once a day in a single e-mail package.

We recommend using the Digest option if your LISTSERV is a high-volume discussion group. Your electronic mailbox stays neat, and it is easier to download all the messages at once.

Moreover, LISTSERV "netiquette" (or the basic rules of courtesy that have developed for exploring the Internet) include these key principles: (1) for subscribing, unsubscribing, stopping delivery, or arranging for delivery of Digests, use *only* the *subscription address* for that LISTSERV; (2) *never* use the *participation address* for any purpose other than communicating with your fellow LISTSERV members; and (3) if you are asking for a specific piece of information or advice that is more of personal than general interest, suggest to your fellow subscribers that they write you directly. As you will quickly discover, people who don't respect these basic principles will clutter your mailbox (and raise your e-mail storage bills) with irrelevant messages.

SEARCHING THE INTERNET

The third and final piece of advice we would offer for making your Internet sessions more efficient is learning how to use the various "search engines." Each Internet communication tool makes these search engines available to you for sifting through the multitude of information resources suddenly at your fingertips over the Internet. As we saw in the last scenario, Ms. Olga Reyes employed the simplest Gopher searching capability (which can be found wherever the symbol <?> is at the end of a Gopher menu item). Every Gopher on any computer network in the world also can be searched with the more sophisticated program called Veronica. While we cannot go into detail about Veronica here, studying an Internet handbook will pay big dividends in getting the most out of Gopher. Similarly, FTP, WAIS, and World Wide Web all have "search engines" that roam the world of the Internet and deliver customized collections of information resources back to the local host computer of your Internet service provider.

What If I Don't Have Full Internet Access?

Every Internet service provider provides e-mail as its most basic communication tool. If yours does not offer the full suite of other programs, including Gopher, World Wide Web, FTP, and Telnet, it may at least offer Telnet. With Telnet, you can connect from your own host computer to another host computer site that does allow you to run its Gopher, World Wide Web, and other Internet information-displaying programs. The Internet addresses of these sites changes constantly; check a recently revised Internet handbook or consult with your school district's computer coordinator for the current networks that offer this service to guest visitors. Out of respect for this generosity, another important rule of Internet "netiquette" is to choose the site that is geographically closest to your own Internet service provider; that way, you are tying up fewer computer networks while you are connected and are helping out with the "traffic problem" that can slow down the speed with which distant computer networks respond to everyone on the Internet at any particular moment in time.

If your service provider offers no-frills e-mail, you still can use a service called "Gophermail" to locate information on the Internet. To use this service, you send an e-mail message to a network that houses the Gophermail program with the computer address of a Gopher that you want to learn about. Gophermail automatically fetches the main menu of that particular Gopher and sends it to your mailbox. You can send Gophermail an e-mail request for any directory that you want to explore. While this takes longer than exploring the Gopher interactively, it does allow users with electronic mail–only accounts to find excellent resources, once they know where to begin their search. Again, Gophermail sites spring up constantly and change addresses; a recent Internet handbook and the advice of your school district's computer coordinator will be your best guides in locating the Gophermail site nearest you.

Internet Reference Books

To receive a monthly update on new Internet handbooks, you can request "The Unofficial Internet Booklist" by sending e-mail to `booklist-request@northcoast.com`. In the "Subject" line, include the word "archive" and in the body of the message the words "send booklist." To receive the Booklist automatically every month, send an e-mail message to `booklist-request@northcoast.com` and simply include the word "subscribe" in the subject line. The booklist is also available on the Web at

`http://www.northcoast.com/savetz/faqs.html`

Dern, D. (1994). *The Internet guide for new users.* New York: McGraw-Hill.

Estrada, S. (1994). *Connecting to the Internet: An O'Reilly buyer's guide.* Sebastopol, CA: O'Reilly and Associates.

Falk, B. (1994). *The Internet roadmap.* San Francisco: Sybex.

Gaffin, A. (1994). *Everybody's guide to the Internet.* Cambridge, MA: MIT Press.

Gilster, P. (1994). *The Internet navigator,* 2nd ed. New York: John Wiley and Sons.

Hahn, H. and Stout, R. (1994). *The Internet complete reference.* Berkeley, CA: Osborne/McGraw-Hill.

Hoffman, P. (1994). *The Internet.* Foster City, CA: International Data Group Company.

Krol, E. (1994). *The whole Internet,* 2nd ed. Sebastopol, CA: O'Reilly Associates.

Levine, J., and Baroudi, C. (1994). *The Internet for dummies,* 2nd ed. Foster City, CA: International Data Group Company.

Wiggins, R. (1995). *The Internet for everyone: A guide for users and providers.* Berkeley, CA: Osborne/McGraw-Hill.

Young, M. and Levine, J.R. (1994). *The Internet for Windows for dummies starter kit.* Foster City, CA: International Data Group Company.

Internet Resources for K–12 Education: Selected Annotated Listings

Introduction

Here we survey and annotate more than 800 human and curricular resources available to parents and educators using the Internet. The following sections are organized by subject areas:

1. Partner-Class Clearinghouses and Project-Oriented Activities
2. Multidisciplinary K-12 Internet Resources
3. Parent Involvement
4. Multicultural Education
5. Bilingualism and Second-Language Acquisition
6. Resources for Students with Special Learning Needs
7. Arts in Education
8. Language Arts
9. Social Studies
10. Mathematics and Science

Under each section, we list resources according to the Internet communication tool that can be used to access them, in the following order: (a) LISTSERVs and electronic mail–based services such as e-newsletters and e-journals; (b) USENET newsgroups; (c) Gophers and World Wide Web

(WWW) information displayers; (d) Telnet; (e) anonymous File Transfer Protocol (FTP); and (f) ERIC Clearinghouses and resources pertinent to each subject area.

Before presenting the resources by subject area, we will discuss some basic information which can assist parents and educators in getting started with each of the Internet communication tools.

LISTSERVS AND ELECTRONIC MAIL–BASED JOURNALS

For each LISTSERV provided, there are two addresses: a subscription address and a participation address. Use the subscription address *only* to subscribe, modify your subscription, or drop your subscription to the LISTSERV discussion group. Use the participation address *only* to contribute to the ongoing discussion.

LISTSERVs are managed by several different computer programs; among the principal ones are LISTSERV, Listproc, and Majordomo. Here are the key commands for each of these programs.

For subscribing:
LISTSERV and Listproc: `SUBSCRIBE listname Firstname Lastname`

Majordomo: `SUBSCRIBE listname youraddress@provider`

For unsubscribing:
LISTSERV and Listproc: `UNSUBSCRIBE listname`

Majordomo: `UNSUBSCRIBE listname youraddress @provider`

For daily digests (for high-volume groups)
LISTSERV: `SET listname DIGEST`

Listproc: `SET listname MAIL DIGEST`

Majordomo: `SUBSCRIBE listname-DIGEST`

`UNSUBSCRIBE listname`

(Note: With Majordomo, `youraddress@provider` means your full Internet e-mail address, including the location of the computer your service provider uses to store your e-mail. Also, you must subscribe to the digest *and* unsubscribe from the regular list in the same message; otherwise, you will receive both formats).

For e-mail newsletters and e-journals, you only need the subscription address, as these are by definition "read-only" LISTSERVs. To subscribe, follow the preceding directions and include and provide the "listname" of the e-journal where indicated.

USENET NEWSGROUPS

To participate in the educational USENET newsgroups, your service provider must subscribe to the "newsfeeds" for each newsgroup. Check to see which newsgroups are provided as part of your Internet service. If your service providers carries USENET newsgroups, the manual you received when you first subscribed will explain how to read and send messages to newsfeeds. If your service provider does not carry K-12 newsgroups, there is a World Wide Web site you can connect to that allows you to read and send messages to USENET newsgroups. (See "Multidisciplinary K-12 Internet Resources.")

GOPHERS AND WORLD WIDE WEB
INFORMATION DISPLAYERS

As with USENET newsgroups, your service provider may include Gopher and one of the World Wide Web "browsers" (such as Lynx, Mosaic, or NetScape) as part of your Internet account. If not, ask if your account provides Telnet. (See the next section.) If you have Telnet, you can connect with another service provider that does have the Gopher program or Web browser.

In the previous "Guide to the Internet," we have provided an overview of how to use Gophers. Here we simply wish to stress the importance of learning how to search Gophers, especially using the powerful Gopher search engine called Veronica. Skill in using Veronica comes with practice and reading the on-line directions provided wherever it appears on your Gopher menu. In addition, any Internet handbook will provide detailed instructions.

To use the World Wide Web, you will need a text-only browser (such as Lynx) or a graphical browser (such as Mosaic or NetScape). The graphical browsers require a high-speed modem; they work best with a Super VGA color monitor and, ideally, a speaker attached to your computer.

In our resources listings, we utilize the standard URL (Uniform Resource Locator) for Gophers, Web sites, Telnet sites, and FTP catalogs. We do so because this is exactly what you will type when you use Lynx or a graphical Web browser to access other computers on the Internet. Here are some examples:

```
gopher://ericir.syr.edu   -->ERIC Digests
                          -->Search ERIC Digests <?>


http://ericir.syr.edu
```

These are the URLs for the Gopher (with subdirectories once you arrive at the Gopher) and the Web site of ERIC, which you would type in using Lynx, Mosaic, or NetScape. If Gopher is part of your Internet account, you would type gopher ericir.syr.edu to activate your local Gopher to go to Syracuse University. (Note: Web sites use the URL prefix http:// and sometimes include the "tilde" symbol [~]. If your keyboard does not include this symbol, substitute the letters %7E wherever the ~ appears. The symbol --> indicates the name of the menu item or highlighted text you should choose to find a particular resource.)

TELNET

Telnet is a program that connects your service provider to another distant service provider on the Internet and allows you to run programs there that your service provider does not carry. Check with your school district's computer coordinator or a recent Internet handbook to find the sites where you can access Gopher or one of the Web browsers, as these change frequently. If you want to upgrade your electronic mail–only account and funds are short, investigate whether your service provider carries Telnet.

With Telnet, you are connecting to a remote computer, and often will be asked to login and give a password. Whenever you see a listing of a Telnet resource, always check to see what login and password are expected; also, be sure you note how to *quit* the remote service provider!

We list Telnet sites using the URL format:

`telnet://nptn.org` and login as `visitor`

ANONYMOUS FILE TRANSFER PROTOCOL (FTP)

The oldest of the Internet communication tools, FTP is the least "parent-" or "teacher-friendly." Our recommendation is to consult a recent Internet handbook for instructions on how to handle the intricacies of accessing FTP catalogs of Internet information resources.

"STAYING ON TOP" OF THE INTERNET

The Internet is constantly growing and changing. One of the key skills for using the Internet involves keeping abreast of latest developments, including new resources that are becoming available and Internet sites that have changed their electronic addresses.

The following LISTSERVs, Gophers, and Web sites are those we have found most useful for keeping up with changes and developments on the Internet.

C-EDRES: An extremely useful resource for parents and educators, C-EDRES evaluates educational LISTSERVs, Gophers, and Web sites, thus saving you the time and expense of reviewing each resource yourself. A searchable companion database, EDRES-DB, archives previous reviews of Internet sites. In addition, EDRES reviews are available (and searchable) on the ERIC Gopher and Web sites at `gopher://gopher.cua.edu` or `http://cspace.unb.ca/c-edres/`, respectively.

Subscriptions: `LISTSERV@unb.ca`

EVERYBODY'S INTERNET UPDATE: Published monthly by the Electronic Frontier Foundation, current and back copies are available at:

```
gopher://gopher.eff.org —>Net Info —>EFF Net Guide—>Updates
http://www.eff.org/pub/Net_info/EFF_Net_Guide/Updates/
```

To receive the updates automatically via e-mail, send a message to LISTSERV@eff.org, leaving the subject line blank, and including in the body of the message the words add net-guide-update.

"HotList of K-12 Internet School Sites": A World Wide Web site maintained by Internet chronicler Gleason Sackman, manager of the comprehensive Net-Happenings LISTSERV. (See below). This Web site is helpful for staying on top of useful K-12 Internet resources in North America and elsewhere.

```
http://toons.cc.ndsu.nodak.edu/~sackmann/k12.html
```

NEW-LIST: This essential service keeps track of new LISTSERVs as they appear on the Internet and sends descriptive information, including how to subscribe and participate. Also useful are the archives of this LISTSERV, which offer information on the focus and scope of existing LISTSERVs. These are accessible with Gopher at gopher://vm1.nodak.edu:7010/.

Subscriptions: LISTSERV@vm1.nodak.edu

NET-HAPPENINGS: Perhaps the most complete day-to-day update of Internet resources. However, "net-happenings" is a high volume LISTSERV that generates dozens of messages each day. The moderator, Gleason Sackman, has also created "sub-lists" to assist subscribers in customizing their participation. "Net-sites" is concerned with new Web sites, Gopher listings, and other Internet site updates. "Net-zines" focuses on electronic journals, magazines and newsletters. "Net-events" centers on upcoming conferences, workshops, and on-line courses. "Net-misc" provides updates of new publications, software, FAQs ("Frequently Asked Questions" fact sheets) and other Internet-related publications. You may want to use the Digest function for these LISTSERVs to manage the e-mail you will receive.

Subscriptions: MAJORDOMO@dsmail.internic.net

SCOUT-REPORT: A weekly digest of changes that are occurring in Internet resources, such as address changes of computers. The Report is available by subscribing to SCOUT-REPORT at

MAJORDOMO@is.internic.net

or it may be viewed at the Web site at

http://rs.internic.net/scout_report-index.html.

Partner-Class Clearinghouses and
Project-Oriented Activities

As we saw in the first pair of portraits in chapter 2, there are basically two approaches to making global learning networks a reality in classrooms: (1) establishing team-teaching partnerships between as few as two teachers who tailor-make their activities to suit the necessities of their students; or (2) creating wider collaborations encompassing many classes, often in several countries, all of which agree to work toward a common learning goal based on a shared project. Here we summarize a few of the most successful efforts to establish global learning networks in either—and often both—of these directions.

We have ranked each project in terms of the costs involved to participate:

- No-cost to low-cost projects: These e-mail-based projects can be reached through no-cost educational electronic bulletin board systems (BBSs) such as Global School Net, K12NET, or any service provider that offers low-cost level 1 connectivity (e-mail-based) to the Internet.
- Moderate-cost projects: These projects require an Internet service provider that offers level 2 connectivity, with a minimum of e-mail and Telnet services. In some cases, a project also may charge a subscription for participation.
- Higher-cost projects: These projects require level 2 or 3 connectivity and charge a higher fee for participation.

Academy One

The National Public Telecomputing Network works to establish "Free-Nets," which are public access computer systems based in communities around the world. Free-Nets share resources and newsgroups over the Internet, and one of their most active components is Academy One, a cluster of project-oriented activities for parents, educators, and students who have access to electronic mail. Recent projects include City Youth

On-line (middle school youth confronting urban problems), Save the Beaches (a comparative environmental activism project linking students in 22 schools in 5 countries), and the Health and Wellness Clinic (physicians around the world responding to students' questions on medical issues). Contact Linda Delzeit of Academy One at LINDA@nptn.org or explore the NPTN Web site at

http://www.nptn.org

BookRead Suite of LISTSERVs

BR_Match: The BookRead Matchmakers LISTSERV run by Western Carolina University as a spin-off of the BookRead project, which puts K-12 teachers and students in touch with authors. BR_Match extends this idea by arranging for partner-class exchanges between teachers who have students reading the same book. A low-cost project.

Subscriptions: LISTPROC@micronet.wcu.edu

Participation: BR_MATCH@micronet.wcu.edu

BR_Review: Devoted to student-authored book reviews, this LISTSERV also provides an archive of previous reviews.

Subscriptions: LISTPROC@micronet.wcu.edu

Participation: BR_REVIEW@micronet.wcu.edu

BR_Cafe: A virtual "coffee shop" (or better yet, milk bar) where students can discuss informally the books they are reading. In order to participate, a student must submit a review to the BR_Review LISTSERV as their "ticket of admission" to the BR_Cafe.

Subscriptions: LISTPROC@micronet.wcu.edu

Participation: BRCAFE@micronet.wcu.edu

DeweyWeb

Based on John Dewey's philosophy of active learning, this World Wide Web site is sponsored by Interactive Communications and Simulations (ICS) and the University of Michigan. It provides activities to encourage students' awareness of global education issues, ranging from simulations to interactions with youth in other countries. A low- to moderate-cost project.

http://ics.soe.umich.edu

ELDERS

A discussion list on intergenerational learning that also matches young people with elder mentors. A no- to low-cost project.

Subscriptions: LISTSERV@sjuvm.stjohns.edu

Participation: ELDERS@sjuvm.stjohns.edu

European Schools Project

Perhaps the most ambitious telecomputing project in Europe, ESP links 300 secondary schools in 21 countries. Based at the University of Amsterdam and codirected by professors Henk Sligte, Pauline Meijer, and Aad Nienhuis, ESP is best known for its "Teletrips," which are multilingual projects between partner schools focusing on a common curricular topic. Teletrips are designed to foster collaboration between domain-specific teachers, foreign language educators, and educational computer specialists. Thus, a multilingual and intercultural focus is maintained throughout all ESP activities, much as in Orillas and I*EARN projects (see below). Recent "teletrips" have centered on such controversial topics as "The Image of the Other" (immigration issues in a European context), "Pollution," "Stories on World War II," "Power Plants," and "Water Quality."

Resources, Information, and Support Centre:
RISC@esp.educ.uva.nl
http://www.educ.uva.nl/ESP
or gopher://gopher.educ.uva.nl

Global Learning Corporation's WorldClassroom

A commercial service that provides on-line support for its subscribers and detailed curriculum unit plans on social studies, language arts, mathematics, foreign languages, and current events, along with special activities, including guest speakers. A "Welcome Center" is provided where a personal host guides a new teacher through introductory activities. A building-level "site license," permitting all teachers in a building to participate, costs around $200 per semester. Participating teachers may log in to an 800 toll-free number, or they may access WorldClassroom via the Internet if they have Telnet capability. A higher-cost project.

Global Learning Corporation
P.O. Box 201361
Arlington, TX 76006, USA
Phone: 800-866-4452 (U.S. and Canada only)
817-792-3385 (all others)
Fax: 817-460-5483

For more information, send e-mail: GLOBAL@glc.dallas.tx.us, and for a free demonstration of the WorldClassroom, telnet to globall.glc.dallas.tx.us and login as demo4.

Global SchoolNet Foundation

Founded in 1985 by Al Rogers, the pioneer of educational telecomputing, the nonprofit Global SchoolNet Foundation offers an entire range of networking activities and continues to define the philosophy, design, culture, and content of educational networking on the Internet. Its stated goals include

the development of a low cost, community-based, distributed electronic data communications network owned by public agencies such as schools, libraries, cities, and other community service organizations, with the goal of providing all citizens equal and free or low-cost access to the basic tools of information access, retrieval, and transmission that are so important in our age of information.[1]

The following sections describe several of Global SchoolNet's most important current initiatives, which cover the entire range of no-cost to higher-cost projects.

FrEdMail: There are currently 200 FrEdMail electronic bulletin board systems (BBSs) located throughout the United States that receive e-mail from teachers during the day and call other FrEdMail systems at night to pass e-mail back and forth to its destination. Recently, the FrEdMail system became even more flexible by adding 12 "gateway" systems around the country that cut the costs of sending e-mail by routing it through the Internet.

Operating on simple Apple IIe/IIgs computers, these BBSs provide access for one user at a time at no cost for each local call to the BBS. Or, if the Apple II computer is equipped with a $350 Digicard, the BBSs can offer multiuser access for up to 500 people. In addition, FrEdMail is compatible with the Novalink Information Server for Macintosh. And for schools with their own computer address on the Internet, FrEdMail is adaptable to Bolt, Baranek and Newman's UNIX-based Copernicus Internet server, permitting the full range of Internet communication tools.

Aside from the teacher- and parent-friendly interface offered by FrEdMail, many users find its *content* the most attractive feature of the network. Organized according to menus, there are numerous class-to-class and multiclass projects, with carefully designed goals and clearly defined deadlines for activities. These projects can serve as models for teachers who wish to generate their own successful projects.

Global SCHLnet Newsgroup Service: Global SchoolNet Foundation also provides a USENET Newsgroup subscription service that includes all of its FrEdMail activities as a "newsgroup feed." Aside from the subscription fee, this requires an Internet service provider that offers the USENET newsgroup reader service.

For more information, contact `FRED@acme.fred.org` about arranging a SCHLnet Newsfeed directly to your own mail/newsgroup server.

HILITES LISTSERV: If your Internet service provider cannot provide direct access to our Global SCHLnet Newsgroups, you can subscribe to the Global SchoolNet Foundation's Projects LISTSERV.

Subscriptions: `FRED@acme.fred.org`

In the body of the message, include a line with the words SUBSCRIBE HILITES. For guidelines on developing your own project and having it posted on HILITES, include a line with the words SEND GUIDELINES. To submit your own project for posting on our International lists, send your complete project description, formatted according to our guidelines, to `CALL-IDEAS@acme.fred.org`. Once validated, it will be sent out around the world over the HILITES LISTSERV and the SCHLnet Newsgroup.

Workshops, On-line Courses and Curriculum Development: The Global SchoolNet Foundation currently conducts two teacher workshops:

- Hello Internet, conducted on-site or on-line, which introduces teachers to Internet resources useful to classroom learning applications. All current, up-to-date resources are covered.
- Managing Global Learning Projects, which equips teachers with the skills and resources to plan, organize, and conduct their own collaborative on-line learning projects.

In addition, it has created numerous curriculum guides and training aids for new users of the Internet, including "TeleSensations," a collection of over 100 classroom activities, and "Teachers 'n Telecommunications (T'nT)," a 15-hour workshop syllabus. The foundation also distributes various training videos and publishes a quarterly newsletter.

Send e-mail to `FRED@acme.fred.org` for more information, or visit the Global SchoolNet Foundation's Web page by pointing your browser to `http://gsn.org`.

Global Schoolhouse Project: The foundation is involved in an important research collaboration through its "Global Schoolhouse," a project funded in part by the National Science Foundation and supported by many local and national businesses. The project consists of connecting schools and students nationally and internationally using the Internet and modeling classroom applications of a variety of Internet tools and resources. Collaborative research is conducted using a variety of Internet tools, including live video conferences via Cornell's CU-SeeMe software, using Macintosh and PC (80386/80486) computers. Internet tools training is being pro-vided by the Clearinghouse for Networked Information Discovery and Retrieval. The live video image is transferred over the Internet or voice telephone circuits with audio being transported by phone or Maven software.

The GSH World Wide Web site can be accessed at:

http://gsn.org or http://www.aldea.com

For more information on Global Schoolhouse, contact Yvonne Marie Andres at ANDRESYV@cerf.net, or by fax at 619-931-5934 or phone at 619-433-3413.

I*EARN: International Education and Resource Network

The purpose of I*EARN (the International Education and Resource Network) is to enable elementary and secondary students to make a meaningful contribution to the health and welfare of the planet. Its coordinators explain, "We want to see students go beyond both simply being 'pen-pals' and working on strictly academic work to use telecom-munications in joint student projects designed to make a difference in the world as part of the educational process." I*EARN is expanding to additional international sites daily and now includes about 500 schools in over 20 countries.

I*EARN projects generally utilize three forms of interaction: (1) video-speaker telephones (low-cost, using regular telephone lines, slow-scan, black and white); (2) electronic mail; and (3) on-line conferencing exchanges.

Participants can join existing structured on-line projects or work with others internationally to create their own projects within the following subject areas: environment and science; arts and literature; social studies, economics, and politics; and interdisciplinary projects. Project facilitators provide on-line support for each project. Further, I*EARN uses extensive on-line conferencing as a means of creating "rooms" for project work. The contents of these rooms are shared automatically with all the international networks that are part of the Association for Progressive Computing, thus minimizing costs and maximizing involvement by students and teachers around the world. Examples of recent student projects include:

- *The Contemporary,* a student-run international news magazine. (See Portrait 8 in chapter 2.)
- *A Vision,* an award-winning literary journal.
- *Planetary Notions,* an environmental newsletter.
- *Liberty Bound,* a human rights newsletter.
- *ICARUS,* an ozone measurement project and newsletter.
- The Holocaust/Genocide Project and Newsletter. (See Portrait 5 in chapter 2.)
- The Rainforest Project.
- Support for children in Bosnia and Somalia. (See Portrait 1 in chapter 2.)
- Building wells for clean water in Nicaragua. (See Portrait 7 in chapter 2.)
- The Family Project, a cross-cultural comparison to promote intergenerational learning.

This is a moderate-cost project. For more information, contact Ed Gragert, I*EARN Director at `ED1@igc.apc.org` or Kristin Brown, projects coordinator, at `KRBROWWN@igc.apc.org`; or you can get additional information, in English and in Spanish, through Gopher at

```
gopher://gopher.iearn.org:7000 -->Education and Youth
-->International Education and Resource Network (I*EARN)
```

International Education and Resource Network (I*EARN)
345 Kear Street
Yorktown Heights, NY 10598
Phone: 914-962-5864

IECC—Intercultural Email Classroom Connections Lists

IECC was originally a single LISTSERV but has grown so rapidly (presently, with 2,000 participants in 30 countries) that is has subdivided into four LISTSERVs, which will be described separately. They are:

IECC	Intercultural Email Classroom Connections
IECC-PROJECTS	IECC Project Announcements
IECC-DISCUSSION	Discussion about Intercultural Exchanges
IECC-HE	IECC Projects in Higher Education

Each of these LISTSERVs is independent and has different goals; they may be subscribed to separately. A no- to low-cost project.

IECC: Intended for teachers seeking partner classrooms for international and cross-cultural electronic mail exchanges. This list is *not* for discussion or for people seeking individual pen pals.

> Subscriptions: `IECC-REQUEST@stolaf.edu`
>
> Participation: `IECC@stolaf.edu`

Once subscribed, teachers are encouraged to request, in an e-mail message to `IECC@stolaf.edu`, a K-12 partner classroom. Use a descriptive subject. For example:

> "Seeking Spanish-speaking 9th-grade classroom"
> or "Looking for 12 6th-grade students in Pakistan"

In the body of the message, be sure to include information about the local classroom and preferences for a partner classroom. IECC suggests giving the following details:

- Who you are, where you are
- How many students you have
- How many students you would like to connect with
- When you would like to connect
- Other special interests
- Desired country/culture (area within a country if appropriate)
- Desired language

This is a busy LISTSERV, so you may wish to subscribe to the DIGEST format for IECC. Send a message containing the word "subscribe" to: `IECC-DIGEST-REQUEST@stolaf.edu`

IECC-PROJECTS: An electronic mailing list where people may announce or request help with specific projects that involve e-mail, internationally or cross-culturally. Subscribers automatically receive IECC-SURVEYS which is devoted to student questionnaires on a variety of topics.

> Subscriptions: `IECC-PROJECTS-REQUEST@stolaf.edu`
> Participation: `IECC-PROJECTS@stolaf.edu`
> `IECC-SURVEYS@stolaf.edu`

IECC-DISCUSSION: Intended for general discussion about questions, issues, and observations in the Intercultural Email Classroom Connections.

> Subscriptions: `IECC-DISCUSSION-REQUEST@stolaf.edu`
> Participation: `IECC-DISCUSSION@stolaf.edu`

IECC-HE: The newest mailing list of the IECC suite of LISTSERVs intended for teachers seeking partner teachers in institutions of higher education for international classroom electronic mail exchanges.

> Subscriptions: `IECC-HE-REQUEST@stolaf.edu`
> Participation: `IECC-HE@stolaf.edu`

The IECC Gopher (updated daily and searchable) can be reached at `gopher://gopher.stolaf.edu` and its World Wide Web address is `http://www.stolaf.edu/network/iecc/`.

KIDLINK

This LISTSERV functions as a project announcement service that coordinates annual "KIDS" projects (KIDS-94, KIDS-95, etc.) for students 10 to 15 years of age. A no- to low-cost project.

> Subscriptions: `LISTSERV@vm1.nodak.edu`
> Participation: `KIDLINK@vm1.nodak.edu`

Kidlink messages are archived on the Web at http://www.kid-link.org/kidlink/listmail.html.

An ongoing KIDLINK effort has been the Multicultural Calendar Project, available from telnet://kids.ccit.duq.edu (login as "gopher") or gopher://kids.ccit.duq.edu.

KIDSPHERE

The oldest of the Internet-based global learning networks, KIDSPHERE was formed by Robert Carlitz to provide a global network for the use of children and teachers in grades K-12. It is a very open forum. Parents and educators can expect discussion on a wide range of topics on every aspect of education, from the specifics of special projects to more expansive explorations of educational philosophy. KIDSPHERE is a moderated list (meaning that offensive or irrelevant messages are intercepted by a moderator). Most discussion takes place between teachers, but parents and students often appear. It is a very busy LISTSERV, and subscribers should be careful to "unsubscribe" if they will be away for significant periods. A no- to low-cost project.

Subscriptions: KIDSPHERE-REQUEST@vms.cis.pitt.edu

Participation: KIDSPHERE@vms.cis.pitt.edu

K12NET

An alternative for schools without direct Internet access for joining a low-cost yet far-ranging global learning network. In K12NET, schools set up their own electronic bulletin board systems that store messages from students and teachers during the day and at night call up the closest K12NET BBS, passing e-mail back and forth. This system permits communication with parents, teachers, and students in many countries, especially nations where direct Internet connections are not readily available. Though K12NET is not on the Internet itself, its e-mail is passed to and from the Internet, thus opening up e-mail-based services such as Gophermail. A no- to low-cost project. For more information:

gopher://rain.psg.com/11/schools/k12net

Orillas

De Orilla a Orilla (Spanish for "From shore to shore") is a teacher-researcher project that has concentrated on documenting promising practices for intercultural and multilingual learning over global learning networks. Since 1985, Orillas has been an international networking project to promote team-teaching partnerships and group projects designed to effect social change.

Research on Orillas has validated projects (using both qualitative and quantitative research designs) that have raised self-esteem among Puerto Rican students in the United States involved in partner-class activities with schools in Puerto Rico, as well as projects that promote intergenerational literacy learning and parental involvement in global learning networks.[2] As a result of this research, Orillas has published articles recommending promising networking practices.[3]

Parents or teachers should contact Orillas if they are interested in participating in learning projects over global learning networks that

1. Promote bilingualism and learning another language.
2. Validate traditional forms of knowledge, such as the oral traditions associated with folklore, folk games, proverbs, and learning from elders through oral history.
3. Advance antiracist multicultural education.
4. Develop new approaches to teaching and learning that encourage students, parents, and communities to take action for social justice and environmental improvement.

Orillas operates over various networks; thus, cost for participation ranges from no-cost to low- and moderate-cost, depending on the type of service provider available to a parent or teacher.

Contact the co-directors Kristin Brown at `KRBROWN@igc.apc.org`, Enid Figueroa at `EFIGUERO@orillas.upr.fred.org`, or Dennis Sayers at `SAYERS@acfcluster.nyu.edu` for more information. The Orillas Web page is located at `http://oeonline.com/~globalvp//gvpmenu.html`.

TCHR-SL

For teachers of learners of English as a Second or Foreign Language (ESL or EFL), this partner-class clearinghouse is based at Latrobe University in

Australia. By subscribing to this LISTSERV, ESL/EFL teachers can find teacher collaborators for curriculum projects in countries around the world through which their students can perfect their English language skills while engaging in intercultural learning. To participate, send a blank e-mail message to `ANNOUNCE-SL@latrobe.edu.au`.

TERC

TERC pioneered in the development of educational networking in K-12 with its creation of the National Geographic Kids Network (elementary and middle-grades science curriculum) and Global Lab, a worldwide network of teachers and students involved in collaborative environmental investigations. Two key projects currently under way include LabNet, an electronic community of K-12 science and math educators dedicated to supporting and encouraging inquiry-oriented, project-based learning; and Testbed for Telecollaboration, which is building on TERC's work in curriculum and software development by supporting teachers and students in collaborative investigations, especially in collecting, sharing, analyzing, and visualizing data. Participating Testbed projects use the Alice Network Software, a powerful set of data analysis tools developed by TERC.

Other current work includes Investigations, an elementary mathematics curriculum; Tabletop, a computer tool for logic, information, graphing, and data analysis; and CamMotion, a new combination of video and computer technologies. These are just a few of more than 30 projects. TERC also runs a Gopher at `gopher://hub.terc.edu` and a Web site at `http://hub.terc.edu`.

These are moderate- to higher-cost projects. For more information on the many projects sponsored by TERC and to subscribe to the TERC newsletter *Hands On!*, contact

TERC Communications
2067 Massachusets Avenue
Cambridge, MA 02140
Phone: 617/547-0430
Fax: 617/349-3535
e-mail: `COMMUNICATIONS@terc.edu`

TUTOR-L and TUTOR-ANNOUNCE-L

Complementary LISTSERVs with the ambitious goal of serving as a clearinghouse to promote "global tutoring," that is, the matching of tutors with learners interested in specific subject matter. TUTOR-L is an unmoderated discussion group, while TUTOR-ANNOUNCE-L is an organizational conference for coordinating tutoring matches.

Subscriptions:	`LISTSERV@edie.cprost.sfu.ca`
Participation:	`TUTOR-L@edie.cprost.sfu.ca`
	`TUTOR-ANNOUNCE-L@edie.cprost.sfu.ca`

Multidisciplinary K–12 Internet Resources

E-JOURNALS AND NEWSLETTERS

CANJEDADPOL-L: The *Canadian Journal of Educational Administration and Policy* is a peer-reviewed e-journal providing educational research of interest to the general public and researchers alike.

Subscriptions: `LISTPROC@cc.umanitoba.ca`

EDPOLYAR: Education Policy Analysis Archives is a professional peer-reviewed e-journal publishing timely articles on educational research.

Subscriptions: `LISTSERV@asu.edu`

Back issues are archived at

`gopher://info.asu.edu`
`http://info.asu.edu/asu-cwis/epaa/welcome.html`
`ftp://info.asu.edu/pub/cwis/epaa`

EDUPAGE: A summary of news on education and information technology, offered three times weekly by Educom.

Subscriptions: `LISTPROC@educom.edu`

LEARNING: E-newsletter of the National Research Center on Student Learning (NRCSL), available semiannually by Gopher or e-mail. Focuses on educational reform and research-based teaching methods. Send e-mail requests to `LEARNING@vms.cis.pitt.edu` and ask for an index of available issues.

`gopher://gopher.pitt.edu ——>News releases, newsletters,`
`and newspapers/ ——>Learning Research and Development Center`

NOVAE: E-newsletter for teachers. To contribute or for further information, contact `C6460101@idptv.idbsu.edu` by e-mail.

> Subscriptions: Send e-mail with your name to
> `MELCHERT@raven.csrv.uidaho.edu`

THE ONLINE EDUCATOR: A monthly publication on using the Internet in educational settings. Send checks, money orders, or school purchase orders, and your e-mail address to:

> The Online Educator
> PO Box 251141
> West Bloomfield, MI 48325

Subscription costs for on-line version: one year, $12, two years, $20. Inquire for costs of print version.

RPTCRD: An essential service of the Education Commission of the States and the National Education Goals Panel, Report Card appears three times a week. A clipping service for education-related news, it summarizes articles in the *New York Times,* the *Wall Street Journal, Education Week,* and major dailies.

> Subscriptions: `LISTSERV@gwuvm.gwu.edu`

WESTERN CENTER NEWSLETTER: Available through the Northwest Regional Education Laboratory Gopher, this e-newsletter provides resources and discussion on the crucial issue of alcohol and drug abuse prevention among youth.

> `gopher://gopher.nwrel.org`

LISTSERVS

AERA LISTSERVs: The American Educational Researchers Association runs a suite of LISTSERVs organized according to its organization's divisions. They are

AERA-A: Administration
AERA-B: Curriculum Studies
AERA-C: Learning and Instruction
AERA-D: Measurement and Research Methodology
AERA-E: Counseling and Human Development
AERA-F: History and Historiography
AERA-G: Social Context of Education
AERA-H: School Evaluation and Program Development
AERA-I: Education in the Professions
AERA-J: Postsecondary Education
AERA-K: Teaching and Teacher Education

Subscription and participation addresses are provided for AERA-A to use as a model for subscribing to any of the AERA lists.

Subscriptions: `LISTSERV@asuvm.inre.asu.edu`
Participation: `AERA-A@asuvm.inre.asu.edu`

A related LISTSERV (but operating on a different server) is the new SIG-INNOVATIONS, the electronic forum for AERA's Special Interest Group (SIG) on Research on Instructional Innovations.

Subscriptions: `LISTPROC@lists.Colorado.edu`
Participation: `SIG-INNOVATIONS@lists.Colorado.edu`

AERA-MI: The discussion LISTSERV of the Standing Committee on the Role and Status of Minorities in Educational Research and Development.

Subscriptions: `LISTSERV@unb.ca`
Participation: `AERA-MI@unb.ca`

CACI: In an effort to open a dialogue in order to prevent censorship or the threat of complete denial of access to networked resources, "Children Accessing Controversial Information" LISTSERV provides a forum for teachers, parents, and students to discuss the challenges posed by free

Internet access for young people. Related information is archived at http://www.zen.org/~brendan/caci.html.

> Subscriptions: CACI-Request@cygnus.com
>
> Participation: CACI@cygnus.com

DEAD TEACHERS SOCIETY: A free-wheeling and far-ranging discussion on any educational topic.

> Subscriptions: LISTSERV@iubvm.ucs.indiana.edu
>
> Participation: DTS-L@iubvm.ucs.indiana.edu

ECENET-L: Forum for educators and parents concerned with education of children from birth to eight years of age.

> Subscriptions: LISTSERV@vmd.cso.uiuc.edu
>
> Participation: ECENET-L@vmd.cso.uiuc.edu

EDEQUITY: A forum for discussion between teachers, policymakers, parents, and equity practitioners who are concerned with attaining equity between men and women of all races in educational settings.

> Subscriptions: MAJORDOMO@confer.edc.org
>
> Participation: EDEQUITY@confer.edc.org

EDNET: One of the most active general education discussion groups.

> Subscriptions: LISTSERV@nic.umass.edu
>
> Participation: EDNET@nic.umass.edu

ERL-L: A discussion group centering on issues of educational research, sponsored by the American Educational Research Association.

> Subscriptions: LISTSERV@asuvm.inre.asu.edu
>
> Participation: ERL-L@asuvm.inre.asu.edu

INCLASS (Using the Internet in the Classroom): Sponsored by Canada's SchoolNet (see "Gophers," below) this forum centers on using the Internet for science teaching, but is rapidly branching out into other subject areas. A bilingual list, in English and French.

Subscriptions: LISTPROC@schoolnet.carleton.ca

Participation: INCLASS@schoolnet.carleton.ca

K12ADMIN: Run by the ERIC Clearinghouse on Information and Technology, this forum centers on issues of interest to K-12 school administrators.

Subscriptions: LISTSERV@suvm.syr.edu

Participation: K12ADMIN@suvm.syr.edu

MIDDLE-L: Forum for teachers in Middle Schools.

Subscriptions: LISTSERV@vmd.cso.uiuc.edu

Participation: MIDDLE-L@vmd.cso.uiuc.edu

MULTIAGE: A forum on multigrade and multiage learning.

Subscriptions: LISTPROC@services.dese.state.mo.us

Participation: MULTIAGE@services.dese.state.mo.us

NETWORK_NUGGETS-L: A discussion group on available Internet resources for all aspects of education.

Subscriptions: LISTSERV@cln.etc.bc.ca

Participation: NETWORK_NUGGETS-L@cln.etc.bc.ca

PRISON-L: A discussion group for those teaching in prisons.

Subscriptions: LISTSERV@listserv.dartmouth.edu

Participation: PRISON-L@listserv.dartmouth.edu

RPE-L: "Restructuring Public Education" discussion list established by AERA (see above).

Subscriptions: `LISTSERV@uhccvm.uhcc.hawaii.edu`

Participation: `RPE-L@uhccvm.uhcc.hawaii.edu`

SUPERK12: A forum sponsored by ERIC for promoting "high-bandwidth" K-12 Internet applications, such as Global SchoolHouse and CoVis.

Subscriptions: `LISTSERV@suvm.syr.edu`

Participation: `SUPERK12@suvm.syr.edu`

WWWEDU: A LISTSERV sponsored by the Corporation for Public Broadcasting and The Center for Networked Information Discovery and Retrieval (CNIDR) to encourage effective use of the World Wide Web in education.

Subscriptions: `LISTPROC@kudzu.cnidr.org`

Participation: `WWWEDU@kudzu.cnidr.org`

USENET NEWSGROUPS

`alt.history.what-if`	Imagining how history could have turned out differently.
`k12.ed.art`	Creative arts forum.
`k12.ed.comp.literacy`	Computer literacy forum.
`k12.ed.health-pe`	Health and physical education forum.
`k12.ed.life-skills`	Home economics and career education forum.
`k12.ed.math`	Mathematics curriculum forum.
`k12.ed.music`	Music and performing arts forum
`k12.ed.special`	Special education discussion group.
`k12.ed.science`	Science education forum. Recently creationism has been declared "off topic" by this newsgroup.
`k12.ed.soc-studies`	Social studies and history forum.

k12.ed.special K-12 Education for students with special needs.
k12.ed.tag K-12 Education for talented and gifted students.
k12.ed.tech Industrial arts and vocational education forum.
k12.chat.teacher General discussion between K-12 teachers.
k12.lang.art Forum for educators and future teachers to discuss language arts teaching.

GOPHERS

The "Best of the INTERNET for Educators": Maintained by Gene Glass of Arizona State University, editor of EDPOLYAR (see "E-journals," above) and manager of the American Educational Research Associations suite of LISTSERVs, this Gopher provides links with many Internet sites of interest to the education profession.

```
gopher://info.asu.edu/11/asu-cwis/education/other
```

Big Sky Telegraph Lesson Plans: Hundreds of lesson plans available in every subject area, with a link to the ERIC Gopher lesson plans.

```
gopher://bvsd.k12.co.us -Educational Resources -->Lesson
Plans -->Big Sky
```

CICnet (Committee on Institutional Cooperation) K-12 Education Collection of Select Internet Resources: Compilation of Internet curriculum resources with a special focus on "at-risk" students.

```
gopher://gopher.cic.net
```

Empire Internet Schoolhouse: A Gopher designed by NYSERNet like a school with subject-area departments and a library. Especially attractive for new users because of its straightforward design.

```
gopher://nysernet.org:3000
```

Gopher Jewels: Subject-area listings of Gopher sites devoted to educational resources and issues.

```
gopher://cwis.usc.edu -->Education and Research
```

I*EARN (The International Education and Resources Network): See description under "Partner-Class Clearinghouses and Project-Oriented Activities" and chapter 2.

```
gopher://gopher.igc.apc.org -->Education and Youth
-->I*EARN
```

International Society for Technology in Education (ISTE): Access to publications of and ordering information for this key professional organization for computer educators.

```
gopher://iste-gopher.uoregon.edu:70
```

Internet into the Curriculum: Evaluations of networking resources by teachers and teacher educators.

```
gopher://sjuvm.stjohns.edu -education and teaching
resources -->resources for K-12 teachers (Nebraska)
-->ideas for infusion into curriculum
```

Internic's K-12 Internet Resources: Extremely comprehensive listing of guides to K-12 networking, this Gopher site is a good place to check for novices and veterans alike. Contains most of the guides listed in the "Anonymous FTP" section, below, but with the ease of use and "previewing" capability of Gophers. See especially "Answers to Commonly asked Primary and Secondary School Internet User Questions, FYI 22," an essential guide from Internic.

```
gopher://is.internic/11/infoguide/resources/k-12
```

Library of Congress: Becoming one of the most important repositories of educational information on the Internet, especially for full-text listings and links to the approximately 700 e-books available here and on other Gophers.

```
gopher://marvel.loc.gov -->Global Electronic Library
-->Language, Linguistics, and Literature -Literature
-->ALEX: A Catalogue of Electronic Texts on the Internet
-->Browse ALEX
```

Maricopa Center for Learning: Complete listing of education resources in all content areas, with a special focus on using technology in the classroom.

```
gopher://tapeats.mcli.dist.maricopa.edu
```

The National School Network Testbed: Coordinated by Bolt Beranek and Newman Inc. (BBN), this site offers resources to help make networking a reality in today's schools. Its audience includes school districts, community organizations, state education agencies, technology developers, and private industry and business.

```
gopher://copernicus.bbn.com
```

Ontario Institute for Studies in Education (OISE) Gopher: Our favorite educational Gopher. Not only are complete resources available on every subject area, including the impressive DARE Directory on multicultural education, but many position papers are presented on the *issues* raised by global learning networks, including censorship and inequity of access to the Internet.

```
gopher://porpoise.oise.on.ca -->OISE's own collection of
On-line Educational Resources
```

Rice University Gopher system "Jughead": A very complete education Gopher with a "Jughead" utility that searches all the Gopher menu items at Rice.

```
gopher://chico.rice.edu -->Information by Subject Area
-->Select: Search All of RiceInfo by Title <jughead>
```

Scholastic Gopher: Archives lesson plans in all subject areas.

```
gopher://scholastic.com:2003 -->Scholastic Internet
Libraries
```

SITT Teacher Education Internet Server: Maintained by the Society for Information Technology and Teacher Education at the University of Virginia and University of Houston, this Gopher contains resources for teacher educators and both preservice and in-service teachers, as well as links to other Internet sites.

```
gopher://state.virginia.edu -->Teacher Education Informa-
tion Server
```

Subject-oriented Internet Guide: Organizes documents by numerous subject areas that detail and evaluate resources available over the Internet.

```
gopher://gopher.lib.umich.edu
```

TENET: Maintained by the Texas State Department of Education, long a pioneer in telecomputing, The Texas K-12 Gopher is a rich listing of resources for parents and teachers encompassing every content area.

```
gopher://gopher.tenet.edu
```

UIUC College of Education Learning Resource: A wealth of education-related resources, especially Internet project listings, in every subject area.

```
gopher://lynx.ed.uiuc.edu -->K-12 Learning Resources/
-->Educational Networking Projects/
```

U.S. Department of Education's Office of Educational Research and Improvement (OERI): Run by the Institutional Communications Network project (INET), this Gopher site provides access to the current status of federal funding programs, educational information, and other curricular resources, including software archives.

```
gopher://gopher.ed.gov
```

University of Massachusets Gopher: One of the earliest and best-stocked Gopher sites of curricular resources in every subject area, located at the home of the EdNet LISTSERV.

```
gopher://k12.ucs.umass.edu -->Telecommunications Projects
```

University of Oregon's Media Literacy Project: Devoted to educational issues raised by media literacy, for parents and educators.

```
gopher://interact.uoregon.edu -Institutes, Projects and
Centers -->Media Literacy
```

University of Virginia's Teacher Education Gopher: Devoted to issues of teacher education, mentoring, and the Internet, with Telnet links to other relevant interactive servers.

```
gopher://state.virginia.edu -->Teacher Education
Information Server (TEIS)
```

Violence In Schools: Devoted to providing resources on this issue, which affects the education of increasing numbers of students at every level of schooling, this Gopher is a service of the Ontario Ministry of Education and Training.

```
gopher://gopher.edu.gov.on.ca -->Schools ... -->Violence
Prevention
```

WORLD WIDE WEB (WWW)

AskERIC Web: This Web site is maintained by the ERIC Clearinghouse on Information and Technology. Along with many of the resources on the AskERIC Gopher, it features a multimedia slide show on ERIC.

```
http://eryx.syr.edu
```

Carrie's Crazy Quilt: A well-organized Web page especially attractive to parents, teachers, and students who are new users of the Internet.

http://www.mtjeff.com/~bodenst/page1.html

Children Now: A nonpartisan policy and advocacy organization for children. This Web site includes resources on children's health and family economic security.

http://www.dnai.com/~children

CNIDR, the Clearinghouse for Networked Information Discovery and Retrieval: Houses the Web version of a number of important networking initiatives: (1) Global Schoolhouse (see description under "Partner-Class Clearinghouses and Project-Oriented Activities"); (2) ARTSEDGE, (see description under "Arts in Education," "Gophers," below; (3) Janice's K12 Cyberspace Outpost, with Janice's RAVES (innovative Web pages submitted by teachers and students); and (4) EdWeb, maintained by Andy Carvin for the Corporation for Public Broadcasting, offering comprehensive resources, such as Carvin's *Educational Resource Guide,* with links to other Internet resources and sites.

http://edweb.cnidr.org

Consortium for School Networking (CoSN): An organization devoted to developing a constituency in order to influence public policy decisions that are favorable to K-12 networking. Complete curricular resources and links to other Gophers are provided.

http://www.cosn.org

Internet Training and Consulting Services (ITCS): "Top tens" are lists of outstanding resources in various areas, including K-12 education and Internet handbooks.

http://www.itcs.com/itcs/topten.html

Internic's FYI 22, "Answers to Commonly asked Primary and Secondary School Internet User Questions": Extremely helpful and comprehensive introductory guide for parents and teachers.

    http://chs.cusd.claremont.edu/www/people/rmuir/rfc1578.html

The Institute for the Learning Sciences' *Engines for Education:* A hypertext book by cognitive scientists Roger Schank and Chip Cleary that takes full advantage of Web hyperlinks to discuss a multitude of educational reform issues ranging from a critique of Hirsch's *Cultural Literacy* to the use and misuse of Case Methods approaches to teaching education.

    http://www.ils.nwu.edu/~e_for_e

KidsCom: Described as "a communication playground for children ages 8-12," the usual links to other interesting sites are supplemented by activities range from seeking help on educational topics from experts to setting up "key pals."

    http://www.spectracom.com/kidscom/

"Magpie" (Educational Resources on the Internet): A unique Web site based at the University of Wales which meshes a database of more than 900 K-12 Internet resources with an array of graphics, documents, and links to sites around the world.

    http://www.dcs.aber.ac.uk/~jjw0/indexht.html

Maricopa Center for Learning: See description under "Gophers," above.

    http://hakatai.mcli.dist.maricopa.edu

On-line Educational Resources: Together with the usual access to other Web sites concerned with education, these pages include information on how to design your own Web pages.

    http://www.nas.nasa.gov/NAS/WebWeavers

Scholastic, Inc. Web Site: See description under "Gophers," above.

`http://scholastic.com:2005/public/Learning-Libraries.html`

SchoolsNet: An Australian Web site with comprehensive links to K-12 Internet resources, SchoolsNet is designed to encourage teachers and students to participate in global networking projects.

`http://www.schnet.edu.au/Docs/Home/Edu/edtoc.html`

United States Department of Education: "Educational Resources" is a complete compendium of live hypertext links to K-12 sites on the Internet.

`http://www.ed.gov/EdRes/EducRes.html`

Vose School Home Page: Comprehensive Web site listing education-related Internet resources in every content area.

`http://www.teleport.com/~vincer/starter.html`

WEB66: An ambitious project of the University of Minnesota, WEB66 seeks to help schools set up their own Internet servers while providing students and teachers with links to other schools with Web sites. WEB66 houses the oldest and most comprehensive registry of schools linked through the Web.

`http://web66.coled.umn.edu`

Wentworth's Cyber WWW Site: Links to many Internet sites, especially those dealing with high technology in classrooms; also, many links to K-12 FreeNets.

`http://wentworth-art.com`

WWW links to K-12 USENET Newsgroups: One of the easiest ways to see what's going on in the Newsgroups in 11 subject areas if your service provider does not subscribe to the USENET newsfeeds.

```
http://osiris.wu-wien.ac.at/news/k12.ed.html
```

WisDPI Home Page: Maintained by the Wisconsin Department of Public Instruction, with links to other education-related Internet sites.

```
http://badger.state.wi.us/0/agencies/dpi/www/dpihome.html
```

TELNET

Book Stacks Unlimited, Inc.: An on-line ordering service for books with complete publishing information in searchable format.

```
telnet://books.com and login by providing information
requested -->(B)ook Store
```

Cleveland Freenet: One of the oldest Freenets, with Academy One and numerous other interactive activity areas. There are one-hour time limits for unregistered users.

```
telnet://freenet-in-c.cwru.edu and login by selecting "A visi-
tor" and "Explore the system" -->The Schoolhouse (Academy
One) -->Academy One Projects Underway
```

Health CHAT: CHAT here stands for Conversational Hypertext Access Technology, which is a program that "answers" questions by retrieving pertinent documents. A useful resource for up-to-date health information, especially for parents and teachers that need to deal with sensitive issues such as AIDS and sex education.

```
telnet://debra.dgbt.doc.ca:3000
```

Teachers*Pages: The huge resource bank of lesson plans and other educational resources is available on the Internet with a searchable database.

> `telnet://psupen.psu.edu` and login in with `TX` —>`choose`
> `Teachers*Pages` —>`Keyword Search` then search the "Idea Bank"
> and "PDE" for general education, or "EISC" for students with
> special learning needs.

University of Massachusetts Web site: See description under "Gophers," above.

> `telnet://kl2.ucs.umass.edu` and login as "guest"

ANONYMOUS FTP

"Cerf_n_Safari" by Yvonne Andres: Well-organized compendium of Internet-based curricular activities.

> `ftp://nic.cerf.net /cerfnet/cerfnet_kl2programs`
> `/cerf_n_safari/safari_guide/safari-guide.txt`

"Educational Networks Survey": An evaluation of available service providers and project-oriented telecomputing groups.

> `ftp://ariel.unm.edu/library/networks-survey`

"FAQ Draft for K12 Telecomputing" by the Internet Education Task Force.

> `ftp://ds.internic.net /internet-drafts/`
> `draft-ietf.isn.faq-02.txt`

"Incomplete Guide to the Internet and Other Telecommunications Opportunities Especially for Teachers and Students K-12," by the NCSA Telnet Group.

```
ftp://ftp.ncsa.uiuc.edu/Education/Education_Resources /In-
complete_Guide
```

Stephen Hodas' "Implementation of the K-12 NREN: Equity, Access, and a Trojan Horse" and "Technology Refusal and the Organizational Culture of Schools": Two key articles by an important thinker on equity of access to networking.

```
ftp://ftp.u.washington.edu /pub/user-supported/horsehorse
```
and get K12NREN1.1 or refuse_1.2

Internet Resource Directory for Educators: A summary of Judi Harris's collaborative efforts to evaluate Internet resources.

```
ftp://tcet.unt.edu//pub/telecomputing-info/IRD/ get IRD-
telnet-sites.txt, IRD-ftp-archives.txt, IRD-listservs.txt,
and IRD-infusion-ideas.txt
```

"K12FYI, Basic Internet Facts for K12 Networking": This extremely comprehensive document from Internic is an important place to start for parents and teachers who are novice users.

```
ftp://ds.internic.net//rfc/rfc1578.txt
```

"Telementoring" by D. J. Wighton: An important article on how the Internet can be used to support teacher education and first-year teachers.

```
ftp://cln.etc.bc.ca/pub/research/telementoring
```

University of Massachusetts at Amherst—The Educator's Guide to Email LISTSERVs and Newsgroups.

```
ftp://nic.umass.edu/pub/ednet
```

University of New Brunswick's Lists of Education Internet Resources:
One of the most complete repositories of reviews of Internet resources in
education, organized by subject areas; maintained by the University of New
Brunswick, home of the useful C-EDRES LISTSERV and EDRES-DB
database of reviews.

> `ftp://jupiter.sun.csd.unb.ca` and login as "anonymous" giving
> your full Internet address as the password. Reviews are at:
> `/pub/faculty.ed/resources` and `/pub/faculty.ed/arts`

THE ERIC CLEARINGHOUSES AND ACCESS ERIC

ERIC Clearinghouse on Adult, Career, and Vocational Education
Ohio State University
Center on Education and Training for Employment
1900 Kenny Road
Columbus, OH 43210-1090
Phone: 614-292-4353
800-848-4815
FAX: 614-292-1260
e-mail: `ERICACVE@magnus.acs.ohio-state.edu`

ERIC Clearinghouse on Assessment and Evaluation
Catholic University of America
210 O'Boyle Hall
Washington, DC 20064-4035
Phone: 202-319-5120
800-464-3742
FAX: 202-319-6692
e-mail:`ASK_AE@cua.edu`
Gopher: `gopher://vmsgopher.cua.edu-->Special Resources`
Web: `http://www.cua.edu./www/eric_ae`

ERIC Clearinghouse for Community Colleges
University of California at Los Angeles (UCLA)
3051 Moore Hall
Los Angeles, CA 90095-1521
Phone: 310-825-3931
800-832-8256
FAX: 310-206-8095
e-mail: EEH3USC@mvs.oac.ucla.edu

ERIC Clearinghouse on Counseling and Student Services
University of North Carolina at Greensboro
School of Education
Greensboro, NC 27412-5001
Phone: 910-334-4114
800-414-9769
FAX: 910-334-4116
e-mail: ERICCASS@iris.uncg.edu
Web: http://www2.uncg.edu/~ericcas2

ERIC Clearinghouse on Disabilities and Gifted Education
Council for Exceptional Children (CEC)
1920 Association Drive
Reston, VA 22091-1589
Phone: 703-264-9474
800-328-0272
FAX: 703-264-9494
e-mail: ERICEC@inet.ed.gov

ERIC Clearinghouse on Educational Management
5207 University of Oregon
Eugene, OR 97403-5207
Phone: 503-346-5043
800-438-8841
FAX: 503-346-2334
e-mail: PPIELE@oregon.uoregon.edu
Web: http://darkwing.uoregon.edu/~ericcem/home.html

ERIC Clearinghouse on Elementary and Early Childhood Education
University of Illinois
805 West Pennsylvania Avenue
Urbana, IL 61801-4897
Phone: 217-333-1386
800-583-4135
FAX: 217-333-3767
e-mail: ERICEECE@ux1.cso.uiuc.edu for general information
         askeric@ericir.syr.edu for Parents AskERIC, an
         Internet-based question-answering service
Gopher: gopher://ericps.ed.uiuc.edu for the National Parent
         Information Network (NPIN)
Web: http://ericps.ed.uiuc.edu/ericeece.html for general
     clearinghouse information
     http://ericps.ed.uiuc.edu/npin/npinhome.html for NPIN
     http://ericps.ed.uiuc.edu/readyweb/readywebhome.html
     for ReadyWeb, on school readiness for youngsters

ERIC Clearinghouse on Higher Education
George Washington University
One Dupont Circle NW, Suite 630
Washington, DC 20036-1183
Phone: 202-296-2597
800-773-3742
FAX: 202-296-8379
e-mail: ERICHE@inet.ed.gov

ERIC Clearinghouse on Information and Technology
Syracuse University
4-194 Center for Science and Technology
Syracuse, NY 13244-4100
Phone: 315-443-3640
800-464-9107
FAX: 315-443-5448
e-mail: ERIC@ericir.syr.edu
        AskERIC@ericir.syr.edu for Internet-based education
        question-answering service

Gopher: gopher://ericir.syr.edu for ERIC Virtual Library
Web: http://ericir.syr.edu for ERIC Virtual Library

ERIC Clearinghouse on Languages and Linguistics
Center for Applied Linguistics (CAL)
1118 22nd Street NW
Washington, DC 20037-0037
Phone: 202-429-9292
800-276-9834
FAX: 202-659-5641
e-mail: ERIC@cal.org
Web: http://ericir.syr.edu/ericcll/

ERIC Clearinghouse on Reading, English, and Communication
Indiana University Smith Research Center, Suite 150
2805 East 10th Street
Bloomington, IN 47408-2698
Phone: 812-855-5847
800-759-4723
FAX: 812-855-4220
e-mail: ERICCS@ucs.indiana.edu
Gopher: gopher://gopher.indiana.edu
Web: http://www.indiana.edu/~eric_rec

ERIC Clearinghouse on Rural Education and Small Schools
Appalachia Educational Laboratory (AEL)
1031 Quarrier Street, P.O. Box 1348
Charleston, WV 25325-1348
Phone: 304-347-0465
800-624-9120
FAX: 304-347-0487
e-mail: ERICRC@ael.org
Gopher: gopher://gopher.ael.org
Web: http://www.ael.org/~eric/
FTP: ftp://ftp.ael.org

ERIC Clearinghouse for Science, Mathematics, and Environmental
Education
Ohio State University
1929 Kenny Road
Columbus, OH 43210-1080
Phone: 614-292-6717
800-276-0462
FAX: 614-292-0263
e-mail: ERICSE@osu.edu
Gopher: gopher://gopher.ericse.ohio-state.edu
Web: http://gopher.ericse.ohio-state.edu

ERIC Clearinghouse for Social Studies/Social Science Education
Indiana University
Adjunct ERIC Clearinghouse for Art Education
Adjunct ERIC Clearinghouse for United States–Japan Studies
Adjunct ERIC Clearinghouse for Law-Related Education
Social Studies Development Center
2805 East 10th Street, Suite 120
Bloomington, IN 47408-2698
Phone: 812-855-3838
800-266-3815
FAX: 812-855-0455
e-mail: ERICS0@ucs.indiana.edu
        JAPAN@ucs.indiana.edu for US-Japan Studies
Web: http://www.indiana.edu/~ssdc/eric-chess.html
      http://www.indiana.edu/~japan for US-Japan Studies

ERIC Clearinghouse on Teaching and Teacher Education
American Association of Colleges for Teacher Education (AACTE)
One Dupont Circle NW, Suite 610
Washington, DC 20036-1186
Phone: 202-293-2450
FAX: 202-457-8095
e-mail: ERICSP@inet.ed.gov

ERIC Clearinghouse on Urban Education
Teachers College, Columbia University
Institute for Urban and Minority Education
Main Hall, Room 303, Box 40
525 West 120th Street
New York, NY 10027-9998
Phone: 212-678-3433
800-601-4868
FAX: 212-678-4048
e-mail: ERIC-CUE@columbia.edu
Web: http://eric-web.tc.columbia.edu

Adjunct ERIC Clearinghouse on Chapter 1 (Compensatory Education)
Chapter 1 Technical Assistance Center
PRC Inc.
2601 Fortune Circle East
One Park Fletcher Building, Suite 300-A
Indianapolis, IN 46241-2237
Phone: 317-244-8160
800-456-2380
FAX: 317-244-7386
e-mail: PRCINC@delphi.com

Adjunct ERIC Clearinghouse on Clinical Schools
American Association of Colleges for Teacher Education
One Dupont Circle NW, Suite 610
Washington, DC 20036-1186
Phone: 202-293-2450
800-822-9229
FAX: 202-457-8095
e-mail: IABDALHA@inet.ed.gov

Adjunct ERIC Clearinghouse on Consumer Education
National Institute for Consumer Education
207 Rackham Building, West Circle Drive
Eastern Michigan University
Ypsilanti, MI 48197-2237

Phone: 313-487-2292
800-336-6423
FAX: 313-487-7153
e-mail: NICE@emuvax.emich.edu
Gopher: gopher://emunix.emich.edu

Adjunct ERIC Clearinghouse for ESL Literacy Education
National Clearinghouse for Literacy Education (NCLE)
Center for Applied Linguistics (CAL)
1118 22nd Street NW
Washington, DC 20037
Phone: 202-429-9292, Ext. 200
FAX: 202-659-5641
e-mail: NCLE@cal.org

ACCESS ERIC offers a toll-free service that provides access to the information and services available through the ERIC system. Staff will answer questions as well as refer callers to other clearinghouses. ACCESS ERIC also produces several on-line publications and reference and referral databases that provide information about both the ERIC system and current education-related issues and research.

ACCESS ERIC
Aspen Systems Corporation
1600 Research Boulevard
Rockville, MD 20850-3172
Phone: 301-251-5506
800-LET-ERIC (538-3742)
FAX: 301-251-5767
e-mail: ACCERIC@inet.ed.gov
Web: http://www.aspensys.com/eric2/welcome.html with links
to all existing ERIC Gophers and Web sites currently available for
the 16 Clearinghouses.

Books and Articles

Computer-Mediated Communication and the On-line Classroom. Overview and Perspectives, Volume 1; Computer-Mediated Communication and the On-line Classroom in Higher Education, Volume Two; and *Computer-Mediated Communication and the On-line Classroom in Distance Learning, Volume 3: Comprehensive Treatment of CMC,* edited by Zane Berge and Mauri Collins, in the form of chapters written by leaders in the field. $54 for the set, $20 per volume. Inquire for shipping and handling costs:

> Hampton Press, Inc.
> 23 Broadway
> Cresskill, NJ 07626
> Phone: 201-894-1686
> FAX: 201-894-8732

An Educator's Guide to Electronic Networking: Creating Virtual Communities (ISBN: 0-937597-37-6), by Barbara Kurshan and Marcia Harrington, revised and updated by Peter Milbury, provides novice users with comparisons of various Internet Service Providers. Intended to help teachers as well as administrators planning to introduce networking into their schools. Also from ERIC: *Information Literacy in an Information Society: A Concept for the Information Age* (ISBN: 0-937597-38-4), by Christina Doyle, discusses networking in its historical and contemporary context by focusing on the transition from an industrial to a services- and information-oriented economy.

> ERIC Clearinghouse on Information & Technology
> 4-194 Center for Science and Technology
> Syracuse University
> Syracuse, NY 13244-4100
> Phone: 800-464-9107
> Fax: 315-443-5448
> Internet: ERIC@ericir.syr.edu

The Educator's Guide To The Internet, by Patrick Golden of the Virginia Space Grant Consortium, provides information for novice K-12 users of the Internet, with examples mostly drawn from science and mathematics education. Accompanying the guide is a NASA videotape on using the Internet in the classroom and a diskette of software (IBM or Macintosh). Current price: $16.

The Virginia Space Grant Consortium
2713-D Magruder Boulevard
Hampton, VA 23666 USA
Phone: 804-865-0726
Internet: VSGC@pen.k12.va.us

The INTERNET Resource Directory for K-12 Teachers and Librarians, 1994-95 Edition, by Elizabeth B. Miller, while focusing on science education, offers useful pointers for parents and teachers new to the Internet.

Libraries Unlimited, Inc.
P.O. Box 6633
Englewood, CO 80155
(800) 237-6124

Way of the Ferret: Finding Educational Resources on the Internet, by Judi Harris, draws on her wealth of experience in evaluating Internet resources in this 1994 revised edition.

International Society for Technology Education
1227 University of Oregon
Eugene, Oregon 97403

Education on the Internet: A Hands-on Book of Ideas, Resources, Projects and Advice, by Jill Ellsworth. This 1994 first edition offers a helping hand to beginners in K-12 networking.

Howard SAMS Publishing
4300 W. 62nd St.
Indianapolis, Indiana 46268

The Student's Guide to the Internet, 1995, by David Clark (ISBN 1-56761-545-7). Intended for high school and university students, this handbook supplements its basic orientation chapters on the Internet information tools with discussion of topics ranging from student political activism to locating financial aid information. An accompanying Web page is available at `http://mcp.com/~dclark/student.html`.

Alpha Books Distributors
303 W. 10th St.
New York, NY 10014

Parent Involvement

LISTSERVS

LEARNER: "Pen pals" between adult learners and their tutors.

>Subscriptions: `LISTSERV@nysernet.org`
>Participation: `LEARNER@nysernet.org`

LITERACY: Adult literacy discussion, with a focus on native speakers of English.

>Subscriptions: `LISTSERV@nysernet.org`
>Participation: `LITERACY@nysernet.org`

NLA National Literacy Alliance: Adult literacy discussion.

>Subscriptions: `MAJORDOMO@world.std.com`
>Participation: `NLA@world.std.com`

TAGFAM: A discussion group for those concerned with supporting families of children who are gifted and talented.

>Subscriptions: `LISTSERV@sjuvm.stjohns.edu`
>Participation: `TAGFAM@sjuvm.stjohns.edu`

VOCNET: Sponsored by the National Network for Curriculum Coordination in Vocational Technical Education, a federally funded national consortium of six curriculum centers and representatives from each state, VOCNET is a moderated LISTSERV discussing issues of vocational education for out-of-school youth and adults.

>Subscriptions: `LISTSERV@cmsa.berkeley.edu`
>Participation: `VOCNET@cmsa.berkeley.edu`

Gophers

National Center for Education Statistics: A Gopher site where documents related to an important longitudinal study on parental involvement, the National Household Education Survey (NHES), can be retrieved.

```
gopher://gopher.ed.gov -National Center for Education
Statistics (NCES)/ -->Elementary and Secondary Education/
-->Surveys and Studies/ -->National Household Education
Survey (NHES)
```

Another useful document here is "Parental Involvement in Education."

```
gopher://gopher.ed.gov -->National Center for Education
Statistics/ -->National Longitudinal Studies/ -->Selected
Publications, Tabulations and Data Files/ -->Parental
Involvement in Education
```

National Parent Information Network: NPIN is a pilot project of the ERIC Clearinghouse on Elementary and Early Childhood Education and the ERIC Clearinghouse on Urban Education. NPIN represents the richest single resource on parental involvement in education. Its main menu includes directories for the weekly newsletter *Parent News,* listings of resources for parent educators, readings in English and Spanish for parents, and model programs for building community involvement.

On this Gopher, ERIC resources are also organized in clear, easy-to-access categories: There is a directory for *all* the ERIC digests pertinent to child development and parental involvement, with subdirectories by children's age, from infancy to adolescence; information on how to use the PARENTS AskERIC question-answering service is easily available; and customized ERIC bibliographies of resources are listed by topic.

```
gopher://gopher.prairienet.org/ -->National Parent
Information Network
```

NCAL Newsletter: From the Literacy Research Center and the National Center on Adult Literacy, a periodical on adult literacy.

```
gopher://listerver.literacy.upenn.edu -->NCAL Newsletter
```

Other interesting materials are found here under:

```
-->Links to other Literacy Resources/ -->Electronic
Journals
```

Ohio Literacy Resource Center: Offers many directories with publications on adult literacy instruction.

```
gopher://archon.educ.kent.edu
```

The Outreach and Technical Assistance Network (OTAN): Serving adult educators in California, its resources are freely available over the Internet.

```
gopher://archon.educ.kent.edu -->Adult Literacy Info
Servers -->OTAN Gopher Server
```

Parent Participation Directory: Contains 23 files focusing on parental involvement and schooling.

```
gopher://gopher psupena.psu.edu -->Alphabetical Keyword
List/ -->P/ -->Parent-Participation/
```

Parents and Goals 2000: As part of its effort to build parent support for the Goals 2000 legislation which was signed into law in 1994, the Department of Education is running a Gopher site with many useful documents. To reach the directory where these documents can be retrieved use the following Gopher path:

```
gopher://gopher.ed.gov -->Department-wide Initiatives/
-->Goals 2000 Initiatives/
```

Other information is found in various sub-directories. Interesting background papers on the importance of parent involvement are found under:

```
-->Satellite Town Meetings and Background Papers/ -->State
Challenges --> Background Papers/ -->Parent and Community
Support and Involvement
```

Suggestions for grass-roots organizing for parents support can be found under:

```
-->An Invitation to Your Community/ -->More Questions: 10
Elements of Your Plan/ -->Parent and Community Support and
Involvement
```

The "Family Involvement" directory contains "Strong Families/Strong School Reports":

```
-->Family Involvement/ -->Strong Families/Strong School
Reports/
```

It also contains model programs that can be replicated, located at:

```
-->Family Involvement/ -->Strong Families/Strong School
Reports/ -->Promising Approaches/
```

and at

```
-->Family Involvement/ -->Examples and Programs
```

Finally, under the "Legislation" directory, this Gopher site offers information for administrators to apply for grants to increase parent and community participation within the school community and on the Parent Information and Resource Centers which will be operational in every state by September, 1998.

```
-->Legislation - The Goals 2000: Educate America Act/
-->Title IV Parent Assistance
```

Parents Role in Integrating Math and Science: How to help with family math and science.

```
gopher://gopher gopher.rbs.org —RBS Announcements,
Newsletters and Updates/ —Parents Role in Integrating Math
and Science
```

PTA: Available from the same Gopher as the National Parent Information Network is this listing of resources for making parent-teacher organizations more effective.

```
gopher://gopher.prairienet.org —>Education Center —>PTA
```

Resources for Parents of Gifted Children: A listing of resources for parents of high-ability learners.

```
gopher://gopher services.dese.state.mo.us
—>Educational Projects —>desenet —>archives desenet
—>Resources for Parents
```

U.S. Department of Education Publications for Parents: This Gopher site lists documents that encourage parental participation with their children's academic achievement, such as "Parental Involvement in Education," "Helping Your Child Improve Test Taking," and "Helping Your Child Learn Geography."

```
gopher://gopher.ed.gov —>U.S. Department of Education/
—>OERI Publications/ —>Education/OERI Publications -
full text/ —>Publications for Parents/
```

WORLD WIDE WEB (WWW)

The Bowen Family: A glimpse at the way the Internet will facilitate new intergenerational learning, not only originating with institutional initiatives but shaped by individual families. The Bowens live in Oxford, England and have created a well-designed Web site that both highlights their own family's artistic and literary output, but provides links to similar intergenerational collaborations in other countries and cultures.

```
http://www.comlab.ox.ac.uk/oucl/users/jonathan.bowen/
children.html
```

National Parent Information Network: See description under "Gophers," above.

```
http://ericps.ed.uiuc.edu/npin/npinhome.html
```

Ohio Literacy Resource Center: See description under "Gophers," above.

```
http://archon.educ.kent.edu/
```

U.S. Department of Education: See descriptions directories in the Department of Education Gopher, above.

```
http://www.ed.gov
```

TELNET

ParentLink Community Connection: A Telnet site with many resources on literacy.

```
telnet://bigcat.missouri.edu —>Community and Social
Services —>Parentlink Community Connection
```

Teacher*Pages of The Pennsylvania Department of Education: Many documents are available by search for keywords such as parent-school-relationship, parent-student-relationship, and parental-involvement. A very active site that is updated monthly.

```
telnet://psupen.psu.edu —>login: tx —>pen pages —>key
word search
```

Multicultural Education

E-JOURNALS AND NEWSLETTERS

Wotanging Ikche (Native American News): A weekly news digest excerpted from NATIVE-L, NAT-EDU, and other sources.

> Subscriptions: GARS@netcom.com

LISTSERVS

ACTIV-L: Forum on civil and human rights, peace, and nonviolence.

> Subscriptions: LISTSERV@mizzou1.missouri.edu
> Participation: ACTIV-L@mizzou1.missouri.edu

AFRICA-L: A forum for those interested in increasing communication of all types to and from Africa.

> Subscriptions: LISTSERV@brufmg.vtvm1.cc.vt.edu
> Participation: AFRICA-L@brufmg.vtvm1.cc.vt.edu

AFRICANA: Discussion focusing on the use of information technologies and networks on the continent of Africa.

> Subscriptions: LISTSERV@wmvm1.cc.wm.edu
> Participation: AFRICANA@wmvm1.cc.wm.edu

AFROAM-L: A discussion group on African American life and culture.

> Subscriptions: LISTSERV@harvarda.harvard.edu
> Participation: AFROAM-L@harvarda.harvard.edu

AMNESTY: Discussion group of Amnesty International.

> Subscriptions: LISTSERV@vms.cis.pitt.edu
> Participation: AMNESTY@vms.cis.pitt.edu

ANTHRO-LIB: This discussion group centers on the anthropology of "third and fourth world peoples and cultures," rejecting colonial and neocolonial approaches to the study of human culture.

> Subscription: LISTPROC@lists.colorado.edu

COMDEV: Discussion of communication and international development.

> Subscriptions: LISTSERV@rpitsvm.bitnet
> Participation: COMDEV@rpitsvm.bitnet

CULTUR-L: Discussion group for those interested in the role of cultural differences in the curriculum.

> Subscriptions: LISTSERV@vm.temple.edu
> Participation: CULTUR-L@vm.temple.edu

DIVERS-L: Discussion encouraging diversity in academic studies.

> Subscriptions: LISTSERV@psuvm.psu.edu
> Participation: DIVERS-L@psuvm.psu.edu

FEMINISM-DIGEST: Forum on women's rights.

> Subscriptions: MAJORDOMO@netcom.com
> Participation: FEMINISM-DIGEST@netcom.com

GLGB-HS: Forum for teachers and secondary students of global studies.

Subscriptions: `LISTSERV@ocmvm.onondaga.boces.k12.ny.us`
Participation: `GLGB-HS@ocmvm.onondaga.boces.k12.ny.us`

GLOBALED: Forum on curriculum issues in global education.

Subscriptions: `LISTSERV@unmvm.bitnet`
Participation: `GLOBALED@unmvm.bitnet`

H-NET: Not a LISTSERV itself but a far-ranging suite of LISTSERVs, managed by the University of Illinois (Chicago) and Michigan State University. Of particular interest for multicultural studies are H-ANTIS (on anti-Semitism), H-URBAN (urban history), and HOLOCAUS (Holocaust studies) out of the University of Illinois and H-AFRICA (African history), H-ASIA (Asian history), H-DEMOG (demographic history), H-ETHNIC (ethnic, immigration and emigration studies), H-JUDAIC (Judaica, Jewish history), H-LATAM (Latin American history), H-RURAL (rural and agricultural history), H-W-CIV (teaching Western civilization), H-WOMEN (women's history), and H-WORLD (world history) at Michigan State University. More H-Net lists are described under "Social Studies."

Subscriptions: `LISTSERV@uicvm.uic.edu` or
`LISTSERV@msu.edu`
Participation: Substitute the actual group name for the word "LISTSERV," e.g. `H-ETHNIC@msu.edu`

HR-L: Forum on international human rights issues.

Subscriptions: `HR-L-REQUEST@vms.cis.pitt.edu`
Participation: `HR-L@vms.cis.pitt.edu`

INDIANnet: Open forum for those interested in Native American issues.

Subscriptions: `LISTSERV@spruce.hsu.edu`
Participation: `INDIANNET@spruce.hsu.edu`

INTCOLED: Devoted to "international collaborative education" using the Internet.

> Subscriptions: LISTSERV@ist01.ferris.edu
> Participation: INTCOLED@ist01.ferris.edu

MEXICO-L: Discussion of Mexican culture, in English and Spanish.

> Subscriptions: LISTSERV@tecmtyvm.bitnet
> Participation: MEXICO-L@tecmtyvm.bitnet

MIGRANT-L: A forum devoted to issues affecting the education of migrant students.

> Subscriptions: LISTSERV@netcom.com
> Participation: MIGRANT-L@netcom.com

MULTC-ED: Forum on Multicultural Education from K-12 through University. Includes educators and parents, covering the full range of diversity, including disability and gender orientation.

> Subscriptions: LISTSERV@umdd.umd.edu
> Participation: MULTC-ED@umdd.umd.edu

NAT-EDU: Principally higher education participation on issues surrounding Native American education.

> Subscriptions: LISTSERV@indycms.iupui.edu
> Participation: NAT-EDU@indycms.iupui.edu

NAT-LANG: Discussion group concerned with Native languages in North America.

> Subscriptions: LISTSERV@tamvm1.tamu.edu
> Participation: NAT-LANG@tamvm1.tamu.edu

NAT-LIT-L: Forum devoted to discussion of Native American literature.

>Subscriptions: `LISTSERV@cornell.edu`
>Participation: `NAT-LIT-L@cornell.edu`

ORTRAD-L: A forum on living oral traditions and texts rooted within oral traditions, with an intercultural, interdisciplinary focus.

>Subscriptions: `LISTSERV@mizzou1.missouri.edu`
>Participation: `ORTRAD-L@mizzou1.missouri.edu`

WOMEN: Gender issues at all levels of education.

>Subscriptions: `LISTSERV@world.std.com`
>Participation: `WOMEN@world.std.com`

WORLD-L: Discussion of non-Eurocentric world history.

>Subscriptions: `LISTSERV@ubvm.cc.buffalo.edu`
>Participation: `WORLD-L@ubvm.cc.buffalo.edu`

Y-RIGHTS: Discussion on the rights of children and adolescents.

>Subscriptions: `LISTSERV@sjuvm.stjohns.edu`
>Participation: `Y-RIGHTS@sjuvm.stjohns.edu`

USENET NEWSGROUPS

The following newsgroups discuss topics of relevance to multicultural education:

```
alt.activism
alt.native
alt.society.civil-liberties
bit.listserv.politics
```

```
soc.culture.african
soc.culture.african.american
soc.culture.arabic
soc.culture.asian.american
soc.culture.canada
soc.culture.caribbean
soc.culture.filipino
soc.culture.indian.american
soc.culture.jewish
soc.culture.korean
soc.culture.native
soc.culture.native.american
soc.culture.taiwan
soc.politics
soc.rights.human
```

GOPHERS

Academy One—Cultural Awareness Projects: K-12 project ideas.

```
gopher://gopher.cic.net -->Other CICNet Projects and Go-
pher Servers/ -->K-12 on the Internet ...Select Education
Resources/ -->Classroom Activities and Projects/ -->Acad-
emy One Project List
```

Arab World and Islamic Resources and School Services: Difficult-to-find curricular materials, reviewed and organized by grade level and subject area.

```
gopher://latif.com -->Muslim Businesses and Educational Or-
ganizations -->Arab World and Islamic Resources and Social
Services
```

Community Learning Network (CLN): Multicultural resources and documentation of the value of "twinning" classes for intercultural learning.

```
gopher://gopher.etc.bc.ca -->CLN Other Partners and Re-
sources/ -->XV Commonwealth Games - on-line Information/
-->Youth & Education Program Materials (Commonwealth
Games)/ -->Windows on Multiculturalism/
```

Computer Professionals for Social Responsibility: Listings of resources on women's and minority concerns.

```
gopher://gopher.cpsr.org -->Computer Professionals for
Social Responsibility Main Directory -->Gender & Minority
Issues
```

Diversity and Anti-racism Resources for Education (DARE) at the Ontario Institute for Studies in Education, Toronto, Canada: The richest Gopher site for resources in multicultural education. Especially useful is the listing of ERIC digests.

```
gopher://porpoise.oise.on.ca -->The Collection of On-line
Education Resources at OISE/ -->Internet Resources for Use
in Education/ -->Internet Resources for Education/ --> Di-
versity and Anti-racism Resources for Education (DARE)/
```

The EE Reference Collection—Multicultural & Environmental Education: Rich resource collection linking two often neglected curricular areas.

```
gopher://nceet.snre.umich.edu -->NCEET's Environmental Edu-
cation Toolbox/ -->The EE Reference Collection/ -->VI.
Multicultural and Environmental Education.
```

Electronic Frontier Foundation Reading Room: Many resources on women's issues.

```
gopher://gopher.eff.org -->Publications -->Internet
Resources by Subject -->Gopher Jewels -->Education, Social
Sciences, Arts & Humanities -->Social Sciences -->Women
-->Women's Studies & Resources - PEG, a Peripatetic, Eclec-
```

```
tic Gopher -->Women's Studies Information *A TREASURY*
(U of Maryland) -->Reading Room
```

Gettysburg Gopher: Many holdings on women's studies, with reviews of international publications and films.

```
gopher://jupiter.cc.gettysburg.edu -->Academic Departments
-->Women Studies
```

Maricopa Community College: A Who's Who listing of entries of famous women.

```
gopher://emc.maricopa.edu -->Teaching & Learning -->Infor-
mation Commons -->Notable Women
```

National Clearinghouse on Development and Environmental Education: Sponsored by the American Forum for Global Education, this Gopher links international education with environmental issues.

```
gopher://nceet.snre.umich.edu
```

Pathfinder for Women's History Research in the National Archives and Records Administration Library: 18-page annotated bibliography of over 100 monographs and research tools.

```
gopher://extsparc.agsci.usu.edu -->Other Select Gopher and
Information Servers -->Gopher Jewels -->Library, Refer-
ence, and News -->Books, Journals, Magazines, Newsletters
and Publications -->Books, Journals, Magazines, Newslet-
ters and Publications (misc.) -->English & Literature Go-
pher, University of Pennsylvania -->Other Gophers -->
Literature & Reference Tools -->National Archives Gopher
-->The NARA Library -->NARA Library News
```

The Southwest Institute for Research on Women (SIROW): Especially concerned with curricula with international perspectives.

```
gopher://inform.umd.edu -->Educational Resources -->Aca-
demic Resources by Topic -->Women's Studies Resources --
>Other Women's Issues Gophers -->Southwest Institute for
Research on Women -->About Southwest Institute for Re-
search on Women
```

Minnesota Extension Service Gopher—Project READ: Responsive Educational Approach to Diversity (READ) seeks to link schools with culturally-diverse communities and families.

```
gopher://tinman.mes.umn.edu -->CYFERNet - National Chil-
dren, Youth and Family Network/ -->Youth at Risk Community-
based Projects/ -->Program Abstracts -->Alaska to Kansas/
-->PROJECT TITLE: Responsive Educational Approach to Diver-
sity.
```

PENN State PENpages: Huge, searchable listing of 13,000 full-text multicultural education resources.

```
gopher://psupena.psu.edu -->Search using keywords ? (best
keywords to use: diversity, pluralism)
```

University of Georgia: Multicultural Resources: Searchable database of resources for multicultural education.

```
gopher://gopher.uga.edu -->EXPLORE... Search All UGA Go-
pher Menus -->Words to search for <multicultural>
or -->About the Multicultural Resources Database.
or -->Bibliography/ -->Search the Bibliography <?>
```

University of Pennsylvania: Access to African Studies resources.

```
gopher://gopher.upenn.edu -->PennInfo via Gopher -->Pen-
nInfo Gateway -->PennInfo -->Interdisciplinary Programs
-->African Studies
```

University of Wisconsin Women's Studies: Bibliographies and curricular support concerning women's issues.

```
gopher://inform.umd.edu -->Educational Resources -->Aca-
demic Resources by Topic -->Women's Studies Resources
-->Other Women's Issues Gophers -->Women's Studies
Librarian's Office, University of Wisconsin -->About the UW
System Women's Studies Librarian's Office
```

University of Wisconsin, Criteria for Evaluating Materials on Africa: Curriculum resources for K-12 African, African American, and Islamic culture, with a search utility.

```
gopher://gopher.adp.wisc.edu -->Course Materials and Other
Educational Resources -->African and African American Cur-
riculum Materials K-12 -->Search African and African Ameri-
can Curriculum Materials K-12 ? -->Search for "bias"
-->Criteria for Evaluating Materials on Africa
```

UMD Women's Studies Resources: Many women's studies resources, including syllabi.

```
gopher://inform.umd.edu -->Educational Resources -->Aca-
demic Resources by Topic -->Women's Studies Resources
```

WORLD LINK NEWSLETTER The December 1994 issue lists African and African American resources for K-12 education.

```
gopher://ericir.syr.edu and search for "World Link Newsletter"
```

WORLD WIDE WEB (WWW)

British Columbia First Nations Studies Curriculum and Planning Guides: An excellent example of a secondary-level antibias curriculum.

```
http://www.etc.bc.ca/native/cont.html
```

CLNET Diversity Page: Includes links to LISTSERVs, Gophers, Web sites, and newsgroups focusing on specific groups.

    http://latino.sscnet.ucla.edu/diversity1.html

Community Learning Network (CLN): See "Gophers," above.

    http://www.etc.bc.ca

The First Perspective: Focuses on a wide range of information and resources concerning the indigenous people of Canada.

    http://www.mbnet.mb.ca/firstper

Library of Congress Country Studies: Summaries and bibliographies on specific countries.

    http://lcweb.loc.gov/homepage/lchp.html -->Select Country
    Studies (Area Handbooks)

Social Science Resources Page: Provides access to Internet sites concerned with multicultural education resources.

    http://galaxy.einet.net/GJ/social.html

The U.S. Holocaust Memorial Museum: Both an overview of the museum in Washington, D.C., and a site where teaching ideas may be found for integrating Holocaust studies into the curriculum.

    http://www.ushmm.org/index.html

Yad Vashem Holocaust Memorial (Jerusalem): Established to coincide with Holocaust Remembrance Day in 1995, this Web site offers documents, graphics, and a facility for "visitors" to leave their comments.

    http://yvs.shani.net

TELNET

INDIANnet Bulletin Board System: Sponsored by Americans for Indian Opportunity, the INDIANnet BBS serves as a clearinghouse of information pertinent to the education of Native American people.

```
telnet://indiannet.sdserv.org
```

Bilingualism and Second-Language Acquisition

E-JOURNALS

AMERICA SIN FRONTERAS—una revista literaria bilingue de la secundaria / *AMERICA WITHOUT FRONTIERS*, a bilingual literary journal for secondary school students: Writings in English and Spanish for "all those who wish to be bilingual," organized by I*EARN. (See "Partner-Class Clearinghouses and Project-Oriented Activities.") Send submissions to WESTMESA@iearn.org.

ENEWS-SL: This LISTSERV is devoted to editorial discussion for an electronic magazine by English as a foreign language/English as a second language (ESL/EFL) students.

> Subscriptions: MAJORDOMO@latrobe.edu.au
>
> Participation: ENEWS-SL@latrobe.edu.au

NCBE NEWSLINE: In addition to discussion groups (see "LISTSERVs," below), the National Clearinghouse for Bilingual Education maintains NEWSLINE as a mechanism for providing up-to-date information on news and resources relating to the education of linguistically and culturally diverse students in the United States. Unlike many e-journals, NEWSLINE is "moderated;" that is, it invites comments from its subscribers which are reviewed for accuracy and pertinence and then posted.

> Subscriptions: MAJORDOMO@cis.ncbe.gwu.edu
>
> Participation: NEWSLINE@cis.ncbe.gwu.edu

ReCALL: Stands for "Re: Computer-Aided Language Learning," this e-newsletter is published by the CTI Centre for Modern Languages: The Computers in Teaching Initiative Centre for Modern Languages (CTICML), at the University of Hull in Ontario.

> gopher://gopher.hull.ac.uk/11/cti

*REVIEW OF BITNET / INTERNET LISTS FOR LANGUAGE LEARN-
ING:* For several years, David Bedell of the University of Bridgeport has
been maintaining an updated list of LISTSERVs and other language
learning resources. For a current listing, send e-mail to `@cse.bridge-
port.edu`. Alternatively, send e-mail to `LISTSERV@ubvm.bitnet` and in the
body of the message include the words GET FLTEACH FLLISTS or to
`LISTSERV@cunyvm.cuny.edu` with the message GET LIST OFLISTS1. The
Review can also be found at `http://ubvm.cc.buffalo.edu:80/~list-
serv/FLTEACH/flteach.fllists`.

*TESLEJ-L: Teaching English as a Second or Foreign Language: An Electronic
Journal* for English as a second language/English as a foreign language
(ESL/EFL) professionals.

> Subscriptions: `LISTSERV@cmsa.berkeley.edu`

Also available through Gopher and the Web. Back issues are archived at:

> `gopher://CUNYVM.CUNY.EDU:70/11 -->CUNY Resources -->esl
> -->Teacher Training Resources -->TESL-EJ`

> `http://cc2000.kyoto-su.ac.jp/information/tesl-
> ej/index.html http://www.well.com/www/sokolik/index.html`

LISTSERVS

AATG: Forum for the American Association of Teachers of German.

> Subscriptions: `LISTSERV@indycms.iupui.edu`
> Participation: `AATG@indycms.iupui.edu`

ARABIC-L: A forum devoted to the linguistics and teaching of Arabic.

> Subscriptions: `MAILSERV@byu.edu`
> Participation: `ARABIC-L@byu.edu`

BILINGUE-L: A forum concerned with developmental bilingual elementary education, or "two-way bilingual programs," where native speakers of English learn all their regular subjects with native speakers of Spanish, with the goal of both groups becoming bilingual while performing academically on grade level. Based on the premise, according to the organizers, that "a second language is best learned not as the object of instruction, but rather as the medium of instruction, through a content-based curriculum."

> Subscriptions: `LISTSERV@Reynolds.k12.or.us`
>
> Participation: `BILINGUE-L@Reynolds.k12.or.us`

CAUSERIE: French for "chat," which is just what this LISTSERV provides in French.

> Subscriptions: `LISTSERV@uquebec.ca`
>
> Participation: `CAUSERIE@uquebec.ca`

CGF-ACTIVITES and **CGF-PRESSE:** LISTSERVs of the "Classe Globale de Francais," for planning classroom projects and for sharing news in French, respectively.

> Subscriptions: `LISTSERV@cren.org`
>
> Participation: `CGF-ACTIVITES@cren.org`
>
> `CGF-PRESSE@cren.org`

CHILD-LITERACY-AND-ESL-DEVEL: Discussion group linking the teaching of reading and writing with the education of immigrant children.

> Subscriptions: `LISTSERV@latrobe.edu.au`
>
> Participation: `CHILD-LITERACY-AND-ESL-DEVEL@latrobe.edu.au`

CHILDRENS-VOICE: An important initiative from the innovators at Canada's SchoolNet which seeks to offer children an electronic publishing outlet for their writings. Teachers are encouraged to submit their students' best efforts and to share the writings they find on the LISTSERV with their classes. Writings in languages other than English and French are encouraged, as are writings of children learning English as a second language.

> Subscriptions: LISTPROC@schoolnet.carleton.ca
>
> Participation: SCHOOLNET.carleton.ca

EDUFRANCAIS: For the exchange of teaching ideas among teachers of French, in French, from France.

> Subscriptions: LISTSERV@univ-rennes1.fr
>
> Participation: EDUFRANCAIS@univ-rennes1.fr

ESPAN-L: A forum mostly in Spanish for Spanish foreign-language teachers.

> Subscriptions: LISTSERV@vm.tau.ac.il
>
> Participation: ESPAN-L@vm.tau.ac.il

EST-L and EST-SL: Discussion LISTSERVs for teachers of and students of English for science and technology, respectively. Students often use EST-SL to receive suggestions for improving their writing skills.

> Subscriptions: LISTSERV@asuacad.bitnet
>
> Participation: EST-L@asuacad.bitnet
> EST-SL@asuacad.bitnet

FLAC-L: Discussion of foreign language learning across the curriculum.

> Subscriptions: LISTSERV@brownvm.bitnet
>
> Participation: FLAC-L@brownvm.bitnet

FLTEACH: The Foreign Language Teaching Forum offers discussion among secondary and university teachers of modern foreign languages.

Subscriptions: `LISTSERV@ubvm.cc.buffalo.edu`

Participation: `FLTEACH@ubvm.cc.buffalo.edu`

FRENCHTALK: Discussion LISTSERV about things French, a service of the French embassy in Washington, D.C.

Subscriptions: `LISTPROC@yukon.cren.org`

Participation: `FRENCHTALK@yukon.cren.org`

FROGPROF: Sponsored by the American Association of Teachers of French and the Scientific Mission of the French Embassy in Washington, D.C., this forum is open to all teachers of French worldwide.

Subscriptions: `LISTSERV@bitnic.educom.edu`

Participation: `FROGPROF@bitnic.educom.edu`

FROGTALK: Open forum on any topic, in French.

Subscriptions: `LISTSERV@bitnic.bitnet`

Participation: `FROGTALK@bitnic.bitnet`

GAKUSEI: This suite of LISTSERVs is designed to provide students of Japanese as a foreign language a forum for practicing their developing language skills. Correspondence takes place in romanized Japanese according to proficiency levels (Gakusei-L, 1-2 years of study: Gakusei2-L, 2-3 years; and Gakusei3-L, advanced and native speakers of Japanese).

Subscriptions: `LISTPROC@uhunix.uhcc.hawaii.edu`

Participation: `GAKUSEI-L@uhunix.uhcc.hawaii.edu`

`GAKUSEI2-L@uhunix.uhcc.hawaii.edu`

`GAKUSEI3-L@uhunix.uhcc.hawaii.edu`

HEBLANG: Discussion group for biblical, medieval, Tiberian and modern Hebrew.

>   Subscriptions: `LISTSERV@israel.nysernet.org`

>   Participation: `HEBLANG@@israel.nysernet org`

IROQUOIS: Forum devoted to the preservation of the Iroquois language.

>   Subscriptions: `LISTSERV@vm.utcc.utoronto.ca`

>   Participation: `IROQUOIS@vm.utcc.utoronto.ca`

HAITI-L: Discussion about Haiti, in French and occasionally Haitian.

>   Subscriptions: `LISTSERV@conicit.ve`

>   Participation: `HAITI-L@conicit.ve`

KIDCAFEJ, KIDCAFEN, KIDCAFEP, KIDCAFES: Japanese, Scandinavian, Portuguese and Spanish language LISTSERVs, respectively, for students from 10-15 years old. For teachers of these languages, there are the corresponding LISTSERVs KIDLEADJ, KIDLEADN, KIDLEADP, and KIDLEADS.

>   Subscriptions: `LISTSERV@vml.nodak.edu`

>   Participation: `KIDCAFEJ@vml.nodak.edu`
>   `KIDCAFEN@vml.nodak.edu`
>   `KIDCAFEP@vml.nodak.edu`
>   `KIDCAFES@vml.nodak.edu`
>   `KIDLEADJ@VMl.nodak.edu`
>   `KIDLEADN@VMl.nodak.edu`
>   `KIDLEADP@VMl.nodak.edu`
>   `KIDLEADS@VMl.nodak.edu`

LCTL ("Less Commonly-Taught Languages") Project: The National Language Resource Center at the University of Minnesota maintains five LISTSERVs for teachers to share teaching ideas: Celtic-T, China-T, Hindi-T, Nordic-T, and Polish-T.

> Subscriptions: `LISTSERV@vm1.spcs.umn.edu`
>
> Participation: `CELTIC-T@vm1.spcs.umn.edu`, or substitute the name of another LISTSERV for CELTIC-T.

LLTI: Discussion of language learning and technology with an international perspective.

> Subscriptions: `LISTSERV@dartcms1.bitnet`
>
> Participation: `LLTI@dartcms1.bitnet`

MENDELE: A forum concerned with Yiddish literature and language. Submissions are accepted in Yiddish or English.

> Subscriptions: `LISTSERV@yalevm.ycc.yale.edu`
>
> Participation: `MENDELE@yalevm.ycc.yale.edu`

MULTI-L: Focusing on issues of language learning and education in multilingual settings.

> Subscriptions: `LISTSERV@barilvm.bitnet`
>
> Participation: `MULTI-L@barilvm.bitnet`

NAT-LANG: Forum devoted to preservation of the languages of indigenous peoples.

> Subscriptions: `LISTSERV@tamvm1.tamu.edu`
>
> Participation: `NAT-LANG@tamvm1.tamu.edu`

NCBE'S Electronic Discussion Groups: The National Clearinghouse for Bilingual Education maintains a number of specialized discussion groups, focusing on: early biliteracy, education reform, educational personnel training, educational technology, language preservation, refugee and immigrant education, research, special education, and a teacher roundtable. In addition, NCBE reference librarians staff a question-answering service (much like AskERIC, see "Multidisciplinary K-12 Internet Resources") via e-mail askncbe@ncbe.gwu.edu.

Subscriptions: MAJORDOMO@cis.ncbe.gwu.edu

Participation: EARBILIT@cis.ncbe.gwu.edu

EDREFORM@cis.ncbe.gwu.edu

EDTRAIN@cis.ncbe.gwu.edu

EDTECH@cis.ncbe.gwu.edu

LANGPRES@cis.ncbe.gwu.edu

REFUGED@cis.ncbe.gwu.edu

RESEARCH@cis.ncbe.gwu.edu

SPECED@cis.ncbe.gwu.edu

TEACHER@cis.ncbe.gwu.edu

"SL" LISTSERVs: Originating out of Latrobe University in Australia, these LISTSERVs offer English language learners a chance to sharpen their emerging skills around a common topic of interest. While designed for college-level students, secondary students can benefit from participation by working with their teachers to send polished texts.

Subscriptions: MAJORDOMO@latrobe.edu.au
(To subscribe to these LISTSERVs, be sure the listname is in capitals).

Participation: CHAT-SL@latrobe.edu.au
(Beginners' Discussion List)

DISCUSS-SL@latrobe.edu.au
(Advanced Discussion List)

BUSINESS-SL@latrobe.edu.au
(on Business & Economics)

ENVIR-SL@latrobe.edu.au
(On the Environment)

ENGL-SL@latrobe.edu.au
(On learning English)

EVENT-SL@latrobe.edu.au
(On Current Events)

MOVIE-SL@latrobe.edu.au
(On the Cinema)

MUSIC-SL@latrobe.edu.au
(On Music)

RIGHT-SL@latrobe.edu.au
(On Human Rights)

SCITECH-SL@latrobe.edu.au
(On Science & Technology)

SPORT-SL@latrobe.edu.au
(On Sports)

TRAVL-SL@latrobe.edu.au
(On Travel)

TCHR-SL@latrobe.edu.au
(For class projects)

SLART-L: Forum for teachers and researchers interested in second- or foreign-language acquisition.

Subscriptions: LISTSERV@cunyvm.cuny.edu

Participation: SLART-L@cunyvm.cuny.edu

SLLING-L: The "Sign Language Linguistics List."

Subscriptions: LISTSERV@yalevm.ycc.yale.edu

Participation: SLLING-L@yalevm.ycc.yale.edu

SWAHILI-L: Discussion for promoting the learning of Swahili.

>Subscriptions: `LISTSERV@relay.adp.wisc.edu`
>
>Participation: `SWAHILI-L@relay.adp.wisc.edu`

TESL-L: English as a second or foreign language discussion group, with numerous subLISTSERVs. Subscribe to TESL-L before subscribing to the subgroups, which consist of TESLCA-L (computer-assisted language learning), TESLFF-L (fluency first and whole language), TESLIE-L (intensive English programs), TESLIT-L (adult education and literacy), TESLJB-L (jobs and employment issues), and TESLMW-L (materials writers).

>Subscriptions: `LISTSERV@cunyvm.cuny.edu`
>
>Participation: `TESL-L@cunyvm.cuny.edu`

TESLK-12: A separate forum for ESL teachers at the elementary and secondary school levels run by TESL-L but not a subLISTSERV; subscribe directly.

>Subscriptions: `LISTSERV@cunyvm.cuny.edu`
>
>Participation: `TESLK-12@cunyvm.cuny.edu`

USENET NEWSGROUPS

The following Usenet newsgroups focus on topics pertinent to second language acquisition.

`k12.lang.esp-eng` Forum for Spanish learners, in Spanish.
`k12.lang.deutsch-eng` German "conversational" practice.
`k12.lang.francais` French language practice.
`k12.lang.japanese` Discussion group for Japanese learners.
`k12.lang.russian` Russian language discussion.
`soc.culture.french` Discussion of French culture.
`soc.culture.german` Discussion of German culture.

GOPHERS

AATF: Run by the American Association of Teachers of French, this Gopher is replete with teaching units. All materials are in French.

```
gopher://utsainfo.jpl.utsa.edu -->AATF-American
Association of Teachers of French/ -->Guide to on-line
Pedagogical Activities in French
```

California Department of Education: Hosts the Bilingual Education Network (BiEN).

```
gopher://goldmine.cde.ca.gov
```

Language Minority Research Institute: A Gopher concerned with bilingual education and the schooling of linguistic minority students.

```
gopher://lmrinet.gse.ucsb.edu
```

NCBE Gopher: The National Clearinghouse on Bilingual Education lists resources and up-to-date information concerning the education of linguistically-diverse students.

```
gopher://gopher.ncbe.gwu.edu
```

The TESL/TEFL Gopher: Provides resources relevant to teachers of English as a second or foreign language.

```
gopher://cunyvm.cuny.edu -->Subject Specific Gopher
-->Teaching English as a Second/Foreign Language
-->Teacher Training Resources
```

WORLD WIDE WEB (WWW)

The E-mail Pen Pal Connection: From the Virtual English Language Center (an on-line resource for students of English as a second or foreign language), this Web site brings together native English speakers and students of English worldwide.

```
http://www.interport.net/~comenius/pen-pal.html
```

The EMBASSY OF SPAIN IN OTTAWA: A web site devoted to contemporary life in Spain, as well as Spanish history and culture. Viewable in English and in Spanish.

```
http://www.civeng.carleton.ca/SiSpain/
```

EXCHANGE: A WWW-based ESL/EFL magazine devoted to publishing writings of ESL/EFL learners and teachers, as well as sharing effective teaching/learning strategies.

For graphical format: `http://www.ed.uiuc.edu/exchange/`
For TEXT ONLY: `http://www.ed.uiuc.edu/exchange/ex-change.html`

The HUMAN-LANGUAGES PAGE: A huge listing of pointers to language learning resources.

```
http://www.willamette.edu/~tjones/Language-Page.html
```

TESL-EJ: The electronic journal for ESL/EFL professionals is also available on the Web. (See "E-journals," above.)

```
http://cc2000.kyoto-su.ac.jp/information/
tesl-ej/index.html
http://www.well.com/www/sokolik/index.html
```

University of Texas Bilingual Education Web Page/Resource Page: Of local interest to Texans working in bilingual education, but with an

"Internet Resource Page" providing links to other sites dealing with bilingual/bicultural education nationally and internationally.

```
http://www.edb.utexas.edu/coe/depts/CI/bilingue/re-
sources.html
```

WebLouvre ANNOUNCE: Located in Paris, this award-winning Web site now houses three on-line exhibits on French medieval art, well-known paintings from famous artists, and a tour of Paris, the Eiffel Tower, and the Champs-Elysees.

```
http://mistral.enst.fr/~pioch/louvre/ or
http://mistral.enst.fr/
```

TELNET

MOO Francais or FrenchMOO: Something like a role-playing game where students assume French identities and visit a "virtual reality" version of Paris.

```
telnet://logos.daedalus.com:8888
```

login as "visiteur" then type the letter "o" and read the guide for new visitors. Direct questions by e-mail to Mark Horan at HORAN@lclark.edu.

BOOKS

Warschauer, Mark (1995). *E-Mail for English Teaching: Bringing the Internet and Computer Learning Networks into the Language Classroom.* TESOL Publications. (Ordering information from <TESOL@tesol.edu>.)

Warschauer, Mark (Ed.) (1995). *Virtual Connections: Online Activities and Projects for Networking Language Learners.* Second Language Teaching and Curriculum Center, University of Hawaii. (Ordering information from <SLTCC@uhunix.uhcc.hawaii.edu>.)

Resources for Students with Special Learning Needs

E-JOURNALS AND NEWSLETTERS

ABILITY: An e-journal concerned with students who are academically, artistically, or athletically talented. A companion LISTSERV, ABLE-L (below), discusses these issues.

> Subscriptions: LISTSERV@asuvm.inre.asu.edu
> Participation: ABILITY@asuvm.inre.asu.edu

ADVOCACY: A discussion list centering on access and civil rights issues of people with disabilities.

> Subscriptions: LISTSERV@sjuvm.stjohns.edu
> Participation: ADVOCACY@sjuvm.stjohns.edu

DEAF-MAGAZINE: E-newsletter concerned with deaf lifestyles.

> Subscriptions: LISTSERV@listserv.deaf-magazine.org
> Participation: DEAF-MAGAZINE@listserv.deaf-magazine.org

DOIT (Disabilities, Opportunities, Internetworking and Technology) *NEWS:* A newsletter produced at the University of Washington designed to recruit and retain students with disabilities into science, engineering, and mathematics academic programs and careers.

> e-mail: DOIT@u.washington.edu

HANDICAP DIGEST: Summaries of articles from a Usenet newsgroup, *Handicap News,* and several conferences dealing with disabilities.

> Subscriptions: WTM@bunker.shel.isc-br.com
> Participation: Address forwarded after subscribing.

INFORMATION TECHNOLOGY AND DISABILITIES: A quarterly journal devoted to all aspects of computer-mediated learning with a special focus on the Internet and broad range of authors.

Journal Subscriptions: `LISTSERV@sjuvm.stjohns.edu`

In the body of the message, type:
`Subscribe itd-jnl <first name> <last name>`

Table of Contents Subscriptions: `LISTSERV@sjuvm.stjohns.edu`
In the body of the message, type:
`Subscribe itd-toc <first name> <last name>`

LISTSERVS

ABLE-L: Companion LISTSERV to the e-journal *Ability* that discusses the education of gifted students.

Subscriptions: `LISTSERV@asuacad.bitnet`

Participation: `ABLE-L@asuacad.bitnet`

ADA-LAW: Discussion of the Americans With Disabilities Act.

Subscriptions: `LISTSERV@listserv@vml.nodak.edu`

Participation: `ADA-LAW@vml.nodak.edu`

ALTLEARN: Concerning alternative approaches to learning, with a focus on assistive technologies.

Subscriptions: `LISTSERV@stjohns.edu`

Participation: `ALTLEARN@stjohns.edu`

ANI-L: Discussion for sharing among autistic people, their families and friends, and to promote civil rights for the autistic.

Subscriptions: `LISTSERV@utkvml.utk.edu`

Participation: `ANI-L@utkvml.utk.edu`

AUTISM: An active discussion group on all types of developmental disabilities.

> Subscriptions: `LISTSERV@sjuvm.stjohns.edu`
>
> Participation: `AUTISM@sjuvm.stjohns.edu`

AXSLIB-L: Discussion on issues of access to libraries.

> Subscriptions: `LISTSERV@sjuvm.stjohns.edu`
>
> Participation: `AXSLIB-L@sjuvm.stjohns.edu`

BEHAVIOR: A forum on behavioral and emotional disorders among youth, focused on attention deficit disorder, with and without hyperactivity, and autism. Includes parents and teachers.

> Subscriptions: `LISTSERV@asuacad`
>
> Participation: `BEHAVIOR@asuacad`

BLIND-L: A forum on adaptive computer use for and by persons who are blind.

> Subscriptions: `LISTSERV@uafysyb.bitnet`
>
> Participation: `BLIND-L@uafysyb.bitnet`

CEC-TAM: A forum sponsored by the Technology and Media Division of the Council for Exceptional Children to discuss the use of technology with special needs learners.

> Subscriptions: `LISTSERV@sjuvm.stjohns.edu`
>
> Participation: `CEC-TAM@sjuvm.stjohns.edu`

COMMDIS: Concerns speech disorders.

> Subscriptions: `LISTSERV@rpitsvm.bitnet`
>
> Participation: `COMMDIS@rpitsvm.bitnet`

COUNSELING: Discussion among counselors, counselor educators, graduate students, and teachers on mental health issues.

> Subscriptions: ICN-REQUEST@ctrvax.vanderbilt.edu
>
> Participation: COUNSELING@ctrvax.vanderbilt.edu

CREA-CPS: A discussion of creativity in education, designed for high school students and adults.

> Subscriptions: LISTSERV@nic.surfnet.nl
>
> Participation: CREA-CPS@nic.surfnet.nl

DADVOCAT: A forum on fathers as advocates for children with disabilities or special health needs.

> Subscriptions: LISTSERV@ukcc.uky.edu
>
> Participation: DADVOCAT@ukcc.uky.edu

DDFIND-L: General discussion on disabilities.

> Subscriptions: LISTSERV@vm1.nodak.edu
>
> Participation: DDFIND-L@vm1.nodak.edu

DEAF-L: Discussion of topics concerning deafness.

> Subscriptions: LISTSERV@siucvmb.bitnet
>
> Participation: DEAL-L@siucvmb.bitnet

DISRES-L: A forum on disability research.

> Subscriptions: LISTSERV@ryevm.ryerson.ca
>
> Participation: DISRES-L@ryevm.ryerson.ca

DSSHE-L: Discussion among service providers for students with disabilities.

> Subscriptions: LISTSERV@ubvm.cc.buffalo.edu
>
> Participation: DSSHE-L@ubvm.cc.buffalo.edu

EASI: The Equal Access to Software and Information forum discusses issues relating to technology use by persons with disabilities.

> Subscriptions: `LISTSERV@sjuvm.stjohns.edu`
> Participation: `EASI@sjuvm.stjohns.edu`

EDSTYLE: Concerns different learning styles and their implications for educating disabled students.

> Subscriptions: `LISTSERV@sjuvm.stjohns.edu`
> Participation: `EDSTYLE@sjuvm.stjohns.edu`

EDUDEAF: For teachers of the deaf and the hard-of-hearing.

> Subscriptions: `LISTSERV@ukcc.uky.edu`
> Participation: `EDUDEAF@ukcc.uky.edu`

GIFTEDNET-L: A forum on approaches to gifted and talented education.

> Subscriptions: `LISTSERVER@listserv.cc.wm.edu`
> Participation: `GIFTEDNET-L@listserv.cc.wm.edu`

GTOT-L: Concerns children under six who are gifted.

> Subscriptions: `MAJORDOMO@eskimo.com`
> Participation: `GTOT-L@eskimo.com`

LD-LIST: Discusses learning disabilities in general.

> Subscriptions: `LD-LIST-REQUEST@east.pima.edu`
> Participation: `LD-LIST@east.pima.edu`

L-HCAP: Like EASI, L-CAP focuses on adaptive computer hardware and software.

> Subscriptions: `LISTSERV@vml.nodak.edu`
>
> Participation: `L-CAP@vml.nodak.edu`

LTCARE-L: Discusses research for policy decision on physical and cognitive disabilities associated with aging.

> Subscriptions: `LISTSERV@nihlist.bitnet`
>
> Participation: `LTCARE-L@nihlist.bitnet`

MOBILITY: Discusses disabilities involving mobility.

> Subscriptions: `LISTSERV@sjuvm.stjohns.edu`
>
> Participation: `MOBILITY@sjuvm.stjohns.edu`

SPEDTALK: Concerned with all topics about disabilities. Includes participation of teachers, students, parents, and professors.

> Subscriptions: `MAJORDOMO@virginia.edu`
>
> Participation: `SPEDTALK@virginia.edu`

STARNET: Discusses innovative strategies for working with "at-risk" students, for parents, educators, and graduate students of education. Previous three months' discussions are archived at `gopher://services.dese.state.mo.us`.

> Subscriptions: `LISTPROC@services.dese.state.mo.us`
>
> Participation: `STARNET@services.dese.state.mo.us`

STUTT-L: A forum on stuttering.

> Subscriptions: `LISTSERV@vm.temple.edu`
>
> Participation: `STUTT-L@vm.temple.edu`

TAG-L: A forum on educating talented and gifted students.

> Subscriptions: `LISTSERV@vml.nodak.edu`
> Participation: `TAG-L@vml.nodak.edu`

TALKBACK: A discussion group for children with disabilities.

> Subscriptions: `LISTSERV@sjuvm.bitnet`
> Participation: `TALKBACK@sjuvm.bitnet`

YOUTHNET: A discussion group for therapists working with youth.

> Subscriptions: `LISTSERV@indycms.iupui.edu`
> Participation: `YOUTHNET@indycms.iupui.edu`

GOPHERS

Books for Gifted Featuring Gifted: Resources in the form of reviews of books for gifted students that feature gifted children as main characters.

```
gopher://gopher ctdnet.acns.nwu.edu -->The Center for
Talent Development -->Book Lists-Reviews -->Bibliography
-->L. Silverman, Counseling the Gifted, etc. -->Books for
Gifted Featuring Gifted
```

British Columbia Ministry of Education: Useful directories for special education in general and especially for parents and teachers of hearing-impaired and deaf children.

```
gopher://cln.etc.bc.ca --> B.C. and Canadian Government
Gophers/ -->Government of British Columbia/ -->BC Ministry
of Education (CLN.TDEB)/ -->Special Education Information
(Under Development)/ -->Special Education Resources/
-->Teacher Resources/ -->Resource Guide: Hard of Hearing &
Deaf Students
```

Cornucopia of Disability Information: The most complete Gopher devoted to resources for the education of people with disabilities.

```
gopher://val-dor.cc.buffalo.edu
```

Duke University's Talent Identification Program: Focused on summer and international programs for talented young people.

```
gopher://gopher arnold.tip.duke.edu -->Duke University
-->TIP
```

ERIC Clearinghouse on Disabilities and Gifted Education: Resources for communication disorders, behavior disorders, developmental disabilities, emotional disturbance, and severe disability.

```
gopher://ericir.syr.edu -->Clearinghouses -->ERIC Clearing-
house on Disabilities and Gifted Education/
```

First Day of GT: A lesson plan for launching a lower elementary gifted and talented class.

```
gopher://gopher bvsd.k12.co.us -->Educational Resources
-->Lesson Plans -->Big Sky -->Misc. lesson plans -->First
Day in GT
```

Gifted Education: A listing of university programs, workshops, and extracurricular activities for gifted students.

```
gopher://gopher.pps.pgh.pa.us -->k12 Net Resources -->Edu-
cational Resources -->Gifted
```

Johns Hopkins Center for Talented Youth: Listings of resources for secondary school academically talented youth.

```
gopher://gopher jhuniverse.hcf.jhu.edu -->Div., Centers,
and Affiliates -->CTY
```

The HEATH Ressource Center: A Federal clearinghouse on information about education and persons with disabilities is now accessible on the internet. It is a significant source of up-to-date information on education, training, funding, legislation, and persons with disabilities.

```
gopher://bobcat-ace.nche.edu -->ACE Departments -->HEATH
Resource Center
```

Kent State University Deaf Education Resource Archive: A Gopher devoted to issues affecting parents and educators of deaf or hard-of-hearing students.

```
gopher://shiva.educ.kent.edu
```

The Library of Congress: Comprehensive bibliography on dyslexia.

```
gopher://marvel.loc.gov -->Search LC MARVEL Menus/
-->Search LC MARVEL menus using Jughead <?>,
```
then type in the search such as Dyslexia.

Missouri Gifted Education Programs: Resources of national interest developed in Missouri for academically gifted students.

```
gopher://gopher services.dese.state.mo.us -->Elementary
and Secondary School Info -->Educational Program -->Gifted
Ed Programs
```

Michigan State University Gopher: A keyword search for "deaf" or "deaf education" from the main menu reveals a wealth of resources.

```
gopher://burrow.cl.msu.edu
```

Project Success Enrichment: A program validated by the National Diffusion Network that develops high-level thinking in art, literature, mathematics, and music.

```
gopher://gopher gopher.ed.gov -->Educational Research
-->NDN -->Educational plans that work -->Gifted
```

Rice University: Contains the OLMIM database.

```
gopher://handicap.afd.olivetti.com -->Disability re-
sources/ -->rare disorders
```

St. Johns University Electronic Rehabilitation Resources Center: Offers access to major software archives and a wide array of other information on the education of students with disabilities.

```
gopher://sjuvm.stjohns.edu
```

Look under "What's New on the SJU Gopher," "Disability and Rehabilitation Resources," or "Education and Teaching Resources."

Stanford University Education Program for Gifted Youth: Documents related to computer-based mathematics education courses for secondary-school gifted students leading to university-level achievement.

```
gopher://gopher kanpai.stanford.edu -->EPGY
```

Syracuse University: Lists documents on facilitated communication.

```
gopher://cwis.syr.edu -->Departmental and other S.U. Serv-
ers -->School of Education -->Facilitated Communication In-
stitute-FC, AUTISM and developmental disability.
```

William and Mary University Center for Gifted Education: Curriculum resources relevant to gifted and talented education programs.

```
gopher://gopher.wm.edu -->School of Education -->Publica-
tions and Ordering -->Information on National Language Arts
```

Science and Mathematics Units may be found at:

```
-->Center for Gifted Education -->Other Resources
```

WORLD WIDE WEB (WWW)

CTY Web Page: The Center for Talented Youth of Johns Hopkins University offers access to its "Writing Tutorials" and provides links to other sites concerned with gifted and talented education and writing.

```
http://jhunix.hcf.jhu.edu/~ewt2
```

EASI Web Page: See description under LISTSERVs, above.

```
http://www.rit.edu/~easi
```

The Gifted Education Center of the National Capitol Area Public Access Network: A general repository for gifted and talented education resources, with a focus on parent involvement.

```
http://www.nas.nasa.gov/HPCC/K12/EDRC23.html
```

Learning Disabilities: Designed for educators, administrators, parents, and daycare workers as a repository of information on identification, assessment, and services for students with learning disabilities.

```
http://www.sped.ukans.edu/speddisabilitiesstuff/speddisabili
ties-child.html
```

NEC*TAS: The National Early Childhood Technical Assistance System maintains a Web site that focuses on policies and programs for young children with disabilities.

```
http://www.nectas.unc.edu/
```

Stanford University Education Program for Gifted Youth: See description under "Gophers," above.

```
http://kampai.stanford.edu/epgy/pamph/pamph.html
```

TELNET

The Gifted Education Center of the National Capitol Area Public Access Network: See description under "World Wide Web," above.

```
telnet://cap.gwu.edu
login: guest
password: visitor
type: go gifted
```

Freenet: A listing of community services available for disability assistance.

```
telnet://leo.nmc.edu -->login: visitor
-->community services
-->resources A-D
   -->disability assistance
```

Prairenet Freenet: A listing of exemplary disability support groups.

```
telnet://firefly.prairienet.org
-->login: visitor
-->community center
-->community health center
-->self-help center
-->listing of disability groups
```

UMD: A resource listing adaptive software, hardware and other disability-related topics. Disability resources are found in the "Reading Room" of "Educational Resources."

```
telnet://info.umd.edu
```

FTP SITES

American Sign Language Software Tutors: Several programs are available through anonymous FTP.

```
ftp://handicap.afd.olevetti.com/cd/pub/hear-
ing/SF600AHD.ZIP, SIGN4TH.ZIP, SIMCGA40.ZIP, ASL-TRAN.ZIP,
and LSIGN25.ZIP
```

Children and Disabilities: Files on children and disabilities, and education for people with handicapping conditions.

```
ftp://handicap.shel.isc.-br.com//pub/children or /educ
```

Handicap News FTP Archives: Over 50 directories of information on a wide range of disabilities.

```
ftp://handicap.afd.olivetti.com/pub
```

North Dakota State University: Stores the archives of several LISTSERVs of interest to the educator of the disabled.

```
ftp://vm1.nodak.edu
```

Arts in Education

LISTSERVs

ASTR-L: Theater history discussion.

> Subscriptions: LISTSERV@uiucvmd.bitnet
> Participation: ASTR-L@uiucvmd.bitnet

CANDRAMA: Canadian theater discussion.

> Subscriptions: LISTSERV@unbvml.bitnet
> Participation: CANDRAMA@unbvml

C-ARTS is a moderated forum where arts-related Internet resources are announced and evaluated. Housed at the University of New Brunswick in Canada, C-ARTS is modeled after the EDRES-L LISTSERV located there. Like C-EDRES, C-ARTS has a companion list, C-ARTSdb, where evaluations are archived. Finally, Internet sites that have been reviewed by C-ARTS are accessible through a Web server at http://cspace.unb.ca/c-arts/ (take care to use the final slash when typing in this URL [Uniform Resource Locator] on your Web browser).

> Subscriptions: LISTSERV@LISTSERV.UNB.CA

CINEMA-L: Discusses the art of film.

> Subscriptions: LISTSERV@american.edu.bitnet
> Participation: CINEMA-L@american.edu.bitnet

DANCE-L: Principally focusing on folk-dance and traditional dances, this discussion group explores the role of computers in cultural development.

> Subscriptions: LISTSERV@hearn.nic.surfnet.nl
> Participation: DANCE-L@hearn.nic.surfnet.nl

IMAGE-L: Discussion of transmitting art graphics through the Internet.

Subscriptions: `LISTSERV@trearn.bitnet`
Participation: `IMAGE-L@trearn.bitnet`

INSEA-L: LISTSERV of the International Society for Education through Art. Book reviews and evaluations of Internet resources.

Subscriptions: `LISTSERV@unbvml.csd.unb.ca`
Participation: `INSEA-L@unbvml.csd.unb.ca`

MEDIA-L: Multimedia arts discussion.

Subscriptions: `LISTSERV@bingvmb.bitnet`
Participation: `MEDIAL-L@bingvmb.bitnet`

MEDIAWEB: A LISTSERV devoted to helping educators negotiate the many WEB sites devoted to film and video.

Subscriptions: `LISTSERV@vm.temple.edu`
Participation: `MEDIAWEB@vm.temple.edu`

NAEATASK: The LISTSERV of the NAEA Art Teacher Education Task Force. Position papers on art education issues. New Internet sites often are announced here.

Subscriptions: `LISTSERV@arizvml.ccit.arizona.edu`
Participation: `NAEATASK@arizvml.ccit.arizona.edu`

NEWMEDIA: A multimedia discussion group.

Subscriptions: `LISTSERV@unb.ca`
Participation: `NEWMEDIA@unb.ca`

PERFORM-L: Performance arts discussion.

>Subscriptions: LISTSERV@acfcluster.nyu.edu
>
>Participation: PERFORM-L@acfcluster.nyu.edu

PhotoForum: Photo/imaging education discussion.

>Subscriptions: LISTSERV@listserver.isc.rit.edu
>
>Participation: PHOTOFORUM@listserver.isc.rit.edu

SHAKSPER: Discusses Shakespeare's poetry and plays.

>Subscriptions: LISTSERV@utoronto.bitnet
>
>Participation: SHAKSPER@utoronto.bitnet

TEACHART: The LISTSERV of the National Museum of American Art. Discussion of art education issues for classroom practitioners. An outgrowth of NMAA's Summer Institutes for Teachers. Ask about "African American Artists: Affirmation Today."

>Subscriptions: LISTSERV@sivm.si.edu
>
>Participation: LISTSERV@sivm.si.edu

THEATRE: Theater arts discussion.

>Subscriptions: LISTSERV@grearn.bitnet
>
>Participation: THEATRE@grearn.bitnet

UAARTED: A supportive discussion group of art educators concerned with day-to-day teaching.

>Subscriptions: LISTSERV@arizvm1.bitnet
>
>Participation: UAARTED@arizvm1.bitnet

USENET NEWSGROUPS

alt.artcom Focuses on visual arts
alt.arts.ballet Performing arts and dance forum.
alt.music General music discussion.
clari.news.arts Announcements of general arts news.
clari.news.music Announcements of music news.
rec.arts.dance Discussion of performing arts and dance.
rec.arts.movies.* Film production and reviews. criticism.
rec.arts.theatre Discussion of theater.
rec.music General music discussion.
rec.photo Discussion of photography

GOPHERS

ArtsEdge Information Gallery: A cooperative project between the John F. Kennedy Center for the Performing Arts, the National Endowment for the Arts, and the U.S. Department of Education. A huge resource for documents on arts education; especially valuable are its newsletter and the program profiles of exemplary arts education curricula that can be replicated.

```
gopher://purple.tmn.com/ -->artsedge information gallery
```

Complete Works of Shakespeare

```
gopher://libnet.wright.edu/ -->Subject Grouping of In-
dexes, Full Text, and Internet Resources -->Fine Arts
(Art, Music, Theatre) -->Internet Resources Grouped by
Subject -->Complete works of Shakespeare
```

Creative Columbia—A Blueprint for Action: A description of an initiative to link city planning with cultural development, with a focus on using arts extensively in education.

```
gopher://bigcat.missour.edu/ -->Government Center -->City
of Columbia -->Columbia City Government Major Reports
-->Creative Columbia
```

Dallas Museum of Art: A repository of graphic images that can be downloaded using "freeware" or "shareware" provided in the Gopher itself; also, an on-line art history reference section.

```
gopher://gopher.unt.edu/ -Denton, Dallas, Ft. Worth Infor-
mation Resources -->Dallas -->Museum of Art - Information
and images
```

Discipline-Based Theatre Education: Developed by the Southeast Institute for Education in Theatre, this dramatic arts curriculum with a focus on social, historical, and multicultural issues can serve as a model for replication.

```
gopher://cecasun.utc.edu/scea/ -->SIET -->Discipline-Based
Theatre Education
```

Guide to Theater Resources on the Internet: Lists resources for schools with theater arts programs.

```
gopher://gopher.umich.edu/ -->Library Resources -->Humani-
ties Resources -->Internet Resource Guides for the Humani-
ties -->Guides on the Humanities -->Theatre
```

Minnesota Center for Arts Information: Arts education resources.

```
gopher://gopher.mcae.k12.mn.us
```

National Standards for Art Education: Developed by a consortium of National Arts Education Associations and funded by the U.S. Department of Education, the National Endowment for the Arts, and the National Endowment for the Humanities, national standards were developed for grades K-4, 5-8, and 9-12 in the areas of dance, music, theater, and the visual arts.

```
gopher://gopher.ed.gov/ -->United States Department of
Education: Publications -->ED-OERI-Publications: Full Text
-->National Standards for Art Education
```

WORLD WIDE WEB (WWW)

ACCAD (the Advanced Computing Center for the Arts and Design) at the Ohio State University Department of Art: The Web site of one of the most important art departments exploring arts on the Internet.

```
http://www.cgrg.ohio-state.edu/COTA/Art/text/
ARTHOMEPAGE.html
```

The Andy Warhol Museum Home Page: A tour of this collection, with samples of various works by the artist.

```
http://www.warhol.org/warhol
```

Ansel Adams Photographs: Images and explanatory text on the artist and his photographic methods.

```
http://bookweb.cwis.uci.edu:8042/AdamsHome.html
```

ArtsEdge (See "Gopher" listing, above, for description.)

```
http://k12.cnidr.org/janicek12/artsedge/artsedge.html
```

Arts Resources Website: Constructed by Marcus Kruse of the Art Gallery of the Ohio State University at Newark, this homepage leads to 200 museums and arts organizations.

```
http://www.cgrg.ohio-state.edu/Newark/artsres.html
```

ArtSource: Networked resources on art and architecture are gathered here for teachers, students, artists, and academics.

`http://www.uky.edu/Artsource/artsourcehome.html`

The Electric Gallery: An on-line museum with eclectic tastes and "wings" ranging from jazz and blues to Haitian art, the Amazon Project (viewer discretion recommended!), and folk art.

`http://www.egallery.com/egallery/`

Emory University, Michael C. Carlos Museum: An on-line museum with virtual exhibitions on ancient Americas, ancient Egypt, ancient Near East, artworks on paper, Asia, Greece and Rome, and sub-Saharan Africa.

`http://www.cc.emory.edu/CARLOS/carlos.html`

Fluxus on-line: An on-line museum most frequently described as "iconoclastic." Be prepared for variety.

`http://www.panix.com:80/fluxus/`

'HypArt': Devoted to the creation, display, and discussion of images created by more than one artist in collaboration.

`http://rzsun01.rrz.uni-hamburg.de/cgi-bin/HypArt.sh`

Institute of Egyptian Art and Archaeology: Visuals and text on the art of ancient Egypt, located at Egypt's University of Memphis.

`http://www.memst.edu/egypt/main.html`

Krannert Art Museum: An on-line museum with a virtual exhibition that links images with texts explaining the artist's work and life.

`http://www.ncsa.uiuc.edu/General/UIUC/KrannertArtMuseum/`
`KrannertArtHome.html`

LaTrobe University Art Museum: Choose "on-line Exhibition" for a guided tour.

> http://www.latrobe.edu.au/Glenn/Museum/ArtMuseumHome.html

Library of Congress Exhibits: Numerous exhibitions accompanied by extensive supporting documentation. See especially "Rome Reborn."

> http://lcweb.loc.gov/homepage/exhibits.html

Musee du Louvre: A silent walk through the Louvre, as little text and no sound is provided yet.

> http://meteora.ucsd.edu/norman/paris/Musees/Louvre

911 Gallery: A museum that features electronic media art, with critical and explanatory text linked to images and music.

> http://www.iquest.net/911/iq_911.html

On-line Museum of Singapore Art and History: Six exhibits, linking images with explanatory text, on art from Singapore.

> http://www.gov.sg/nhb/museum.html

Surrealist Homepage: Images and music are featured at this Web site; also a brief tour of the Dali Museum.

> http://pharmdec.wustl.edu/juju/surr/surrealism/
> surrealist.html

WebLouvre: Especially noteworthy is the exhibition on the Impressionists that takes full advantage of improving Web software to explore "threads" of sequenced paintings and focus in on details of individual works of art.

> http://mistral.enst.fr/~pioch/louvre/

Wentworth Gallery: Reproductions of original oil paintings, limited edition serigraphs, lithographs and sculptures from artists around the world.

```
http://wentworth-art.com
```

TELNET

Arizona State University on-line Public Catalogue: Two databases can be searched for keywords, the Theatre for Youth database and the American Alliance for Theatre and Education database.

```
telnet://carl.lib.asu.edu/ -->CARL -->Other ASU Libraries
Specialized Collections and Databases -->Theatre for Youth
```

FTP SITES

Fine Art Forum Directory of On-Line Resources: An enormous archive of art education and appreciation resources.

```
ftp://ra.msstate.edu//pub/archives/finearton-line/
on-lineDirectory
```

FUNET (Finnish University) Archive: A bibliography of arts education related resources.

```
ftp://ftp.funet.fi/pub/doc/library/artbase.txt.Z
```

University of New Brunswick: Arts education resource listing.

```
ftp://jupiter.sun.csd.unb.ca/pub/faculty.ed/arts
```

Language Arts

E-JOURNALS AND NEWSLETTERS

News From the Windowsill (formerly **WEB On-line Review**): Reviews of children's literature by Wendy E. Betts and others, with theme issues and genre-specific issues. To subscribe, send e-mail to KIDSBOOK-RE-QUEST@armory.com and in the body of the message include your name and e-mail address. For back issues, see the New Mexico State University Gopher site, below.

LISTSERVS

BOOKBRAG: Discussion on book reviews, author reviews, and teaching suggestions.

> Subscriptions: `BOOKBRAG-REQUEST@scholastic.com`
> Participation: `BOOKBRAG@scholastic.com`

CANLIT-L: Bilingual in English and French, this LISTSERV is devoted to Canadian children's literature and literature in general. Uses the rare MAILSERV program for subscriptions. Include the words "subscribe CANLIT-L" in the body of your subscription message, and keep the welcoming message.

> Subscriptions: `MAILSERV@nlc-bnc.ca`
> Participation: `CANLIT-L@nlc-bnc.ca`

CHILDLIT: Discussion among parents and teachers of children's literature.

> Subscriptions: `LISTSERV@rutvml.bitnet`
> Participation: `CHILDLIT@rutvml.bitnet`

CHILDRENS-VOICE: See description of this important project in "Bilingualism and Second-Language Acquisition."

Subscriptions: LISTPROC@schoolnet.carleton.ca

Participation: SCHOOLNET.carleton.ca

CREWRT-L: Forum on creative writing pedagogy for teachers and students.

Subscriptions: LISTSERV@umcvmb.missouri.edu

Participation: CREWRT-L@umcvmb.missouri.edu

CSRNOT-L: A LISTSERV maintained by the Center for the Study of Reading at the University of Illinois at Urbana-Champaign.

Subscriptions: LISTSERV@vmd.cso.uiuc.edu

Participation: CSRNOT-L@vmd.cso.uiuc.edu

ENGLISH: Discussion on using computers to teach English literature and composition.

Subscriptions: LISTSERV@utarlvml.uta.edu

Participation: ENGLISH@utarlvml.uta.edu

ENGLISH-TEACHERS: Forum for discussion of the teaching of language arts from Kindergarten through University.

Subscriptions: MAJORDOMO@uxl.cso.uiuc.edu or
MAJORDOMO@listserv.cso.uiuc.edu

Participation: ENGLISH-TEACHERS@uxl.cso.uiuc.edu

ERIC-L: Discussion group focusing on the teaching and study of literature.

Subscriptions: LISTSERV@iubvm.ucs.indiana.edu

Participation: ERIC-L@iubvm.ucs.indiana.edu

FOLKLORE: Discussion of all aspects of folklore.

> Subscriptions: `FOLKLORE@tamvm1.tamu.edu`
>
> Participation: `LISTSERV@tamvm1.tamu.edu`

KIDLIT-L: A discussion list of children's literature.

> Subscriptions: `LISTSERV@bingvm.cc.binghamton.edu`
>
> Participation: `KIDLIT-L@bingvm.cc.binghamton.edu`

T-AMLIT: Teaching The American Literatures is a discussion group about teaching the expanding canon of literary arts.

> Subscriptions: `LISTSERV@bitnic.educom.edu`
>
> Participation: `T-AMLIT@bitnic.educom.edu`

USENET NEWSGROUPS

`alt.books.review` A forum for writers of book reviews.

`comp.edu.compositions` Discussion on writing and the potential of the Internet for encouraging composition skills.

`rec.arts.books.childrens` Discussion of articles and reviews written by members of this newsgroup on children's literature.

GOPHERS

American Folklore Society: Catalogs electronic texts on folklore, including a full directory of fairy tales.

```
gopher://panam.edu -->American Folklore Society -->Other
Gophers -->Folklore, Folklife, and Ethnomusicology (via
MARVEL) -->E-Texts Related to Folklore and Mythology
```

Books for Children and Young Adults: Focusing on environmental themes, compiled by the American Association for the Advancement of Science (AAAS).

```
gopher://freenet.victoria.bc.ca -->Environment and Science
Information -->Environmental Education Books and Learning
Resources -->Books for Children and Young Adults
```

Children's Literature—A Library Timesaver: A Gopher that gives a parent or educator a tutorial on using a library with an on-line Public Access Catalog (OPAC) to find children's literature resources.

```
gopher://cwis.sfu.ca -->Library Catalogue, Electronic
Library, Library Info -->Humanities Handouts -->Children's
Literature: A Library Timesaver
```

To practice using OPACs, utilize the world's central Gopher site at the University of Minnesota. Through this Gopher it is possible to Telnet to any of the OPAC listings at libraries around the world. Indiana University is one rich site for children's literature resources and is keyword searchable to help with curriculum planning.

```
gopher://hafnhaf.micro.umn.edu --> Libraries --> Library
Catalogs via Telnet --> Library Catalogs from Other Insti-
tutions --> Catalogs Listed by Location --> Americas -->
United States --> Indiana --> Indiana University
```

and login as "guest," or

```
telnet://consultant.micro.umn.edu
```

and login as "gopher" and follow the path above.

The Children's Literature Center of the Library of Congress: Complete listings of resources available over the Internet.

```
gopher://marvel.loc.gov -->Research and Reference (Public
Services) -->Reading Rooms of the Library of Congress
(Under Construction) -->Children's Literature Center
-->About the Children's Literature Center
```

Georgetown University's Catalogue of Projects in Electronic Text (CPET): Cataloguing dozens of curriculum projects that focus on using computers and the Internet for the study of literature, this Gopher site is an excellent "companion resource" to the Library of Congress ALEX Gopher catalogue of electronic texts. (See "Multidisciplinary K-12 Internet Resources.")

```
gopher:///liberty.uc.wlu.edu/0/library/human/eng/cpet
```

MBNet—On-line Canadian Writing: Located in Manitoba Province, this Gopher provides resources on Canadian authors and writing for all grade levels.

```
gopher://access.mbnet.mb.ca -->Services Provided by Mem-
bers of MBnet -->on-line - Canadian Writing
```

The New Mexico State University Library Electronic Resources on Children's Literature: The largest Gopher listing devoted to many facets of children's literature. Available are reviews and ordering information for Caldecott and Children's Choice award winners, full-text books listed by author's names, a directory of author's birthdays to help sequence the language arts curriculum, public-domain folktales, resource listings, and book reviews. Especially valuable is the directory "Internet Resources for Children's Literature" with links to other Gophers around the world.

```
gopher://lib.nmsu.edu -->NMSU Library -->Resources by
Subject -->Education -->Children's Literature: Electronic
Resources
```

In this directory can be found *News From the Windowsill* (formerly WEB On-line Review): Reviews of children's literature by Wendy E. Betts and others, with theme issues and genre-specific issues. To subscribe, send e-mail to `KIDSBOOK-REQUEST@armory.com` and in the body of the message include your name and e-mail address. For back issues:

```
-->Electronic Journals and Book Reviews -->Notes From the
Windowsill (formerly WEB On-line Review)
```

Reader's Theater Scripts: Based on folktales from around the world. To have future scripts delivered to you, send an e-mail message to `AARONSHEP@aol.com`.

```
-->Papers, Booktalks, and Reader's Theater -->Reader's
Theater Scripts by Aaron Shepard
```

On-line Writers Workshop & Reference Tools: Students have access to a writer's lab for help with developing writing skills, and a range of reference tools from *Roget's Thesaurus* to the *American English Dictionary*.

```
gopher://dept.english.upenn.edu -->other gophers -->
literature+reference tools
```

Scholastic Reading and Language Arts Library: Teaching ideas for language arts.

```
gopher://scholastic.com 2003 -->Scholastic Internet Li-
brary -->Reading and Language Arts Library -->Teaching
With Literature -->Lesson Plans -->We Love Literature Les-
son Plans
```

Scottish Folktales: A collection of eight Scottish folktales.

```
gopher://almac.co.uk -->Everything About Scotland
-->Dalriada Celtic Heritage Society -->Myths
```

U.S. Library of Congress: ALEX, a catalogue of electronic texts on the Internet, lists and provides links to Gophers with all the major e-text holdings available on-line, now 700 titles and growing.

```
gopher://marvel.loc.gov -->Global Electronic Library
-->Language, Linguistics, and Literature -->Literature
-->ALEX: A Catalogue of Electronic Texts on the Internet
-->Browse by Author or Title
```

Wolf Study Project: A curriculum unit centered on children's books, folktales, and nonfiction illustrating negative stereotyping and more realistic portrayals.

```
gopher://tiesnet.ties.k12.mn.us -->Best of the K-12 Inter-
net Resources -->WOLF STUDY PROJECT -->Timber Wolf Unit
Study Guide -->Pre-Visit Activities -->Wolves in Children's
Literature
```

A study guide and bibliography is also available under

```
-->WOLF STUDY PROJECT -->Timber Wolf Unit Study Guide
-->Bibliography
```

WORLD WIDE WEB (WWW)

The Children's Literature Web Guide: An enormous compendium of information and activities centering on children's literature, including first chapters of Newbery award winners, listings of banned books (most of which are children's titles), "choose your own adventure" labyrinths, slide shows of fairy tales for those with graphical browsers, and hyperlinked mythology pages.

```
http://www.ucalgary.ca/~dkbrown/index.html
```

KidPub: A site devoted to publishing children's writings and introducing young people to using the Internet for learning.

```
http://www.en-garde.com/kidpub
```

MidLink Magazine: A bimonthly e-magazine for ages 10 to 15, written by and for students, both in fiction and nonfiction.

```
http://longwood.cs.ucf.edu/~MidLink/
```

For more information or to participate, e-mail to

```
<MCCULLEN@aquarius.cc.ucf.edu>.
```

TELNET

Buffalo Freenet Children's Literature Resources

```
telnet://freenet.buffalo.edu and login as "freeport" -->Li-
brary -->Books and Book Talks -->Booklists -->Recommended
New Children's Books
```

Cleveland Freenet: Offers bulletin boards for children and young adults to share their writings.

```
telnet://freenet-in-a.cwru.edu or telnet://freenet-
in-b.cwru.edu or telnet://freenet-in-c.cwru.edu -->A visi-
tor -->Explore the system -->The Schoolhouse (Academy One)
-->Academy One Projects Underway -->PROJECT: Kid Lit
(Student Writing Projects)
```

Hawaii FYI: Features a searchable, on-line magazine index with nearly half the articles available in full text. "Children's literature" is a useful keyword.

```
telnet://fyi.uhcc.hawaii.edu and press Enter/Return twice
-->Information Service Directory -->Public Library System
(screen 5 of 9 screens of choices) -->Connect to Service
-->HSL (Main) -->Magazine Index
```

Heartland Freenet: An annotated bibliography of young adult titles, with reviews.

```
telnet://heartland.bradley.edu and login as "bbguest"
-->Library Center -->Young Adult Book Reviews - Peoria
Public Library
```

Social Studies

Readers also may find helpful the resources listed under "Multicultural Education."

E-JOURNALS AND NEWSLETTERS

Global Village News: A moderated, student-authored newspaper, providing opportunities for worldwide student journalism that operates as a USENET newsgroup.

```
news://k12.sys.channel11
```

New South Polar Times: A biweekly newsletter written by Lt. Tom Jacobs at the Amundsen-Scott South Pole Station, South Pole, Antarctica. Available over the World Wide Web, the NSPT homepage also offers lesson plans and other resources for teachers and students interested in Antarctica.

```
http://www.deakin.edu.au/edu/MSEE/GENII/NSPT/NSPThome
Page.html
```

LISTSERVS

CANALA-L: Forum for exchanges to encourage Canadian-Latin America educational partnerships.

Subscriptions: `LISTPROC@cunews.carleton.ca`
Participation: `CANALA-L@cunews.carleton.ca`

H-NET: Actually a suite of LISTSERVs managed by the University of Illinois (Chicago) and Michigan State University. Discussion groups from the University of Illinois (Chicago) are H-IDEAS (intellectual history) and IEAHCNET (American colonial history); LISTSERVs out of Michigan

State University include H-ALBION (British and Irish history), H-AMSTDY (American studies), H-CANADA (Canadian history), H-CIVWAR (U.S. Civil War), H-DIPLO (diplomatic history), H-FILM (cinema studies), H-GERMAN (German history), H-HIGH-S (teaching high school social studies), H-LABOR (labor history), H-LAW (legal and constitutional history), H-LOCAL (state and local history and museums), H-NZ-OZ (New Zealand and Australian history), H-PCAACA (Popular Culture Association and the American Culture Association), H-REVIEW (H-Net book reviews), H-RUSSIA (Russian history), H-SHGAPE (U.S. Gilded Age and Progressive Era), H-SOUTH (U.S. South), H-SURVEY (teaching U.S. history). and H-WEST (U.S. frontier history).

Subscriptions: LISTSERV@uicvm.uic.edu or
LISTSERV@msu.edu

Participation: Substitute the actual group name
for the word"LISTSERV," e.g.
H-SOUTH@msu.edu

NCSS-L: The National Council for Social Studies' LISTSERV focuses on sharing ideas about social studies teaching as well as improving teacher preparation in social studies.

Subscriptions: LISTSERV@bgu.edu
Participation: NCSS-L@bgu.edu

OUTDOR-L: Discusses comparative geography based on sharing information on participants' locales.

Subscriptions: LISTSERV@ulkyvm.louisville.edu
Participation: OUTDOR-L@ulkyvm.louisville.edu

SOCSTUD-L: The K-12 Social Studies LISTSERV.

Subscriptions: MAILSERV@hcca.ohio.gov
Participation: SOCSTUD-L@hcca.ohio.gov

TAMHA: Teaching American History is a forum for teachers interested in bringing United States history to life in the classroom.

Subscriptions: `LISTSERV@cms.cc.wayne.edu`

Participation: `TAMHA@@cms.cc.wayne.edu`

USENET NEWSGROUPS

`can.schoolnet.socsci.sr`   The social science newsgroup that is part of Canada's SchoolNet suite of newsgroups.

`clari.apbl.today_history`   *Today in History* summarizes important events that have happened on given dates as well as famous people's birthdays that fall on each date. `

`news:clari.news.top`   Headline news from Associated Press. Clari.news is the prefix for many up-to-the-minute compilations of special-interest reporting.

GOPHERS

The Community IDEA-Net (CINet): Designed for senior high students, this Gopher focuses on community-based strategies for making governments more effective.

```
gopher://149.10.96.2 -->K-12 resources -->Social Studies
-->Classroom Activities
```

Geography and Weather Gopher: Collects information, including satellite images, pertaining to recent natural disasters.

```
gopher://wx.atmos.uiuc.edu -->Case Studies
```

The U.S. Holocaust Memorial Museum: Both an overview of the Museum in Washington, D.C., and a site where teaching ideas may be found for integrating Holocaust studies into the curriculum.

```
http://www.ushmm.org/index.html
```

WORLD WIDE WEB (WWW)

Canadian Open Government WWW: Designed to help explain the workings of Canadian governmental bodies.

```
http://debra.dgbt.doc.ca/opengov
```

The ERIC Clearinghouse for Social Studies/Social Science Education (ERIC/ChESS): A WWW site which highlights the services of ERIC/ChESS and offers links to valuable Internet resources for social studies education.

```
http://www.indiana.edu/~ssdc/eric-chess.html
```

Heritage Post Interactive: A bilingual (French/English) Canadian history Web site. Netscape or Mosaic browsers are recommended.

```
http://heritage.excite.sfu.ca/hpost.html
```

Social Science Resources Page: Covers the range of social studies, providing resource documents and links to other pertinent Internet sites.

```
http://galaxy.einet.net/GJ/social.html
```

Social Sciences WWW Virtual Library: Based in Geneva, Switzerland, this site offers direct access to more than 260 of the world's leading on-line information facilities for social sciences and humanities.

```
http://coombs.anu.edu.au/WWWVL-SocSci.html
```

Southwest Ohio Council for the Social Studies: Maintained by Paul Filio of the Cincinnati Public Schools, this homepage features one of the most extensive listing of links to Web sites concerned with social studies.

```
http://iac.net/~pfilio
```

The United Nations and Voices of Youth: Developed during the March 1995 World Summit for Social Development, this Web site features writings of youth on issues poverty, homelessness, famine and ethnic and social conflict. For more information about United Nations initiatives in educational networking, send mail to <unicef@igc.apc.org>.

```
http://www.iisd.ca/linkages/un/feedback.html
```

TELNET

HNSOURCE: An interactive server devoted to issues of history teaching and research, HNSOURCE provides access to other Internet sites, including newsgroups focusing on historical issues.

```
telnet://ukanaix.cc.ukans.edu and login with "history"
```

ANONYMOUS FTP

Geography Resources: The many files here will need to be "unzipped," a skill you can learn from your local computer coordinator or from an Internet manual.

```
ftp://relay.cs.toronto.edu/doc/geography/world-factbook.Z
or ftp://relay.cs.toronto.edu/doc/geography/world
```

World Constitutions: An invaluable site for students and teachers of comparative government.

```
ftp://wiretap.spies.com/gov/world
```

Mathematics and Science

E-JOURNALS AND NEWSLETTERS

Earth and Sky: This is a monthly e-digest of the script for the nationally broadcast radio show produced by the National Oceanic and Atmospheric Administration. For more information, send e-mail to Deborah Byrd at DBYRD@pinet.aip.org directly. For subscriptions, send e-mail to MAJOR-DOMO@lists.utexas.edu and in the body of the message write SUBSCRIBE EARTHANDSKY followed by your full Internet address.

FAM-MATH: Monthly e-newsletter published by Lawrence Hall of Science at University of California (Berkeley), to encourage mathematics relevant to students and their families and communities as well as to encourage mathematics careers for girls and culturally diverse students.

Subscriptions: LISTSERV@uicvm.cc.uic.edu

Participation: FAM-MATH@uicvm.cc.uic.edu

Vocal Point: Student-edited on-line e-newsletters devoted to linking environmental issues and technology. Contact Jill Tucker at JTUCKER@knightridder.com for more information.

http://bvsd.k12.co.us/cent/newspaper/newspaper.html

E-MAIL AND LISTSERVS

ASCD-SCI (Alliance for Teaching of Science): Forum for discussion of all branches of science teaching.

Subscriptions: LISTSERV@psuvm.psu.edu

Participation: ASCD-SCI@psuvm.psu.edu

Ask-A-Geologist: This is an e-mail service offered by the U.S. Geological Survey. Questions about geology are referred to the "geologist of the day" who responds within two days. Send e-mail with your own Internet address in the body of the message to

ASK-A-GEOLOGIST@octopus.wr.usgs.gov

Ask Mr. Science: This question-answering service is staffed by the Advanced Placement Chemistry Class at Christiansburg High School, Christiansburg, Virginia, but questions can be on any science topic. Send e-mail to:

APSCICHS@radford.vak12ed.edu

BIOPI-L (Secondary Biology Teacher Enhancement): Focus on innovative practices within biology teaching.

Subscriptions: LISTSERV@ksuvm.ksu.edu
Participation: BIOPI-L@ksuvm.ksu.edu

BIOSPH-L: Forum for discussion on the Biosphere project.

Subscriptions: LISTSERV@ubvm.bitnet
Participation: BIOSPH-L@ubvm.bitnet

CHEMCOM: Chemistry in the Community shares curriculum ideas for making chemistry more relevant to students' lives.

Subscriptions: LISTSERV@ubvm.cc.buffalo.edu
Participation: CHEMCOM@ubvm.cc.buffalo.edu

CHEMED-L: Chemistry Education is a forum on curriculum issues for teachers of chemistry in high schools and colleges.

Subscriptions: LISTSERV@uwf.bitnet
Participation: CHEMED-L@uwf.bitnet

ECOLOGY: Forum for environmental discussion, with a focus on political implications.

> Subscriptions: `LISTSERV@emuvml.bitnet`
>
> Participation: `ECOLOGY@emuvml.bitnet`

EFLIST: Discussion group on environmental education for teachers, educators, administrators, students, activists and parents.

> Subscriptions: `EFLIST-REQUEST@htbbs.com`
>
> Participation: `EFLIST@htbbs.com`

Galileo: A discussion group for K-12 science teachers. In addition, Galileo has a lesson plan distribution LISTSERV at `MAJORDOMO@unr.edu` that can be joined by sending e-mail to that address and including SUBSCRIBE GALILEO followed by your full Internet address.

> Subscriptions: `LISTSERV@unr.edu`
>
> Participation: `GALILEO@unr.edu`

IMSE-L: Discussion group run by the Institute for Math and Science Education.

> Subscriptions: `LISTSERV@uicvm.cc.uic.edu`
>
> Participation: `IMSE-L@@uicvm.cc.uic.edu`

PHYS-STU: Forum for students of physics.

> Subscriptions: `LISTSERV@cc.uwf.edu`
>
> Participation: `PHYS-STU@cc.uwf.edu`

SAIS-L: Discusses promoting science awareness among students.

> Subscriptions: `LISTSERV@unb.ca`
>
> Participation: `SAIS-L@unb.ca`

SCHOOL SCIENCE: Based in the United Kingdom, this LISTSERV is a clearinghouse of teaching ideas for science teachers.

Subscriptions: `LISTSERV@vollans.demon.co.uk`

Participation: `SCHOOSCIENCE@vollans.demon.co.uk`

SHARING-NASA: "Passport To Knowledge" sponsors such projects as "Virtual Field Trip To Antarctica" and "Live From The Hubble Space Telescope." In the body of your e-mail message send the words "subscribe sharing-nasa" to

Subscriptions: `LISTMANAGER@quest.arc.nasa.gov`

USENET NEWSGROUPS

`can.schoolnet.earth.jr` Ecology discussion group for teachers, students and researchers.

`can.schoolnet.math.sr` Secondary math issues discussed by teachers and students.

`can.schoolnet.*` All other SchoolNet newsgroups can be found with this prefix.

`clari.apbl.weather` Daily weather statistics for sites around the world. Useful from upper elementary grades and higher.

GOPHERS

EcoGopher: Listings of resources for environmental education.

`gopher://ecosys.drdr.virginia.edu`

EE-Link: A listing of environmental education curriculum units for K-12 classes, with a special focus on recycling, grouped by appropriate grade levels.

```
gopher://nceet.snre.umich.edu -->Activities and Lesson
Plans for EE/ -->Solid Waste Activities (Cornell)/
```

The EE Reference Collection—Multicultural & Environmental Education: See listing under "Gophers" in "Multicultural Education."

EnviroGopher: The archive of the EnviroLink Network, this Gopher lists many environmental education resources.

```
gopher://envirolink.org -->EnviroInformation- A Library of
Environmental Information -->EnviroScience -->Ecology
```

Florida Technical University Education Gopher: Serves as a link to many other science education-related Gophers.

```
gopher://sci-ed.fit.edu
```

Minnesota Valley National Wildlife Refuge Wildlife Lesson Plans: While specific to Indiana, these K-12 lesson plans often are adaptable to other regions and countries.

```
gopher://informns.k12.mn.us/11/mn-k12/mvnwr/lessons/elem
```

NASA Quest Gopher and the Mendocino Unified School District Lesson Units: A model curriculum unit for middle school that teaches "science across the curriculum" using Internet resources to conduct and publish research conducted by small groups of students using cooperative learning techniques.

```
gopher://quest.arc.nasa.gov -->Internet Resources/
-->Mendocino's Curriculum by Topics/
```

National Aeronautics and Space Administration (NASA) on-line Resources: NASA has so many resources useful for science and math educators that the best place to start is its "Guide to NASA on-line Resources." The on-line version of the guide is searchable.

```
gopher://naic.nasa.gov -->Guide to NASA on-line Resources
http://naic.nasa.gov/naic/guide/
```

National Clearinghouse on Development and Environmental Education: See description under "Gophers" in "Multicultural Education."

SchoolNet: Sponsored by Industry and Science Canada, this rich resource listing focuses mainly on the teaching of science and math but is expanding into other curricular areas.

```
gopher://schoolnet.carleton.ca
```

Scientists on a Disk: Listings of documents that center on the history of science.

```
gopher://gopher.hs.jhu.edu
```

University of California–San Diego InternNet Lesson Plans: Focuses on science education activities from upper elementary grades and higher.

```
gopher://ec.sdcs.k12.ca.us -->Lesson Plans -->UCSD
InternNet Lesson Plans
```

WhaleNet: Aimed at middle school, this Gopher subdirectory offers unit plans and opportunities to interact with classes on whale-sighting field trips.

```
gopher://ericir.syr.edu and search for "WhaleNet."
```

WORLD WIDE WEB (WWW)

Collaborative Visualization Project (CoVis): Like Global SchoolHouse, CoVis seeks to link networking with advanced visualization software that can be shared over distances. However, CoVis principally links high school teachers and their students, while Global SchoolHouse finds partner classes across age levels.

    http://www.covis.nwu.edu

Dinosaur Fossil Exhibition: With a graphical Web browser such as Mosaic, students can access full-color images made from replicas of fossils at New York's American Museum of Natural History.

    http://www.hcc.hawaii.edu/dinos/dinos.1.html

Earth and Planetary Studies: Maintained by The Center for Earth and Planetary Studies at the Smithsonian Institute's National Air and Space Museum, this site focuses on the geologies of Earth and other bodies in the solar system. Many spectacular images culled from space missions are accessible.

    http://ceps.nasm.edu:2020/homepage.html

EE-Link: See description under "Gophers," above.

    http://www.nceet.snre.umich.edu

EnviroLink: K-12 environmental resources on the Internet.

    http://envirolink.org/enviroed/envirok12.html

Geometry Forum: Rich Web site at Swarthmore College, with many curriculum and software resources, including the "Ask Dr. Math" question-answering service and access to math newsgroups and a "Forum News Gateway" where Web homepages relevant to mathematics education are shared.

```
http://forum.swarthmore.edu
```

The Jason Project: This widely-publicized project permits students to participate in "virtual expeditions" with real explorers through technology-mediated "telepresence."

```
http://seawifs.gsfc.nasa.gov/JASON/JASON.html
```

Math & Science On-line Resources: Not only lists and describes mathematics and science Internet resources, but provides links to those sites with further information.

```
http://life.anu.edu.au:80/education/mathsci.html
```

MegaMath: For teachers and students in grades 2-12, activities are surveyed that include elementary statistics, graphing, and math through drama and literature.

```
http://www.c3.lanl.gov/mega-math/
```

Mercury-Story: Definitely requiring a graphical browser such as Mosaic, this Web site simulates a nuclear accident and its aftermath, requiring a robot to reconnoiter a radioactive desert landscape. In fact, the robot is real and students (who have to pass an operator's test) can control its movement, which is monitored through Mercury-Story Web.

```
http://www.usc.edu/dept/raiders/story/mercury-story.html
```

SchoolNet: See description under "Gophers," above.

```
http://schoolnet.carleton.ca/schoolnet/hmpage.html.
```

SciEd: "Science and Mathematics Education Resources" seeks to bring together as many resources as possible in science and mathematics education, with links to important Internet Gophers and WWW sites.

```
http://www.halcyon.com/cairns/science.html
```

Space and Planets: With links to the European Space Agency and NASA, this Web site sequences full-color graphics and text in a way that allows students with access to Mosaic to conduct a tour of the solar system.

```
http://www.c3.lanl.gov/~cjhamil/SolarSystem/homepage.html
```

The Virtual Frog Dissection Kit: Takes students through the classic biology project, with images based on digitized color photos of real dissections.

```
http://george.lbl.gov/ITG.hm.pg.docs/dis-
sect/whole.frog.html
```

WebStars—Astrophysics in Cyberspace: A fully multimedia Web site that incorporates sound, moving images, and hypertext to create an exciting context for K-12 teachers and students to explore astronomy through NASA's educational resources; best experienced with Mosaic, Cello, or NetScape and speakers.

```
http://guinan.gsfc.nasa.gov
```

TELNET

Classroom Earth BBS: Funded by NASA, Classroom Earth seeks to link K-12 students with both access to information on environmental education and access to people interested in environmental action.

```
telnet://classroomearth.ciesin.org 2010
```

EE-Link: See description under "Gophers," above.

```
telnet://nceet.snre.umich.edu, then login with "eelink" and
give your e-mail address as the password. -->Activities
and Lesson Plans for EE/ -->Solid Waste Activities
(Cornell)/
```

The Eisenhower National Clearinghouse (ENC) for Mathematics and Science Education: ENC has established its own on-line database of curriculum resources to assist teachers in selecting materials.

```
telnet://enc.org
```

NASA Spacelink: Current information and background on NASA projects in the news.

```
telnet://Spacelink.msfc.nasa.gov
```

Newton: Used by many science educators, this bulletin board system provides access to resources and to potential collaborators; also, an entire directory of "Ask the Scientist" question-answering services is available.

```
telnet://newton.dep.anl.gov and follow login and
registration instructions carefully.
```

SpaceMet: Devoted to the history and current status of space exploration.

```
telnet://SpaceMet.phast.umass.edu and press Enter/Return.
```

ANONYMOUS FTP

NASA's Space-related Images: Space photographs available in .GIF format. (Check with your district's computer coordinator on how to get and view them.)

```
ftp://explorer.arc.nasa.gov/pub/SPACE/GIF
```

Notes

Chapter 1

1. Schlesinger (1991).
2. Bigelow (1991, p. 29).
3. These data are documented in a recent report from the National Center for Children in Poverty, which puts the number of children living in poverty at a record high of 6 million. According to the press release:

   > J. Lawrence Aber, the group's director, said the findings, based on the U.S. Census Bureau's 1993 supplement to the 1990 census, reflected a 20-year trend that is having "devastating consequences" on youth.
   >
   > "The significance of these figures for our society's social landscape cannot be overstated, because we will pay the costs of these poverty rates for the next two decades," Aber said. (*Toronto Star,* January 30, 1995)

4. Freire (1975).
5. Hirsch (1987).
6. McLuhan (1965).
7. For insightful discussion of current interethnic conflicts, see Ignatieff (1993).

Chapter 2

1. Kozol (1991).
2. Neuman (1991, p. 2). The gaps between the technological haves and the have-nots are glaring. While an increasing number of computers are being placed in schools, early surveys reported wealthy districts with a 54:1 student-computer ratio while poor ones had a ratio of 73:1 (Hood et al., 1985), and more recent surveys show this pattern persisting (Becker, 1990). Female students and those from low income backgrounds and ethnic and linguistic minorities tend not to have the same access to computers as do their male, middle-income, nonminority counterparts (Gerver, 1990). Generally, the more exciting programs are reserved for students in the upper tracks; when lower track and minority students *do* get access, they are much more likely to be assigned to drill and practice rather than to problem-solving activities (Becker, 1987; Mehan et al., 1985; Sayers, 1993).
3. Copen, personal communication (January 31, 1995).

4. Figueroa/Sayers/Brown (1990).

5. DeVillar/Faltis (1991, p. 116).

6. Orillas and I*EARN are among the only major global learning networks that have an official policy which encourages participants to write in languages other than English, on the theory that when schools receive communications in other languages, this will serve as a stimulus for exploring local linguistic and cultural resources to assist in translation and in understanding other cultural realities.

7. The events outlined in this portrait are depicted in the videotape "A Global Gateway for Kids," produced by the Southwest Educational Development Laboratory under a contract with the Office of Educational Research and Improvement of the U.S. Department of Education. Ordering information available from SEDL, 211 East 7th Street, Austin, Texas 78701, USA.

8. Vives, personal communication (September 9, 1994).

9. Ibid.

10. Ibid.

11. Ibid.

12. Ibid.

13. For another example of successful "cross-cultural" communication between students from the same culture, see Sayers (1991).

14. See Cummins (1994) for a review of the research literature.

15. Much of the information on intergenerational literacy presented here is drawn from data collected, analyzed and discussed in publications by the Orillas codirectors, Kristin Brown, Enid Figueroa, and Dennis Sayers. Examples presented here have appeared previously in fuller exposition in Brown (1993) and Sayers/Brown (1994).

16. This portrait reflects an extensive collaboration between the authors and Kristin Brown, co-director of Orillas and project coordinator of I*EARN, and Juan Carlos Cuellar, Bilingual Resource Specialist for the San Francisco Unified School District, who contacted teachers involved in this prejudice reduction project. Quotations are drawn from personal communications through electronic mail between February 10-17, 1995.

17. Allport (1954).

18. Brown/Cuellar, personal communication, February 12, 1995.

19. Miller, personal communication, February 11, 1995.

20. Sayers (1994a).

21. Brown/Cuellar, personal communication, February 12, 1995.

22. Ibid.

23. Ibid.

24. Ibid.

25. Ibid.

26. Ibid.

27. Miller, personal communication, February 12, 1995.

28. Sayers/Brown (1994), p. 180. All quotes which follow of children's and parents' writings are taken from this source.

29. Ibid., p. 180.

30. Figueroa/Brown/Sayers, personal communication, February 17, 1995.

31. *An End to Intolerance,* June 1994, p. 4.

32. *I*EARN Holocaust/Genocide Project* (1993), p. 5.

33. Kern, personal communication, October 8, 1994.
34. Lee (1992).
35. Salza, personal communication, September 7, 1994.
36. Ibid.
37. Gragert, personal communication, September 20, 1994.
38. *The Contemporary,* January 1994, p. 4.
39. Lucas, personal communication, September 20, 1994.
40. *The Contemporary,* January 1994, p. 22.
41. Ibid.
42. *The Contemporary,* January 1994, pp. 23-24, source for all letters which follow.
43. Lucas, personal communication, September 20, 1994.
44. *The Contemporary,* January 1994, pp. 23-24.
45. Ibid.
46. Lucas, personal communication, September 20, 1994.
47. *The Contemporary,* January 1994, p. 4.
48. "Aftermath of a Massacre: An Introduction," *The Contemporary,* May 1994, p. 18.
49. Ibid., p. 18.
50. Ibid., pp. 20-21. This and other students' writings are taken from the Middle East Section of the May 1994 *Contemporary,* pp. 18-27.
51. Ibid., p. 21.
52. Ibid., p. 21.
53. Ibid., p. 22.
54. Ibid., p. 19.
55. Ibid., p. 23.
56. Lucas, personal communication, September 20, 1994.
57. *The Contemporary,* January 1994, p. 4.
58. Gragert, personal communication, September 20, 1994.
59. Copen, personal communication, January 31, 1995.
60. Gragert, personal communication, September 20, 1994.

Chapter 3

1. An apocalyptic and influential vision of the future was presented by Robert D. Kaplan in his *Atlantic Monthly* article entitled "The Coming Anarchy" (February 1994). The brief description on the magazine cover page presents the essence of the argument: "The coming anarchy: Nations break up under the tidal flow of refugees from environmental and social disaster. As borders crumble, another type of boundary is erected—a wall of disease. Wars are fought over scarce resources, especially water, and war itself becomes continuous with crime, as armed bands of stateless marauders clash with the private security forces of the elites." This preview of the future is disputed by Marcus Gee in *The Globe and Mail* (April 9, 1994). Gee reviews extensive United Nations data on indicators such as world child mortality, life expectancy, adult literacy, trade, population trends, food, environment, and military expenditure reductions that show progress in virtually all areas. We suspect that future realities will probably emerge somewhere between these competing visions.

2. Hodgkinson (1991, pp. 9-16).

3. William Gibson, the science fiction writer who first coined the term "cyberspace," expressed a similar perspective in a speech to the Convocation on Technology and Education organized by the National Academy of Sciences (May 10, 1993). In strongly supporting proposals to link U.S. public schools to the Internet, he suggests that the survival of democracy in the United States might well depend on this process. The major threat to democracy, he argues, stems "from a single and terrible fact: there currently exists in this nation a vast and disenfranchised underclass, drawn, most shamefully, along racial lines, and whose plight we are dangerously close to accepting as a simple fact of life, a permanent feature of the American landscape." He suggests that provision of free access for public schools to the Internet "may well represent nothing less than this nation's last and best hope of providing something like a level socio-economic playing field for a true majority of its citizens."

   Gibson goes on to argue that requiring telephone companies to provide unlimited free access for public schools to the Internet as a basic operation requirement would cost us nothing as a society. Similarly, requiring that companies provide public school teachers with free copies of software, on demand, for professional use in schools would entail only a loss of potential revenue "for some of the planet's fattest and best-fed corporations." In fact, provision of these services and products would represent enlightened self-interest for multinational corporations:

   > Having thrived under democracy, in a free market, the time has come for these corporations to demonstrate an enlightened self-interest, by acting to assure the survival of democracy and the free market—and incidentally, by assuring that virtually the entire populace of the United States will become computer-literate potential consumers within a single generation.

   Gibson sums up his message by urging American business to "stop devouring your children's future in order to meet your next quarterly report."

4. Fine (1991).

5. Barlett & Steele (1992).

6. Williams & Snipper (1990).

7. Hirsch (1987).

8. Apple (1993, pp. 46-47). Australian scholar R. W. Connell expresses a similar point as follows:

   > Each particular way of constructing the curriculum (i.e. organizing the field of knowledge and defining how it is to be taught and learned) carries social effects. Curriculum empowers and dis-empowers, authorizes and de-authorizes, recognizes and mis-recognizes different social groups and their knowledge and identities. For instance, curriculum developed from academic institutions controlled by men has, in a variety of ways, authorized the practices and experiences of men and marginalized those of women. Curriculum defined by representatives of a dominant ethnic group is liable to exclude or de-authorize the knowledge and experience of dominated groups, or to incorporate them on terms that suit the dominant group. (1994, pp. 140-141)

9. Peterson (1993, p. 8).

10. Shor (1992, p. 129).

11. Cited in *Rethinking Schools* (1994), vol. 9, n2, p.9.
12. Barlett & Steele (1992).
13. Ada (1988, p. 236).
14. Ferdman (1990, pp. 181-204).
15. Fordham (1990, p. 259).
16. The distinction that University of California anthropologist, John Ogbu (1978, 1992) makes between voluntary and involuntary minorities is helpful in understanding why some minority groups experience persistent educational difficulties whereas the difficulties of other groups are short-term. Voluntary minorities have moved more or less voluntarily to another society in search of greater economic opportunities and/or political or religious freedom. They tend to have positive attitudes both toward their own culture and toward the host society. Ogbu argues that voluntary minorities may experience initial problems due to cultural and language differences but these problems are usually short lived. He suggests that Punjabi and Chinese immigrant groups are examples of this pattern. By contrast, involuntary minorities were originally brought to the new society against their will; for example, through slavery, conquest, colonization or forced labor. According to Ogbu, "thereafter, these minorities were often relegated to menial positions and denied true assimilation into the mainstream society" (1992, p. 8). In addition to the economic and cultural barriers erected by the dominant group, cultural and language boundaries were often also maintained by minority group members as a way of reinforcing their collective identity and insulating themselves from further subordination. Ogbu suggests that these differences in the historical and sociopolitical situation of voluntary and involuntary minorities can explain the marked differences in educational achievement between some recent immigrant groups and historically subordinated groups such as African Americans, Latinos, and Native Americans. See Cummins (1995) for further analysis of these issues.
17. Olsen et al. (1994); Stedman (1987).
18. For a sobering documentation of the tragic outcomes of CIA covert operations that brought down democratically elected governments around the world and propped up military dictatorships from the 1950s through the 1980s, see the many works of Noam Chomsky. The ease with which domestic assent for these illegal actions was manufactured attests to the strength of the internalized anti-Communist discourse among the American people during this period.
19. National Commission on Excellence in Education (1983, p. 1). Surveys of literacy levels in North America have fueled the "literacy crisis" rhetoric. Statistics Canada (1990), for example, reported that while a majority (62 percent) of Canadians between the ages of 16 and 69 were judged to have adequate reading skills, a substantial number (38 percent) had either very limited reading skills or some degree of difficulty in reading when the task became more complex. In the United States context, Stedman and Kaestle (1987) synthesized the findings of seven national studies to conclude that about 30 percent of the adult population have either minimal or marginal functional literacy skills.
20. Certainly not all efforts at school restructuring reflect a "back-to-basics" orientation. Theodore Sizer's Coalition for Essential Schools, Henry Levin's Accelerated Schools, and James Comer's School Development Project all endorse far greater power for teachers and parents in school decision making as well as high expectations and a challenging curriculum for all students. However while the promising nature of these efforts is occasionally

acknowledged by policymakers and media commentators, their impact and promise tend to be submerged by the quick-fix, back-to-basics discourse that has succeeded in scapegoating schools for virtually all of society's social and economic ills.

21. Cuban (1994).
22. Barlow & Robinson (1994); Hodgkinson (1991); Cuban (1993, 1994); Weisman (1993). Federal social priorities in the United States during the past 15 years can be seen from the fact that between 1980 and 1995, Military expenditures increased by $1,116 billion and Corrections by $59 billion, while Education lost $59 billion, Aid to Cities lost $101 billion, and Housing lost $390 billion (*Rethinking Schools* [1995], p. 15).
23. Cuban (1993, p. 11).
24. Cuban (1994, p. 44). A similar pattern of competitiveness discourse allied to calls for back-to-basics pedagogy is evident in the Canadian context. Andrew Nikiforuk, the *Globe and Mail* education correspondent for several years, puts the case for "bad schools cause a bad economy" bluntly: "If Canada plans to enter the twenty-first century without becoming another battered Argentina or a hungry Brazil, its $50-billion school system will have to deliver something better than illiterate graduates, progressive promises and a 30-per-cent dropout rate" (1991, A14). The apparent plausibility of this Canadian version of the education/economy equation suffers when exposed to the evidence. In the first place, national dropout figures have been revised substantially downward (to less than 20 percent) to take account of student reentry into high school. Also, contrary to what is implied by "literacy crisis" claims, literacy levels of younger Canadians are higher than those of previous generations and levels of education attained by Canadians have increased significantly (Baril and Mori, 1991).

   In a scathing attack on the Canadian version of the "Great School Scam," William Hynes (1994) cites data from the Japan Productivity Center that Canadian and U.S. workers are 1.34 and 1.31 times more productive than Japanese workers respectively and, per person-hour, North Americans outproduce the Japanese about 5 to 3. Hynes also points out that North America now has more mathematicians, engineers, and scientists than business knows how to employ.
25. Rotberg (1990).
26. O'Reilly (1992).
27. Weisman (1993, p. 368).
28. Baril & Mori (1991, p. 17).
29. Stedman & Kaestle (1985, p. 209).
30. Carson, Huelskamp & Woodall (1993); Frazier (1993).
31. Iris Rotberg (1990) has also argued convincingly that the apparent inferior performance of U.S. schools in international comparisons is at least partially an artifact of sampling problems in the studies. Educational systems that are elitist insofar as they retain fewer students in academic streams at the secondary level will tend to do better than educational systems that retain a much larger number of students in academic streams. Similarly, systems that have large numbers of second language learners who typically require upwards of five years to reach grade level expectations in the academic aspects of the language of instruction (Collier, 1987; Cummins, 1984) will tend to perform more poorly than systems whose student body is more linguistically homogenous. On both these counts, North American schools are less elitist and less homogenous than many of the school systems that attain higher rankings.

32. Cuban (1994, p. 44).
33. Hynes (1994, p. 104).
34. Barlow & Robertson (1994).
35. In spite of the recent corporate concern for the nation's educational health, the financial contribution of U.S. business to public education has been drastically reduced in recent decades. Robert Reich (1991), for example, points out that in 1989 only 6 percent of corporate donations to education went to public schools while the corporate share of local property taxes, which are the main source of most school budgets, declined from 45 percent in 1957 to about 16 percent in 1990 (see also Folbre, 1992).
36. The renewed call for a return to the basics echoes the attack on the alleged excesses of progressive education in the 1950s. The fundamentally different philosophical and psychological assumptions of traditional and progressive education are lucidly expressed by John Dewey (1963), widely regarded as the "father" of progressive education:

    The history of educational theory is marked by opposition between the idea that education is development from within and that it is formation from without; . . . [according to traditional education], the subject matter of education consists of bodies of information and of skills that have been worked out in the past; therefore the chief business of the school is to transmit them to the new generation. . . . Since the subject-matter as well as standards of proper conduct are handed down from the past, the attitude of pupils must, on the whole, be one of docility, receptivity, and obedience. Books, especially textbooks, are the chief representatives of the lore and wisdom of the past, while teachers are the organs through which pupils are brought into effective connection with the material. Teachers are the agents through which knowledge and skills are communicated and rules of conduct enforced." (pp. 18-19)

    By contrast, Dewey's progressive education emphasized expression and cultivation of individuality rather than imposition of knowledge and rules from above, free activity as opposed to external discipline, learning from experience rather than from texts and teachers, and acquiring skills and knowledge from activities to which pupils are personally committed rather than learning isolated skills and facts through drill and practice activities. In particular, progressive educators promoted a more open democratic classroom atmosphere in which instruction built on the interests and needs of students.
37. Ravitch & Finn (1987).
38. The most prominent opponent of progressive education in the 1950s was Vice-Admiral Hyman Rickover, who presided over the development of the atomic submarine within the American navy. Rickover's best-selling book *Education and Freedom* and numerous popular articles that he wrote condemned both the American school system and professional educators for their lack of rigorous standards and their preoccupation with frivolous subjects rather than with basic academic disciplines. Rickover argued that standards of excellence had been abandoned throughout the American educational system in order to keep the majority of students in school until their late teens. By contrast, the standards enforced by the Soviet school system were reflected in their technological advantage (illustrated by the launch of Sputnik in 1957), which threatened America's position as leader of the "free world." According to Rickover,

Russian education proves one thing conclusively: properly motivated and deftly taught by competent teachers who know their subjects thoroughly, average children can reach far higher levels of education than even our talented children have achieved in most American public schools. Failure to bring American pupils to levels of performance comparable to those of other advanced industrial countries is in large part a consequence of progressive educationist theories and practices. (1959, p. 137)

In a somewhat contradictory vein, Rickover goes on to note that "fortunately, progressive educational methods have not found too wide application in our schools—thanks primarily to the heroic resistance and good judgement of our teachers" (p. 137), but they have influenced teachers' colleges and state boards of education resulting in the "steady deterioration of secondary-school curricula" (p. 138). A consequence of progressive methods is that education becomes "stuck in the concrete and unable to carry the child from there to abstract concepts and ideas. Our young people are therefore deprived of the tremendous intellectual heritage of Western civilization which no child can possibly discover by himself." (p. 139)

Rickover's attacks on the permissiveness of American education continued the earlier attacks of the McCarthy era in which schools "were accused of being the handmaiden of communist efforts to corrupt the will of the American people" (Lauderdale, 1987, p. 24). However, many of his arguments have been echoed 30 years later in the writings of Hirsch and other neo-conservative educational reformers.

A number of scholars (e.g., Lauderdale, 1987; Postman & Weingartner, 1981) have pointed out that although Dewey was probably regarded as the foremost educational philosopher by his contemporaries, it was not true that practice in American schools strongly reflected Dewey's ideas (as acknowledged by Rickover). Progressive educators certainly raised public consciousness of the needs of the individual child but the philosophy of progressive education never dominated policy or practice in public education. Postman and Weingartner point out that "the school curriculum was substantially the same in 1957 as it was in 1917" (p. 8). Goodlad's (1984) and Ramirez's (1992) data suggest that the same conclusion held true in the 1980s. One of the more enlightening discussions of the history of pedagogical debate can be found in Kalantzis and Cope (1993).

39. Stedman & Kaestle (1985, p. 208).
40. Goodlad (1984); Ramirez (1992); Sirotnik (1983); Sizer (1984).
41. Goodlad (1984, p. 230).
42. Sirotnik (1983, pp. 16-17).
43. Sirotnik (1983, p. 26).
44. Hirsch (1987); Rickover (1959). It is worth noting that aspects of whole-language approaches also have been criticized by researchers and theorists who would probably characterize themselves as left-of-center in political perspective (Delpit, 1988; Kalantzis and Cope, 1993; Reyes, 1992). These critics are concerned about issues such as (1) the lack of explicit focus in much whole-language pedagogy on development of critical literacy that would foster students' awareness of issues of social justice; (2) the need for direct instruction to provide students with access to the "genres of power;" in other words, to teach students how to use language for socially powerful purposes; (3) the need to affirm more explicitly culturally diverse students' cultural knowledge and to promote

multicultural awareness. Delpit clearly expresses the importance of integrating skills and process perspectives in arguing for the need "to help students to establish their own voices, but to coach those voices to produce notes that will be heard clearly in the larger society" (1988, p. 296). Kalantzis and Cope (1993) similarly argue that neither traditional "teacher-centered" pedagogy nor its nemesis, progressive "child-centered" pedagogy, are capable of preparing students to think and act in the powerful ways necessary to function in this increasingly fragmented global reality. They acknowledge the "cultural arrogance and blindspots" of the traditional curriculum but insist, contrary to much progressive practice, that explicit instruction in powerful ways of knowing and using language is of central importance. As outlined in subsequent chapters, our pedagogical orientation is consistent with the "explicit pedagogy for inclusion and access" advocated by Cope and Kalantzis (1993).

45. Kirsch & Jungeblut (1986)
46. Newman & Beverstock (1990, p. 77).
47. Mullis, Campbell, & Farstrup (1993).
48. Dunn (1987); Porter (1990).
49. Barlett & Steele (1992). Among the data they compiled are the following:
    - During the 1980s, salaries of people earning $20,000 to $50,000 increased by 44 percent while salaries for those earning $200,000 to $1 million increased by 697 percent.
    - During the 1950s, the corporate share of U.S. income tax collected was 39 percent compared to 61 percent for individuals; in the 1980s, the corporate share had dropped to 17 percent while individuals' share rose to 83 percent.
    - The percentage of workers receiving fully paid health insurance fell from 75 percent to 48 percent between 1982 and 1989.
50. Comer (1980); Levin (1988); Sizer (1984).
51. Olsen et al. (1994, p. 31).
52. Olsen et al. (1994, p. 30).
53. Barlett & Steele (1992); Barlow & Robertson (1994). Cross-national comparisons from 1991 show that in the United States, 20.4 percent of children live in poverty compared to 9.3 percent in Canada, 9 percent in Australia, 8.4 percent in the United Kingdom, 4.6 percent in France, 3.8 percent in the Netherlands, 2.8 percent in West Germany, and 1.6 percent in Sweden (Bracey, 1995).

    Howe (1991) has similarly pointed to the hypocrisy of the America 2000 goals that fail to acknowledge the impact of poverty on "school failure, job failure, emotional imbalance, and social rejection." His criticism applies equally to the Clinton administration's Goals 2000 document:

    > There is not even a whisper in the document to suggest that the troubles of children and youth are closely related to the rapid growth of poverty in our society over the last two decades. The number of children who experience poverty in the U.S. . . . is headed for one child in four in 2000. That means that, before the close of this century, fully one-fourth of all children in this country will be beleaguered by some combination of inadequate housing, lack of family support, poor health care, and inattention to personal and social development—a level of social trauma that is not approached by any other major industrialized nation in the world. . . . The unstated expectation

of America 2000 is that this growing army of poverty-stricken children and young people will take the new tests, meet the new standards, benefit from the new model schools, and use the leverage of choice to find schools that will best serve their interests and needs. That expectation is a pipe dream. (1991, p. 201)

54. Cummins (1995); Ogbu (1992).

55. Hacker (1995, p. 229).

56. Blauner (1969).

57. Skutnabb-Kangas (1984).

58. Olsen et al. (1994, p. 9).

59. Kennedy (1993, p. 305).

60. Hodgkinson (1991). The shift in funds from education to corrections during the past 15 years is evident when federal elementary, secondary, and job training spending is compared to federal corrections spending. Between 1980 and 1995, education spending dropped from $27 to $16 billion while corrections spending climbed from $8 to $20 billion (Slavin, 1995).

Barlow and Robertson (1994) make a similar point with reference to the Canadian situation: "We have strange priorities. It costs taxpayers nearly $70,000 to keep one young offender in secure custody for one year—and this figure does not include treatment or rehabilitation. There are few young offenders whose lives would not have been put on a different course if a fraction of this money had been invested in prevention; yet the public outcry is centred not on early intervention, but on tougher measures for young offenders." (p. 250)

61. Natriello, McDill, & Pallas (1990, p. 43).

62. Ibid., p. 41.

63. Schweinhart, Weikart, & Larney (1986).

64. Kennedy (1993, p. 304).

65. Waldman (1990).

66. The Stanford Working Group on Federal Education Programs for Limited-English-Proficient Students have pointed to the counterproductive nature of the deficit orientation in U.S. language policies:

The United States, however, remains an underdeveloped country when it comes to multiple language skills and knowledge of other countries. The American Council on the Teaching of Foreign Languages estimates that "only 3 percent of American high school graduates, and only 5 percent of our college graduates, reach a meaningful proficiency in a second language—and many of these students come from bilingual homes." By contrast, virtually all of our trading partners require all of their graduates to attain proficiency in two, three, or more languages. . . . Recent foreign policy initiatives have been hindered by shortages of U.S. military and diplomatic personnel who are proficient in Arabic, Somali, and Serbo-Croatian. The Central Intelligence Agency now has difficulty meeting its needs for critical language skills, even in commonly taught languages such as Spanish. (1993, p. 12)

67. It is in this context that we can understand statements such as the following from Arthur Schlesinger, Jr., (1991) in his book *The Disuniting of America:*

In recent years the combination of the ethnicity cult with a flood of immigration from Spanish-speaking countries has given bilingualism new impetus. . . . Alas, bilingualism has not worked out as planned: rather the contrary. Testimony is mixed, but indications are that bilingual education retards rather than expedites the movement of Hispanic children into the English-speaking world and that it promotes segregation rather than it does integration. Bilingualism shuts doors. It nourishes self-ghettoization, and ghettoization nourishes racial antagonism. . . . Using some language other than English dooms people to second-class citizenship in American society . . . . Monolingual education opens doors to the larger world. . . . institutionalized bilingualism remains another source of the fragmentation of America, another threat to the dream of "one people." (pp. 108-9)

The claims that "bilingualism shuts doors" and "monolingual education opens doors to the wider world" are laughable if viewed in isolation, particularly in the context of current global interdependence. They become interpretable only in the context of a societal discourse that is profoundly disquieted by the fact that the sounds of the "other" have now become audible and the hues of the American social landscape have darkened noticeably.

68. Two recent examples of this are cited by Wirth (1993): "For example, an action by the Texas legislature made Texas teachers subject to a $50 fine if they were caught teaching reading without an approved textbook, and legislators in Florida passed a law making basal materials 'the only legal means to provide reading instruction'." (p. 363)

69. Barlow & Robertson (1994); Folbre (1992); Reich (1991).

70. *Business Week,* July 13, 1992.

71. *New York Times,* December 4, 1992, p. A1.

72. National Coalition of Advocates for Students (1988).

73. Kennedy (1993, p. 313). The anti-immigrant sentiment that resulted in the passing of Proposition 187 in California in 1994 is fueled by misperceptions of the economic costs of immigration. In fact, *Business Week* (July 13, 1992) reports that at least 11 million immigrants are working and from their earnings of $240 billion are paying more than $90 billion annually in taxes, a great deal more than the $5 billion they are estimated to receive in public assistance. Despite their difficult economic situation as new arrivals, only 8.8 percent of immigrants receive public assistance, compared with 7.9 percent of the general population. Furthermore, the average immigrant family pays $2,500 more in tax dollars annually than they receive in public services (*New York Times,* June 27, 1993, p. A1).

The American Council on Civil Liberties (ACLU) also has summarized data regarding the economic impact of immigration; among the information it compiled is the following:

- In a 1990 American Immigration Institute Survey of prominent economists, four out of five said that immigrants had a favorable impact on economic growth. None said that immigrants had an adverse impact on economic growth.

- According to a Los Angeles *Times* analysis summarizing the best available research, "Immigrants contribute mightily to the economy, by paying billions in annual taxes, by filling low-wage jobs that keep domestic industry com-

petitive, and by spurring investment and job-creation, revitalizing once-de-
caying communities. Many social scientists conclude that the newcomers,
rather than drain government treasuries, contribute overall far more than they
utilize in services" (January 6, 1992).

- Studies by the Rand Corporation, the University of Maryland, the Council
  of Economic Advisors, the National Research Council and the Urban Institute all show that immigrants do not have a negative effect on the earnings
  and employment opportunities of native-born Americans. A 1989 Department of Labor study found that neither U.S. workers in complementary jobs,
  nor most minority workers, appear to be adversely affected by immigration.
  (ACLU, Department of Public Education, June 10, 1994).

74. Stedman (1987).
75. Ruiz (1990).
76. Rubenson (1989). The Secretary's Commission on Achieving Necessary Skills (1991).
77. Reich (1991).
78. Barlow & Robertson (1994, pp. 72-73).
79. Wirth (1993, p. 361).
80. Ibid., p. 365.
81. Barlow & Robertson (1994, p. 67).
82. Wirth (1993, p. 365).
83. Connell (1994); Taylor & Piché (1991).
84. Goodlad (1984); Ramirez (1992).
85. Barlow & Robertson (1994); Booth (1992); Moffett (1989).
86. Barlow & Robertson (1994, p. 136).

Chapter 4

1. Translations into English from the works of the Modern School Movement and the
   Cooperative Education Movement are those of the authors.
2. Lodi (1974) and Tonucci (1981).
3. Lodi (1977).
4. C. Freinet (1969/1975), p. 45.
5. Lodi (1977), note p. 13.
6. Sayers (1990).
7. Among those who recognized Freinet's contribution was Paulo Freire. As reported by
   Lee (1983), Freire acknowledged important affinities between his own and Freinet's
   work: "I am flattered to have my work associated with that of Célestin Freinet" and
   regarded Freinet as "one of the great contemporaries in education for freedom." See also
   Lee (1993) and Sayers (1990) for other contemporary Freinet scholarship in English;
   for Freinet studies in French, consult Clanche/Testanière (1989) of the Centre de
   Recherce sur Freinet et L'École Moderne at University of Bordeaux II (3 Place de la
   victoire, 33076, Bordeaux).
8. With the exception of a brief anthology (C. Freinet 1990a) and two short volumes of
   philosophical writings (C. Freinet 1990b and C. Freinet 1990c), little has appeared in
   the English language.

9. Lee (1993).
10. Ibid.
11. Ibid.
12. C. Freinet (1986), p. 67.
13. É. Freinet (1975), pp. 168-69.
14. C. Freinet (1986), pp. 64-65.
15. Ibid. pp. 53-54.
16. Balesse/C. Freinet (1973), p. 89.
17. C. Freinet (1986), pp. 54-55.
18. Ibid., p. 50.
19. Gervilliers/Berteloot/Lemery (1977), pp. 23.
20. Balesse/C. Freinet (1973), pp. 64-65.
21. Kristin Brown (in press) has written about one critical moment in the history of the Modern School Movement which illustrates the potential of global learning networks as contexts for language learning, of special relevance for foreign language teaching and bilingual education:

> The advantages of networking for bilingual students is best illustrated by a short but intriguing chapter in the history of Freinet's school when it became a bilingual school. During the years of the Spanish Civil War, students at Freinet's school included both local French children and refugees from Spain who lived at the school. At end of the 1936-37 school year and during the following academic year, the Spanish children outnumbered the French (Bens-Freinet, 1991).
>
> Élise Freinet describes the effectiveness of Freinet's techniques for students learning a second language. At the end of each class, after a walk, activity or discussion—an experience which all members in the class shared and which provided a common referent—the students collectively dictated a collective "free text" and then typeset the text so that a new page could be added to the class book. One day the text was written in Spanish by students from Spain, the next day it was written in French by students from France.
>
> In this way the children came to know the essential characteristics of the foreign language, its original syntax, its vocabulary, and other unknown aspects of the language that, thanks to the "free text," had the spontaneous quality of spoken language and the more cognitively demanding quality of written language. (É. Freinet, 1977, p. 359).
>
> An interscholastic exchange which linked the immigrant students with their homeland provided additional opportunities for linguistic and cultural learning. The children corresponded with a class at the Freinet school in Barcelona, exchanging school newspapers as well as cultural packages. These packages contained a wealth of information about the minerology, flora, and fauna of Spain as well as a selection of literary, pedagogical, and scientific reference books which became part of the permanent collection at the school in France.
>
> The personal writing of the immigrant children from Spain was powerful and sad and, as a result, compelling reading for the children of France. They received young childrens' accounts of the war, fear of the planes that

flew overhead and information about the shelters where they were forced to take refuge. A motivated context for writing practice evolved as the children in France collaborated with their Spanish classmates in writing letters of support to and comparing community portraits with the children in Northern Spain. "There came a moment when many of the children could dictate texts with equal facility in French or Spanish" (É. Freinet, 1977, p. 362).

22. Lodi (1977), note p. 13.
23. Tonucci (1981), p. 61.
24. In Tonucci (1981), pp. 46-47.
25. Tonucci (1981), p. 41.
26. Lee (1983).
27. Ibid., pp. 86-87.
28. Ibid., p. 87.
29. Ibid.
30. Cohen (1986), Devillar/Faltis (1991), Holt (1992), and Kessler (1992).
31. Calkins (1986) and Graves (1983).
32. Goswami/Stillman (1987).
33. Gervilliers/Berteloot/Lemery (1977), p. 31.
34. The concept of "pedagogies of distancing" in the work of both Célestin Freinet and Paulo Freire has been elaborated by Dennis Sayers and Kristin Brown (1993). Both Freinet and Freire have employed technology to amplify the impact of distancing on students' literacy development.

After the military coup of April 1964, the Brazilian popular educator Paulo Freire was arrested, imprisoned, and eventually forced into exile. Government authorities were reacting to Freire's successes in mounting massive literacy campaigns among illiterate adults. Freire's Popular Culture Movement (PCM) had been expanding to include 20,000 "Culture Circles," each serving 25 to 30 rural and urban slum residents who were working to build both their literacy skills and an awareness of their collective ability to generate change in their communities.

Literacy instruction in Freire's campaigns was divided into two parts: a pre-literacy phase and a literacy-building phase. In both phases, audiovisual media served to focus the discussion which took place within Culture Circles. In the pre-literacy phase, slides were created that depicted culture as a vital social process in which the community plays an active, determining role; no words were shown, just line drawings of community life. During the literacy-building phase, the slides used both graphic and written representations of key community concerns—called "generative themes"—which literacy workers had identified after weeks of research with local residents. . . . Freire felt that the use of educational media played a central role in the democratization of culture by making the slide's image "shareable" among all participants. Indeed, Freire felt that

> [when a] representation is projected as a slide, the learners effect an operation basic to the act of knowing: *they gain distance from the knowable object.* This experience is undergone as well by the educators, so that educators and learners together can reflect critically on the knowable object which mediates between them (p. 15).

For Freire, audiovisual technology played a large role in fostering reflective distancing. Certainly, this point was not lost on the military junta who sought to extirpate Freire's influence. Not surprisingly, they burned all the printed materials from the literacy campaign that they could lay their hands on. With this action, the junta merely joined ranks with book burners from reactionary regimes throughout history, frightened by "subversive" ideas contained in published materials. But the military government took a further step which clearly shows they appreciated the dangers in Freire's use of educational technology: they also destroyed the slide projectors whose only crime was to display images for thousands of Culture Circles. (pp. 13, 32-33)

35. This was the fate of the RAPPI project that operated in Canada in 1985 and 1986. RAPPI is an acronym for *reseau d'ateliers pédagogiques pilote international* (international educational computer conferencing network). Funded by the Canadian Department of Communications (1986), RAPPI linked 45 schools across Canada with schools in France, Britain and Italy. Two forms of communication were possible through RAPPI: (1) open discussion mode where any participant could comment on any topic; and (2) designated mode where two classes were paired according to similar interests and grade level. Participants exchanged information in English, French, and Italian. The evaluation identified several benefits that some teachers and students felt they derived from the project, including high student motivation, enjoyment of group activity, increased social communication skills for students, and improved reading and writing skills. However, students and teachers received little guidance with respect to either technical or pedagogical issues and many became frustrated by intermittent or non-existent responses to their communications. As expressed by the evaluators: "the technical, curricular, and human support system required by the RAPPI project was never properly in place" (1986, p. 35). As a result of this lack of curricular guidance, exchanges frequently degenerated into "pen-pal" letters that were not sustained by any strong motivation.

36. Plato (1973).

37. Ong (1982) and Postman (1992).

38. Douglas (1995), Marvin (1990), and Resnick & Resnick (1977).

39. Willinsky (1991).

40. Cited by Willinsky (1991, p. 132).

Chapter 5

1. Goodlad (1984); Ramirez (1992).

2. Freire (1983).

3. Brophy & Good (1986). These assumptions are perhaps most clearly realized in the widely used DISTAR program aimed at providing direct instruction to students considered at risk. Becker (1977), for example, argued that DISTAR was the most effective of eight compensatory program models evaluated by Abt Associates (1977). Direct Instruction approaches tend to be highly structured and teacher-centered and allow little opportunity for active language use or problem-solving by students other than what has been prescripted into the program.

   Closer examination of the data reviewed by Becker (1977) suggests that his conclusions are overly optimistic. He notes, for example, that there is a progressive decline among the DISTAR group in reading comprehension scores, from the 70th percentile at the end of grade 1 to the 56th percentile at grade 2, to the 40th percentile at grade 3. Students drop to around the 30th percentile by grades 5 and 6, despite maintaining their superior performance in decoding and spelling.

These data suggest that the apparent success of Direct Instruction programs may be an artifact of the narrow band of skills assessed by most standardized tests and the fact that students are drilled in test-related content. Thus, decoding and math computation skills can be effectively drilled into students by this approach, but higher-level skills and knowledge of vocabulary and concepts, central to literacy development after the early grades, cannot be developed through direct instruction methods. These higher-order thinking and literacy skills can be developed only when students are intrinsically motivated to engage in tasks that require these skills (reading extensively, creative writing, problem-solving, etc.). (See Cummins, 1984; Krashen, 1993).

4. Becker (1990).
5. Hirsch (1987)
6. Brophy (1992, pp. 5-6).
7. Prawat (1992). A large number of other researchers have also emphasized that learning is maximized in collaborative contexts. Wells and Chang-Wells (1992), for example, in describing how classroom communities of literate thinkers are created, suggest that "equal outcomes for all children can best be maximized regardless of cultural and linguistic background, by providing collaborative learning opportunities that integrate a wide range of uses of oral and written language with action and reflection" (p. 120). McCaleb (1994) has similarly focused on collaboration among teachers, students, families, and community as a means of building communities of learners in which the academic development of low-income students can be accelerated. James Moffett (1994) also has emphasized the importance of decentralized communities of learning in his recent book *The Universal Schoolhouse: Spiritual Awakening Through Education.*
8. Goodlad (1984); Ramirez (1992); Sirotnik (1983).
9. Sirotnik (1983, p. 29).
10. A transmission approach to pedagogy is also clearly more appropriate for the previous industrial age than the current information age. The impossibility of transmitting even a tiny fraction of the available information was expressed more than a decade ago by Patricia Cross (1984): "Between 6,000 and 7,000 scientific articles are written each day, and information doubles every five and a half years. By the time the average physician completes his or her training, half of all the information acquired in medical school is obsolete" (p. 172).
11. Howard Zinn, author of *A People's History of the United States,* discusses this point in response to a question about how textbooks are incorporating multicultural and anti-racist perspectives:

> What I find is a bland eclecticism where everything has equal weight. You add more facts, you add more continents, you add more cultures, you add more people. But then it becomes a confusing melange in which you've added a lot of different elements but without any real emphasis on what had previously been omitted. . . . You need the equivalent of affirmative action in education. What affirmative action does is to say, look, things have been slanted one way for a long time. We're going to pay special attention to this person or to this group of people because they have been left out for so long. . . . I think it is important to pay special attention to the history of black people, of Indians, of women, in

> a way that highlights not only the facts but the emotional intensity of such issues
> .... [With respect to instruction], the most important thing is to get students
> to do independent reading and research. Tell the students, "Pick something that
> interests you, pick out a person that interests you." ... I find that when students
> have a research project of their own they can get excited about it—especially if
> they are allowed to choose from a complex set of possibilities (pp. 154-155).

Along the same lines, Robert Hughes (1993) warns against substituting one set of dogmas and myths for another (e.g. Afrocentric versus Eurocentric) in constructing and teaching history:

> The need for absolute goodies and absolute baddies runs deep in us, but it
> drags history into propaganda and denies the humanity of the dead: their
> sins, their virtues, their efforts, their failures. .... You cannot remake the past
> in the name of affirmative action. But you can find narratives that haven't
> been written, histories of people and groups that have been distorted or
> ignored, and refresh history by bringing them in. (pp. 127-128)

12. Moffett (1989, pp. 75-76). A more recent example of the same type of confrontation revolved around the *Impressions* literature-based reading series published in Canada but popular throughout North America. Christian fundamentalists objected to fairy tales that depicted witches (in Halloween-related stories) and demanded that the series be removed from classrooms. Newspaper columnist Andrew Nikiforuk (1994) found its whole-language philosophy and its "disdain for even minimal teaching" (p. 133) even more scary. See Booth (1992), McConaghy (1992), and Nikiforuk (1994) for perspectives on this recent outbreak of curriculum censorship.

13. Moffett (1989, pp. 76-77).

14. Ibid., pp. 86-87.

15. Ibid., p. 84.

16. Schlesinger (1991, p. 127). It is hardly coincidence that the dust jacket of *The Disuniting of America* reflects the apocalyptic tone and racial counterpoint of the entire book: As the red and white stripes of the American flag are falling off one by one, they change color and become a dull brown!

The possessive attitude toward the origins of democratic ideals articulated by many of those who assert the superiority of Western civilization would be more convincing if democratic principles were applied more consistently by Western powers. (See, for example, Chomsky and Herman, 1979; Macedo, 1993, 1994). Whether governments are left-wing or right-wing, European or non-European, democratic ideals are very much secondary to perceived self-interest in the actions of governments. To take just two examples: in South Africa during this century, democracy was long demanded by Black Africans and resisted by European-origin Whites; Western governments, including the left-wing government of Gough Whitlam in Australia, acquiesced in the Indonesian annexation of East Timor in the mid-1970s and in the subsequent (and continuing) genocide of the East Timorese people in which one-third of the population has been slaughtered. The European tradition of respect for human rights is obviously not significant enough to jeopardize the economic partnerships that Indonesia has forged with many Western countries. (See Chomsky, 1987.)

17. One of the most influential approaches to learning theory within North America is currently based on the ideas of Soviet psychologist Lev Vygotsky. Vygotsky argued that

learning takes place within the "zone of proximal development" (ZPD), defined as the distance between children's developmental levels as determined by individual problem-solving without adult guidance and the levels of potential development as determined by their problem-solving under the influence of, or in collaboration with, more capable adults or peers. Thus, the social context is crucial for children's learning and cognitive development. Children internalize concepts, cognitive capacities, and learning strategies in the context of an apprenticeship relationship with adults or peers. Other cognitive approaches to learning that do not draw their inspiration from Vygotsky also emphasize the importance of meaningful inquiry supported by efficient learning strategies (e.g. Chamot and O'Malley, 1994; Pressley and Associates, 1990).

18. See Krashen (1993) for a comprehensive review.

19. The most common issue to surface in the popular press in relation to whole language is its rejection of isolated phonics instruction and the reciprocal rejection of whole language by phonics advocates. To us, this is largely a nonissue; students in the early grades do need to acquire an awareness of phonic regularities; and most students can do so through the type of phonics instruction given in whole-language classes, which draws attention to phonic regularities as students read and write. However, more formal attention to phonics may be beneficial for students who encounter difficulty in picking up reading skills. Certainly, isolated phonics instruction in the early grades is unlikely to cause permanent psychic damage (as sometimes implied by a few extreme whole-language advocates), provided that students quickly get into extensive reading of literature. Unfortunately, literature is often largely absent from the basal readers that form the foundation of skills-based reading programs. The culprit, however, is not isolated phonics instruction per se (although for most students it is probably a waste of time) but the failure to promote extensive reading and writing in a variety of genres.

20. Holt (1993); Johnson & Johnson (1994); Kessler (1992). Cooperative learning is actually not a recent instructional strategy. Its origins go back to the last great "multicultural" upheaval in United States schools, the aftermath of the landmark Supreme Court decision of *Brown v. Board of Education* in 1954, which mandated integration of American classrooms. At that time, educators and social scientists collaborated in the development of cooperative learning approaches, stressing small-group work among races, as a major vehicle for promoting effective learning while reducing prejudice between racial groups working together in integrated classrooms, often for the first time (Allport, 1979; Cook, 1978). Cooperative learning is receiving renewed attention from contemporary educators as an important vehicle for promoting multicultural education and intercultural understanding. The Socioacademic Achievement Model of DeVillar and Faltis (DeVillar and Faltis, 1991; DeVillar, Faltis, and Cummins, 1994) is noteworthy as a recent effort to generate a theoretical framework for promoting academic achievement among culturally diverse students. This model is based on three interdependent components—integration, communication, and coop-eration—reflecting respectively the work of Gordon Allport (1954) on racial integra-tion and prejudice reduction, Lev Vygotsky (1962) on social interaction as crucial to cognitive and academic development, and a variety of researchers who have demon-strated that cooperative learning enhances academic development and acts to equalize status relationships among students from different cultural and racial backgrounds (Holt, 1993; Kessler, 1992).

21. Artigal (1991); Moll (1990); Moll et al. (1992); Newman, Griffin and Cole (1989); Poplin (1988); Tharp and Gallimore (1991); Wells and Chang-Wells (1992). In support of "inquiry" approaches to learning, Robert Sternberg of Yale University suggests that "the single most helpful thing we can do to help children develop their intelligence is a simple one: take their questions seriously, and turn these questions into golden opportunities to think and learn" (1994, p. 138). He describes seven levels of responding to children's questions and notes that "as we move up the levels, we go from rejecting children's questions, at one extreme, to encouraging the formation and testing of hypotheses at the other. We go from no learning, to passive rote learning, to analytic and creative learning" (p. 138).

22. Levin (1993). The instructional approaches implemented in accelerated schools are reinforced by the reanalysis of the "effective schools" literature carried out by Lawrence Stedman (1987). Stedman focused on case studies of schools that achieved grade-level success with low-income students and maintained this success over several years. The following factors were highlighted as crucial for student academic success:

   - *Cultural pluralism*—affirmation of the ethnic and racial identity of students.
   - *Parental participation*—frequent communication with parents and encouragement of parental participation in school governance.
   - *Academically rich programs*—students are encouraged to become actively involved in learning through tasks that challenge them cognitively and engage their personal experiences.

   Other factors Stedman highlighted are: (1) shared governance between administrators, parents, and teachers; (2) skilled use and training of teachers within a collaborative school climate; (3) personal attention to students through the use of volunteers and community resources; and (4) student responsibility for student affairs.

23. Delpit (1988); Kalantzis & Cope (1993); Reyes (1992).

24. Delpit (1988, p. 296).

25. Kalantzis & Cope (1993).

26. Our intent here is not to deny that there are epistemological and social presuppositions and implications in progressive pedagogy. There clearly are; in fact, Dewey devoted considerable energy to discussing the social goals of education. Our point is that most of those who are currently implementing forms of pedagogy that we have categorized as "progressive" are not overly concerned with these broader presuppositions and implications. Their goal is simply to help children develop academic skills as effectively as possible. With considerable research support, they see active inquiry, peer collaboration, and experiential learning as central to this goal.

   Articulating the social assumptions of progressive pedagogy has been left to theorists whose links to the classroom are often tenuous. In discussing these theorists and their social (and pedagogical) assumptions, Kalantzis and Cope (1993) distinguish two forms of progressivist pedagogy: that of modernism and experience, and that of postmodernism and difference. The former is derived directly from Dewey's work and prescribes a pedagogy of activity and experience so that students will be better able to contribute to social progress in a world that is rapidly changing. The latter, according to Kalantzis and Cope, rejects universal objective truths in favor of a relativism that attempts to legitimate the different cultural experiences that children (and adults) bring to the classroom. Kalantzis and Cope are highly critical of both forms of progressivism on the grounds that they romantically equalize all types of diversity and fail to come to grips with issues of how relations of power are manifested in language, culture, and curriculum. Their *explicit pedagogy for inclusion and access* attempts to overcome the limitations of both traditional and progressive pedagogies. See also Cazden (1992) for a balanced and insightful discussion of whole-language pedagogy.

27. Reyes (1992).

28. Although whole-language theorists have not neglected issues related to bilingualism (e.g. Edelsky, 1986; Goodman, Goodman, & Flores, 1979; Hudelson, 1989), in practice, relatively little attention has been devoted to the instructional modifications required to adapt whole-language approaches for second-language learners. Two excellent books by David and Yvonne Freeman (1992, 1994) have begun to address this gap.

29. Bigelow et al. (1994). Individual copies of *Rethinking Our Classrooms* are available for $6 (U.S.) plus $3.50 shipping and handling, from Rethinking Schools, 1001 E. Keefe Ave., Milwaukee, WI 53212, USA; 414-964-9646. Substantial discounts are offered on orders of 10 or more.

30. Peterson (1994, p. 30).

31. Bigelow et al. (1994, pp. 4-5).

32. Peterson (1994, p. 33).

33. Peterson (1994, pp. 36-37). For many other illustrations of critical teaching, see Frederickson (1995) and Shor (1992). Theoretical discussions of these issues can be found in Giroux (1992, 1993) and McLaren (1995a, 1995b).

34. Poplin & Weeres (1992, pp. 12-13).

35. Poplin & Weeres (1992, p. 13).

36. Poplin & Weeres (1992, p. 15).

37. Delpit (1992, p. 245). Several outstanding books on multicultural education emphasize the importance of infusing the core curriculum with a multicultural perspective: see Banks (1988); Nieto (1992). Sonia Nieto (1992), in her book *Affirming Diversity,* defines multicultural education as follows:

> Multicultural education is a process of comprehensive school reform and basic education for all students. It challenges and rejects racism and other forms of discrimination in schools and society and accepts and affirms the pluralism (ethnic, racial, linguistic, religious, economic, and gender among others) that students, their communities, and teachers represent. Multicultural education permeates the curriculum and instructional strategies used in schools, as well as the interactions among teachers, students and parents, and the very way that schools conceptualize the nature of teaching and learning. Because it uses critical pedagogy as its underlying philosophy and focuses on knowledge, reflection, and action (praxis) as the basis for social change, multicultural education furthers the democratic principles of social justice. (p. 208)

A comprehensive account of multicultural education can be found in Banks and Banks, eds., *Encyclopedia of Multicultural Education* (1995).

Although they are rightly suspicious of certain forms of "multicultural education," the explicit pedagogy for inclusion and access articulated by Kalantzis and Cope (1993) shares the essential features of Nieto's description of multicultural education. Kalantzis and Cope describe their approach as follows:

> A pedagogy that shunts backwards and forwards between: on the one hand, explicit exposition of the common cultural contents and social experience of industrial society, to allow social access and critique for all social groups; and, on the other hand, the experience of diversity, starting with student experience, the ethics and epistemology of pluralism. A culturally open yet socially purposeful pedagogy. . . . it is the role of schools to induct students into those discourses and genres that are the most powerful in society (pp. 82-83).

They suggest that education must initiate a dialogue between dominant ways of knowing (e.g., the Western canon) and other marginal discourses such that both core and margins are transformed.

38. Moffett (1989, p. 85).
39. Giroux (1992, pp. 28-34). See Peter McLaren (1995a, 1995b) for additional insightful discussions of multiculturalism and "border disputes." Sonia Nieto (personal communication, March 22, 1995) points out that the notion of "border crossing" needs to acknowledge that crossing cultural and linguistic boundaries is a daily normal experience for the many bilingual and bicultural students and teachers in schools around the world. Unfortunately, dominant groups frequently have restricted minority groups' ability to cross boundaries by erecting barriers to full participation in schools and other societal institutions controlled by the dominant group.
40. Poplin & Weeres (1992, p. 11).
41. Hughes (1993, pp. 88-100).

Chapter 6

1. Postman (1993).
2. Barlett & Steele (1992).
3. Carson, Huelskamp, & Woodall (1993).
4. Barlett & Steele (1992).
5. Moll et al. (1992); Olsen et al. (1992); Poplin & Weeres (1992).
6. Moffett (1989, 1994).
7. Noble (1994, p. 69).
8. The rise and fall of Chris Whittle, former chairperson of Whittle Communications, has been amply documented (Apple, 1993; DeVaney, 1994; Kozol, 1993). Whittle carved out a huge public school audience for his commercial television programming effort, Channel One. In return for Channel One's paying for the installation of a satellite dish on the school's roof (wired to a free television monitor in each classroom), districts must agree to require 90 percent of its students to watch the shows first thing in the morning 90 percent of the time. More than 8 million students—fully a third of all junior and senior high students in the United States—in 12,000 schools located in 47 states are required to watch 12 minutes of Whittle's commercial programming. What's in it for Whittle Communications? Channel One brings in $630,000 a day in advertising fees.

   Whittle's next venture, the Edison Project, was far less successful. First proposed as a chain of 1,000 technology-intensive private schools, the project, in its heyday, attracted considerable attention to the volatile issue of privatizing education. Its board of directors, headed by Benno Schmidt, former president of Yale University, includes two of the principal proponents of school vouchers, Chester Finn, former Bush and Reagan appointee to numerous posts, and John Chubb, who also serves as director of curriculum. But financing woes at Whittle Communications forced a shift in focus to securing contracts to run public schools (none of which has been implemented to date). Financial uncertainties among potential investors eventually led to Whittle's ouster as CEO.

But the Edison Project is by no means the sole player in the corporate drive to privatize education. Chief among high-profile rivals is the Minneapolis-based Educational Alternatives, Inc. (EAI), headed by John Golle (1994). In 1987, Golle set out to open 20 private elementary schools within five years, projecting $30 million in profits annually. Like the Edison Project, EAI proposed to save costs by keeping teacher-student ratios high through increased use of computers as "teaching machines." After managing single schools for years, EAI secured the first major coup for school privatization corporations: a multischool contract in Baltimore, Maryland, to run eight elementary schools and a single middle school (Miner, 1993).

In spite of a scandal in spring of 1994 involving EAI's erroneous reporting of exaggerated improvements in Baltimore students' test scores, Golle hit the privatization jackpot in another eastern city; he managed to convince the school board of Hartford, Connecticut, to turn over all of its 32 schools to EAI's control, beginning with the 1994-95 school year (Schmidt, 1994). With partners and backers like KPMG Peat Marwick (the largest accounting firm in the world, which offers accounting and financial consultation to EAI schools) and Johnson Controls Worldwide (providing $5 billion in food services, maintenance, and secretarial services), all at nonunion rates, EAI is poised to bring privatization schemes to school districts all over North America.

Golle's EAI is playing its "technology card" even more strongly than Whittle did. Its third principal financial backer and partner is Computer Communication Corporation (CCC), a division of Simon & Schuster, the world's largest publisher, in turn owned by Paramount Communications, with $4.2 billion in revenues in 1992. CCC is the provider of the rote-learning computer laboratories that plug children at EAI schools into electronic workbook programs rather than more socialized learning projects involving collaborative critical inquiry (Miner, 1993).

9. Noble (1994, p. 65).
10. Apple (1993), Barlow & Robertson (1994), Christian-Smith (1991), Noble (1994), Olson (1987), and Sullivan (1983), among others.
11. Barlow & Robertson (1994, pp. 89-90).
12. Apple (1993, p. 117).
13. Hodas (1992).
14. "Measure Insuring Schools Access to "Information Highway" Dies," *Education Week,* October 5, 1994.

In both the United States and Canada, schools are just in the beginning stages of getting access to the Internet. According to a report from Education Secretary Richard Riley (1995), only about one-third of U.S. schools have access to the Internet, and "the information superhighway is rarely available for daily learning in the classroom, even for those schools that do have Internet access. . . . schools cite limited funding, lack of, or inadequate equipment, and too few access points in the school building as the main reasons why they do not have or use advanced telecommunications."

In Canada, as reported by Robert Sheppard (1995a), the federal government has been strongly proactive during the past few years in establishing links between education and the information highway. We quote at some length from Sheppard's report:

By most standards, that little node on the communications highway known as SchoolNet has been an unqualified success.

Set up two years ago by the federal government and the provinces so that teachers and students could "talk" to each other in an Internet-ish way across the computer miles, SchoolNet is already used by about a quarter of Canada's 16,000 elementary and secondary schools. The system is "accessed" about 100,000 times a month by its users, and its use is growing at a phenomenal rate.

But behind this promising start is a serious rupture in the educational superhighway. In recent months, a number of school boards—mostly rural, with the biggest ones in Nova Scotia—have been disconnected from the SchoolNet system for a very simple reason: The long-distance and connect charges were running the tab to about $10,000 a year, too much for a small school board to bear. (p. A13)

Sheppard points out that urban schools in cities that have a freenet node to access the larger system can have virtually unlimited access for about $300 (Canadian) a year, but rural schools must bear the long-distance charges to connect to the system. While provinces such as Ontario and Manitoba are taking steps to address the problem (Ontario is paying $5 million a year to rent trunk lines from Bell Canada to provide access to rural isolated schools), a comprehensive solution is required, according to Sheppard. He points out that

A century ago we built a railway to knit the country together and open our frontiers to all comers. And we did it by sharing the branch and trunk-line costs of these connections among a variety of public and private users. The information networks are today's equivalent of that railway. It's not right that some Canadian schools get pretty close to a free ride on this new information highway while others are barred from it, essentially because of geography. . . . The phone companies want adaptable, computer-sophisticated employees for the future—not to mention a new generation of network users who will be paying for the current trunk-line investment in years to come.

There may even be education-tax savings for businesses if they help schools keep their costs down. But the biggest advantage is simply to have a school system that encourages students to chit-chat electronically with their peers across the country and get a real taste of the differences that both separate us and drive us together. (1995a, p. A13)

Sheppard (1995b) lauds the province of New Brunswick, which has already connected every elementary school to the Internet despite being regarded as one of the "have-not" Canadian provinces. By contrast, Ontario has about 300 schools connected to the Internet, representing only about one-tenth of the total number of schools that could be connected.

15. Kadi (1995).
16. During the last quarter of the nineteenth century, change in communications technology was extremely rapid, paralleling today's explosion of computing and networking tech-

nologies. In quick succession, a string of what Carolyn Marvin (1990) has termed "proto-mass media" were introduced: the telephone, phonographic recording, the radio and the cinema. Marvin's portrait of the spirit of those times is startlingly parallel to what we are experiencing today. The appearance of the telephone and the shock waves it occasioned in the social order at the end of the nineteenth century is particularly instructive.

One hundred years ago, the telephone was an invention that inspired both admiration and fear. On the one hand, it was cheered as ushering in a new era of world unity in which people throughout the world would be connected through voice signals; on the other hand, two-way communication through telephony generated discomfort among those citizens interested in safeguarding cherished traditions of Western civilization. Marvin notes that "the early history of electric media is less the evolution of technical efficiencies in communication than a series of arenas for negotiating issues crucial to the conduct of social life; among them, who is inside and outside, who may speak, who may not, and who has authority and may be believed." (p. 4)

Telephone technology held the promise—and the threat—of permitting two-way communication between people from different cultures located anywhere on the planet, and on a basis dangerously approaching equal terms. Marvin details the concern and confusion which greeted the introduction of telephones in terms that evoke the partisan debates of our own times on the place of multiculturalism in schools:

> Chaotic and creative experiments . . . attempted to reduce and simplify a world of expanding cultural variety to something more familiar and less threatening. That impulse fixed on one-way communication from familiar cultural, social, and geographic perimeters as a preferred strategy to two-way exchange, with its greater presumption of equality and risks of unpredictable confrontation. . . . New kinds of encounters collided with old ways of determining trust and reliability, and with old notions about the world and one's place in it: about the relation of men and women, rich and poor, black and white, European and non-European, experts and publics. (pp. 5-6)

Indeed, Marvin notes, "the prospect of media that made senders and receivers proximate and seemed to eliminate many of the barriers that kept them safely separated excited profound xenophobic anxiety" (pp. 200-1). If barriers to international communication were to come tumbling down in the face of telephone technology, there was widespread concern that the new terms of intercultural discourse should be negotiated in ways which favored a particular world view. According to Marvin, "instantaneous communication augured a universal language, usually thought to be English, and . . . this distinctly Anglophile solution reflected a conviction that the provincialism of English-speaking peoples was the sensibility of the world" (p. 193).

Marvin summarizes her critical review of nineteenth century popular and professional literature on the potential societal impact of the telephone as follows:

> The capacity to reach out to the Other seemed rarely to involve any obligation to behave as a guest in the Other's domain, to learn or appreciate the Other's customs, to speak his [or her] language, to share his [or her] victories and disappointments, or to change as a result of any encounter with him [or her]. For their part, peripheral Others were expected to do all these things, to communicate on terms provided by the center, and to converse

with representatives of European civilization without saying much back in the course of the conversation about their own unique cultures. (p. 195)

History appears to be repeating itself as computers become linked in far-ranging networks at the end of the twentieth century. For example, among modern computer learning networks, Orillas and I*EARN are two of the few electronic communities of learners that have explicit language policies that encourage participation in languages other than English in all their projects. Indeed, many networking projects have explicitly banned the use of languages other than English as the medium of exchange. The question of which language (or what mix of languages) to employ as the "coin of the realm" when teachers and students participate in today's computer-based global learning networks is too often answered, without hesitation or reflection, with a single alternative: English. In this sense, little appears to have changed between the turn of the last century and the coming of the next.

17. Nader (1995, p. 74).

Internet Basics

1. The technically sophisticated may be concerned at our effort toward simplification in this guide. We have coined a few terms, such as "Internet communication tool," to cover a huge variety of networking activity, from e-mail and LISTSERVs to client-server and browsing programs for the Web. Our goal has been to offer a rudimentary print-media introduction that helps the novice parent, teacher, and student take a first step into networking.

2. Here we concentrate on the Gopher information displayer because it is more text-based and depends on menu hierarchies; representing the myriad possibilities of Hypertext in a printed book such as you are now holding in your hands is much harder to do. Yet Hypertext browsers, such as Mosaic or Netscape for the Web, are becoming increasingly popular, especially for transmitting multimedia information. Web sites use the URL prefix http:// and sometimes include the "tilde" symbol [~]. If your keyboard does not include this symbol, substitute the letters %7E wherever the ~ appears.)

3. Even without a full-service account that included the ability to use Gopher directly, Ms. Reyes could have arrived at this menu; we will explore alternatives for parents and educators who do not have full Internet connectivity in the last paragraphs of this guide.

4. Some documents will be forwarded not to a mailbox but to a file directory, but for simplicity's sake we discuss only documents forwarded in the form of electronic mail.

5. There are other approaches, such as XModem, Kermit, or FTP utilities, but here we focus on the most straightforward way to capture simple text.

Internet Resources for K–12 Education

1. Rogers, personal communication, November 14, 1994.
2. Sayers (1991), Sayers (1994a), and Sayers/Brown (1994).
3. Figueroa/Sayers/Brown (1990).

Bibliography

Abt Associates. (1977). *Education as experimentation: A planned variation model. Vol. IV.* Cambridge, MA: Abt Associates.

Ada, A. F. (1988). The Pajaro Valley experience: Working with Spanish-speaking parents to develop children's reading and writing skills in the home through the use of children's literature. In T. Skutnabb-Kangas & J. Cummins, eds., *Minority education: From shame to struggle,* pp. 223-238. Clevedon, England: Multilingual Matters.

Allport, G. (1954). *The nature of prejudice.* Cambridge, MA: Addison-Wesley.

An End to Intolerance. (1994). Cold Spring Harbor, NY: Cold Spring Harbor High School.

Apple, M. W. (1993). *Official knowledge: Democratic education in a conservative age.* New York: Routledge.

Artigal, J. P. (1991). *The Catalan immersion program: A European point of view.* Norwood, NJ: Ablex Publishing Corporation.

Balesse, L., & Freinet, C. (1973). *La lectura en la escuela por medio de la imprenta.* F. Beltran, trans. Barcelona: Editorial Laia. (Original work published 1961 as *La lecture par l'imprimerie a l'école.* [Reading through printing in schools]).

Baril, A., & Mori, G. A. (1991). Educational attainment of linguistic groups in Canada. *Canadian Social Trends,* Spring, 17-18.

Barlett, D. L., & Steele, J. B. (1992). *America: What went wrong?* Kansas City, KS: Andrews & McMeel.

Barlow, M., & Robertson, H.-J. (1994). *Class warfare: The assault on Canada's schools.* Toronto: Key Porter Books.

Becker, H. J. (1987). Using computers for instruction. *BYTE, 12*(2), 149-162. ERIC: EJ 349 598.

Becker, H. J. (1990). How computers are used in United States schools: Basic data from the 1989 I.E.A. computers in education survey. Baltimore, MD: Johns Hopkins University, Center for Social Organization of Schools.

Becker, W. C. (1977). Teaching reading and language to the disadvantaged: What we have learned from field research. *Harvard Educational Review, 47*(4), 518-543.

Bens-Freinet, M. (1994). Three critical moments in the life of the Freinet school. In J. Sivell, ed., *Freinet pedagogy: Theory and practice,* pp. 105-127. Lewiston, NY: Edwin Mellon Press.

Bigelow, B. (1991). Once upon a genocide . . . Christopher Columbus in children's literature. In B. Bigelow, B. Miner, & B. Peterson, eds., *Rethinking Columbus: Teaching about the*

500th anniversary of Columbus's arrival in America, pp. 23-30. Milwaukee, WI: Rethinking Schools.

Bigelow, B., Christensen, L., Karp, S., Miner, B., & Peterson, B. (1994). *Rethinking our classrooms: Teaching for equity and justice.* Milwaukee, WI: Rethinking Schools.

Blauner, R. (1969). Internal colonialism and ghetto revolt. *Social Problems, 16,* 393-408.

Booth, D. (1992). *Censorship goes to school.* Markham, ON: Pembroke.

Bracey, G. (1995). Debunking the myth that the U.S. spends more on schools. *Rethinking Schools, 9*(4), p. 7.

Brophy, J. (1992). Probing the subtleties of subject-matter teaching. *Educational Leadership,* April, 4-8.

Brophy, J. & Good, T. (1986). Teacher behavior and student achievement. In M. Wittrock, ed., *Handbook of research on teaching,* 3rd ed., pp. 328-375. New York: Macmillan.

Brown, K. (1993). Balancing the tools of technology with our own humanity: The use of technology in building partnerships and communities. In A. F. Ada & J. Tinajero, eds., *The power of two languages: Literacy and biliteracy for Spanish-speakers,* pp. 178-198. New York: Macmillan.

Brown, K. (In press). "Curriculum innovations: Gaining control over technology in bilingual/multicultural classrooms." In D. Sayers, ed., *Bilingual/multicultural education teacher resource handbook.* Ontario, CA: California Association for Bilingual Education.

Brown, K., & Cuellar, J. L. (1995). Personal communication, February 12.

Bruner, J. S. (1966). *Toward a theory of instruction.* Cambridge, MA: The Belknap Press of Harvard University Press.

Carson, C. C., Huelskamp, R. M., & Woodall, T. D. (1993). Perspectives on education in America. *Journal of Educational Research, 86,* 257-312.

Cazden, C. (1992). *Whole language plus: Essays on literacy in the United States and New Zealand.* New York: Teachers College Press.

Chamot, A. U., & O'Malley, J. M. (1994). *The CALLA handbook: Implementing the cognitive academic language learning approach.* Reading, MA: Addison-Wesley.

Chomsky, N. (1987). The manufacture of consent. In J. Peck, ed., *The Chomsky reader,* pp. 121-136. New York: Pantheon Books.

Chomsky, N., & Herman, E. (1979). *The Washington connection and third world fascism: The political economy of human rights, Volume 1.* Montreal: Black Rose Books.

Christian-Smith, L. (1991). Texts and high tech: Computers, gender, and book publishing. In M. W. Apple & L. K. Christian-Smith, eds., *The politics of the textbook,* pp. 41-55. New York: Routledge.

Cohen, E. (1986). *Designing groupwork.* New York: Teachers College Press.

Collier, V. P. (1987). Age and rate of acquisition of second language for academic purposes. *TESOL Quarterly, 21,* 617-641.

Comer, J. P. (1980). *School power: Implications of an intervention project.* New York: The Free Press.

Connell, R. W. (1994). Poverty and education. *Harvard Educational Review, 64*(2), 125-149.

The Contemporary. (1994). January and May issues. Cold Spring Harbor, NY: Cold Spring Harbor High School.

Copen, P. (1995). Personal communication. January 31.

Cook, S. (1978). Interpersonal and attitudinal outcomes in cooperating interracial groups. *Journal of Research and Development in Education, 12*(1), 98-113.

Cope, B., & Kalantzis, M. (1993). The power of literacy and the literacy of power. In B. Cope & M. Kalantzis, eds., *The powers of literacy: A genre approach to teaching writing*, pp. 63-89. London: The Falmer Press.

Cross, K. P. (1984). The rising tide of school reform reports. *Phi Delta Kappan, 66*(3), 167-172.

Cuban, L. (1993). Unemployment, recession, and other economic ills: Are public schools to blame? *Rethinking Schools, 7*(4), p. 11.

Cuban, L. (1994). The great school scam: The economy's turned around, but where is the praise? *Education Week, 13*, June 15, p. 44.

Cummins, J. (1984). *Bilingualism and special education: Issues in assessment and pedagogy*. Clevedon, England: Multilingual Matters.

Cummins, J. (1994). Primary language instruction and the education of language minority students. In C. Leyba, ed., *Schooling and language minority students: A theoretical framework*, 2nd ed., pp. 3-46. Los Angeles: Evaluation, Dissemination, and Assessment Center.

Cummins, J. (1995). *Negotiating identities: Education for empowerment in a diverse society*. Ontario, CA: California Association for Bilingual Education.

Cummins, J., & Sayers, D. (1990). Education 2001: Learning networks and educational reform. In C. Faltis & R. DeVillar, eds., *Language, minority students and computers*, pp. 1-29. New York: The Haworth Press.

Delpit, L. D. (1988). The silenced dialogue: Power and pedagogy in educating other peoples's children. *Harvard Educational Review, 58*(3), 280-298.

Delpit, L. D. (1992). Education in a multicultural society: Our future's greatest challenge. *Journal of Negro Education, 61*, 237-249.

Department of Communications, Government of Canada. (1986). *An evaluation report of the RAPPI project, September 1985–June 1986: An international computer conferencing network*. Ottawa: Government of Canada.

DeVaney, A. (1994). *Watching Channel One: The convergence of students, technology, and private business*. Albany, NY: SUNY Press.

DeVillar, R. A., & Faltis, C. J. (1991). *Computers and cultural diversity: Restructuring for school success*. Albany, NY: SUNY Press.

DeVillar, R. A., Faltis, C. J., & Cummins, J., eds. (1994). *Cultural diversity in schools: From rhetoric to practice*. Albany, NY: SUNY Press.

Dewey, J. (1963). *Experience and education*. New York: Collier Books.

Douglas, F. (1941). *Life and times of Frederick Douglass: Written by himself*. New York: Pathway Press.

D'Souza, D. (1991). *Illiberal education: The politics of race and sex on campus*. New York: Vintage Books.

Dunn, L. (1987). *Bilingual Hispanic children on the U.S mainland: A review of research on their cognitive, linguistic, and scholastic development*. Circle Pines, MN: American Guidance Service.

Edelsky, C. (1986). *Writing in a bilingual program.* Norwood, NJ: Ablex.

Ferdman, B. (1990). Literacy and cultural identity. *Harvard Educational Review, 60*(2), 181-204.

Figueroa, E. (1988). "Efectos del adiestramiento en redaccion computadorizada en las actitudes del personal de Tecnologia Educativa (DIP) hacia la ensenanza de la redaccion." Unpublished typescript. Rio Piedras: University of Puerto Rico.

Figueroa, E., Brown, K., & Sayers, D. (1995, February 17). "International proverbs project." Unpublished manuscript.

Figueroa, E., Sayers, D., & Brown, K. (1990). Red multilingue para el apprendizaje: De Orilla a Orilla (A multilingual learning network: From Shore to Shore). *Micro Aula: El maestro y la computadora* (Micro-classroom: The teacher and the computer), *8,* 27-30.

Figueroa, E., Brown, K., & Sayers, D. (In press). "De Orilla a Orilla: A decade of multilingual teacher-as-researcher projects over global learning networks." *NABE News.*

Fine, M. (1991). *Framing drop-outs: Notes on the politics of an urban public high school.* Albany, NY: SUNY Press.

Folbre, N. (1992). Business to the rescue? *The Nation, 255*(8), September 21, 281-282.

Fordham, S. (1990). Racelessness as a factor in Black students' school success: Pragmatic strategy or pyrrhic victory? In N. M. Hidalgo, C. L. McDowell, & E. V. Siddle, eds., *Facing racism in education,* pp. 232-262. Reprint series No. 21, *Harvard Educational Review.*

Frazier, K. (1993). The state of American education: Sandia study challenges misconceptions. *Rethinking Schools, 8*(2), 16-17.

Frederickson, J. (Ed.) (1995). *Reclaiming our voices: Bilingual education, critical pedagogy, & praxis.* Ontario, CA: California Association for Bilingual Education.

Freeman, D. E., & Freeman, Y. S. (1994). *Between worlds: Access to second language acquisition.* Portsmouth, NH: Heinemann.

Freeman, Y. S., & Freeman, D. E. (1992). *Whole language for second language learners.* Portsmouth, NH: Heinemann.

Freinet, C. (1974). *Las tecnicas audio-visuales.* J. Colome, trans. Barcelona: Editorial Laia.

Freinet, C. (1986). *Por una escuela del pueblo.* J. Alcobe, trans. Barcelona: Editorial Laia. (Original work published 1969 as *Pour l'ecole du peuple: Guide practique pour l'organisation materielle, technique et pedagogique de l'ecole populaire* [For a school of the people: A practical guide for the material, technical, and pedagogical organization of a popular school].)

Freinet, C. (1990a). *Cooperative learning & social change: Selected writings of Célestin Freinet.* D. Clandfield & J. Sivell, eds. Toronto: Our Schools/Our Selves.

Freinet, C. (1990b). *Education and work: A model for child-centered learning.* John Sivell, trans. Lewiston, NY: Edwin Mellen Press.

Freinet, C. (1990c). *The wisdom of Matthew: An essay in contemporary French educational theory.* John Sivell, trans. Lewiston, NY: Edwin Mellen Press.

Freinet, É. (1975). *Nacimiento de una pedagogia popular: Historia de una escuela moderna.* Pere Vilanova, trans. Barcelona: Editorial Laia. (Original work published 1969 as *Naissance d'une pedagogie populaire* [Birth of a popular pedagogy].)

Freinet, É. (1977). *La escuela Freinet: Los niños en un medio natural.* Santiago Puig, trans. Barcelona: Editorial Laia.

Freire, P. (1969). *La educación como práctica de la libertad.* Mexico, D.F.: Siglo XXI.

Freire, P. (1975). *Cultural action for freedom.* Cambridge, MA: Harvard Educational Review.

Freire, P. (1983). Banking education. In H. Giroux & D. Purpel, eds., *The hidden curriculum and moral education: Deception or discovery?,* pp. 283-291. Berkeley, CA: McCutcheon Publishing Corporation.

Freire, P., & Macedo, D. (1987). *Literacy: Reading the word and the world.* South Hadley, MA: Bergin & Garvey.

Gee, M. (1994). Apocalypse deferred. *Globe & Mail,* April 9, pp. D1-D3.

Gerver, E. (1990). Computers and gender. In T. Forester, ed., *Computers in the human context: Information technology, productivity and people,* pp. 481-501. Cambridge, MA: Massachusetts Institute of Technology Press.

Gervilliers, D., Berteloot, C., & Lemery, J. (1977). *Las correspondencias escolares.* Barcelona: Editorial Laia.

Gibson, W. (1993, May 10). "Presentation to the Convocation on Technology and Education, National Academy of Sciences." Unpublished manuscript.

Giroux, H. (1992). *Border crossings: Cultural workers and the politics of education.* New York: Routledge.

Giroux, H. (1993). *Living dangerously: Multiculturalism and the politics of difference.* New York: Peter Lang.

Golle, J. (1994). You must take care of your customer. *Education Week, 13*(29), June 22, 44-45.

Good, T., & Brophy, J. (1986). School effects. In M. Wittrock, ed., *Handbook of research on teaching,* 3rd ed., pp. 570-602. New York: Macmillan.

Goodlad, J. I. (1984). *A place called school: Prospects for the future.* New York: McGraw-Hill.

Goodman, K. S., Goodman, Y. M., & Flores, B. (1979). *Reading in the bilingual classroom: Literacy and biliteracy.* Rosslyn, VA: National Clearinghouse for Bilingual Education.

Goswami, D., & Stillman, P. (1987). *Reclaiming the classroom: Teacher research as an agency for change.* Portsmouth, NH: Heinemann.

Gragert, E. (1994). Personal communication, September 20.

Graves, D. (1983). *Writing: Teachers and children at work.* Exeter, NH: Heinemann Educational Books.

Hacker, A. (1995). *Two nations: Black and white, separate, hostile, unequal.* New York: Ballantine Books.

Hirsch, E. D., Jr. (1987). *Cultural literacy: What every American needs to know.* Boston: Houghton Mifflin Co.

Hodas, S. (1992, January). "Implementation of the K-12 NREN: Equity, access, and a Trojan horse." Unpublished manuscript.

Hodgkinson, H. (1991). Reform versus reality. *Phi Delta Kappan, 73*(1), September, 9-16.

Holt, D., ed. (1993). *Cooperative learning: A response to linguistic and cultural diversity.* Washington, DC: Center for Applied Linguistics.

Hood, J. F., et al. (1985, May). Microcomputers in schools, 1984-85: A comprehensive survey and analysis. Westport, CT: Market Data Retrieval. ERIC no. ED 265 822.

Howe, H. II. (1991). America 2000: A bumpy ride on four trains. *Phi Delta Kappan, 73*(3), November, 192-203.

Hudleson, S. (1989). *Write on: Children writing in ESL.* Englewood Cliffs, NJ: Prentice Hall.

Hughes, R. (1993). *Culture of complaint: A passionate look into the ailing heart of America.* New York: Warner Books.

Huxley, A. (1932). *Brave new world.* London: Chatto & Windhus.

Hynes, W. A. A good idea and its enemies: Part 2. The best kept secrets of North American education. *Our Schools, Our Selves, 5*(3), 95-107.

I*EARN Holocaust/Genocide Project (1993). White Plains, NY: I*EARN Publications.

Ignatieff, M. (1993). *Blood and belonging: Journeys into the new nationalism.* London: Penguin.

Itzkan, S. (1993). *Student recommendations for global networking in schools.* Washington, DC: World Future Society General Assembly.

Johnson, D. W., & Johnson, R. T. (1994). Cooperative learning in the culturally diverse classroom. In R. A. DeVillar, C. J. Faltis, & J. P. Cummins, eds., *Cultural diversity in schools: From rhetoric to practice,* pp. 57-74. Albany, NY: SUNY Press.

Kadi, M. (1995). Welcome to Cyberia. *Utne Reader,* No. 68, March-April, 52-59.

Kalantzis, M., & Cope, B. (1993). Histories of pedagogy, cultures of schooling. In B. Cope & M. Kalantzis, eds., *The powers of literacy: A genre approach to teaching writing,* pp. 38-62. London: The Falmer Press.

Kalantzis, M., Cope, B., Noble, G., & Poynting, S. (1990). *Cultures of schooling: Pedagogies for cultural difference and social access.* London: The Falmer Press.

Kaplan, R. D. (1994). The coming anarchy. *Atlantic Monthly,* February, 44-76.

Kennedy, P. (1993). *Preparing for the twenty-first century.* New York: HarperCollins Publishers Ltd.

Kessler, C., ed. (1992). *Cooperative language learning: A teacher's resource book.* Englewood Cliffs, NJ: Prentice-Hall Regents.

Kirsch, I. S., & Jungeblut, A. (1986). *Literacy: Profiles of America's young adults.* Princeton, NJ: Educational Testing Service.

Kozol, J. (1991). *Savage inequalities: Children in America's schools.* New York: Crown Publishers.

Kozol, J. (1992). Whittle and the privateers, *The Nation, 255*(8), September 21, 272 ff.

Krashen, S. (1993). *The power of reading.* Englewood, CO: Libraries Unlimited.

Krol, E. (1992). *The whole Internet: User's guide and catalog.* Sebastopol, CA: O'Reilly Associates.

Lauderdale, W. B. (1987). *Educational reform: The forgotten half.* Bloomington, IN: The Phi Delta Kappan Foundation.

Lee, E. (1992). Pump project proves old adage: All's well that ends well. *The Contemporary, 3*(1), 10.

Lee, W. B. (1983). Célestin Freinet, the unknown reformer. *Educational Forum, 48*(1), 97-113.

Lee, W. B. (1994). John Dewey and Célestin Freinet: A closer look. In J. Sivell, ed., *Freinet pedagogy: Theory and practice,* pp. 13-27. Lewiston, NY: Edwin Mellon Press.

Levin, H. M. (1988). *Accelerated schools for at-risk students.* New Brunswick, NJ: Center for Policy Research in Education.

Levin, H. M. (1993, January). "Accelerated schools after six years." Paper presented at the conference entitled "The Contributions of Instructional Innovation to Understanding Learning," University of Pittsburgh.

Lodi, M. (1977). *El pais errado.* Maria Dolors Badia, trans. Barcelona: Editorial Laia. (Original work published in 1970 as *Il paese sbagliato.* Turin: Giulio Einaudi.)

Lodi, M. (1981). *Cronica pedagogica.* Rosa Marcela Pericas, trans. Barcelona: Editorial Laia. (Original work published 1972 as *C'esperanza se questo accade al Vho.* Turin: Giulio Einaudi.)

Lucas, K. (1994). Personal communication, September 20.

Macedo, D. P. (1993). Literacy for stupidification: The pedagogy of big lies. *Harvard Educational Review, 63*(2), 183-207.

Macedo, D. P. (1994). *Literacies of power: What Americans are not allowed to know.* Boulder, CO: Westview Press.

Marvin, C. (1990). *When old technologies were new: Thinking about electric communication in the late nineteenth century.* New York: Oxford University Press.

McCaleb, S. P. (1994). *Building communities of learners: A collaboration among teachers, students, families and community.* New York: St. Martin's Press.

McConaghy, T. (1992). A witch hunt bedevils a Canadian reading series. *Phi Delta Kappan, 73*(8) April, 649-651.

McLaren, P. (1995a). *Critical pedagogy and predatory culture.* New York: Routledge.

McLaren, P. (1995b). Critical multiculturalism, media literacy, and the politics of representation. In J. Frederickson, ed., *Reclaiming our voices: Bilingual education, critical pedagogy, & praxis,* pp. 99-138. Ontario, CA: California Association for Bilingual Education.

McLuhan, M. (1965). *Understanding media: The extensions of man.* New York: McGraw-Hill.

Mehan, H., Moll, L., & Riel, M. (1985). *Computers in classrooms: A quasi-experiment in guided change.* [NIE Report 6-83-0027]. La Jolla, CA: Interactive Technology Laboratory.

Miller, T. (1995). Personal communication, February 11.

Miner, B. (1993). Education for sale? For-profit firms target public schools. *Rethinking Schools, 7*(4), 1, 14-17.

Moffett, J. (1988). *Storm in the mountains: A case study of censorship, conflict, and consciousness.* Carbondale, IL: Southern Illinois University Press.

Moffett, J. (1989). Censorship and spiritual education. *English Education, 21,* 70-87.

Moffett, J. (1994). *The universal schoolhouse: Spiritual awakening through education.* San Francisco: Jossey-Bass.

Moll, L. C. (1990). *Vygotsky and education: Instructional implications and applications of sociohistorical psychology.* Cambridge, UK: Cambridge University Press.

Moll, L. C., Amanti, C., Neff, D., & Gonzalez, N. (1992). Funds of knowledge for teaching: Using a qualitative approach to connect homes and classrooms. *Theory into Practice, 31*(2), 132-141.

Mullis, I. V. S., Campbell, J. R., & Farstrup, A. E. (1993). *Executive summary of the NAEP 1992 reading report card for the nation and the states.* Report No. 23-ST08. Washington, DC: Office of Educational Research and Improvement, U.S. Department of Education.

Nader, R. (1995). Citizens and computers. *Utne Reader,* No. 68, March-April, 74.

National Coalition of Advocates for Students. (1988). *New voices: Immigrant students in U.S. public schools.* Boston: National Coalition of Advocates for Students.

National Commission on Excellence in Education. (1983). *A nation at risk: The imperative for educational reform.* Washington, DC: U.S. Government Printing Office.

Natriello, G., McDill, E. L., & Pallas, A. M. (1990). *Schooling disadvantaged children: Racing against catastrophe.* New York: Teachers College Press.

Neuman, D. (1991). Technology and equity. *ERIC Digest,* EDO-IR-91-8. ERIC No. ED339400.

Newman, A. P., & Beverstock, C. (1990). *Adult literacy: Contexts & challenges.* Newark, DE: International Reading Association.

Newman, D., Griffin, P., & Cole, M. (1989). *The construction zone.* Cambridge, MA: Cambridge University Press.

Nieto, S. (1992). *Affirming diversity: The sociopolitical context of multicultural education.* New York: Longman.

Nieto, S. (1995). Personal communication, March 22.

Nikiforuk, A. (1991). Fifth Column: Education. Andrew Nikiforuk offers a recipe for reforming the school system. *The Globe & Mail,* December 27, A14.

Nikiforuk, A. (1992). Fifth Column: Education. Andrew Nikiforuk explains why half a Piaget isn't better than none. *The Globe & Mail,* April 3, A20.

Nikiforuk, A. (1994). *If learning is so natural, why am I going to school?* Toronto: Penguin.

Noble, D. (1994). The regime of technology in education. *Our Schools, Our Selves, 5*(3), 49-72.

Ogbu, J. U. (1978). *Minority education and caste.* New York: Academic Press.

Ogbu, J. U. (1992). Understanding cultural diversity and learning. *Educational Researcher, 21*(8), 5-14, 24.

Olsen, L., Chang, H., De La Rosa Salazar, D., Leong, C., McCall Perez, Z., McClain, G., & Raffel, L. (1994). *The unfinished journey: Restructuring schools in a diverse society.* San Francisco: California Tomorrow.

Olson, C. P. (1987). Who computes? In D. W. Livingstone, ed., *Critical pedagogy & cultural power,* pp. 179-204. South Hadley, MA: Bergin & Garvey.

Ong, W. J. (1982). *Orality and literacy: The technologizing of the word.* London: Methuen.

O'Reilly, B. (1992). Your new global work force. *Fortune,* December 14, 52-66.

Peterson, B. (1993). What should kids learn? A teacher looks at E. D. Hirsch's work on "cultural literacy." *Rethinking Schools, 8*(2), 1, 8-11.

Peterson, B. (1994). Teaching for social justice: One teacher's story. In B. Bigelow, L. Christensen, S. Karp, B. Miner, & B. Peterson, eds., *Rethinking our classrooms: Teaching for equity and justice,* pp. 30-33. Milwaukee, WI: Rethinking Schools.

Plato. (1973). *The Phaedrus of Plato.* New York: Arno Press.

Poplin, M. (1988). Holistic/constructivist principles of the teaching/learning process: Implications for the field of learning disabilities. *Journal of Learning Disabilities, 21*(7), 401-416.

Poplin, M., & Weeres, J. (1992). *Voices from the inside: A report on schooling from inside the classroom.* Claremont, CA: Institute for Education in Transformation at the Claremont Graduate School.

Porter, R. P. (1990). *Forked tongue: The politics of bilingual education.* New York: Basic Books.

Postman, N. (1993). *Technopoly: The surrender of culture to technology.* New York: Vintage Books.

Postman, N., & Weingartner, C. (1981). *How to recognize a good school.* Bloomington, IN: The Phi Delta Kappan Foundation.

Prawat, R. S. (1992). From individual differences to learning communities: Our changing focus. *Educational Leadership,* April, 9-13.

Pressley, M., & associates. (1990). *Cognitive strategy instruction that really improves children's academic performance.* Cambridge, MA: Brookline Books.

Ramirez, J. D. (1992). Executive summary. *Bilingual Research Journal, 16,* 1-62.

Ravitch, D., & Finn, C. E. (1987). *What do our 17-year olds know? A report on the first national assessment of history and literature.* New York: Harper & Row.

Reich, R. (1991). *The work of nations: Preparing ourselves for 21st century capitalism.* New York: Knopf.

Reyes, M. de la Luz. (1992). Challenging venerable assumptions: Literacy instruction for linguistically different students. *Harvard Educational Review, 62*(4), 427-446.

Rickover, H. G. (1959). *Education and freedom.* New York: Dutton.

Riley, R. (1995, February 8). *Report card. 3,* No. 296. Washington, DC: Department of Education.

Rogers, A. (1994). Personal communication, November 14.

Rotberg, I. C. (1990). I never promised you first place. *Phi Delta Kappan, (72)*4, December, 296-303.

Rowse, A. L., ed., (1988). *The annotated Shakespeare: The comedies, histories, sonnets and other poems, tragedies, and romances complete.* New York: Greenwich House.

Rubenson, K. (1989). The economics of adult basic education. In M. C. Taylor & J. A. Draper, eds., *Adult literacy perspectives,* pp. 387-398. Toronto: Culture Concepts, Inc.

Ruiz, R. (1990). Orientations in language planning. In S. L. McKay & S. C. Wong, eds., *Language diversity: Problem or resource?,* pp. 3-26. New York: Newbury House.

Salza, D. (1994). Personal communication, September 7.

Sayers, D. (1989). Bilingual sister classes in computer writing networks. In D. Johnson & D. Roen, eds., *Richness in writing: Empowering ESL writers,* pp. 130-145. New York: Longman.

Sayers, D. (1990, November 17). "School-to-school exchanges in Celestin Freinet's Modern School Movement: Implications for computer-mediated global learning networks." Keynote Address, First North American Freinet Congress, St. Catharine's, Ontario.

Sayers, D. (1991). Cross-cultural exchanges between students from the same culture: A portrait of an emerging relationship mediated by technology. *Canadian Modern Language Review, 47,* 678-696.

Sayers, D. (1993). Helping students find their voice in non-fiction writing: Team-teaching partnerships between distant classes. In J. Tinajero and A. F. Ada, eds., *The power of two languages: Literacy and biliteracy for Spanish-speaking children,* pp. 164-177. New York: Macmillan/McGraw-Hill.

Sayers, D. (1994a). Bilingual team-teaching partnerships over long distances: A technology-mediated context for intra-group language attitude change. In C. Faltis, R. DeVillar and J. Cummins, eds., *Cultural diversity in schools: From rhetoric to practice,* pp. 299-331. Albany, NY: State University of New York Press.

Sayers, D. (1994b). "Computer literacy" v. computer networking: Equity issues for bilingual education. *NABE News, 17*(5), 14 ff.

Sayers, D. (1994c). Computer networks and distance team-teaching. *TESOL Journal, 3*(1), 19-23.

Sayers, D., & Brown, K. (1987). Bilingual education and telecommunications: A perfect fit. *The Computing Teacher, 17,* 23-24.

Sayers, D., & Brown, K. (1993). Freire, Freinet and "distancing": Forerunners of technology-mediated critical pedagogy. *NABE News, 17*(3), 13 ff.

Sayers, D., & Brown, K. (1994). Putting a human face on educational technology: Inter-generational bilingual literacy through parent-child partnerships in long-distance networks. In D. Spener, ed., *Adult biliteracy in the United States: A national clearinghouse for literacy education forum,* pp. 171-189. Washington, DC: Co-published by the Center for Applied Linguistics and Delta Systems Company.

Schlesinger, A., Jr. (1991). *The disuniting of America.* New York: W. W. Norton.

Schmidt, P. (1994). Hartford asks E.A.I. to help fund its district. *Education Week, 13*(40), August 3, 1.

Schweinhart, L. J., Weikart, D. P., & Larney, M. B. (1986). Consequences of three preschool curriculum models through age 15. *Early Childhood Research Quarterly, 1,* 15-45.

The Secretary's Commission on Achieving Necessary Skills. (1991). *What work requires of schools: A SCANS report for America 2000.* Washington, DC: U.S. Department of Labor.

Sheppard, R. (1995a). Working without a SchoolNet. *Globe & Mail,* February 13, A13.

Sheppard, R. (1995b). Slow boat to digital education. *Globe & Mail,* February 14, A23.

Shor, I. (1992). *Empowering education: Critical teaching for social change.* Chicago: University of Chicago Press.

Simon, P. (1980). *The tongue-tied American.* New York: Continuum.

Sirotnik, K. A. (1983). What you see is what you get—consistency, persistency, and mediocrity in classrooms. *Harvard Educational Review, 53*(1), 16-31.

Sizer, T. R. (1984). *Horace's compromise: The dilemma of the American high school.* Boston: Houghton Mifflin.

Skutnabb-Kangas, T. (1984). *Bilingualism or not: The education of minorities.* Clevedon, England: Multilingual Matters.

Slavin, R. (1995). How can we target programs that work? Making money make a difference. *Rethinking Schools, 9*(4), 10 ff.

Stanford Working Group. (1993). *Federal education programs for limited-English-proficient students: A blueprint for the second generation.* Stanford, CA: Report of the Stanford Working Group, Stanford University.

Statistics Canada. (1990). *Survey of literacy skills used in daily activities.* Ottawa: Statistics Canada.

Stedman, L. C. (1987). It's time we changed the effective schools formula. *Phi Delta Kappan,* 69(3), November, 215-224.

Stedman, L. C., & Kaestle, C. F. (1985). The test score decline is over: Now what? *Phi Delta Kappan,* 67(3), November, 204-210.

Stedman, L. C., & Kaestle, C. F. (1987). Literacy and reading performance in the United States from 1800 to the present. *Reading Research Quarterly, 22,* 8-46.

Sternberg, R. J. (1994). Answering questions and questioning answers: Guiding children to intellectual excellence. *Phi Delta Kappan, 76*(2), October, 135-137.

Sullivan, E. V. (1983). Computers, culture, and educational futures: A critical appraisal. *Interchange, 14*(3), 17-26.

Taylor, W. L., & Piché, D. M. (1991). *A report on shortchanging children: The impact of fiscal inequality on the education of students at risk.* Washington, DC: U.S. House of Representatives, Committee on Education and Labor.

Tharp, R. G. & Gallimore, R. (1991). *The instructional conversation: Teaching and learning in social activity.* Santa Cruz, CA: National Center for Research on Cultural Diversity and Second Language Learning.

Tonucci, F. (1981). *Viaje alrededor de "El Mundo": Un diario de clase de Mario Lodi y sus alumnos.* M. Vassallo, trans. Barcelona: Editorial Laia. (Original work published 1980 as *Un giornalino di classe* [A classroom newspaper]. Roma Bari: Guis, Laterza and Figli Spa.)

Vives, Narcis. (1994). Personal communication, September 9.

Vygotsky, L. S. (1978). *Mind in society: The development of higher psychological processes.* M. Cole, V. John-Steiner, S. Scibner, & E. Souberman, eds. Cambridge, MA: Harvard University Press.

Waldman, M. (1990). *Who robbed America? A citizen's guide to the Savings & Loan scandal.* New York: Random House.

Weisman, J. (1993). Skills in the schools: Now it's business' turn. *Phi Delta Kappan, 74*(5), January, 367-369.

Wells, G., & Chang-Wells, G. L. (1992). *Constructing knowledge together: Classrooms as centers of inquiry and literacy.* Portsmouth, NH: Heinemann.

Williams, J. D., & Snipper, G. C. (1990). *Literacy and bilingualism.* New York: Longman.

Willinsky, J. (1991). A literacy more urgent than literature: 1800-1850. *Our Schools, Our Selves, 3*(1), 110-135.

Wirth, A. G. (1993). Education and work: The choices we face. *Phi Delta Kappan, 74*(5), January, 360-366.

Zinn, H. (1994). Why students should study history: An interview with Howard Zinn. In B. Bigelow, L. Christensen, S. Karp, B. Miner, & B. Peterson, eds., *Rethinking our classrooms: Teaching for equity and justice,* pp. 150-156. Milwaukee, WI: Rethinking Schools, Ltd.

Index

electronic mail and LISTSERV
management techniques, 207-209,
214
reference books, 211
searching, 209
service providers and levels of connectivity, 182-185
updating Internet resources, 217-219

literacy
computer, 340
critical, 87-82, 97, 104, 108, 114, 116,
149, 154-155, 162, 168-169, 171-
172, 344
cultural, 9-11, 13, 88-89, 92, 98, 106,
107, 115, 166
functional, 8, 86, 92, 100-101, 104, 107,
116, 168, 171, 341
instruction, 91, 98-100
intercultural, 9-11, 116, 160
intergenerational, 45-50, 50-57
skills, 11, 15, 82, 84, 116
standards, 99
Lodi, Mario, 121-122, 131-134, 136-138

minority groups, 11, 13, 87, 100-104, 107,
109
multicultural education, 4, 9, 82, 100, 103,
153, 155, 159-162, 169, 356

Orillas (De Orilla a Orilla), 22-23, 338

pedagogy
border, 161
for intercultural learning, 6, 9
progressive, 98-100, 143-144, 150-154,
157, 343-345, 355-356
traditional, 99-100, 142-150, 153-154,
159, 343, 345, 356
transformative, 143-144, 153-157, 172
phonics, 98, 99, 145, 354
poverty, 8, 83, 103, 106, 115, 154, 337,
345-346
precursors of contemporary global learning
networks
See Freinet, Célestin
See Lodi, Mario
prejudice reduction
The Holocaust/Genocide Project, 58-62
interethnic prejudice, 34-45, 337, 338
privatization of public schools and technology, 357-358

social justice, 144, 149, 154-157, 171-172,
344, 356

team-teaching partnerships over distances
binary partnerships, 23, 30-34, 34-45
network-wide collaborations, 23, 25-30,
45-79

whole language methods, 98-100, 107, 116,
150, 152-153, 344, 353, 354, 356